DICTATING THE AGENDA

DICTATING THE AGENDA

THE AUTHORITARIAN RESURGENCE IN WORLD POLITICS

ALEXANDER COOLEY
AND
ALEXANDER DUKALSKIS

OXFORD
UNIVERSITY PRESS

OXFORD
UNIVERSITY PRESS

Oxford University Press is a department of the University of Oxford.
It furthers the University's objective of excellence in research, scholarship,
and education by publishing worldwide. Oxford is a registered trade mark of
Oxford University Press in the UK and in certain other countries.

Published in the United States of America by Oxford University Press
198 Madison Avenue, New York, NY 10016, United States of America.

© Oxford University Press 2025

All rights reserved. No part of this publication may be reproduced, stored in a retrieval system,
transmitted, used for text and data mining, or used for training artificial intelligence, in any form or
by any means, without the prior permission in writing of Oxford University Press, or as expressly
permitted by law, by license or under terms agreed with the appropriate reprographics rights
organization. Inquiries concerning reproduction outside the scope of the above should be sent
to the Rights Department, Oxford University Press, at the address above.

You must not circulate this work in any other form
and you must impose this same condition on any acquirer.

Library of Congress Cataloging-in-Publication Data
Names: Cooley, Alexander, 1972- editor | Dukalskis, Alexander editor
Title: Dictating the agenda : the authoritarian resurgence in world
politics / Alexander Cooley and Alexander Dukalskis.
Description: New York, NY : Oxford University Press, 2025. | Includes
bibliographical references and index.
Identifiers: LCCN 2024059539 (print) | LCCN 2024059540 (ebook) |
ISBN 9780197776360 hardback | ISBN 9780197776384 epub | ISBN 9780197776391
Subjects: LCSH: Authoritarianism | Mass media–Political aspects |
Boycotts–Political aspects | Freedom of the press |
World politics–1989-
Classification: LCC JC480 .D53 2025 (print) | LCC JC480 (ebook) |
DDC 320.53–dc23/eng/20250404
LC record available at https://lccn.loc.gov/2024059539
LC ebook record available at https://lccn.loc.gov/2024059540

DOI: 10.1093/oso/9780197776360.001.0001

Printed by Sheridan Books, Inc., United States of America

The manufacturer's authorised representative in the EU for product safety is
Oxford University Press España S.A. of El Parque Empresarial San Fernando de
Henares, Avenida de Castilla, 2 – 28830 Madrid (www.oup.es/en or
product.safety@oup.com). OUP España S.A. also acts as importer into
Spain of products made by the manufacturer.

CONTENTS

List of Figures ix
List of Tables x
Acknowledgments xi
About the Companion Website xvi

Chapter 1. Introduction: Dictating the Agenda 1
  What's So New About Authoritarianism Today? 5
    Authoritarian Resurgence and Internal Contestation 8
    Authoritarian Interconnectedness: Global Interactions
      Rewired 14
  The Argument in Brief 18
  The Plan of This Book 20

Chapter 2. The 1990s Origins and the Acceleration of
  Transnational Liberal Influence 25
  Transnational Liberal Influence in the 1990s 32
  Two Paths for Promoting Liberal Values Globally: Liberal
    Democratic Primacy and Transnational Activism 34
  Three Hidden Assumptions of Liberal Influence 39
    Efficacious Authority 39
    Market Power 43

vi   CONTENTS

Autonomy and Political Independence   46

Taking Stock of the Unipolar Moment   49

Chapter 3. Authoritarian Resurgence and Influence in the 2020s   51

The Vulnerabilities of the 1990s Model in the Cold Light of the 2020s   57

The West Is No Longer Perceived as Best   61

Market Power Shifts Eastward   65

Questioning Embedded Autonomy and Cracking Down in Plain Sight   66

Countering Liberal Influence Globally   70

Authoritarian Learning and Emulation   71

Rewiring Global Governance   73

The Internal Demand for Illiberal Alternatives   75

The New Authoritarian Offensive: Openly Contesting Liberal Influence   77

Chapter 4. Authoritarian Snapback Explained   79

From Spiraling Toward Liberal Change to Dictating the Agenda?   80

Tactic 1: Stigmatize   83

Tactic 2: Shield   87

Tactic 3: Reframe Engagement and Set New Ground Rules   90

Tactic 4: Project Control and Influence Outward   92

Tactic 5: Dictate the Agenda   96

Coda: Transmit Success Back to Domestic Audience   100

Illustrative Example: China and Human Rights   101

Tactic 1: Stigmatize   101

Tactic 2: Shield   102

Tactic 3: Reframe Engagement and Set New Ground Rules   103

Tactic 4: Project Control and Influence Outward   104

Tactic 5: Dictate the Agenda   106

Coda: Transmit Success Back to Domestic Audience   108

CONTENTS   vii

Chapter 5. Reconfiguring Global Media Influence   110
    Authoritarian Amplification: New Realities of Pro-
        Authoritarian Media   112
    The Visible and Hidden Global Reach of Authoritarian
        Media: A Closer Look   119
        Wire Services and the Proliferation of Global Content-Sharing
            Agreements   122
    What Do Authoritarians Say?   127
    Learning and Adapting to Be More Effective   130
        The Importance of Online and Social Media   132
        Authoritarian Learning and Snapback in the Global Media
            Sphere   135
    Authoritarian Silencing: Repression of Foreign
        Journalists   138
        The Authoritarian Restrictions on Foreign Journalists (ARFJ)
            Data Set   142
    Conclusion: Reconfiguration and Response   147

Chapter 6. Repurposing Global Consumer
Activism   149
    Consumer Activism and Transnational Advocacy
        Movements   151
        Snapback Against Liberal Campaigns, New Authoritarian
            Assertiveness, and Boycotts   153
    Two Cases of Apparel-Related Transnational Activism
        and Boycotts   157
        Nike and the Anti-Sweatshop Campaigns of the 1990s   157
    Activism and Snapback, 2017–2022: Repression
        in Xinjiang, Cotton Standards, and H&M   162
        Background: Repression in Xinjiang and Activist Campaigns   162
        Cotton Standards, Activism, and Corporate Self-Regulation   169
        H&M and Party-Supported Consumer Backlash   175
        Xinjiang, Forced Labor, and the Authoritarian Snapback   179
    Conclusion: Pro-Authoritarian Consumer Activism   182

viii CONTENTS

Chapter 7. Harnessing Global Higher Education 184

The Ascendence of the Liberal Model in Global Higher
Education 188

Indicators of Global Influence: People, Donations, and
Rankings 190

Internationalization Evolving on Whose Terms? 192

The Rise of the Transnational Campus 195

The Rise of the Democratic-Authoritarian Transnational
Campus 196

Whose Norms and Sovereignty Are Influencing
Whose? 200

Transnational Challenges 201

The Fate of Transnational Partnerships: Finances and Academic
Freedom 205

Dictating the Educational Agenda: The Rise and Decline of
the Central European University 207

A Liberal Education Paradigm for Central Europe 208

The Escalating Stages of Authoritarian Snapback: Orbánism and the
CEU 209

External Reactions: Liberal Outrage and Illiberal Allies 211

The Global Erosion of the Liberal Education Model 213

Chapter 8. Rewriting the Playbook: Global Sports 217

Globalization and the Internationalization of Sport 219

The NBA Goes to China: But Who Changed Whom? 221

International Mega-Events and Liberal Projections 225

Authoritarian Emergence and the New Sportswashing 227

New Authoritarian Markets, New Authoritarian Partners 229

Formula One Expands Its Frontiers 234

From Speaking Out to Remaining Neutral: Voice
and Protest in Global Sport 236

Protesting Beijing's Crackdowns: Snapback Against the NBA
and Premier League 239

The Qatar World Cup and LGBTQ Advocacy   244

Saudi Arabia Enters the Global Arena   247

The Unfolding LIV-PGA Partnership   250

Conclusion   252

Chapter 9. Conclusion   254

Applying the Argument to Emerging Global Issues   259

The Emerging Politics of Greenwashing   260

Genderwashing   262

Governing AI   265

Where Are We Going? Liberalism, Geopolitics, and
Multipolarity   269

What Should Be Done?   272

Index   279

LIST OF FIGURES

1.1 GDP of Most and Least Liberal Democratic States (V-Dem), 1991 and 2021	10
1.2 Global Liberal Democracy (V-Dem), 1980 to 2023	13
4.1 Authoritarian Snapback Illustrated	82
5.1 Offices of Russian State Media State Outlets as of 2023	120
5.2 Offices of Chinese State Media Outlets as of 2023	121
5.3 Content-Sharing Agreements with Chinese State Media (302 total)	126
5.4 Content-Sharing Agreements with Russian State Media (99 total)	127
5.5 Trends in Harassment of Journalists According to V-Dem	140
5.6 Yearly Count of Restrictions on Foreign Journalists in ARFJ Database	145
7.1 Transnational University Campuses of Liberal Democratic Sending Countries in Authoritarian Host Countries, as of 2023	197
8.1 Saudi Arabian Sports Sponsorships Active in 2021 and 2023	248

LIST OF TABLES

3.1 Global Media Attention to Human Rights in Two Beijing Olympics 56
5.1 Most Frequent Actions in the ARFJ, 1999–2023 145
5.2 Most Frequent Countries in the ARFJ, 1999–2023 146
8.1 Authoritarian Ownership in Highest Revenue Generating Football Clubs, as Valued by Deloitte Football Money League 2024 231

ACKNOWLEDGMENTS

Like many others, this academic collaboration was born of common interests and fortuitous timing. After crossing paths in a few virtual forums about transnational repression and reputation laundering, Alex D. and Alex C. began brainstorming the contours of this project in the spring of 2021. We shared the view that, during the first year of the Biden administration, we were witnessing more assertive challenges to US soft power and liberal activism coming from China, Russia, and other authoritarian countries.

Both of us had previously researched topics that related to authoritarianism, global governance, and international order, and as we observed the world struggle under lockdown, we were struck with the boldness of some of Beijing's and Moscow's antidemocratic rhetoric and restrictions. In the midst of a global pandemic, these countries were no longer just defending their governance practices and mounting repression from Western accusations—they were publicly portraying critical messengers such as NGOs and journalists from liberal democracies as geopolitical agents and threats to their national and global security.

We also were struck by how this backlash was informing areas not traditionally explored by international relations scholarship, especially the world of sports (particularly the National Basketball Association), higher education, and consumer activism. The structure and initial research framework for the book came together quickly, and we embarked on a remarkable three-year intellectual journey during which

xii

we uncovered new political connections, found new rabbit holes to go down, regularly learned from one another, and even had a few laughs. Toward the completion of the project, Alex C. became a participant-observer of the "authoritarian snapback" phenomenon we identify in the book when in March 2024 he was sanctioned by the government of the Russian Federation, along with hundreds of other academic colleagues and analysts, for his alleged involvement "in conceiving, carrying out and justifying the anti-Russia policy adopted by the current administration of the United States."

Such is the state of our world, where undertaking research about authoritarianism is no longer separable from the geopolitical threats that authoritarians push back against. And yet, more than ever, it is critical that we not only identify these global political shifts but also document them in a way that scholars, journalists, and policymakers can access and appreciate. As this book went to press the two of us watched on either side of the Atlantic as the United States voted Donald Trump back into the White House, underscoring the importance of understanding the dynamics of the globe's rising illiberal tide. Supported by a range of new right-wing and digital media platforms, Trump has promised to bend American institutions to enact his agenda which includes levying a new round of tariffs on imports, dismantling the Department of Education, and enacting a large-scale deportation program of immigrants. As these and likely other events unfold, neither of us are equipped with the ability to see into the future, but we briefly address what we think are the implications of Trump's return for our book's main arguments as best we can with the knowledge we have as we write in November 2024.

As authors in a time of political turbulence, we are blessed to be part of a community of scholars and institutions that helped make this book possible. We thank colleagues and audiences at invited talks and lectures at the Air War College, Barnard College, Chatham House in London, Columbia University, Heidelberg University, Oxford University, Trinity College Dublin, University College Dublin, University of Exeter, University of Glasgow, University of Toronto, and Uppsala University for giving our arguments a hearing (many thanks also to colleagues at the University of Manchester for arranging a talk even though it was canceled due to strike action). We appreciate your generosity

xiv ACKNOWLEDGMENTS

and feedback, especially those of you who listened while we road-tested early versions of the argument and discussed them with us.

Likewise, we thank colleagues at multiple conferences for valuable feedback. The European Consortium for Political Research Joint Sessions of Workshops is unique among academic conferences for the intensity of focus given to each project, and so we thank especially Maria Joshua, Erik Vollman, Aykut Öztürk, Yoni Abramson, Julia Bader, Una Bērziņa-Čerenkova, and other participants for their helpful comments in 2022 on our early thinking about the snapback model. We thank Marianne Kneuer, Rachel Vanderhill, and Thomas Ambrosio for helpful comments at the 2023 International Studies Association convention in Montreal, the members of the Offshore Research Group, as well as Karl Gustafsson and other panelists and audience members at the 2022 Pan-European Conference on International Relations in Athens.

This research was supported in part by a grant awarded from the Research Council of Norway to the Norwegian Institute of International Affairs (NUPI; R&D project 314604 Chinese Anger Diplomacy). We are grateful to the entire NUPI project team, including Morten Andersen, Bjørnar Sverdrup-Thygeson, Wrenn Yennie Lindgren, Ole Jacob Sending, Minda Holm, and Oliver Turner for their feedback at multiple stages over the project cycle. We also thank NUPI for organizing and supporting a daylong book workshop in Oslo in December 2023. For that meeting, Fiona Adamson and David Lewis read an entire draft manuscript and provided firm but friendly criticism that helped improve the book in countless ways, including brainstorming over dinner about the title of the book. In addition to our NUPI colleagues, Natalie Koch, Adam Scharpf, and Tena Prelec gave insightful and tremendously helpful comments on draft chapters. We are also grateful for feedback on various portions of the manuscript and points of fact or interpretation. For this we owe many thanks to Thomas Ambrosio, Finbarr Bermingham, Clifford Coonan, Kirsten Han, John Heathershaw, Ian Hurd, Joakim Kreutz, Louisa Lim, Paul Musgrave, Filip Reyntjens, Maria Snegovaya, Ben Tonra, Leslie Vinjamuri, Adrian Zenz, and Pär Zetterberg. As is customary, we note that all errors remain our responsibility and we apologize if we have missed anybody.

Alex D.'s fieldwork in Sweden was supported by the UCD Output Based Research Support Scheme and the Uppsala University Forum on

Democracy, Peace, and Justice (many thanks, again, to Joakim Kreutz for hosting and organizing). For help facilitating fieldwork and making introductions, many thanks to Benjamin Katzeff Silberstein and Wrenn Yennie Lindgren, and to interviewees who took the time to talk. Alex C. remains grateful for the vibrant intellectual culture that has enriched his thinking and supported his risk-taking, including the support of his remarkable colleagues in the Barnard and Columbia political science departments, the Harriman Institute, the Saltzman Institute at the School of International and Public Affairs, the University Consortium, and Columbia Global. Two external reviewers at Oxford University Press gave critical and important feedback at the project's formative stage.

Dave McBride showed great trust and then a good deal of faith in the project, and we are delighted to once again have partnered with him and the talented team at Oxford University Press. The painstaking multiyear compilation of our data and sources was at various points undertaken by Natalie Hall, Rachel Amman, and Boyang Liu. Over the project's final year, Emma Julia Larson provided extraordinary research support, helping us not only to complete our collection of findings on global media hubs, content-sharing agreements, repression of journalists, higher-education agreements, and sports investments, but also to identify and address numerous empirical and analytical challenges. Remy Chwae conscientiously designed the graphics, including the maps and figures. Dave Prout once again compiled a masterful index, and the production of the book was generously supported by a Faculty Publication Grant from the Harriman Institute.

Finally, of course, we thank our families for putting up with us during this process. Alex C. thanks his wife Nicole for her indispensable support through yet another consuming project. Over the course of writing the book, their daughter Greta entered high school and began her own journey into advocacy and understanding the high-stakes political contests of our time. Alex D. thanks his wife Laura for being an honest voice about everything, especially the title and cover. Trying to explain this book to a six-year-old is a humbling experience, but Alex D. thanks his son Felix for even asking and for living through another book by dad (and for the historical record: you were impressed by the number of pages, what the book factory that prints it might look like, and the

xvi   ACKNOWLEDGMENTS

fact that the other author was also called Alex). Frankie joined the family during this project and while she's only forming her first words now, we hope that when they're adults both she and Felix will live in a world where democracy and freedom of expression are protected.

November 2024
New York City and Dublin, Ireland

ABOUT THE COMPANION WEBSITE

A companion website housing the following appendixes referenced in the book can be found at https://www.alexanderacooley.com/books.

Appendix 5.1. Offices of Russian Media Outlets (RT, TASS, Sputnik) as of 2023

Appendix 5.2. Offices of Chinese Media Outlets (Xinhua and CGTN) as of 2023

Appendix 5.3. Content-Sharing Agreements with Chinese State Media

Appendix 5.4. Content-Sharing Agreements with Russian State Media

Appendix 5.5. Authoritarian Restrictions on Foreign Journalists (ARFJ) Data Set

Appendix 7.1. List of Discontinued Liberal Democratic-Authoritarian Transnational Higher-Education Partnerships

Appendix 8.1. Authoritarian State-Based Airline Sponsorship Deals of Sports Clubs

Appendix 8.2. Saudi Arabian Investment in Global Sports, 2023

Chapter 1

Introduction
Dictating the Agenda

After winning a bruising presidential election in 2020 that his defeated opponent refused to concede, US President Joe Biden prioritized the renewal of global democracy as a driver of his foreign policy. In launching the December 2021 global Summit for Democracy, Biden cited evidence from Freedom House and the International Institute of Democracy and Electoral Assistance that global democracy was in danger. He welcomed participants in the virtual meeting of representatives from countries around the world by saying, "This gathering has been on my mind for a long time for a simple reason: In the face of sustained and alarming challenges to democracy, universal human rights . . . all around the world, democracy needs champions."[1]

The view from Beijing and Moscow was quite different. Chinese Foreign Minister Wang Yi accused the United States of using the summit to draw ideological lines between democracies and non-democracies and

---

[1] White House, "Remarks by President Biden at the Summit for Democracy Opening Session," December 9, 2021, https://www.whitehouse.gov/briefing-room/speeches-remarks/2021/12/09/remarks-by-president-biden-at-the-summit-for-democracy-opening-session.

argued that "the US' purpose lies not in democracy but hegemony. . . . The US seeks to meddle in internal affairs of other countries under the banner of democracy and abuse democratic values to create divides."[2] Not content to let summit participants define democracy, the People's Republic of China released a white paper the week of the gathering with the title *China: Democracy That Works*.[3] It claimed, contrary to Biden's statements, that "today's world is facing challenges of excessive democracy, democracy implemented in great haste, democratic deficit and fading democracy." The true threats were not from rising authoritarians but from democracy promoters. Russia's foreign minister, Sergei Lavrov, advanced a similar critique, saying of the summit: "In recent times, we have witnessed attempts to establish an international order . . . to impose upon everyone new rules that have been drawn up in non-inclusive bodies and circles."[4]

Leaders of non-democratic states like China and Russia frequently view the spread of liberal ideas associated with democracy and human rights, and the global networks and practices that advocate for these principles, as threatening.[5] The fact that a geopolitical rival champions democracy certainly amplifies the sense of threat, but these liberal ideas and values themselves sit at odds with the way politics is organized

---

[2] Zhao Jia, "FM Denounces 'Democracy Summit' as Exercise in Hypocrisy," *China Daily*, December 4, 2021, https://global.chinadaily.com.cn/a/202112/04/WS61ab4358a310cdd39bc7960a.html.

[3] Embassy of the People's Republic of China in the United States of America, *China: Democracy That Works*, 2021, http://us.china-embassy.gov.cn/eng/zgyw/202112/t20211204_10462468.htm.

[4] Philippe Rater, "Russia Slams U.S. Proposal for 'Summit for Democracy,'" *Moscow Times*, May 7, 2021, https://www.themoscowtimes.com/2021/05/07/russia-slams-us-proposal-for-summit-for-democracy-a73839.

[5] The scholarly literature on autocracy promotion and democracy prevention makes this point. See, for example, Rachel Vanderhill, *Promoting Authoritarianism Abroad* (Lynne Rienner Publishers, 2013); Christian von Soest, "Democracy Prevention: The International Collaboration of Authoritarian Regimes," *European Journal of Political Research* 54, no. 4 (2015): pp. 62–63, https://doi.org/10.1111/1475-6765.12100; Laurence Whitehead, "Antidemocracy Promotion: Four Strategies in Search of a Framework," *Taiwan Journal of Democracy* 10, no. 2 (2014): pp. 1–24; Julia Bader et al., "Would Autocracies Promote Autocracy? A Political Economy Perspective on Regime-Type Export in Regional Neighborhoods," *Contemporary Politics* 16, no. 1 (2010): pp. 81–100; Oisin Tansey, "The Problem with Autocracy Promotion," *Democratization* 21, no. 1 (2016): pp. 141–63, https://doi.org/10.1080/13510347.2015.1095736.

in authoritarian regimes. Therefore, the global networks and actors that promote those ideas are dangers that must be confronted and neutralized.

Beijing and Moscow have said so themselves. In 2013 a leaked inner-party circular called *Communiqué on the Current State of the Ideological Sphere*, more popularly known as Document Number 9, spelled out the ideas the Chinese Communist Party (CCP) found threatening to its continued authority: constitutional democracy, universal human rights, a free press, and civil society, among others.[6] In subsequent years the CCP acted on most of these points by clamping down on a wide array of ideas and activities. Russia's Vladimir Putin took a slightly different tack in a 2019 interview with the *Financial Times*, arguing that liberal ideas are "obsolete" and that "traditional values are more stable and more important for millions of people than this liberal idea, which, in my opinion, is really ceasing to exist."[7] Even so, liberal political ideas and the transnational networks and practices that advocate them were apparently threatening enough for Russia to enact a series of laws that at first restricted and then outright banned an array of actors promoting liberal values, including well-known domestic human rights organizations such as Memorial,[8] Western philanthropic organizations such as the Open Society Foundations,[9] and Bard College's 20-year high-profile academic liberal arts program with St. Petersburg State University.[10] After Russia's full-scale invasion of Ukraine in February 2022, Russia kicked

---

[6] "Document 9: A ChinaFile Translation," ChinaFile, November 8, 2013, https://www.chinafile.com/document-9-chinafile-translation (accessed September 17, 2021).

[7] Lionel Barber and Henry Foy, "Vladimir Putin Says Liberalism Has Become Obsolete," *Financial Times*, June 28, 2019, https://www.ft.com/content/670039ec-98f3-11e9-9573-ee5cbb98ed36; "Putin Says Liberal Values Are Obsolete: Financial Times," Reuters, June 27, 2019, https://www.reuters.com/article/us-russia-putin-europe-values-idUSKCN1TS2UF.

[8] "Memorial: Russia's Civil Rights Group Uncovering an Uncomfortable Past," BBC, January 2, 2022, https://www.bbc.com/news/world-europe-59853010.

[9] Jennifer Ablan, "Russia Bans George Soros Foundation as State Security 'Threat,'" Reuters, November 30, 2015, https://www.reuters.com/article/idUSL1N13P22Y/.

[10] Stephanie Saul, "Russia Bans Bard College, and Other Universities Ask What's Next," *New York Times*, August 5, 2021, https://www.nytimes.com/2021/08/05/us/bard-college-russia-ban-undesirable.html.

4   DICTATING THE AGENDA

out remaining international nongovernmental organizations and foundations like Amnesty International, Human Rights Watch, and the Carnegie Endowment for International Peace.[11] It reached abroad and designated Meduza, the independent news organization operating in exile in Riga, Latvia, since 2014 that had broken important stories during the war such as the Bucha Massacre, an "undesirable organization," effectively criminalizing any contacts between Russian citizens and its reporters.

These examples and many others like them show how authoritarian states now are more aggressively cracking down on these "threatening" transnational networks of liberal influence. While in the 1990s and early 2000s networks and practices operated in a global context in which democratic states were more dominant, today NGOs, journalists, activists, universities, and for-profit companies must operate in a world of authoritarian advance, the spread of illiberal ideas, democratic backsliding, and the rise of authoritarian great powers.[12] Autocracies express shared understandings, learning, and tactical cooperation

---

[11] Amnesty International, "Russia: Authorities Close Down Amnesty International's Moscow Office," April 8, 2022, https://www.amnesty.org/en/latest/news/2022/04/russia-authorities-close-down-amnesty-internationals-moscow-office/ (accessed March 7, 2023).

[12] The literature documenting this trend is by now vast. On surging authoritarianism, see research produced by the Sweden-based Varieties of Democracy research institute: Anna Lührmann and Staffan I. Lindberg, "A Third Wave of Autocratization Is Here: What Is New About It?," *Democratization* 26, no. 7 (2019): pp. 1095–113, https://doi.org/10.1080/13510347.2019.1582029; Seraphine F. Maerz et al., "State of the World 2019: Autocratization Surges—Resistance Grows," *Democratization* 27, no. 6 (2020): pp. 909–27, https://doi.org/10.1080/13510347.2020.1758670; Sebastian Hellmeier et al., "State of the World 2020: Autocratization Turns Viral," *Democratization* 28, no. 6 (2021): pp. 1053–74, https://doi.org/10.1080/13510347 .2021.1922390. On backsliding within democratic states, see Stephan Haggard and Robert Kaufman, *Backsliding: Democratic Regress in the Contemporary World* (Cambridge University Press, 2021). On the rise of authoritarian great powers and their impact on global governance, see Alexander Cooley and Daniel Nexon, *Exit from Hegemony: The Unraveling of the American Global Order* (Oxford University Press, 2020); Gregorio Bettiza and David Lewis, "Authoritarian Powers and Norm Contestation in the Liberal International Order: Theorizing the Power Politics of Ideas and Identity," *Journal of Global Security Studies* 5, no. 4 (2020): pp. 559–77, https://doi .org/10.1093/jogss/ogz075; Nana de Graaff et al., "China's Rise in a Liberal World Order in Transition: Introduction to the FORUM," *Review of International Political Economy* 27, no. 2 (2020): pp. 191–207, https://doi.org/10.1080/09692290.2019 .1709880.

INTRODUCTION 5

in confronting the transnational "threat" of democracy and the actors that promote its norms.[13] In February 2022, just weeks before Russia's invasion, and on the same day as the Opening Ceremony of the 2022 Beijing Winter Olympics, Russia and China announced an agreement that codified their perspective on rejecting the global advance of liberal democratic ideas, seeing it mostly as a cynical US plot to preserve Washington's power and therefore as a threat to the international order.[14]

What's So New About Authoritarianism Today?

The perceived threat of liberal political influence is not new. After all, during the Cold War the two camps engaged in a long-run ideological battle to delegitimize one another's systems and elevate their own,

[13] Thomas Ambrosio, "Constructing a Framework of Authoritarian Diffusion: Concepts, Dynamics, and Future Research," *International Studies Perspectives* 11, no. 4 (2010): pp. 375–92, https://doi.org/10.1111/j.1528-3585.2010.00411.x; Stephen G. F. Hall and Thomas Ambrosio, "Authoritarian Learning: A Conceptual Overview," *East European Politics* 33, no. 2 (2017): pp. 143–61, https://doi.org/10.1080/21599165.2017.1307826; Marlies Glasius et al., "Illiberal Norm Diffusion: How Do Governments Learn to Restrict Nongovernmental Organizations?," *International Studies Quarterly* 64, no. 2 (2020): pp. 453–68, https://doi.org/10.1093/isq/sqaa019; Stephen G. F. Hall, *The Authoritarian International: Tracing How Authoritarian Regimes Learn in the Post-Soviet Space* (Cambridge University Press, 2023).

[14] The statement read: "Certain States' attempts to impose their own 'democratic standards' on other countries, to monopolize the right to assess the level of compliance with democratic criteria, to draw dividing lines based on the grounds of ideology, including by establishing exclusive blocs and alliances of convenience, prove to be nothing but flouting of democracy and go against the spirit and true values of democracy. Such attempts at hegemony pose serious threats to global and regional peace and stability and undermine the stability of the world order." President of Russia, "Joint Statement of the Russian Federation and the People's Republic of China on the International Relations Entering a New Era and the Global Sustainable Development," February 4, 2021, http://en.kremlin.ru/supplement/5770. In May 2024, the two governments issued another joint statement, this time called "Joint Statement of the People's Republic of China and the Russian Federation on Deepening the Comprehensive Strategic Partnership of Coordination for the New Era in the Context of the 75th Anniversary of China-Russia Diplomatic Relations"; see "Xi, Putin Hold Talks in Beijing, Charting Course for Enhanced Ties," State Council of the People's Republic of China, May 17, 2024, https://english.www.gov.cn/news/202405/17/content_WS66469c33c6d0868f4e8e72bb.html (accessed May 27, 2024).

6   DICTATING THE AGENDA

aligning with regimes and interfering in the elections and domestic affairs of targeted states.[15] Going back centuries, political authorities have perceived threat from ideas circulating internationally that might challenge their own grip on power.[16]

But in other ways, there are strikingly novel features of what we argue is a renewed global authoritarian backlash against transnational liberal influence. This is particularly true if we take the 1990s as our starting point. At that time, the United States had emerged from the Cold War as an unchallenged global power that created an international environment in its own image: a world in which liberal democratic ideas, values, and standards could proliferate through advocacy organizations like NGOs and foundations, new global media broadcasts, the overseas expansion of American companies and US consumerism, new international programs and global partnerships of major universities, and global mega-events in democracies that seemingly showcased this new post–Cold War era. A network of transnational liberal influence permeated across global social and political life that sought to promote values that included human rights, democracy, marketization, gender equality, and freedom of the press.[17]

Leaders of non-democratic states, even if they perceived transnational liberal influence as a threat—and indeed many did[18]—were mostly playing defense in the global order of the 1990s. Some, including China, even felt compelled to explicitly welcome democracy promotion efforts in the 1990s from the likes of the Carter Center and the Asia Foundation but sought to steer and limit them, showing how authoritarian states "creatively coped with external pressure for

---

[15] Dov H. Levin, *Meddling in the Ballot Box: The Causes and Effects of Partisan Electoral Interventions* (Oxford University Press, 2020).

[16] John M. Owen IV, *The Clash of Ideas in World Politics: Transnational Networks, States, and Regime Change, 1510–2010* (Princeton University Press, 2010); Chad E. Nelson, *Revolutionary Contagion and International Politics* (Oxford University Press, 2022).

[17] For an early review of scholarship on these themes, see Richard Price, "Transnational Civil Society and Advocacy in World Politics," *World Politics* 55, no. 4 (2003), pp. 579–606, https://doi.org/10.1353/wp.2003.0024.

[18] For example, see John W. Garver, *China's Quest: The History of the Foreign Relations of the People's Republic of China* (Oxford University Press, 2016), pp. 23, 484–85, and 812–14.

liberal democracy."[19] The pressure was real and seemingly unrelenting, as well-known scholarly models of human rights socialization envisioned transnational forces naming and shaming authoritarian states to adhere to liberal standards of behavior.[20] As it turns out, recent scholarship suggests that domestic-transnational civil society linkages really do increase the chances of autocratic governments democratizing, indicating that transnational networks of liberal influence present a genuine "threat" to dictatorships.[21]

To be sure, there was always a disconnect—even a hypocritical one—between the public rhetoric and actual behavior of states touting liberal democratic ideas and order. The United States and other liberal democracies have not always practiced what they preached, selectively allying with and supporting authoritarian leaders.[22] But liberal norms enjoyed a dominant status after the end of the Cold War, and the regimes that signaled accordance with those values enhanced their status. Furthermore, transnational networks of NGOs, media outlets, companies, universities, and other actors spread many of those ideas and values globally, including by turning their gaze on shortcomings in liberal

---

[19] Sungmin Cho, "Why Non-Democracy Engages with Western Democracy-Promotion Programs: The China Model," *World Politics* 73, no. 4 (2021): p. 777, https://doi.org/10.1017/S0043887121000137.

[20] The seminal texts in this area are Margaret E. Keck and Kathryn Sikkink, *Activists Beyond Borders: Advocacy Networks in International Politics* (Cornell University Press, 1998); Thomas Risse et al., eds., *The Power of Human Rights: International Norms and Domestic Change* (Cambridge University Press, 1999).

[21] Christian Davenport and Benjamin J. Appel, *The Death and Life of State Repression: Understanding Onset, Escalation, Termination, and Recurrence* (Oxford University Press, 2022), p. 86. More generally, rights such as freedom of association, speech, and the press can provide the foundation for collective action that can challenge authoritarian regimes; see Abel Escribà-Folch, "Repression, Political Threats, and Survival Under Autocracy," *International Political Science Review* 34, no. 5 (2013), pp. 543–60, https://doi.org/10.1177/0192512113488259.

[22] On hypocrisy and the "liberal order," see George Lawson and Ayse Zarakol, "Recognizing Injustice: The 'Hypocrisy Charge' and the Future of the Liberal International Order," *International Affairs* 99, no. 1 (2023): pp. 201–17, https://doi.org/10.1093/ia/iiac258; John M. Owen IV, "Liberalism and Its Alternatives, Again," *International Studies Review* 20, no. 2 (2018): p. 311, https://doi.org/10.1093/isr/viy026; Martha Finnemore, "Legitimacy, Hypocrisy, and the Social Structure of Unipolarity: Why Being a Unipole Isn't All It's Cracked Up to Be," *World Politics* 61, no. 1 (2009): pp. 58–85, https://doi.org/10.1353/wp.2009.0005.

democratic states.[23] Scholarship on human rights noted their transnational spread,[24] and authoritarian states seemed to be in a defensive crouch. Authoritarians may have tried to hide their repressive behavior or deny their culpability for specific atrocities, but the prevailing view was that they tacitly accepted the authority of transnational actors to criticize human rights practices.

Authoritarian Resurgence and Internal Contestation

But the international environment has changed since the 1990s. As Snyder writes with regard to human rights promotion, the "period of liberal near-hegemony and great ambitions for the global human rights movement turned out to be short-lived."[25] Threats to liberal influence also come from within democracies, for example in the form of populism and eroding popular support for democratic norms, a topic to which we return below.[26]

For starters, authoritarian states are economically resurgent. One simple way to capture this shift is to measure the relative global economic clout of polities that are more liberal democratic versus those that are less liberal democratic. We use data from the Varieties of Democracy (V-Dem) project, specifically its Liberal Democracy Index (LDI), to reveal the shift from the 1990s to the 2020s. The LDI accounts for protections for civil liberties, rule of law, judicial independence,

---

[23] For example, the United States was the top target of press releases by Amnesty International between 1986 and 2000 according to James Ron et al., "Transnational Information Politics: NGO Human Rights Reporting, 1986–2000," *International Studies Quarterly* 49, no. 3 (2005): pp. 557–588, https://doi.org/10.1111/j.1468-2478.2005.00377.x.

[24] Oona Hathaway, "Why Do Countries Commit to Human Rights Treaties?," *Journal of Conflict Resolution* 51, no. 4 (2002): pp. 588–621, https://doi.org/10.1177/0022002707303046; Christine Min Wotipka and Kiyoteru Tsutsui, "Global Human Rights and State Sovereignty: State Ratification of International Human Rights Treaties, 1965–2001," *Sociological Forum* 23, no. 4 (2008): pp. 724–54, https://doi.org/10.1111/j.1573-7861.2008.00092.x; Zachary Elkins et al., "Getting to Rights: Treaty Ratification, Constitutional Convergence, and Human Rights Practice," *Harvard International Law Journal* 54, no. 1 (2013): pp. 61–95, https://ssrn.com/abstract=2296607.

[25] Jack Snyder, *Human Rights for Pragmatists: Social Power in Modern Times* (Princeton University Press, 2022), p. 2.

[26] For example, see Yascha Mounk, "The End of History Revisited," *Journal of Democracy* 31, no. 1 (2020): pp. 22–35, https://doi.org/10.1353/jod.2020.0002.

electoral democracy, and checks and balances to portray the extent to which the ideal of "liberal democracy" is achieved in a given country in a given year.[27] We combined this with gross domestic product (GDP) data from the World Bank to get a rough picture of the global economic balance of power between more liberal democratic states and less liberal democratic states.

The results are striking.[28] In 1991, states above the global median LDI score accounted for a whopping 89.6% of global GDP. These included the United States, Japan, Germany, and the United Kingdom. Correspondingly, states below the global median LDI score in 1991 accounted for the remaining roughly 10.4% of global GDP. Thirty years later, in 2021, the share of global GDP for states above the global median LDI had declined to about 64.7%, while states with governments below the global median LDI had grown to account for 35.2% of global GDP.

The results are even more remarkable if we slice the data by quartiles, as represented in Figure 1.1. In 1991, the top quartile of states in the LDI—in other words the 25% "most liberal democratic"—accounted for about 84% of global GDP. The bottom quartile—the 25% "least liberal democratic"—accounted for only about 4% of global GDP.

Fast-forward to 2021 and the shift is dramatic. The top quartile of LDI states accounted for about 58.8% of global GDP, while the bottom quartile accounted for 26.4% of global GDP. In fact, in 2021, nine states were in the global *bottom* 25% in terms of liberal democracy but in the global *top* 25% in terms of aggregate GDP: China, Russia, Saudi Arabia, Türkiye, Thailand, Bangladesh, United Arab Emirates, Egypt, and Vietnam. Iran is only one spot below the top quartile for GDP and is also in the bottom 25% for liberal democracy.[29] Of course, the trend toward authoritarians enjoying a greater share of the global economic pie is not predestined to continue, but it is clear that since the 1990s the relative

---

[27] Michael Coppedge et al., "V-Dem Codebook v11.1," *Varieties of Democracy (V-Dem) Project* (2021), p. 44.

[28] We only include states for which both V-Dem and the World Bank have data for the relevant year. In 1991, this was 149 states (74 above the median LDI, 74 below), while in 2021 it was 165 states (82 above the median LDI, 82 below).

[29] Tiny but economically influential Qatar does not make this grouping only because of its small population. Regional leaders near the bottom of the LDI like Rwanda are influential in their neighborhoods but do not make the top tier of global economic listings.

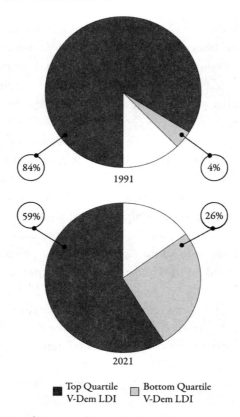

FIGURE 1.1 GDP of Most and Least Liberal Democratic States (V-Dem), 1991 and 2021.

power of liberal democracies has been in decline. Others have organized the data differently but arrive at a similar essential point: Liberal democracies have lost their once dominant share of global economic power.[30] And although this exercise illustrates changes in economic power only, these shifts can facilitate other forms of influence and leverage abroad.[31]

---

[30] Felix Wiebrecht et al., "State of the World 2022: Defiance in the Face of Autocratization," *Democratization* 30, no. 5 (2023): pp. 775–76, https://doi.org/10.1080/13510347.2023.2199452.

[31] The latter is the central point of research on economic statecraft. For recent research on China's economic statecraft, for example, see among others William J. Norris, *Chinese Economic Statecraft: Commercial Actors, Grand Strategy, and State Control* (Cornell University Press, 2016); Yi Edward Yang and Wei Liang, "Introduction to China's Economic Statecraft: Rising Influences, Mixed Results," *Journal of Chinese Political Science* 24, no. 3 (2019): pp. 381–85, https://doi.org/10.1007/s11366-019-09614-1; Stephen Noakes and Charles Burton, "Economic Statecraft and

Unlike the Cold War, when geopolitical competition created clearly demarcated and ideological blocs, the growing global power of authoritarian states is actually fueled, not diminished, by their deepened interconnectedness in the global economy and their embrace of international markets and transnational supply chains. China is the world's largest exporting nation and the top trading partner, investor, and development assistance provider for many countries around the world.[32] The rise of global telecommunications and the internet, easier and cheaper air travel, the globalization of higher education and study-abroad opportunities, and a global financial system in which non-democratic states are entwined all means that the societal, political, and economic "linkages," to borrow a term from Levitsky and Way, between today's major democracies and non-democracies are vastly deeper, broader, and more complex than they ever were during the Cold War. Even in the case of Russia, Moscow's full-scale invasion of Ukraine in 2022 resulted in comprehensive sanctions and Russia's economic estrangement from much of the West, but global interconnectedness and trade networks have allowed Moscow to find willing buyers for its oil and gas in parts of Europe, China, the Middle East, and India and forge new regional re-export channels for the import of restricted technologies.[33] And because of the changing economic realities illustrated in Figure 1.1, the "leverage," the other side of influence in Levitsky

---

the Making of Bilateral Relationships: Canada-China and New Zealand–China Interactions Compared," *Journal of Chinese Political Science* 24, no. 3 (2019): pp. 411–31, https://doi.org/10.1007/s11366-018-09602-x; James Reilly, *Orchestration: China's Economic Statecraft Across Asia and Europe* (Oxford University Press, 2021); Scott L. Kastner and Margaret Pearson, "Exploring the Parameters of China's Economic Influence," *Studies in Comparative International Development* 56, no. 1 (2021): pp. 18–44, https://doi.org/10.1007/s12116-021-09318-9.

[32] On trade, for example, China is the largest partner for 120 countries; see Mark A. Green, "China Is the Top Trading Partner to More Than 120 Countries," *Wilson Center Stubborn Things*, January 17, 2023, https://www.wilsoncenter.org/blog-post/china-top-trading-partner-more-120-countries.

[33] On Western sanctions and the global response, see Agathe Demarais, *Backfire: How Sanctions Reshape the World Against US Interests* (Columbia University Press, 2022). On how the Russian oil trade post-2022 and global oil market have evolved to circumvent sanctions, see Chris Miller et al., "Sanctions on Russia and the Splintering of the World Oil Market," American Enterprise Institute, February 20, 2024, https://policycommons.net/artifacts/11344860/sanctions-on-russia-and-the-splintering-of-the-world-oil-market/12233991/. On the use of neighbors and regional countries to re-export restricted goods, see Maxim Chupilkin et al., "The Eurasian Roundabout: Trade Flows into Russia Through the Caucasus and Central

12   DICTATING THE AGENDA

and Way's conceptual device, that liberal democratic states have over authoritarian states is fading.[34]

Not only is potential for leverage fading but the willingness of liberal democratic states to use it may be, too. It is not just illiberal authoritarian states that have grown in power since the 1990s. Illiberal movements internal to both established and precarious democracies also contest the values of liberal democracy.[35] Snyder identifies this moment as one of "double equipoise," with contestation "between liberal and illiberal states in the international system and between liberal and illiberal social forces within powerful transitional states."[36] The rise of illiberal movements and leaders, mostly of the far-right variety, in the United States and Western Europe grabs much of the attention, perhaps none more so than Donald Trump's decisive election victory in 2024. But illiberal political leaders and movements have risen to power in recent years in important non-US or European democracies, including India, Brazil, Türkiye, Israel, and the Philippines, while leaders of already illiberal dictatorships have clamped down on liberalism even further, including most importantly Xi Jinping in China and Vladimir Putin in Russia.

Figure 1.2 illustrates the point. It shows V-Dem's measure of liberal democracy from 1980 to 2023 weighted by population.[37] A liberal democratic plateau emerges around 1999 and lasts until around 2012. The global level of liberal democracy on a scale of 0–1 hit a zenith of .39 in 2003,[38] but fast-forward two decades and in 2023 it was .29.[39] These

---

Asia," European Bank for Reconstruction and Development, October 2023, https://users.ox.ac.uk/~econ0247/Roundabout.pdf.

[34] Steven Levitsky and Lucan A. Way, "Linkage Versus Leverage. Rethinking the International Dimension of Regime Change," *Comparative Politics* 38, no. 4 (2006): pp. 379–400, https://doi.org/10.2307/20434008. Authoritarian states are also often tightly linked with one another and thereby able to help stabilize each other; see Oisín Tansey et al., "Ties to the Rest: Autocratic Linkages and Regime Survival," *Comparative Political Studies* 50, no. 9 (2017): pp. 1221–54, https://doi.org/10.1177/0010414016666859.

[35] For a seminal statement on the contemporary crisis of liberalism and the rise of illiberalism see Ivan Krastev and Stephen Holmes, *The Light That Failed: A Reckoning* (Penguin 2019).

[36] Snyder, *Human Rights for Pragmatists*, p. 239.

[37] For coding specifics, see Coppedge et al., "V-Dem Codebook v11.1," p. 44.

[38] With a confidence interval of .35–.43.

[39] With a confidence interval .26–.32. Many related indicators, such as freedom of expression, media censorship, and civil society autonomy, reveal similar patterns.

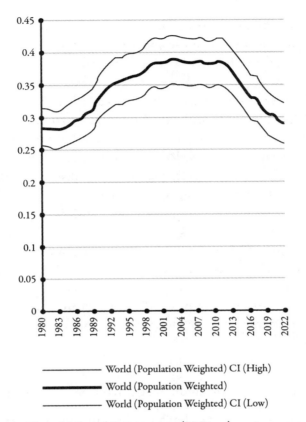

FIGURE 1.2 Global Liberal Democracy (V-Dem), 1980 to 2023.

data include a huge population over a long time period, so shifts are gradual and mask a lot of complexity, but with the data sliced a bit differently, V-Dem researchers observe that the level of democracy for the average global citizen in 2022 was about the same as it was in 1986.[40]

---

[40] Weibrecht, "State of the World 2022," pp. 770–71. There is significant debate about the nature and scope of "democratic backsliding" globally. What all observers appear to agree on is that, at minimum, levels of democracy globally have flatlined even if they have not declined as such. See Andrew T. Little and Anne Meng, "Measuring Democratic Backsliding," *PS: Political Science & Politics* 57, no. 2 (2024): pp. 149–61, https://doi.org/10.1017/S104909652300063X; Steven Levitsky and Lucan Way, "The Resilience of Democracy's Third Wave," *PS: Political Science & Politics* 57, no. 2 (2024): pp. 198–201, https://doi.org/10.1017/S1049096523000914; Michael K. Miller, "How Little and Meng's Objective Approach Fails in Democracies." *PS: Political Science & Politics* 57, no. 2 (2024): pp. 202–7, https://doi.org/10.1017/S1049096523001063.

Underscoring the link between liberalism and democracy, they find that freedom of expression is the underlying component of democracy that eroded the most in the 10 years prior to 2022.[41]

Importantly, the growing power of illiberal authoritarian states and the rise of illiberal movements can feed one another. Illiberal populists assail the "liberal international order" as contrary to the sovereignty and tradition that they ostensibly value, while illiberal authoritarian powers undermine elements of the order that advance liberal democratic values and thus threaten their rule.[42] Illiberal populists routinely express support for systematically engaging China, Russia, and other non-democratic states, arguing that embracing "multipolarity" strengthens state sovereignty by mollifying liberal criticism about domestic illiberal transgressions.[43] The affinity that Donald Trump and his followers seem to have with the views of Russian authorities when it comes to liberalism and nationalism is a case in point. The result is that liberal democratic values, actors, institutions, and networks are squeezed between illiberal movements within democracies and resurgent authoritarian state actors.

Authoritarian Interconnectedness: Global Interactions Rewired

Contra initial assumptions about the liberalizing pressures of globalization, the last 30 years have revealed that globalized linkages are not inherent forces for promoting liberal democracy or liberal values. Authoritarian states can work from within them to cauterize the influence of liberal ideas, silence criticisms of authoritarian politics,

---

[41] Weibrecht, "State of the World 2022," p. 774.

[42] Alexander Cooley and Daniel H. Nexon, "The Illiberal Tide: Why the International Order Is Tilting Toward Autocracy," *Foreign Affairs*, March 26, 2021. On illiberalism as an ideology that professes to value sovereignty and tradition see Marlene Laruelle, "Illiberalism: A Conceptual Introduction," *East European Politics* 38, no. 2 (2022): p. 309, https://doi.org/10.1080/21599165.2022.2037079.

[43] On "multipolar populism," see Alexander Cooley and Daniel Nexon, "Why Populists Want a Multipolar World," *Foreign Policy*, April 20, 2020, https://foreignpolicy.com/2020/04/25/populists-multipolar-world-russia-china/.

and, most importantly, repurpose transnational networks and institutions to advance illiberal aims.[44] In the economic sphere, authoritarian states "are not simply defending themselves against liberalism, they are using its global rules as an offensive strategy to fortify illiberalism at home."[45] Actors with illiberal goals use the toolkit of global activism to advance their aims.[46] Overall, as Glasius observes, "It has become clear in the last two decades that various forms of globalization are fiercely compatible with authoritarianism."[47] In some respects globalization can even accelerate authoritarianism by taking advantage of "asymmetric openness," or "the strange reality that the contemporary liberal order works better for authoritarian regimes than it does for liberal democracies."[48]

Examples are almost too numerous to catalog. Authoritarian states like Russia and China advance illiberal norms via international organizations to help reduce the free flow of information on the internet internationally.[49] The rule-of-law protections that accompany proceedings in financial hubs of New York and London can be used by autocrats to target political opponents.[50] When students are sent from Saudi Arabia or China to study in "the West," government programs attempt to ensure their political loyalty upon departure and return and monitor

---

[44] Alexander Cooley and John Heathershaw, *Dictators Without Borders: Power and Money in Central Asia* (Yale University Press, 2017); Alexander Dukalskis, *Making the World Safe for Dictatorship* (Oxford University Press, 2021).

[45] Nikhil Kalyanpur, "An Illiberal Economic Order: Commitment Mechanisms Become Tools of Authoritarian Coercion," *Review of International Political Economy* 30, no. 4 (2023): p. 1239, https://doi.org/10.1080/09692290.2023.2211280.

[46] Clifford Bob, *The Global Right Wing and the Clash of World Politics* (Cambridge University Press, 2012).

[47] Marlies Glasius, *Authoritarian Practices in a Global Age* (Oxford University Press, 2023), p. 220.

[48] Alexander Cooley and Daniel H. Nexon, "The Real Crisis of Global Order: Illiberalism on the Rise," *Foreign Affairs* 101, no. 1 (2022): p. 106.

[49] Daniëlle Flonk, "Emerging Illiberal Norms: Russia and China as Promoters of Internet Content Control," *International Affairs* 97, no. 6 (2021): pp. 1925–44, https://doi.org/10.1093/ia/iiab146.

[50] Kalyanpur, "An Illiberal Economic Order," pp. 1243–45.

their activities while abroad.[51] China can use the threat of curtailing market access to enforce censorship or punish political speech abroad in a range of industries, from academic publishing[52] to sports[53] to films[54] to university partnerships.[55] Turkish authorities can use Western social media platforms to reach across borders to silence diaspora newspapers in Europe critical of Ankara.[56] Likewise Saudi and Emirati officials can appear tolerant of political pluralism by letting their citizens use X (formerly Twitter) but distort the transnational discussion through spin, policing, and surveillance.[57] Extradition treaties and transnational crime-prevention mechanisms can be abused to pursue critics of authoritarian politics abroad.[58] Global media arms of authoritarian states like Russia's RT are keen to highlight perceived failures of liberal actors and networks, from the destructive consequences of the 2008 financial crisis to the hypocrisy of Western support of strategically important non-democratic states to the rise within the West itself of social movements that oppose liberal causes like reproductive rights, LGBTQ

---

[51] Yan Xiaojun and Mohammed Alsudairi, "Guarding Against the Threat of a Westernising Education: A Comparative Study of Chinese and Saudi Cultural Security Discourses and Practices Towards Overseas Study," *Journal of Contemporary China* 30, no. 131 (2021): pp. 803–19, https://doi.org/10.1080/10670564.2021.1884962.

[52] Nicholas Loubere, "The New Censorship, the New Academic Freedom: Commercial Publishers and the Chinese Market," *Journal of the European Association for Chinese Studies* 1 (2020): pp. 239–52, https://doi.org/10.25365/jeacs.2020.1.239-252.

[53] William D. O'Connell, "Silencing the Crowd: China, the NBA, and Leveraging Market Size to Export Censorship," *Review of International Political Economy* 29, no. 4 (2021): pp. 1112–34, https://doi.org/10.1080/09692290.2021.1905683.

[54] Aynne Kokas, "How Beijing Runs the Show in Hollywood," *Journal of Democracy* 33, no. 2 (2022): pp. 90–102, https://doi.org/10.1353/jod.2022.0020.

[55] Eva Pils, "Complicity in Democratic Engagement with Autocratic Systems," *Ethics & Global Politics* 14, no. 3 (2021): pp. 142–62, https://doi.org/10.1080/16544951.2021.1958509.

[56] Glasius, *Authoritarian Practices*, pp. 39–71.

[57] Robert Uniacke, "Authoritarianism in the Information Age: State Branding, Depoliticizing and 'De-Civilizing' of Online Civil Society in Saudi Arabia and the United Arab Emirates," *British Journal of Middle Eastern Studies* 48, no. 5 (2021): pp. 979–99, https://doi.org/10.1080/13530194.2020.1737916.

[58] Cooley and Heathershaw, *Dictators Without Borders*; Edward Lemon, "Weaponizing Interpol," *Journal of Democracy* 30, no. 2 (2019): pp. 15–29, https://doi.org/10.1353/jod.2019.0019; Daniel Krcmaric, "Nowhere to Hide? Global Policing and the Politics of Extradition," *International Security* 47, no. 2 (2022): pp. 7–47, https://doi.org/10.1162/isec_a_00444.

rights, and the separation of religion and the state.[59] Pro-authoritarian media outlets advance their narratives, while Western media outlets are banned in autocracies and journalists harassed or imprisoned.[60] And companies must now not only consider the reputational damage from being targeted by activists campaigns from civil society in democracies but also the risk of losing access to large consumer markets in authoritarian states like China.[61]

The interconnectedness wrought by globalization combined with the resurgence of authoritarian states (and their illiberal bedfellows within democracies) opens the possibility not only that networks and processes of transnational *liberal* influence can be tamed but also that those very networks and processes can be repurposed or reconfigured for transnational *illiberal* influence. Examples like those above of the "artful exploitation of globalization by authoritarian regimes" are emblematic of authoritarians' capacity to adapt to new environments, often learning from one another to diffuse and improve their methods.[62] As Guriev and Triesman observe, dictatorships "try to use interdependence to advance their interests and weaken democracy,"[63] objectives that are facilitated by their resurgent global power. These efforts can co-opt otherwise pro-democracy actors and enmesh them in networks and processes that hinder liberal influence or even advance authoritarianism.[64]

---

[59] Erin Baggott Carter and Brett L. Carter, "Questioning More: RT, Outward-Facing Propaganda, and the Post-West World Order," *Security Studies* 30, no. 1 (2021): pp. 49–78, https://doi.org/10.1080/09636412.2021.1885730.

[60] Dukalskis, *Making the World Safe.*

[61] O'Connell, "Silencing the Crowd."

[62] Quotation from Glenn Tiffert, "The Authoritarian Assault on Knowledge," *Journal of Democracy* 31, no. 4 (2020): p. 29. On authoritarian learning and emulation, see footnote 13 and Lee Morgenbesser, "The Menu of Autocratic Innovation," *Democratization* 27, no. 6 (2020): pp. 1053–72, https://doi.org/10.1080/13510347. 2020.1746275.

[63] Sergei Guriev and Daniel Treisman, *Spin Dictators: The Changing Face of Tyranny in the 21st Century* (Princeton University Press, 2022), p. 201.

[64] Pils, "Complicity in Democratic Engagement." To this point, Gurol and colleagues note that "interconnectedness also reminds us of the need to look more closely at the multiple ways in which formally democratic actors are implicated in authoritarian practices." See Julia Gurol et al., "Authoritarian Power and Contestation Beyond the State," *Globalizations* 21, no. 6 (2023): p. 3, https://doi.org/10.1080/14747731 .2022.2162290

The Argument in Brief

All these factors combined mean that autocrats increasingly dictate the global agenda in a range of transnational domains. This book attempts to make sense of these patterns and show how once-liberal networks, across many global issue areas, have been repurposed to advance illiberalism. By way of definition we understand political liberalism as a set of ideas that at their core value basic political human rights, individual liberty, and democracy.[65] Applied to the international level, liberalism is concerned with the "international space" that facilitates the survival of liberal democracy domestically.[66] Illiberalism cuts against political rights, individual liberty, and democracy, and international illiberalism seeks to reshape the international environment to be friendlier to authoritarian rule.

Authoritarians are pushing back against global liberalism, actively repurposing the tools, techniques, networks, and actors once associated with advancing liberalism to reclaim control and influence over key global issues. The authoritarian backlash is robust and multifaceted, as important drivers of transnational liberal influence in the 1990s are confronting the resurgent power of newly confident contemporary authoritarian states looking to exploit weaknesses, often with an assist from illiberal allies in democracies. They do not always succeed in dictating the agenda, but they are learning fast.

Our core theoretical contribution is a framework that we call the *authoritarian snapback*. We define it as a process in which non-democratic states at minimum attempt to block the networks and processes associated with transnational liberal influence at home and more maximally attempt to repurpose those same networks and processes to advance illiberal authoritarian aims abroad. We chart the process of authoritarian

---

[65] Michael Freeden, "Liberalism," in *The Routledge Handbook to Social and Political Philosophy*, edited by Gerald F. Gaus and Fred D'Agostino (Taylor & Francis, 2012), pp. 231–42. For an informative discussion about the liberal "script" and contestations within it, see Michael Zürn and Johannes Gerschewski, "Sketching the Liberal Script: A Target of Contestations," SCRIPTS Working Paper No. 10, 2021, https://www.scripts-berlin.eu/publications/working-paper-series/Working-Paper-No_-10-2021/index.html.

[66] G. John Ikenberry, *A World Safe for Democracy: Liberal Internationalism and the Crises of Global Order* (Yale University Press, 2020), pp. xiii–xiv.

snapback by identifying a stylized model involving five steps of escalating ambition—stigmatizing, shielding, reframing, projecting outward, and dictating the agenda—with each subsequent step facilitated by the power and ambition of the authoritarian state.

Empirically, we apply these arguments to the post–Cold War evolution of four global issue areas: media, consumer activism, higher education, and international sports. We choose these areas for three reasons. First, they are domains in which nonstate entities are the primary actors and which are sometimes overlooked. While international organizations (IOs) have always been a core topic in the study of global politics, and NGOs have received a great deal of attention from international relations and comparative politics scholars since the 1990s, the areas of media, consumer action, higher education, and sports are not always central to debates in these fields.[67] Our aim is to open new avenues for thinking about authoritarian influence in global politics.

Second, they are areas that vary in the salience of different liberal values. Journalism and higher education are in large measure premised on values such as freedom of the press, speech, association, academic freedom, and related protections. Consumer behavior and sports, on the other hand, are not built on liberal values as such but rather have witnessed advocacy efforts strategically attached to them given the public prominence of corporate brands and athletic competitions. Conceptually the rights that underlie such advocacy, such as media freedom and access, civil society's freedom to organize, and academic freedom, are among the first targets of autocratizing governments.[68]

Third and finally, we choose them because the authoritarian snapback is still unfolding in all of these areas. So are responses to the snapback. The danger of writing a book that addresses current events is that the latter may overtake the former. However, we think these domains are important not only for academics to understand but also for policymakers and citizens. The normative ground of what is considered

---

[67] There are excellent exceptions, and we engage with these in the chapters that follow. For an analysis on the relations between IOs, NGOs, and transnational contentious politics see Sidney Tarrow, "Transnational Politics: Contention and Institutions in International Politics," *Annual Review of Political Science* 4, no. 1 (2001): pp. 1–20, 10.1146/annurev.polisci.4.1.1.

[68] Wiebrecht et al., "State of the World 2022," p. 778.

politically legitimate and routine is rapidly shifting across all of them. Rather than search for historical analogies to analyze in the hopes that lessons may transfer to the contemporary period, we address our current moment head on.

Theoretically, our research speaks to debates at the nexus of comparative politics and international relations, sketching out the changing transnational dimensions of authoritarian rule, transnational influence networks, and the evolving international order. For each domain we discuss the extent and scope of authoritarian influence, agenda-setting, repression, and sponsorship in these areas of governance. For data we rely on a variety of sources, including publicly available media and NGO reports, company annual reports and statements, statements and speeches by political leaders, purpose-built databases, media analysis, semi-structured interviews, process-tracing, and secondary literature. The approach is designed both to substantiate our theoretical claims and to stimulate new thinking and analysis by other scholars and analysts concerned with the nexus between liberal democratic norms, global order, and authoritarian resilience and advance.

The Plan of This Book

The next three chapters advance our theoretical arguments with greater precision. Chapter 2 opens with a description of transnational influence in the lead-up to the 2008 Summer Olympics in Beijing, during which China's authoritarian governance was scrutinized by global liberal actors and transnational campaigns. Coming amid the plateau of liberal democracy identified in Figure 1.2, the event reveals the liberal influence toolkit of the period as well as its limitations. Stepping back, we show how transnational liberal influence was globally promoted in two ways: the emulative attraction of American "soft power" and the dynamic agency of liberal activists who set the global advocacy agenda around promoting liberal causes and universal norms across transnational civil society networks. Analytically, Western soft power was effective because it was perceived as embodying expertise, channeling consumer trends, and allowing for free expression and autonomy for a wide variety of actors inside and outside of the formal political system.

The global environment for promoting liberalism was propitious, and transnational actors were emboldened to pressure recalcitrant governments to adopt liberal reforms and values.

Chapter 3 identifies just how much things have changed since the 1990s and 2000s and how they look in the 2020s. We open the chapter by contrasting the run-up to the 2022 Beijing Winter Olympics to the 2008 Summer Olympics, showing how Beijing successfully neutered the transnational actors and campaigns that previously had exerted pressure. Zooming out, our analysis reveals that Western models are no longer viewed as monopolizing expertise, market power has shifted toward authoritarian states, and the independence of transnational actors has been curtailed. The power of illiberal states has accelerated that erosion and has established new foundations to ensure that large areas of global governance are less susceptible to liberal influence.

Chapter 4 then lays out the *authoritarian snapback* model. In sequence, it reveals how states *stigmatize* liberal political ideas at home as well as the individuals and institutions associated with them. This prepares the ground to *shield* the public from transnational liberal influence by banning platforms that disseminate it, outlawing certain transnational linkages, and in general deepening control over and surveillance of liberal political discourse. The next escalation is for the authoritarian state to *reframe engagement and set new ground rules* for transnational entities, including businesses, universities, and entertainment figures. By elevating criticisms of the country's human rights or political practices as an attack on "the people" or "the nation," the state attempts to showcase its popular credentials and browbeat the critic into silence. The final two steps entail the outward projection of illiberal influence beginning with *projecting control and influence outward*, often by co-opting or silencing the very institutions that were thought to facilitate the spread of liberal ideas in the first place. The process culminates in the most ambitious step to *dictate the agenda* by actively using repurposed transnational networks to advance illiberal alternatives across a range of areas. This reclamation project is then fed back into the domestic information sphere to help legitimate the regime's ideas as internationally respected. We illustrate the model with an account of how China has sought to mitigate liberal pressure on human rights by transforming these very institutions and networks of global human rights governance, with considerable success.

The next four chapters illustrate and evaluate the arguments by exploring how this authoritarian contestation is occurring in global domains long assumed to be dominated by liberal ideas and liberal actors. Chapter 5 examines important transformations in global media, discussing how since 2008 authoritarian states have amplified their reach and adapted their methods to insert their messages into the global discussion. We present data on the global reach of Russia's RT, TASS, and Sputnik and China's CGTN and Xinhua as well as an original data set of content sharing agreements concluded between Chinese and Russian state media on the one hand and foreign media outlets on the other. The flip side of proffering the pro-authoritarian message is to silence those who might call it into question. The second part of the chapter presents our original data set of all instances in which independent foreign journalists have had their access to authoritarian states officially denied. These 1,020 instances—surely an underestimate given that we rely on publicly available data—show how autocrats try to control flows of transnational information so that their preferred images and messages receive less scrutiny.

Chapter 6 turns to consumer activism. Here we use a paired-case study methodology to compare two consumer boycotts concerned with labor rights and standards in Asia. In the 1990s the American footwear company Nike was the target of consumer and NGO activism regarding labor standards in its factories, some of which were in non-democratic or transitioning states in Asia, including China, South Korea, and Indonesia. The campaign came at the height of liberal democratic soft power and is widely considered to be an effective effort, having forced the US-based apparel-manufacturing giant to change its practices and helped to usher in broader global corporate social responsibility and the introduction of new voluntary compliance standards in global manufacturing. This case is contrasted with activism around forced labor in the Xinjiang cotton industry after 2017, when international reports first revealed China's systemic detention of perhaps one million Uyghurs and other minorities in re-education camps. In contrast to the 1990s episode, in this campaign, authoritarian snapback led to the contestation of this boycott campaign and strikingly different reactions by global companies. The PRC's powerful and nationalistic consumer market facilitated by a confident and vocal party-state created a different context, and we focus on Swedish company H&M and the industry group, the Better Cotton Initiative, to explore what changed between the 1990s and the 2020s.

In Chapter 7 we focus on trends in global higher education, a domain often overlooked in discussions about global governance and rising authoritarianism. After outlining how the perceived global dominance of Western elite universities is eroding, we present descriptive statistics from a newly constructed database of higher-education branch campuses in non-democratic states. We address the drive by China, Singapore, and the Gulf States in the 2000s to secure partnerships and build elite US and European universities and analyze the contradictory imperatives faced by the leadership of its Western partners on key issues such as academic freedom, labor standards, LGBTQ rights, and gender equality. Finally, we illustrate how the stages of authoritarian snapback apply to the largest single overseas investment made in liberal education following the Cold War by tracing the rise and fall of Central European University's campus in Hungary. The institution, founded through donations by liberal philanthropist George Soros, was ultimately expelled by the illiberal government of Viktor Orbán.

In Chapter 8, we consider the realm of international sports. We show how authoritarian states, with their new assertiveness and growing market power, became important players in transforming global sports, across both national competitions and the professional club levels. Authoritarian countries began to engage in what critics call "sportswashing" by hosting major international sporting events such as the Olympics and the World Cup but also influencing aspects of Western sports leagues through their acquisition of individual clubs, media rights, and sponsorship deals with clubs and individual athletes. This newfound authoritarian power in the sports world comes from being networked and embedded in the leagues, associations, and markets that globalized beginning in the 1990s. We show how this has transformed political influence in global sports through closer looks at the US-based National Basketball Association's relationship with China, the English Premier League's embrace of authoritarian-backed ownership groups as well as its own collision with China over free speech,

Formula 1's global expansion, Qatar's squelching of a campaign about LGBTQ rights in the run-up to the 2022 FIFA men's World Cup, and, finally, Saudi Arabia's dramatic investments in global sports.

Chapter 9 reflects upon just how far trends in global governance have strayed from the assumptions of the 1990s, showing how expectations that technology and consumerism would act as liberal agents of change have been proven wrong. We use our framework to discuss how authoritarian states are transforming new areas of global governance and transnational cooperation, including global efforts on climate change, the push for more gender equality, and emerging global governance over artificial intelligence. We present initial thoughts on the evolving relationship between liberalism and geopolitics and provide recommendations for how governments can navigate the challenges of a multipolar world while upholding liberal principles and values.

Chapter 2

The 1990s Origins and the Acceleration of Transnational Liberal Influence

The 2008 Beijing Summer Olympics reveal a lot about how transnational liberal influence worked from the 1990s to the mid-2000s. The methods used by various liberal actors and the responses by Chinese authorities are emblematic of the era, and recalling them now with hindsight shows how much has changed since the early 2000s. Here we open with a look at the lead-up, culmination, and aftermath of the event before stepping back to examine the underlying processes that shaped what we observed.

In the lead-up to 2008, liberal NGOs successfully lobbied the International Olympic Committee (IOC), as well as corporate sponsors and the global media, to make liberal human rights advocacy a core issue of China's showcase.[1] The link between the Chinese regime's human rights practices and the staging of the Olympics had first been raised in September 1993, when Sydney was narrowly awarded the 2000 Summer Games by just two votes over Beijing. The IOC itself

---

[1] The pressure and calls for political change linked with the Olympics were "deafening" when compared to the much-touted case of pressure on Korea to liberalize in the lead-up to the 1988 Summer Olympics. This according to Victor D. Cha, *Beyond the Final Score: The Politics of Sport in Asia* (Columbia University Press, 2009), p. 128.

cited the adverse human rights situation in China as an important factor in its decision to award the Olympics to Australia.[2] Eight years later, after a renewed international campaign, Beijing easily won the competition for the 2008 Games at the IOC meeting in Moscow in 2001. The committee expressed the hope that the seven years run-up would both accelerate China's embrace of the world and improve the human rights situation, opening the door to several liberal actors to launch sustained advocacy campaigns.[3] As the Games approached, some observers expressed optimism that the IOC, with its authority and influence, could help ensure that China improved its human rights record, even if only for public relations and self-interested purposes.[4] Liu Jingmin, vice president of the Beijing Olympic Bid Committee, said as China was making its pitch to host in 2008: "By allowing Beijing to host the Games, you will help the development of human rights."[5]

As a result, from the moment that the Games were awarded to Beijing, leading international human rights organizations planned to use the international media spotlight strategically. The IOC's own public statements about hopes for human rights progress and the Chinese government's perceived quest for international approval could serve as important sources of leverage. The IOC's Coordination Committee for the Olympics, which met with the Beijing Organizing Committee regularly from 2001 to 2008 to discuss preparations, was frequently targeted by human rights NGOs with reports of the inadequacy of Chinese reform efforts.[6] For their part, both Human Rights Watch and Amnesty

---

[2] Jean-Loup Chappelet, "The Olympics' Evolving Relationship with Human Rights: An Ongoing Affair," *Sport in Society* 25, no. 1 (2022): pp. 1–22, https://doi.org/10.1080/17430437.2022.2005289.

[3] Jere Longman, "Olympics: Beijing Wins Bid for 2008 Games," *New York Times*, July 14, 2001.

[4] Julie H. Liu, "Lighting the Torch of Human Rights: The Olympic Games as a Vehicle for Human Rights Reform," *Northwestern Journal of International Human Rights* 5, no. 2 (2007): pp. 213–35.

[5] Quoted in Elizabeth C. Economy and Adam Segal, "China's Olympic Nightmare: What the Games Mean for Beijing's Future," *Foreign Affairs* 87, no. 4 (2008): p. 50.

[6] Susan Brownell, "Human Rights and the Beijing Olympics: Imagined Global Community and the Transnational Public Sphere," *British Journal of Sociology* 63, no. 2 (2012): pp. 316–19, https://doi.org/10.1111/j.1468-4446.2012.01411.x.

ORIGINS AND ACCELERATION OF LIBERAL INFLUENCE 27

International strategically used the attention on the Games and their access to the IOC to mount liberal advocacy campaigns on a broad scope of human rights-related issues.[7] In the years leading up to the Games, these groups would publicly assess the state of "human rights reforms" that Chinese officials had committed to as hosts, and,[8] in the immediate year prior to the Games, they released a wave of reports spotlighting general human rights shortcomings, such as the crackdown on human rights activists and Tibet campaigners,[9] continued use of the death penalty,[10] and denial of media access to politically threatening topics.[11] These groups also mounted advocacy campaigns about specific government policies related to preparations for the staging of the Games, including the use of migrant labor to construct facilities,[12] the forced relocation of urban residents in Beijing,[13] and the government's pledge to the IOC to guarantee media freedoms for foreign journalists covering the Games.[14] External advocates also issued international

---

[7] Brownell, "Human Rights," p. 316.

[8] Amnesty International, "China: The Olympic Countdown: Three Years of Human Rights Reform?," August 4, 2005, https://www.amnesty.org/en/documents/asa17/021/2005/en/; Amnesty International, "China: The Olympics Countdown: Failing to Keep Human Rights Promises," September 20, 2006, https://www.amnesty.org/en/documents/asa17/046/2006/en/.

[9] Amnesty International, "People's Republic of China: The Olympics Countdown: Crackdown on Tibet Protestors," April 1, 2008, https://www.amnesty.org/en/documents/asa17/070/2008/en/; Amnesty International, "China: The Olympics Countdown: Crackdown on Activists Threatens Olympics Legacy," April 1, 2008, https://www.amnesty.org/en/documents/asa17/050/2008/en/.

[10] Amnesty International, "Stop Executions: China's Choice, Legacy of the Beijing Olympics," February 26, 2008, https://www.amnesty.org/en/documents/asa17/029/2008/en/.

[11] Human Rights Watch, "You Will Be Harassed and Detained: Media Freedoms Under Assault Ahead of the 2008 Beijing Olympic Games," August 6, 2007, https://www.hrw.org/reports/2007/china0807/china0807webwcover.pdf; Human Rights Watch, "China's Forbidden Zones: Shutting the Media out of Tibet and Other 'Sensitive' Stories," July 6, 2008, https://www.hrw.org/report/2008/07/06/chinas-forbidden-zones/shutting-media-out-tibet-and-other-sensitive-stories.

[12] Human Rights Watch, "'One Year of My Blood': Exploitation of Migrant Construction Workers in Beijing," March 11, 2008, https://www.hrw.org/report/2008/03/11/one-year-my-blood/exploitation-migrant-construction-workers-beijing/.

[13] Human Rights Watch, "Demolished: Forced Evictions and the Tenants' Rights," March 25, 2004, https://www.hrw.org/sites/default/files/reports/china0304.pdf.

[14] Human Rights Watch, "You Will Be Harassed."

press guides and "media kits" that detailed Beijing's commitments about maintaining open international press coverage. Brownell notes that in a risk assessment undertaken one year before the event, the IOC identified 28 different NGOs that planned to use the 2008 Games to highlight advocacy causes.[15]

Despite concerted effort by Chinese security and intelligence services,[16] several high-profile protests and global incidents, particularly about Tibet, grabbed international media headlines in the run-up to the Games. In March 2008, Tibet experienced its most serious demonstrations and crackdown since the 1980s, as Tibetan monks in Lhasa clashed with Chinese police, who killed at least ten demonstrators.[17] The episode prompted a wave of global protests, renewed media scrutiny on Tibet, and a statement by Olympic President Jacques Rogge that the events there were "a matter of concern to the IOC."[18] The most notable protest occurred in Paris on April 6, 2008, when Olympic officials were forced to extinguish the flame during the Olympic torch relay after pro-Tibet activists tried to seize it.[19] Along the torch route, Tibet protesters gained attention in Athens, London, San Francisco, and Delhi, although on stops after Paris in the route, pro-Beijing counterprotesters began to outnumber their pro-Tibet counterparts, such as in Bangkok, Seoul, and Canberra.[20] At the Games themselves Students for a Free Tibet staged protest actions in Beijing, including projecting "Free Tibet" in lights near the National Stadium. Around 40 activists were detained and deported because of these actions, but a spokesperson

---

[15] Brownell, "Human Rights," p. 307.

[16] Roger Faligot, *Chinese Spies: From Chairman Mao to Xi Jinping* (Hurst Publishers, 2022), pp. 405–27.

[17] Jim Yardley, "Violence in Tibet as Police Clash with Tibetan Monks," *New York Times*, March 15, 2008, https://www.nytimes.com/2008/03/15/world/asia/15tibet.html.

[18] "Statement by Jacques Rogge President of the International Olympic Committee," International Olympic Committee, March 23, 2008, https://olympics.com/ioc/news/statement-by-jacques-rogge-president-of-the-international-olympic-committee.

[19] "Protestors Snuff Out Olympic Torch in Paris," Reuters, April 6, 2008, https://www.reuters.com/article/us-china-tibet/protests-snuff-out-olympic-torch-in-paris-idUSSP23296420080407.

[20] "Timeline: Olympic Torch Protests Around the World," Reuters, April 28, 2008, https://www.reuters.com/article/us-olympics-torch-disruptions-idUSSP17070920080428 (accessed January 16, 2023).

ORIGINS AND ACCELERATION OF LIBERAL INFLUENCE   29

for the group said that "considering how badly the Chinese leadership doesn't want Tibet to be talked about, I think [the protest actions] would be considered a success."[21]

Another issue that garnered international attention was China's support for Sudan and its dictator Omar al-Bashir, who had been sanctioned and would soon be indicted by the International Criminal Court (ICC), for launching a campaign of genocide in the Darfur area. Director Steven Spielberg resigned in February 2008 as an artistic adviser to the Olympics over the Darfur issue after concerted activist pressure and after Spielberg himself lobbied for change, including writing letters to Chinese leader Hu Jintao.[22] International media and advocacy pressure continued right up until the opening ceremony in August, with Amnesty International releasing public assessments acknowledging some progress in the area of death penalty reform but sharply criticizing Beijing for failing to live up to its other major human rights commitments.[23]

Transnational liberal influence appeared to yield moderate successes in conditions for foreign press coverage, where Chinese authorities relented and agreed to relax some restrictions on foreign journalists covering the preparations for the Games and the event itself, some of which were eventually made permanent.[24] The PRC publicly committed to allowing an uncensored internet for journalists reporting on the event, though it did not follow through completely.[25] In a further sign that China felt compelled to show it was playing by something resembling liberal rules, it allowed three "demonstration zones" to be

---

[21] Andrew Jacobs and Colin Moynihan, "5 Americans Are Arrested for Protests in Beijing," *New York Times*, August 19, 2008, https://www.nytimes.com/2008/08/20/sports/olympics/20china.html (accessed January 16, 2023).

[22] Helene Cooper, "Spielberg Drops Out as Adviser to Beijing Olympics over Darfur Conflict," *New York Times*, February 13, 2008, https://www.nytimes.com/2008/02/13/world/asia/13china.html (accessed March 7, 2023).

[23] Amnesty International, "The Olympics Countdown—Broken Promises," July 28, 2008, https://www.amnesty.org/en/documents/asa17/089/2008/en/.

[24] The more liberal measures still mask quite a few restrictions on foreign journalists in China, which, consistent with the themes of this book, appear to be getting more, not less restrictive. See assessments from the Foreign Correspondent's Club of China, https://fccchina.org/.

[25] Nick Mulvenney, "IOC Admits Internet Censorship Deal with China," Reuters, July 30, 2008, https://www.reuters.com/article/us-olympics-idUSN3039947420080730 (accessed March 7, 2023).

30   DICTATING THE AGENDA

established around Beijing where people could highlight their causes. However, demonstrators had to apply for a permit to do so. Ultimately zero permits were granted. After the Games, a Chinese Olympic official said that some applications were rejected because they were against the law, but that most of them saw the applicants' problems solved "after consultations between relevant authorities and the applicants."[26]

The conclusion of the 2008 Summer Olympics marked an important inflection point but not toward liberal expansion as had been hoped. Rather than substantially *change* Beijing's human rights policies and governance, the Games, with a few partial exceptions, underscored *the limits* of transnational liberal influence and gave Beijing lessons it could learn. At the conclusion of the Games on August 24, 2008, as if reflecting on the IOC's inability to effectively press Beijing for reforms, Rogge observed that "the IOC and the Olympic Games cannot force changes on sovereign nations or solve all the ills of the world. But we can, and we do, contribute to positive change through sport." In a now often-quoted watering down of prior expectations, he proclaimed that "the world has learned about China, and China has learned about the world, and I believe this is something that will have positive effects for the long term."[27]

Coming as it did at a fulcrum point in the path of global liberalism, Beijing 2008 reveals both the patterns and the limitations of transnational liberal influence. The power of liberal democratic states created an enabling environment, while transnational liberal advocacy organizations operated as ideational carriers, pressuring Beijing on matters of human rights, press freedom, and foreign policy. These two paths for promoting liberal influence—the power of liberal democratic states and the dynamism of transnational liberal advocacy—took shape in the 1990s and were powerful but had hidden assumptions: the efficacious authority of the "West" and in particular the United States, its outsized market power, and an assumed political autonomy for ideational carriers. This 1990s-rooted model of transnational liberal influence on

---

[26] "China Says Headed Off Olympic Protest Permits," Reuters, September 18, 2008, https://www.reuters.com/article/us-olympics-china-protest-idUSPEK91 59120080918 (accessed January 16, 2023).

[27] "IOC President Says Olympics Opened Up China," NBC News, August 24, 2008, https://www.nbcnews.com/id/wbna2637163.

ORIGINS AND ACCELERATION OF LIBERAL INFLUENCE 31

display when it came to Beijing 2008 was powerful, and it put authoritarian states in a defensive posture, feeling compelled to justify their practices, make tactical concessions, and, at the very least, talk the talk of liberal human rights.

But the 2008 Olympiad also reveals the limitations of the 1990s model as well as the seeds of the authoritarian snapback. The idea that transnational liberal influence posed a threat to Beijing was a strong undercurrent of the Games despite the authorities' positive words about human rights and press freedom. The Games also saw China begin to use its market power to respond to perceived political affronts, as when Chinese consumers boycotted French products after the Olympic torch was subject to pro-Tibet protests in Paris and President Nicholas Sarkozy was publicly contemplating a boycott of the Games.[28] The prospect of consumer boycotts become a regular feature of engagement with China by the 2020s, a topic addressed in detail later in this book.

The 2008 Summer Olympics were widely billed as China's "coming-out party." As external actors spotlighted the country's human rights practices, their advocacy methods and strategy were premised on models that emerged in the 1990s. Those models faced a moment of truth in Beijing in 2008. By now it is clear that the triumphalism about liberal democratic ideas and the international order they underpinned was misplaced and that the triumph itself is questionable.[29]

---

[28] "Carrefour Faces Chinese Online Boycott Bid," France 24, April 15, 2008, https://www.france24.com/en/20080415-carrefourfaces-chinese-online-boycott-bid-; Canhui Hong, Wei-Min Hu, James Prieger, and Dongming Zhu, "French Automobiles and the Chinese Boycotts of 2008: Politics Really Does Affect Commerce," *B.E. Journal of Economic Analysis & Policy* 11, no. 1 (2011), https://doi.org/10.2202/1935-1682.2681.

[29] Even advocates of international liberalism acknowledge that it is in crisis, with Ikenberry, for example, arguing that the globalization of the liberal order got shorn of its social meaning and equated with security and capitalism rather than liberal political values. See John G. Ikenberry, *A World Safe for Democracy: Liberal Internationalism and the Crisis of Global Order* (Yale University Press, 2020). See also John G. Ikenberry, "The End of Liberal International Order?," *International Affairs* 94, no. 1 (2018): pp. 7–23, https://doi.org/10.1093/ia/iix241. For analyses from various perspectives on the theme of the "liberal international order" and its contemporary moment, see Milan Babic, "Let's Talk About the Interregnum: Gramsci and the Crisis of the Liberal World Order," *International Affairs* 96, no. 3 (2020): pp. 767–86, https://doi.org/10.1093/ia/iiz254; Tanja A. Börzel and Michael Zürn, "Contestations of the Liberal International Order: From Liberal Multilateralism to Postnational Liberalism,"

Transnational Liberal Influence in the 1990s

It is useful to evaluate the 1990s as a time when the power of authoritarian states in the aggregate was relatively low. With the benefit of hindsight, we examine the foundations of transnational liberal influence that emerged in the 1990s and identify what, precisely, about the international environment facilitated the spread of liberal influence and how, exactly, it changed or broke down.

In retrospect, the height of post–Cold War liberal-democratic soft power was closely tied with the United States' lone superpower status and the rise of the unipolar moment. The discrediting of communism across the former Soviet bloc spotlighted liberal democracy as ideologically victorious with no obvious rival. This view was captured most influentially by the American political scientist Francis Fukuyama, who wrote that the collapse of communism as a major political ideological competitor left democracy as the sole surviving major political ideology.[30] In China, the 1989 massacre at Tiananmen Square seemed to reveal the weakness of the CCP's grip on power, with only force appearing to keep it afloat. And just a few years after scholars had predicted the demise of the United States because of its large budget deficits and Cold War spending, the United States began to run budget surpluses and pushed for unfettered liberalization of trade and financial flows throughout the world in what became known as globalization.

International Organization 75, no. 2 (2021): pp. 282–305, https://doi.org/10.1017/S0020818320000570; Henry Farrell and Abraham L. Newman, "The Janus Face of the Liberal International Information Order: When Global Institutions Are Self-Undermining," *International Organization* 75, no. 2 (2021): pp. 333–58, https://doi.org/10.1017/S0020818320000302; Jessica Chen Weiss and Jeremy L. Wallace, "Domestic Politics, China's Rise, and the Future of the Liberal International Order," *International Organization* 75, no. 2 (2021): pp. 635–64, https://doi.org/10.1017/S002081832000048X; and Alexander Cooley and Daniel H. Nexon, "The Real Crisis of Global Order: Illiberalism on the Rise," *Foreign Affairs* 101, no. 1 (2022): pp. 103–18. For an introduction to a special issue of *International Organization* on challenges to the liberal international order, see David A. Lake et al., "Challenges to the Liberal Order: Reflections on International Organization," *International Organization* 75, no. 2 (2021): pp. 225–57, https://doi.org/10.1017/S0020818320000636.

[30] Francis Fukuyama, "Reflections on the End of History, Five Years Later," *History and Theory* 34, no. 22 (1995): pp. 27–43, https://doi.org/10.2307/2505433.

ORIGINS AND ACCELERATION OF LIBERAL INFLUENCE   33

The global rise of Western-led liberalism also reflected the widespread belief that authoritarianism, if not doomed, was certainly discredited and increasingly embattled by trends associated with modernization and the opportunity costs of not globalizing. Norms of preserving state sovereignty eroded as global governance practices themselves began to permit and even demand specific forms of intervention, monitoring, and conditioning of domestic affairs.[31] For example, Hyde has shown how throughout the 1990s even authoritarian rulers accepted a new international norm of inviting external election observers from independent groups to assess the quality of their elections, even if they strongly suspected that such assessments would undermine them.[32]

All this meant that the global environment for promoting liberal democratic ideas was propitious. Authoritarian powers were weakened, the world was interconnected politically and informationally in new ways but with democracies controlling key elements of the infrastructure, and globally liberal standards of appropriate behavior had become prized. These aspects of what Guriev and Treisman call the "modernization cocktail" generated liberalizing pressures on authoritarian states and meant that they had to change their strategies to survive and thrive.[33]

Of course, our account of global liberalism in the 1990s is an oversimplification. Many commentators at the time sounded important notes of caution about the triumph of political liberalism. In general, though, these accounts focused on liberal democracy as pitted against forces other than powerful autocracies. Barber's influential essay and subsequent book *Jihad vs. McWorld*, for example, were concerned about the social backlash that globalization would engender.

---

[31] Representative works on globalization and the erosion of sovereignty include Saskia Sassen, *Losing Control? Sovereignty in the Age of Globalization* (Columbia University Press, 1996); Jessica Matthews, "Power Shift," *Foreign Affairs* 76, no. 1 (1997): pp. 50–66, https://doi.org/10.2307/20047909; and David Held et al., "Globalization," *Global Governance* 5, no. 4 (1999): pp. 483–96, https://www.jstor.org/stable/27800244.

[32] Susan D. Hyde, *The Pseudo-Democrat's Dilemma: Why Election Observation Became an International Norm* (Cornell University Press, 2011).

[33] Sergei Guriev and Daniel Treisman, *Spin Dictators: The Changing Face of Tyranny in the 21st Century* (Princeton University Press, 2022), p. 179.

34   DICTATING THE AGENDA

He observed that opposition did not come from states but rather from local groups and minority movements who would leverage these economic dislocations to undermine the traditional nation-state.[34] In his much-maligned set of articles and ultimately 1996 book *Clash of Civilizations*, Huntington argued for a resurgence of "civilization" as the axis around which global conflict would revolve.[35] For some, political Islam was a contender.[36] The 1990s also saw a challenge from the transnational left that emerged as the World Social Forum, which advocated for a different version of social justice.[37] But crucially, very few appeared concerned that the main challenge to democracy globally would come from the re-emergence of powerful authoritarian states.

Two Paths for Promoting Liberal Values Globally: Liberal Democratic Primacy and Transnational Activism

The transnational liberal influence of the 1990s was built on distinct foundations that had converged in the aftermath of the Cold War. In general, liberal influence was transmitted globally in two ways: the emulative attraction of US-led Western "soft power" and the work of activists who promoted liberal values on specific campaigns across transnational civil society networks.

First, US soft power was attractive because it was triumphant and so clearly dominant. Joseph Nye's seminal argument about the importance of soft power in *Bound to Lead* (1990) was intended as a rebuttal to the prevailing gloomy predictions of US overextension and decline, as

---

[34] Benjamin R. Barber, "Jihad vs. McWorld," *The Atlantic*, March 1992, https://www.theatlantic.com/magazine/archive/1992/03/jihad-vs-mcworld/303882/; Benjamin R. Barber, *Jihad vs. McWorld: Terrorism's Challenge to Democracy* (Random House, 1995).

[35] Samuel P. Huntington, *The Clash of Civilizations and the Remaking of World Order* (Simon & Schuster, 1996).

[36] For a review, see the analytical essay Fiona B. Adamson, "Global Liberalism Versus Political Islam: Competing Ideological Frameworks in International Politics," *International Studies Review* 7, no. 4 (2005), pp. 547–69, https://doi.org/10.1111/j.1468-2486.2005.00532.x.

[37] See Jackie Smith, "The World Social Forum and the Challenges of Global Democracy," *Global Networks* 4, no. 4 (2004): pp. 413–21, https://doi.org/10.1111/j.1471-0374.2004.00102.x.

ORIGINS AND ACCELERATION OF LIBERAL INFLUENCE   35

advanced by historian Paul Kennedy and others in the mid-1980s.[38] By the time Nye's paperback edition had been revised, world events, including the Soviet collapse, had dramatically proven the declinists wrong for the time being.

"Soft power" emphasized the non-coercive power to influence through positive appeal and attraction at precisely the moment in which America had secured an unprecedented global leadership role. Specifically, Nye pointed to the broad areas of culture, political values, and foreign policy as key influence vectors and would continue to refine the concept over a series of books and writings, as well as stints of service in the US government.[39] Nye retroactively credited US soft power with explaining the final stages of the Cold War, claiming, "The Berlin Wall ultimately collapsed in 1989 not under a barrage of artillery but from hammers and bulldozers wielded by people whose minds had been affected by Western soft power."[40]

Nye maintained that soft power is "value neutral," meaning that competitors like China and Russia could also potentially wield it effectively. However, he also observed that unless these attractive qualities came from an empowered civil society in these authoritarian regimes, government-sponsored propaganda would lack popular appeal and legitimacy. Subsequent understandings of soft power have emphasized that it is often linked to the interests of a particular state via state policy, regardless of the actors involved in doing the implementation work.[41]

---

[38] See Joseph S. Nye Jr., *Bound to Lead: The Changing Nature of American Power* (Basic Books, 1990); Joseph S. Nye Jr., "Soft Power," *Foreign Policy*, no. 80 (1990): pp. 153–71, https://doi.org/10.2307/1148580; and Paul Kennedy, *The Rise and Fall of Great Powers: Economic Change and Military Conflict from 1500 to 2000* (Random House, 1987).

[39] Joseph S. Nye Jr., *Soft Power: The Means to Success in World Politics* (PublicAffairs, 2004) and Joseph S. Nye Jr., "Soft Power and American Foreign Policy," *Political Science Quarterly* 119, no. 2 (2004): pp. 255–70, https://doi.org/10.2307/20202345.

[40] Joseph S. Nye Jr., "Soft Power: The Evolution of a Concept," *Journal of Political Power* 14, no. 1 (2021): p. 5, https://doi.org/10.1080/2158379X.2021.1879572. For an argument that human rights activism following on from the 1975 Helsinki Final Act helped catalyze the Soviet collapse, see Daniel C. Thomas, *The Helsinki Effect: International Norms, Human Rights, and the Demise of Communism* (Princeton University Press, 2001).

[41] Peter S. Henne, "What We Talk About When We Talk About Soft Power," *International Studies Perspectives* 23, no. 1 (2022): pp. 94–111, https://doi.org/10.1093/isp/ekab007; Maria Repnikova, *Chinese Soft Power* (Cambridge University Press, 2022).

36   DICTATING THE AGENDA

The appeal of a successful state practice or idea is not confined to liberal democratic states, as shown in interwar Europe.[42] However, scholarship on the rise and fall of global communism shows that by the 1980s and early 1990s, state-led single-party communist rule had lost its global standing and power to inspire.[43] Even China's surviving communist leadership, looking for lessons for its own continuity, drew the conclusion that lack of economic dynamism and an unappealing ideology were two of the main contributors to the Soviet collapse.[44] The Western model's pillars had renewed appeal, while its main ideological rival had become a spent force.[45]

Liberal values were not just passively diffused by US and Western prominence. A second branch of research and commentary observed how civil society leaders and activists promoted liberal values globally. They allied with like-minded activists in the Global South

---

[42] Benjamin O. Fordham and Victor Asal, "Billiard Balls or Snowflakes? Major Power Prestige and the International Diffusion of Institutions and Practices," *International Studies Quarterly* 51, no. 1 (2007): pp. 31–52, http://www.jstor.org/stable/4621700. On interwar Europe, see John M. Owen IV, *The Clash of Ideas in World Politics: Transnational Networks, States, and Regime Change, 1510–2010* (Princeton University Press, 2010), p. 201; Seva Gunitsky, *Aftershocks: Great Powers and Domestic Reforms in the Twentieth Century* (Princeton University Press, 2017); and Jørgen Møller et al., "International Influences and Democratic Regression in Interwar Europe: Disentangling the Impact of Power Politics and Demonstration Effects," *Government and Opposition* 52, no. 4 (2017): pp. 559–86, https://doi.org/10.1017/gov.2015.37.

[43] Archie Brown, *The Rise and Fall of Communism* (Vintage, 2010); A. James McAdams, *Vanguard of the Revolution: The Global Idea of the Communist Party* (Princeton University Press, 2017); George W. Breslauer, *The Rise and Demise of World Communism* (Oxford University Press, 2021). Kotkin notes that while the onslaught of images of Western consumerism in the Soviet Union were attractive, most people retained an allegiance to the goals of socialism and "simply wanted the Soviet regime to live up to its promises." See Stephen Kotkin, *Armageddon Averted: The Soviet Collapse, 1970–2000* (Oxford University Press, 2008), p. 44.

[44] David Shambaugh, *China's Communist Party: Atrophy and Adaptation* (University of California Press, 2008).

[45] Of course, as Dimitrov makes clear, communism did not "collapse" entirely as a form of political organization, but as Dukalskis and Gerschewski, among others, note, the single-party communist states that survived and thrived adapted their ideologies to changing circumstances in the 1980s and 1990s to de-emphasize Marxist themes and emphasize nationalist ones. See Martin K. Dimitrov, *Why Communism Did Not Collapse: Understanding Authoritarian Regime Resilience in Asia and Europe* (Cambridge University Press, 2013); and Alexander Dukalskis and Johannes Gerschewski, "Adapting or Freezing? Ideological Reactions of Communist Regimes to a Post-Communist World," *Government and Opposition* 55, no. 3 (2020): pp. 511–32, https://doi.org/10.18452/22420.

ORIGINS AND ACCELERATION OF LIBERAL INFLUENCE 37

and networked with committed representatives of international organizations and friendly states to pressure reluctant governments to enact liberal changes. While the power of liberal democracies provided the overarching political environment, transnational networks of activists openly spread liberal ideas about politics and individual rights.[46] Their work was facilitated by increasing interconnectivity in the global information environment and international organizations that were no longer geopolitically stalemated due to the Cold War.[47]

The global scope and transformative nature of these transnational networks are captured in the "spiral model" as developed by Risse, Roppe, and Sikkink.[48] This influential model explains how even initially reluctant authoritarians eventually complied with international human rights norms. Transnational activism initiated a dynamic sequence of events, or "spiral." In their bid to stave off major change, authoritarians offered strategic concessions that ultimately trapped them into accepting substantive liberal reforms.[49] By attempting to respond strategically, authoritarians eventually succumbed to transnational pressures and became norm compliant. The spiral model greatly influenced how scholars and advocates thought about human rights advocacy in the 1990s.

It also shaped understanding about how global governance and transnational networks could spread liberal or universal values across

---

[46] See, for example, Christine Min Wotipka and Kiyoteru Tsutsui, "Global Human Rights and State Sovereignty: State Ratification of International Human Rights Treaties, 1965–2001," *Sociological Forum*, 23, no. 4 (2008): pp. 724–54, https://doi.org/10.1111/j.1573-7861.2008.00092.x ; David R. Davis et al., "'Makers and Shapers': Human Rights INGOs and Public Opinion," *Human Rights Quarterly* 34, no. 1 (2012): pp. 199–224, http://www.jstor.org/stable/41345476; and Dongwook Kim, "International Nongovernmental Organizations and the Global Diffusion of National Human Rights Institutions," *International Organization* 67, no. 3 (2013): pp. 505–39, https://doi.org/10.1017/S0020818313000131.

[47] Margaret E. Keck and Kathryn Sikkink, *Activists Beyond Borders* (Cornell University Press, 1997).

[48] Thomas Risse et al., eds., *The Power of Human Rights: International Norms and Domestic Change* (Cambridge University Press, 1999).

[49] The spiral sequence includes repression (information about norm violation reaches external actors and media); denial (the government denies the accounts and rejects external intervention); tactical concessions (small concessions are made to outside and domestic observers, allowing for inquiry); prescriptive status (the government publicly comes out affirming the norm even if reluctant to completely implement it); and, finally, rule-consistent behavior (norms become institutionalized).

38   DICTATING THE AGENDA

a range of issue areas. A variation on the spiral model is Keck and Sikkink's acclaimed "boomerang" model. This model highlights how local advocacy NGOs, when stymied by autocrats, can leverage pressure from liberal states, international organizations, and prominent transnational NGOs to pressure governments.[50] Finnemore and Sikkink further developed the concept of a "norm cascade," emphasizing the role of "norm entrepreneurs" in diffusing new norms or global governance practices.[51]

These approaches to global governance and liberal influence of the 1990s shared the understanding that autocrats passed through stages of political calculations and external pressures before succumbing to liberal influence and changing their behavior. Liberal diffusion models anticipated that a targeted authoritarian government would act defensively against multiple sources of external and internal pressure. Governments could try to hide their repressive actions, defy external advocacy, or even make tactical concessions, but the key assumption was that they were on the defensive, responding to outside pressure and susceptible to trending liberal norms.

However, over time it became clear that global commitments to liberal principles outpaced compliance with them. With the partial exception of women's rights,[52] evidence began to show the limited effectiveness of human rights socialization in changing state behavior in cases of entrenched authoritarianism.[53] In situations where human rights violations were perceived as crucial to regime survival,

---

[50] Keck and Sikkink, *Activists Beyond Borders.*

[51] Martha Finnemore and Kathryn Sikkink, "International Norm Dynamics and Political Change," *International Organization* 52, no. 4 (1998): pp. 887–917, https://doi.org/10.1162/002081898550789.

[52] Beth A. Simmons, *Mobilizing for Human Rights: International Law in Domestic Politics* (Cambridge University Press, 2009); Daniel W. Hill Jr., "Estimating the Effects of Human Rights Treaties on State Behavior," *Journal of Politics* 72, no. 4 (2010): pp. 1161–74, https://doi.org/10.1017/S0022381610000599; Neil A. Englehart and Melissa K. Miller, "The CEDAW Effect: International Law's Impact on Women's Rights," *Journal of Human Rights* 13, no. 1 (2014): pp. 22–47, https://doi.org/10.1080/14754835.2013.824274.

[53] Oona Hathaway, "Why Do Countries Commit to Human Rights Treaties?," *Journal of Conflict Resolution* 51, no. 4 (2002): pp. 588–621, https://doi.org/10.1177/0022002707303046; Emilie M. Hafner-Burton and Kiyoteru Tsutsui, "Justice Lost! The Failure of International Human Rights Law to Matter Where Needed Most," *Journal of Peace Research* 44, no. 4 (2007): pp. 407–25, https://doi.org/10.1177/0022343307078942.

ORIGINS AND ACCELERATION OF LIBERAL INFLUENCE   39

leaders typically chose to violate rights rather than relinquish power.[54] Yet few scholars or policymakers in democracies anticipated that autocrats would defiantly embrace illiberal policies or propagate them abroad.

Three Hidden Assumptions of Liberal Influence

These two powerful channels of influence, direct liberal activism and diffuse soft power born of the primacy of the United States and other liberal democratic states, bolstered transnational liberal influence throughout the 1990s and early 2000s. The general spread of liberalism across Europe, through waves of European Union and NATO expansion and accession negotiations (culminating in the large expansions of 2004), underscored that liberal influence rested on an entire political ecosystem that promoted, disseminated, and reinforced liberal norms and values across different regional and global organizations.[55] It seemed to work. As noted in the previous chapter, the world reached new liberal democratic heights as it emerged from the 1990s. The number of democracies around the world continued to increase, while the societies and polities of the post-communist world became qualitatively freer.

But a closer look suggests that the twin channels of influence rested upon three foundations that critically converged to advance liberal ideas transnationally: effective authority, market power, and a belief in the value of political autonomy. Each set of assumptions can be seen in both the prevailing liberal environment (power of liberal democracies) and liberal agents (activists and transnational networks).

Efficacious Authority

First, the tone was set by the perception of US efficacious authority, that is, the legitimacy that comes from being perceived as effective

---

[54] Hill, "Estimating the Effects."

[55] Alexander Cooley, "Ordering Eurasia: The Rise and Decline of Liberal Internationalism in the Post-Communist Space," *Security Studies* 28, no. 3 (2019): pp. 588–613, https://doi.org/10.1080/09636412.2019.1604988.

40 DICTATING THE AGENDA

or highly competent.[56] As America promoted its liberal values in the 1990s, its own agents and tools were widely accepted as having the utmost expertise to enact these specific reforms and transformations. US-based economists became the architects for the massive market transitions and privatization programs in countries such as Russia, Ukraine, and Poland,[57] with the "technical assistance" delivered by the influx of US and Western experts extended into almost every sphere of state-building and social transformation, from constitutional design to reforms and standard setting. In the area of new technologies, US firms were at the frontier and set standards in new geopolitically influential domains that included the internet, software, finance, semiconductor development, international law, intellectual property (which was successfully and controversially embedded in the World Trade Organization), and biohealth and pharmaceutical development.[58] Expertise and efficacious legitimacy also reinforced US material power when these were codified into a robust intellectual property regime that benefited US firms. As Schwartz has pointed out, the United States' active shaping and protection of the intellectual property regime allowed US firms "to capture a disproportionate part of the value creation in global commodity chains."[59] In parallel, the rise of the assessment of governance practices was abetted by the proliferation of international rankings and ratings that measured governance reforms according to idealized liberal-oriented benchmarks.[60] Within states, such diverse social and political phenomena as civil society development, media openness, and control over corruption could now be diagnosed and assessed comparatively, thereby further empowering experts in these domains

---

[56] On different types of authority and their role in global governance, see Deborah D. Avant et al., eds., *Who Governs the Globe?* (Cambridge University Press, 2010).

[57] J. R. Wedel, *Collision and Collusion: The Strange Case of Western Aid to Eastern Europe* (St. Martin's Press, 1998).

[58] On state power, standard-setting, and globalization, see Walter Mattli and Tim Büthe, "Setting International Standards: Technological Rationality or Primacy of Power?," *World Politics* 56, no. 1 (2003): pp. 1–42, https://doi.org/10.1353/wp.2004 .0006. On the global diffusion of US legal practices, see Daniel R. Kelemen and Eric C. Sibbitt, "The Globalization of American Law," *International Organization* 58, no. 1 (2004): pp. 103–36, https://doi.org/10.1017/S0020818304581043.

[59] Mark Herman Schwartz, "American Hegemony: Intellectual Property Rights, Dollar Centrality, and Infrastructural Power," *Review of International Political Economy* 26, no. 3 (2019): p. 507, https://doi.org/10.1080/09692290.2019.1597754.

[60] Alexander Cooley and Jack Snyder, eds., *Ranking the World: Grading States as a Tool of Global Governance* (Cambridge University Press, 2015).

to provide advisory and consulting services to countries wanting to improve their international rankings and images.

The transnational liberal networks forged by activists were buttressed by the global expansion of US soft power across several domains. As American movies and entertainment, culture, sports, and education spread globally, they were now widely acknowledged as culturally dominant, though this was by no means accepted universally as a positive trend. During the Cold War, the superpowers had prized the efficacious authority derived from triumphing in global competitions. For example, the Soviet quest to lead the medal count at the Olympics was done for reasons of prestige, but also to prove that the communist system actually produced superior athletes, just like its best educational institutions purportedly produced the world's best scientists and mathematicians, and cultural institutions the world's best concert pianists and dancers.[61] The Soviet bloc athletes that topped the medal count at the 1992 Summer Games in Barcelona competed as the "Unified Team," not the Soviet Union; despite their competitive success, most media coverage emphasized the terminal states, financial insecurity, and uncertainty now facing the once formidable Soviet sports machine.[62] Tellingly, the biggest stars of the 1992 Summer Olympics were not the flagless former Soviet athletes but members of the inaugural US Dream Team, which for the first time saw the US men's national basketball team compete with professional NBA superstars, who demolished all competitors en route to a gold medal.[63]

In the realm of higher education, US institutions and models now functioned as ideals for the remaking of post-communist societies, but also as possible models for global expansion and international transplantation. Communist and state-run academies, once prestigious globally, were now widely viewed as decrepit and unable to provide the necessary instruction and new courses to prepare post-communist

---

[61] Kiril Tomoff, *Virtuosi Abroad: Soviet Music and Imperial Competition During the Early Cold War, 1945–1958* (Cornell University Press, 2015).

[62] Karen E. Riggs et al., "Manufactured Conflict in the 1992 Olympics: The Discourse of Television and Politics," *Critical Studies in Media Communication* 10, no. 3 (1993): pp. 253–72, https://doi.org/10.1080/15295039309366867.

[63] The closest game was the gold medal final between the United States and Croatia, which the Dream Team won by 32 points.

42   DICTATING THE AGENDA

citizens for a liberalizing and globalizing world.[64] Western-supported institutions rapidly filled this void. The Central European University (CEU), recipient of at least $500 million in funding (including $250 million in endowment funds) was founded in 1991 in Budapest, Hungary, from the charitable foundation of billionaire George Soros. It not only eclipsed the budget and endowment of any other institution in Eastern and Central Europe, but unlike state universities that reported to their respective ministries of education, CEU was accredited by the New York Board of Regents.[65] The same accreditation model had been adopted by the influential American University in Beirut and the American University in Cairo.[66] Similar high-profile American-style universities were introduced in Bulgaria and Kyrgyzstan in the early 1990s, each as private institutions supported by US partnerships with host governments and substantial support from the Open Society Foundations and other US-based philanthropies, but not always with an appreciation of how they fit into the national regulatory context.[67] The undisputed global position of American higher education in the 1990s and 2000s would set the stage for the wave of global partnerships and new international branches negotiated by elite US universities.[68]

The point is critical: Across different sectors such as media, sports, education, and culture, American institutions and even the so-called American way of life held sway because for many they were viewed as the gold standard. Tellingly, global surveys of public attitudes from Pew conducted in 2002 and 2003—when global opinion about the United

---

[64] In his memoir about the founding of the CEU, Alfred Stepan, CEU's first rector, framed the challenge of university reform as "purge or petrification." See Alfred Stepan, "The Early Years of Central European University as a Network: A Memoir," *Social Research: An International Quarterly* 76, no. 2 (2009): p. 688, https://doi.org/10.1353/sor.2009.0032.

[65] Stepan, "Early Years," pp. 689–90.

[66] Rasmus G. Bertelsen, "Private Foreign-Affiliated Universities, the State, and Soft Power: The American University of Beirut and the American University in Cairo," *Foreign Policy Analysis* 8, no. 3 (2012): pp. 293–311, https://doi.org/10.1111/j.1743-8594.2011.00163.x.

[67] See Tereza Pospíšilová, "Transnational Philanthropy and Nationalism: The Early Years of Central European University," *Monde(s)* 6, no. 2 (2014): pp. 129–46.

[68] Philip G. Altbach and Patti McGill Peterson, "Higher Education as a Projection of America's Soft Power," in *Soft Power Superpowers*, edited by Watanabe Yasushi and David L. McConnell (M. E. Sharpe, 2008), pp. 37–53.

ORIGINS AND ACCELERATION OF LIBERAL INFLUENCE 43

States had plummeted because of the Iraq War—indicated that "solid majorities" still expressed positive views of US science and technology, as well as positive views of American culture such as movies, television, and music.[69]

Market Power

Second, liberal diffusion was premised on the market power of the United States and its liberal democratic allies in a globalizing economy, where new emerging markets were still being pioneered, and during which overall consumption was still heavily concentrated in the markets of the United States, Japan, and the European Union. The collapse of the communist bloc shifted the economic consensus away from accepting a role for government regulation and protection and toward the "Washington Consensus" of unambiguously favoring open trade and capital flows.[70] The International Monetary Fund (IMF) and World Bank embodied these liberalizing norms, while the conditionality of the IMF as a lender became stricter as countries in economic distress had no systemic alternative lenders to turn to.[71] This was not just a US initiative, as economic liberalization became locked into the membership rules of expanding Western organizations such as the European Union and the Organisation for Economic Co-operation and Development.[72] In 1997, the Asian financial crisis rocked the region and stymied talk of a more regulated, state-sponsored capitalism, especially as the IMF itself demanded even more stringent neoliberal policy prescriptions from countries including Indonesia and Thailand that had been devasted by rapid capital outflows during the crisis.[73] In late 2001,

---

[69] *Views of a Changing World: Pew Global Attitudes Project* (Pew Research Center For The People & The Press, 2003), https://www.pewresearch.org/wp-content/uploads/sites/2/2003/06/Views-Of-A-Changing-World-2003.pdf, pp. 23–24.

[70] Joseph Stiglitz, *Globalization and Its Discontents* (W. W. Norton, 2002).

[71] Thad Dunning, "Conditioning the Effects of Aid: Cold War Politics, Donor Credibility, and Democracy in Africa," *International Organization* 58, no. 2 (2004): pp. 409–23, https://doi.org/10.1017/S0020818304582073.

[72] Rawi Abdelal, *Capital Rules: The Construction of Global Finance* (Harvard University Press, 2007).

[73] See Robert Wade, "The Asian Debt-and-Development Crisis of 1997–?: Causes and Consequences," *World Development* 26, no. 8 (1998): pp. 1535–53.

44   DICTATING THE AGENDA

after years of drawn-out negotiations, China joined the WTO, effectively opening its economy to overseas investment and competition in services and its retail sector to Western goods. Global trade, finance, and marketization were spreading unrelentingly.[74]

Popular current-affairs books hammered home the theme that the nation-state was under inexorable assault from these global marketizing pressures, with *New York Times* columnist Tom Friedman writing in 1999 how the imperatives of global economic integration represented a new international system that would undermine the old Cold War system of nation-state rivalry and war.[75] State sovereignty appeared doomed, and global interdependence was becoming a new reality, one that would seemingly assimilate all participants.

The triumph of market economics and the rise of unfettered globalization also underscored the central role that sclerotic centrally planned economies had played in delegitimizing the communist system. Writing in 1993 Deudney and Ikenberry noted how the distinctive "political logic" of the West stemmed from how its market networks reinforced civic networks. They observed:

> Make no mistake, the body of the civic union is capitalism. The business of the West is business. Western Europe, Japan and the United States are thoroughly permeated by market relations, mentalities and institutions. As the importance of the market grows in these societies, their character converges. As the market erodes and level pre-capitalist social and economic formations, an increasingly encompassing capitalist society is being created.[76]

The assumption that increased international marketization would inevitably produce political and societal convergence along Western models was widely held among academics, policymakers, and popular

---

[74] Jagdish Bhagwati, *In Defense of Globalization: With a New Afterword* (Oxford University Press, 2004).

[75] Thomas L. Friedman, *The Lexus and the Olive Tree: Understanding Globalization* (Farrar, Straus, and Giroux, 2000).

[76] Daniel Deudney and John G. Ikenberry, "The Logic of the West," *World Policy Journal* 10, no. 4 (1993): p. 18, http://www.jstor.org/stable/40209331.

ORIGINS AND ACCELERATION OF LIBERAL INFLUENCE   45

commentators throughout the post–Cold War era.[77] Such arguments were used to justify a range of international policies designed to integrate authoritarian polities into the global economy and its governing institutions, from the likely liberalizing political impact of China's joining the world trading system to the importance of continuing high-level cooperation between Western energy giants and the Putin regime even as it became increasingly repressive. International economic integration would inevitably force these countries, despite their growing criticism of liberalism, to "play by our rules" or "play our game."[78]

One lingering result of this reasoning is that it blinded many analysts to the potential transformative consequences of expanding consumer markets in emerging powers, especially in China itself. Marketization was widely viewed as a one-way process in which Western companies, products, tastes, and accompanying rules would be imposed in new frontier markets, with little regard to local customs, traditions, or social fabrics.[79] Even champions of free trade and globalization expressed concern at its potential to disrupt and transform.[80]

Asymmetrical market power enabled the liberal advantage in wielding resources, especially through its large philanthropical donors, to fund and promote the supposedly non-economic realm of civil society promotion. In emphasizing the principles that bound together like-minded activists, they downplayed the asymmetrical material or economic backdrop against which campaigns were taking place, even as more critical scholars observed that NGOs in post-communist states that were adept at mastering the grant applications and speaking English consistently received Western funding over other deserving

---

[77] Although many pointed to the success of East Asian economies that featured a heavy role for the state, the 1997 Asian financial crisis eventually damaged the image of the East Asian developmental state model, at least for a time. See Joseph Wong, "The Adaptive Developmental State in East Asia," *Journal of East Asian Studies* 4, no. 3 (2004): pp. 345–62, http://www.jstor.org/stable/23417946.

[78] Edward Steinfel, *Playing Our Game: Why China's Rise Doesn't Threaten the West* (Oxford University Press, 2010).

[79] For a cautionary warning that Chinese capitalism would not precipitate political liberalization, see Kellee Tsai, *Capitalism Without Democracy: The Private Sector in Contemporary China* (Cornell University Press, 2007).

[80] Bhagwati, *In Defense of Globalization*.

46   DICTATING THE AGENDA

domestic counterparts.[81] Grant-making by US-based foundations sky-rocketed during the 1990s, as private foundation grants for international projects increased from $996 million in 1994 to $1.6 billion in 1998.[82] As Bob observed early in the 2000s, many NGO campaigns were shaped by southern groups adjusting their advocacy and messaging so that they could be supported by Western donors and their strategic priorities.[83]

Autonomy and Political Independence

The third assumption of the post–Cold War spread of liberal political influence was that of political autonomy. The support for political autonomy was disseminated in two related forms across global governance networks. The first was upholding freedom of expression, especially for actors outside of the formal political realm. Nongovernmental actors such as athletes, artists, actors, activists, and journalists were broadly afforded the space and right to exercise their freedom of expression and political critique, on both domestic issues and foreign policy issues. In fact, the antiglobalization movement and protests that surrounded the Group of Seven summits in Seattle 1999 and Genoa 2001 were explained as movements for the "globalization of rights" to counter or hold to account economic globalization.[84] As with America's efficacious authority and marketization, the appeal of political autonomy, including freedom of expression, was viewed as an important driver in the collapse of the communist bloc. The mass demonstrations that brought down Eastern Europe's socialist regimes in the fall of 1989 were

---

[81] Sarah Henderson, *Building Democracy in Contemporary Russia: Western Support for Grassroots Organizations* (Cornell University Press, 2003)

[82] Kim D. Reimann, "A View from the Top: International Politics, Norms and the Worldwide Growth of NGOs," *International Studies Quarterly* 50, no. 1 (2006): p. 54, https://doi.org/10.1111/j.1468-2478.2006.00392.x.

[83] Clifford Bob, "Merchants of Morality," *Foreign Policy* 129 (2002): pp. 36–45, https://doi.org/10.2307/3183388. On the impact of financial pressures on NGO behavior, see Alexander Cooley and James Ron, "The NGO Scramble: Organizational Insecurity and the Political Economy of Transnational Action," *International Security* 27, no. 1 (2002): pp. 5–39, https://doi.org/10.1162/016228802320231217.

[84] Donatella Della Porta, ed., *Globalization from Below: Transnational Activists and Protest Networks* (University of Minnesota Press, 2006), pp. 7–10.

widely understood as led by reconstituted civil society involved in associational life in late communism and served as an important cautionary tale for those autocrats still standing.[85]

For many observers, civil society had established itself as a vital and independent actor beyond the state and the private or corporate sector, which was also rapidly globalizing. Nestled in the enabling environment of liberal democratic primacy, actors independent of their governments could advance their preferred values of human rights, democracy, and political liberalism. Networks of transnational activists pressured states to better adhere to these standards. This was even the case on causes or issues, such as America's stance toward the ICC or its erosion of civil liberties protections for suspected terrorists during the global war on terror, when the US government itself rejected the norms that its own civil society groups were promoting.[86]

The proliferation of new media outlets and information technologies, including across Russia, reinforced the belief that previous monopolies of state-controlled propaganda and social messaging were no longer desirable or perhaps even possible. Private television stations, radio channels, and, soon after, blogs and internet sites, all with initial editorial independence, exploded across the country, with many supported via seed grants from Western sources. However, their economic sustainability and independence were challenged as oligarchs and connected elites began to weaponize their own independent media holdings.[87] Nevertheless, broad optimism was only further reinforced by the growth of the internet and the World Wide Web in the second half of the 1990s, with early observers remaining optimistic that

---

[85] Michael Bernhard, "Civil Society and Democratic Transition in East Central Europe," *Political Science Quarterly* 108, no. 2 (1993): pp. 307–26, https://doi.org/10.2307/2152014. However, also see Kotkin's revisionist account that emphasizes the importance of Communist Party decay and bureaucratic defections: Stephen Kotkin, *Uncivil Society: 1989 and the Implosion of the Communist Establishment* (Modern Library, 2009).

[86] Kim Lane Scheppele, "Law in a Time of Emergency: States of Exception and the Temptations of 9/11," *University of Pennsylvania Journal of Constitutional Law* 6 (2003): p. 1001.

[87] Laura Belin, "The Russian Media in the 1990s," *Journal of Communist Studies and Transition Politics* 18, no. 1 (2002): pp. 139–60, https://doi.org/10.1080/13523270209696371.

the internet would promote a borderless world free of government interference and empower democratic activists and civil society platforms worldwide.[88] Surveys from that time revealed broad optimism across the United States that life would improve in the 21st century as a result of these new technologies.[89] Early skeptics identified a direct line from the Cold War triumphalist belief about the superiority of Western media to prevailing assumptions that the expansion of cyberspace and proliferation of online technologies would promote freedom of association based on liberal values.[90]

In addition to freedom of expression, the importance of embedding political autonomy and institutional independence within a new constitutional order was viewed as a key step of the post-communist transition.[91] Comparative models and guides outlining best practices regularly drew upon other countries or systems in the liberal West as institutional models, and the very personnel who provided such advisory and technical assistance were themselves important transnational actors forming new international communities. As Johnson has shown in the case of central banking, the norms of guaranteeing price stability and maintaining complete independence from the executive were disseminated through a "wormhole" network, a very small group of internationally connected central bankers and economists who, from the early 1990s in international gatherings, actively trained and socialized the regulators of even the economically least developed of the post-communist states into such "best practices."[92]

In some international domains, norms of autonomy and noninterference were not so much invented as recovered from older standing principles that had not been widely enforced during the ideologically charged Cold War. For example, the IOC had first discussed

---

[88] For a legal overview and initial critique, see Jack Goldsmith and Timothy Wu, *Who Controls the Internet? Illusions of a Borderless World* (Oxford University Press, 2006).

[89] Pew Research Center, "Optimism Reigns, Technology Plays a Key Role: Introduction and Summary," October 24, 1999, https://www.pewresearch.org/politics/1999/10/24/optimism-reigns-technology-plays-key-role/.

[90] Evgeny Morozov, *The Net Delusion: The Dark Side of Internet Freedom* (PublicAffairs, 2012).

[91] Jon Elster et al., *Institutional Design in Post-Communist Societies: Rebuilding the Ship at Sea* (Cambridge University Press, 1998).

[92] Juliet Johnson, *Priests of Prosperity* (Cornell University Press, 2016).

the principles of "independence and autonomy" in 1949 and added such language to Article 24 of its charter in 1955 as part of its decision to recognize the Soviet and Communist National Olympic Committees,[93] threatening to withhold participation in the 1958 event to any noncompliant members. During the Cold War, member countries regularly intervened in all aspects of sporting life and national policy with little consequence, but these norms were recodified at IOC meetings from 1989 onward, while other major international sporting federations raised the question of government interference with greater frequency. For example, FIFA, the governing body of world football, in the early 1990s began to promptly respond to reports of government interference by suspending federations until such interventions were reversed.[94] Perhaps uniquely in the 1990s, freedom of expression among athletes appeared safeguarded, while the political autonomy of their sporting bodies was maintained.

Taking Stock of the Unipolar Moment

In sum, transnational liberal influence of the 1990s was advanced in an environment characterized by US and Western power and underpinned by three critical assumptions: efficacious authority of the United States, expanding market power, and political autonomy for key transnational actors. This not only led to liberal democratic states promoting their political norms but also allowed liberal-minded transnational civil society actors to operate in a relatively conducive global context.

During this "unipolar moment" there appears to have been little enthusiasm for self-reflection about the pillars on which liberal influence rested and how it was spread. Having emerged decisively victorious from the hot and cold wars of the 20th century, an unchallenged superpower was remaking the world in its image along with its allies.

---

[93] Jean-Loupe Chappelet, *Autonomy of Sport in Europe* (Council of Europe Publishing, 2010), https://rm.coe.int/autonomy-of-sport-in-europe/168073499f, pp. 11–12.

[94] J. Gordon Hylton, "How FIFA Used the Principle of Autonomy of Sport to Shield Corruption in the Sepp Blatter Era," *Maryland Journal of International Law* 32 (2017): p. 137.

50   DICTATING THE AGENDA

Some analysts urged caution.[95] Even Krauthammer in his seminal *Foreign Affairs* article emphasizes that the unipolar moment is just that—a moment—and that, "no doubt, multipolarity will come in time."[96] From the vantage point of the 1990s, although debates proliferated about the resurgence of religion, the role of civilizational categories in global conflict, and the effects of global capitalism, few foresaw serious illiberal authoritarian challengers ahead. Most observers of the liberal diffusion model did not reckon with the possibility that transnational advocacy networks could be repurposed and used to advance illiberal values and politics.[97] But by the time the Winter Olympics were held in Beijing in 2022, the shakiness of all these assumptions about the vectors of transnational influence had been exposed; the resurgent authoritarian power of China and others stood ready to challenge them along multiple dimensions.

---

[95] Christopher Layne, "The Unipolar Illusion: Why New Great Powers Will Rise," *International Security* 17, no. 4 (1993): pp. 5–51, https://doi.org/10.2307/2539020.

[96] Charles Krauthammer, "The Unipolar Moment," *Foreign Affairs* 70, no. 1 (2002): p. 23, https://doi.org/10.2307/20044692.

[97] An important exception was Clifford Bob, who in his seminal 2012 book argued that transnational advocacy networks were ideologically diverse and could be used to advance right-wing causes such as gun rights and pro-life advocacy just as they advance liberal human rights causes. See Clifford Bob, *The Global Right Wing and the Clash of World Politics* (Cambridge University Press, 2012).

Chapter 3

Authoritarian Resurgence and Influence in the 2020s

In comparison to the years before 2008, when liberalism was still on its plateau, the run-up to the 2022 Winter Olympic Games in Beijing was no less controversial in terms of China's actual human rights policies. If anything, they had deteriorated in many areas. However, the international response was considerably more muted and involved fewer global actors when compared with 2008. In many respects, the People's Republic of China (PRC) successfully reframed the Olympiad and international sport as an apolitical domain.

By 2022, the international spotlight had shifted away from Tibet (in large measure because of China's media restrictions on the region) and toward China's western region of Xinjiang, where most of the country's minority Uyghur population reside. In 2017 reports emerged, later confirmed by firsthand testimonies, primary documentation, and satellite imagery, that Chinese authorities had constructed a network of re-education camps in which Uyghur and other minorities were forcibly detained and subjected to intensive indoctrination, coerced interrogations, and sometimes even allegedly torture and sexual abuse.[1]

---

[1] See Adrian Zenz, "'Thoroughly Reforming Them Towards a Healthy Heart Attitude': China's Political Re-Education Campaign in Xinjiang," *Central Asian Survey* 38,

52   DICTATING THE AGENDA

Beijing's crackdown on democratic activists, politicians, and media outlets in Hong Kong, codified in the 2020 National Security Law, also fueled concerns about human rights conditions there as China subsumed a previously quasi-liberal democratic city more firmly under Chinese Communist Party (CCP) rule.[2]

The Biden administration announced in December 2021 that it would diplomatically boycott the 2022 event; the United States would send athletes as planned but not government officials. White House Press Secretary Jenn Psaki declared the boycott was in response to the "PRC's ongoing genocide and crimes against humanity in Xinjiang."[3] The day after the US announcement, PRC Foreign Ministry spokesperson Zhao Lijian questioned US moral authority and credibility, claiming that "in the US society, racism is deeply entrenched, white supremacy is rampant, and ethnic equality remains beyond reach." He stated that the boycott "gravely violates the principle of political neutrality enshrined in the Olympic Charter" and cautioned that the "US should stop politicizing sports."[4] In the end, despite a considerable diplomatic effort to enlist the support of other allies, the boycott was joined by only a handful of other countries (Canada, United Kingdom, Norway, Sweden, Australia, Lithuania, Kosovo, Belgium, Denmark,

---

no. 1 (2019): pp. 102–28, https://doi.org/10.1080/02634937.2018.1507997; Joanne Smith-Finley, "Securitization, Insecurity and Conflict in Contemporary Xinjiang: Has PRC Counter-Terrorism Evolved into State Terror?," *Central Asian Survey* 38, no. 1 (2019): pp. 1–26, https://doi.org/10.1080/02634937.2019.1586348; and Darren Byler, *In the Camps: Life in China's High-Tech Penal Colony* (Columbia University Press, 2022).

[2] Victoria Tin-bor Hui, "Crackdown: Hong Kong Faces Tiananmen 2.0," *Journal of Democracy* 31, no. 4 (2020): pp. 122–37, https://doi.org/10.1353/jod.2020.0060; Sonny Lo, "Hong Kong in 2020: National Security Law and Truncated Autonomy," *Asian Survey* 61, no. 1 (2021): pp. 34–42, https://doi.org/10.1525/as.2021.61.1.34; Brian C. H. Fong, "Exporting Autocracy: How China's Extra-Jurisdictional Autocratic Influence Caused Democratic Backsliding in Hong Kong," *Democratization* 28, no. 1 (2021): pp. 198–218, https://doi.org/10.1080/13510347.2020.1851202.

[3] Vincent Ni and Joan E. Greve, "US Confirms It Will Stage Diplomatic Boycott of Beijing Winter Olympics," *The Guardian*, December 6, 2021, https://www.theguardian.com/sport/2021/dec/06/china-denounces-possible-us-olympic-boycott-as-provocation.

[4] Foreign Ministry of the People's Republic of China, Foreign Ministry Spokesperson Zhao Lijian's Regular Press Conference, December 7, 2021, https://www.fmprc.gov.cn/mfa_eng/xwfw_665399/s2510_665401/2511_665403/202112/t20211207_10463627.html.

and Estonia did not send leaders; nor did India but because of ongoing border clashes with China, not over Xinjiang repression).[5]

Strikingly, the effort to expand the boycott mostly failed to garner the support of other global actors. The private sector, especially international corporate sponsors, steered clear of commenting on Xinjiang or Chinese policies. Eleven of 13 major corporate sponsors did not respond to a *Financial Times* inquiry about their plans to reconsider sponsorship.[6] Perhaps most tellingly, the new president of the International Olympic Committee (IOC) itself, which before 2008 had proudly championed its potential to act as a catalyst for positive change, stated in July 2021, "As a non-governmental organisation, we have neither the mandate, nor the capability, to change laws of sovereign countries. We cannot solve human rights issues which generations of politicians were unable to solve."[7] A group of nongovernmental organizations (NGOs) did attempt to mount an international campaign to support the US-led boycott but were not able to generate the same scope or intensity in the lead-up to the February 2022 Olympics as in 2008.

As Chinese officials publicly dismissed the boycott effort, members of the Chinese organizing committee warned that foreign athletes could face punishment if they violated Chinese law, including its restrictions on criticizing certain political topics.[8] Concerns that international athletes were under surveillance were heightened when a Canadian tech watchdog warned that the MY2022 App, whose download and use was required of all Olympic athletes, contained significant

---

[5] "Beijing Winter Olympics Boycott: Why Are the Games So Controversial?," BBC, February 4, 2022, https://www.bbc.com/news/explainers-59644043.

[6] Demetri Sevastopulo et al., "Olympic Sponsors Duck Questions over Beijing 2022 as Boycott Calls Grow," *Financial Times*, May 6, 2021, https://www.ft.com/content/bf07dfb7-f70a-4008-8ab1-2b23bfbfb84d.

[7] International Olympic Committee, "The Unifying Power of the Olympic Games to Bring the World Together in Peaceful Competition," July 7, 2021, https://olympics.com/ioc/news/the-unifying-power-of-the-olympic-games-to-bring-the-world-together-in-peaceful-competition.

[8] Jessica Dou, "China Warns Foreign Olympic Athletes Against Speaking Out on Politics at Winter Games," *Washington Post*, January 19, 2022, https://www.washingtonpost.com/sports/olympics/2022/01/19/china-winter-olympics-politics-speech/.

54   DICTATING THE AGENDA

vulnerabilities that allowed external access to personal medical and travel information as well as built-in censorship of over 2,000 political terms and phrases.[9]

Beijing also mounted influence campaigns on social media within the West itself to promote the Olympics and dismiss their "politicization." One such campaign was reportedly coordinated by the New Jersey–based firm Vippi Media, the recipient of a $300,000 contract paid by the Chinese Consulate in New York.[10] Most of the influencer posts on Instagram and Tik-Tok were intended to focus on "Beijing and China elements," including Chinese history and culture, and 20% on "cooperation and any good things in US-China relations." A *New York Times* and *Pro Publica* investigation identified a network of 3,000 "inauthentic-looking" Twitter accounts that appeared to be coordinating posts with Chinese media entities, including criticizing the boycott and lauding Chinese policies in Hong Kong.[11] To be sure, the PRC used Western public relations firms to boost the 2008 Games as well,[12] but the shift in methods and tone were both notable.

As events that capture the impact of transnational liberal influence, the run-up to the two Beijing Olympics were starkly different, despite the Beijing government clampdown on domestic dissent in both cases. In 2008, NGOs and civil society led a broad human rights advocacy campaign, bolstered by the authority of having direct discussions with members of the IOC. They successfully put human rights on the international agenda and into the global media spotlight and prompted Beijing to defensively respond to various reports and allegations of unfulfilled commitments. By contrast, in 2022 it was the US government,

---

[9] Jeffry Knockel, "Cross-Country Exposure: Analysis of the MY2022 Olympics App," Citizen Lab, University of Toronto, January 18, 2022, https://citizenlab.ca/2022/01/cross-country-exposure-analysis-my2022-olympics-app/.

[10] Anna Massoglia, "Chinese Government Deploying Online Influencers amid Beijing Olympics Boycotts," OpenSecrets, December 13, 2021, https://www.opensecrets.org/news/2021/12/chinese-government-deploying-online-influencers-amid-beijing-olympics-boycotts/.

[11] Steven Lee Myers et al., "Bots and Fake Accounts Push China's Vision of Winter Olympic Wonderland," *New York Times*, February 18, 2022, https://www.nytimes.com/2022/02/18/technology/china-olympics-propaganda.html.

[12] Anne-Marie Brady, "The Beijing Olympics as a Campaign of Mass Distraction," *China Quarterly* 197 (2009): p. 8, https://doi.org/10.1017/S0305741009000058.

not the NGO or the private sector, that was most visibly vocal, actively leading a diplomatic boycott that, as it turned out, was relatively ineffective and lacked significant global backing. In addition, the PRC was more forceful and vocal in responding to detractors and proactive in setting the agenda.

To illustrate the impact of these changes, we construct a rough measure of global media attention to linkages between human rights and the two Olympics. We used LexisNexis's "Major World Publications" search tool, which contains about 120 leading publications from around the world, and conducted searches for the period from August 8, 2007, to August 8, 2008 (the year before the 2008 Beijing Summer Olympics) and from February 4, 2021, to February 4, 2022 (the year before the Beijing Winter Olympics).[13]

The results in Table 3.1 show how global media attention to the links between human rights, including repression of ethnic minorities, and the Olympics was much lower in 2022 relative to 2008. Crucially, this is not explained by Summer Olympics being more popular than Winter Olympics, as each period contained a similar number of articles mentioning the Olympics generally. The take-home message appears to be that even though many activists and Western governments tried hard to make the PRC government's repression of Uyghurs in Xinjiang (and beyond) and human rights generally a central issue of the 2022 Olympics, much less attention was generated than the PRC government's repression of Tibetans or its general human rights practices in 2008.[14]

Tellingly, both the IOC and Beijing appeared to have learned similar lessons from the 2008 Olympics. The IOC itself expressed deep skepticism about the campaigns of NGOs in 2008, with Coordination Commission chairman Hein Verbruggen himself lamenting in an interview that the IOC's initial deference drew attention away from

---

[13] The search was most recently performed and validated on May 31, 2024, using the Nexis Advance library account of University College Dublin. The total number of articles on any subject in each year was about 3.3 million.

[14] Different regions were chosen for the different years to reflect the more discussed issue at the time. In the 2007–8 sample, 750 articles appear for Xinjiang and Olympics, while in 2021–22, 382 articles appear for Tibet and Olympics. Thus, even for the "less salient" region in each time period, attention decreased in the later sample.

DICTATING THE AGENDA

Table 3.1 Global Media Attention to Human Rights in Two Beijing Olympics

	No. of articles on "human rights" and Olympics	No. of articles on Tibet/Xinjiang and Olympics	No. of articles mentioning Olympics
Aug. 8, 2007–Aug. 8, 2008	5,459	6,336 (Tibet)	89,074
Feb. 4, 2021–Feb. 4, 2022	3,761	1,563 (Xinjiang)	92,144

the general sporting principles at stake.[15] The IOC's response was to withdraw from politics altogether, even as Beijing more aggressively threatened the free speech of athletes and sparred with critics. Of course, Human Rights Watch and Amnesty International still condemned China's abuses, but as the media analysis and IOC statements both suggest, they were far more marginalized, if not outright ignored, by a variety of global actors.

China also learned important lessons. Four months after the 2008 Summer Games, the director of the CCP's Propaganda Department acknowledged that China's international communications surrounding the Games had been "weak," allowing overly critical media to frame international coverage of the event.[16] The foreign attention to Tibet in 2008 "served as a jolt to the system," and the party's approach to information campaigns about international human rights issues began to change.[17] The 2008 Olympics was a "watershed moment" that shaped Beijing's subsequent global media strategy.[18] The year 2008 more generally was an important turning point that saw the CCP begin to

---

[15] Susan Brownell, "Human Rights and the Beijing Olympics: Imagined Global Community and the Transnational Public Sphere," *British Journal of Sociology* 63, no. 2 (2012): pp. 306–27, https://doi.org/10.1111/j.1468-4446.2012.01411.x.

[16] Brownell, "Human Rights."

[17] Jamie J. Gruffydd-Jones, *Hostile Forces: How the Chinese Communist Party Resists International Pressure on Human Rights* (Oxford University Press, 2022), p. 53.

[18] Johan Lindberg et al., "The World According to China: Capturing and Analysing the Global Media Influence Strategies of a Superpower," *Pacific Journalism Review* 29, nos. 1–2 (2023): p. 185, https://doi.org/10.24135/pjr.v29i1and2.1317.

more assertively push back against liberal values.[19] Domestically, after ramping up to ensure a smooth Olympics, "The internal security bureaucracy never loosened up again."[20] Starting in early 2009, the CCP began investing billions in its international propaganda streams, such as CCTV International (later CGTN), Xinhua, and *Global Times*.[21]

The contrast between 2008 and 2022, in terms of both transnational liberal influence efforts and illiberal state response, is illustrative of deeper shifts. The 2022 Winter Olympics displayed a range of techniques to neutralize and counter the channels of liberal activism that had surrounded the lead-up to the 2008 Games and the event itself. A new form of contested politics—what we later describe as authoritarian snapback—was in evidence in 2022 in ways that it was not 14 years prior. A powerful illustration of this new politics is that Xi Jinping and Vladimir Putin declared their "no limits friendship" on the opening day of the 2022 Olympics, including their shared viewpoints on opposing the imposition of liberal democracy and pushing back against the West.[22]

The Vulnerabilities of the 1990s Model in the Cold Light of the 2020s

Changes in global politics have altered the modalities of transnational liberal influence. As power has shifted toward autocracies, the assumptions sustaining liberal influence and its enabling environment have also been challenged.[23] In the 1990s and 2000s when autocracies

---

[19] Susan Shirk, *Overreach: How China Derailed Its Peaceful Rise* (Oxford University Press, 2023), p. 85.

[20] Shirk, *Overreach*, p. 160.

[21] Anne-Marie Brady, "China's Foreign Propaganda Machine," *Journal of Democracy* 26, no. 4 (2015): pp. 51–59, https://doi.org/10.1353/jod.2015.0056.

[22] Tony Munroe et al., "China, Russia Partner Up Against West at Olympics Summit," Reuters, February 4, 2022, https://www.reuters.com/world/europe/russia-china-tell-nato-stop-expansion-moscow-backs-beijing-taiwan-2022-02-04/.

[23] Contrasting the global environment for sustaining democracy in the 1990s versus the 2020s, Levitsky and Way make a succinct case: "Most important, the geopolitical balance of power has shifted dramatically. The post–Cold War era of Western liberal hegemony—in which the United States and Western Europe were the world's undisputed military, economic, and ideological powers—is over. The rise of China

58 DICTATING THE AGENDA

transitioned, they did so to democracy more often than not,[24] but this no longer appears to be the case.[25] This changing global context has empowered authoritarian states to contend with transnational liberal advocacy in new ways, often by plugging or reversing the very channels of influence that originally spread liberal norms. Autocrats are increasingly trying to dictate the agenda on a range of issues in world politics.

Authoritarians are now also aided by certain actors within liberal democracies themselves who stigmatize liberal activism and contest what types of norms the West should adhere to and spread. In a prescient essay written nearly ten years ago, Boyle argued that the challenge to global liberalism had domestic as well as international sources.[26] On this account, "Populist leaders mobilize around visions of state sovereignty that challenge the [liberal international order] by promoting alternative illiberal orders."[27] The domestic challenge comes not just from democracies in "the West,"[28] but the skepticism toward international forms of liberalism is most striking there given that Western states were in large measure responsible for advancing global liberalism after World War II. Donald Trump's 2024 election, which followed

---

and the renewed power and aggressiveness of Russia and other illiberal states (e.g., Iran and Saudi Arabia) have created an international environment that is far less favorable to democracy—and more favorable to autocracy—than that which existed during the heady 1990s. Unlike during the immediate post–Cold War period, democracy is not 'the only game in town.'" The authors argue that despite these threats, democracy has proved surprisingly resilient. See Steven Levitsky and Lucan Way, "The Resilience of Democracy's Third Wave," *PS: Political Science & Politics* 57, no. 2 (2024): pp. 198–201, https://doi.org/10.1017/S1049096523000914.

[24] Barbara Geddes et al., "Autocratic Breakdown and Transitions: A New Data Set," *Perspectives on Politics* 12, no. 2 (2014): p. 316, https://doi.org/10.1017/S1537592714000851.

[25] Felix Wiebrecht et al., "State of the World 2022: Defiance in the Face of Autocratization," *Democratization* 30, no. 5 (2023): pp. 775–76, https://doi.org/10.1080/13510347.2023.2199452.

[26] Michael J. Boyle, "The Coming Illiberal Order," *Survival* 58, no. 2 (2016): p. 37, https://doi.org/10.1080/00396338.2016.1161899.

[27] See the argument by Jenne and Laroche in Angelos Chryssogelos et al., "New Directions in the Study of Populism in International Relations," *International Studies Review* 25, no. 4 (2023): p. 5, https://doi.org/10.1093/isr/viado35.

[28] Fredrik Söderbaum et al., *Contestations of the Liberal International Order: A Populist Script of Regional Cooperation* (Cambridge University Press, 2021).

a campaign filled with illiberal promises, is the latest and potentially most important example. Trubowitz and Burgoon have charted how the embrace of pro-globalization economic policies by both Western center-right and center-left governments during the 1990s and 2000s fueled subsequent discontent, nationalism, and calls to break from liberal economic and foreign policy orthodoxy.[29] The result is that international liberalism is under dual attack from politicians and voters within liberal democratic states as well as from illiberal authoritarian governments.[30]

As a result, authoritarianism now appears to be on the front foot globally. Led in many respects by the examples of China and Russia, autocracies openly celebrate their partnerships in opposition to political liberalism and have learned to protect their autocracies abroad or even sometimes promote autocracy,[31] cooperate and learn from one another,[32] and diffuse apparently "successful" authoritarian methods and practices.[33] Autocracies actively promote illiberal norms in

---

[29] Peter Trubowitz and Brian Burgoon, *Geopolitics and Democracy: The Western Liberal Order from Foundation to Fracture* (Oxford University Press, 2023).

[30] Rebecca Adler-Nissen and Ayşe Zarakol, "Struggles for Recognition: The Liberal International Order and the Merger of Its Discontents," *International Organization* 75, no. 2 (2021): pp. 611–34, https://doi.org/10.1017/S0020818320000454.

[31] See references in footnote 5 in Chapter 1. See also Kurt Weyland, "Autocratic Diffusion and Cooperation: The Impact of Interests vs. Ideology," *Democratization* 24, no. 7 (2017): pp. 1235–52, https://doi.org/10.1080/13510347.2017.1307823; Carlos de la Torre, "Hugo Chavez and the Diffusion of Bolivarianism," *Democratization* 24, no. 7 (2017): pp. 1271–88, https://doi.org/10.1080/13510347.2017.1307825; Katsiaryna Yakouchyk, "Beyond Autocracy Promotion: A Review," *Political Studies Review* 17, no. 2 (2019): pp. 147–60, https://doi.org/10.1177/1478929918774976. For a skeptical view, see Jason Brownlee, "The Limited Reach of Authoritarian Powers," *Democratization* 24, no. 7 (2017): pp. 1326–44, https://doi.org/10.1080/13510347.2017.1287175.

[32] Oisín Tansey, *International Politics of Authoritarian Rule* (Oxford University Press, 2016); Oisín Tansey et al., "Ties to the Rest: Autocratic Linkages and Regime Survival," *Comparative Political Studies* 50, no. 9 (2017): pp. 1221–54, https://doi.org/10.1177/0010414016666859; and Stephen G. F. Hall, *The Authoritarian International: Tracing How Authoritarian Regimes Learn in the Post-Soviet Space* (Cambridge University Press, 2023).

[33] On this theme see Seva Gunitsky, *Aftershocks: Great Powers and Domestic Reforms in the Twentieth Century* (Princeton University Press, 2017); Jørgen Møller et al., "International Influences and Democratic Regression in Interwar Europe: Disentangling the Impact of Power Politics and Demonstration Effects," *Government and*

international organizations once designed to monitor human rights and other liberal values.[34] They use regional organizations to safeguard their regimes[35] and to road-test normative changes in emerging domains like internet governance.[36] They forge simultaneously subnational but transnational networks, such as party-to-party exchanges in Africa financed by the CCP.[37] Russia has also systematically sought to both erode liberal norms and push alternative norms like Eurasianism, civilizational diversity, and "traditional" values in global forums[38]

Opposition 52, no. 4 (2017): pp. 559–86, https://doi.org/10.1017/gov.2015.37; Kurt Weyland, *Assault on Democracy: Communism, Fascism, and Authoritarianism During the Interwar Years* (Cambridge University Press, 2021).

[34] Alexander Cooley, "Countering Democratic Norms," *Journal of Democracy* 26, no. 3 (2015): pp. 49–63, https://doi.org/10.1353/jod.2015.0049; Rana Siu Inboden, "China and Authoritarian Collaboration," *Journal of Contemporary China* 31, no. 136 (2022): pp. 505–17, https://doi.org/10.1080/10670564.2021.1985828; Rana Siu Inboden, *China and the International Human Rights Regime, 1982–2017* (Cambridge University Press, 2021); Alexander Dukalskis, "A Fox in the Henhouse: China, Normative Change, and the United Nations Human Rights Council," *Journal of Human Rights* 22, no. 3 (2023): pp. 334–50; Rosemary Foot, "Institutional Design and Rhetorical Spaces: China's Human Rights Strategies in a Changing World Order," *Journal of Contemporary China* (2024): pp. 1–14, https://doi.org/10.1080/10670564.2023.2299958; Anna M. Meyerrose and Irfan Nooruddin, "Trojan Horses in Liberal International Organizations? How Democratic Backsliders Undermine the UNHRC," *Review of International Organizations* (2023): pp. 1–32, https://doi.org/10.1007/s11558-023-09511-6.

[35] Maria J. Debre, "The Dark Side of Regionalism: How Regional Organizations Help Authoritarian Regimes to Boost Survival," *Democratization* 28, no. 2 (2021): pp. 394–413, https://doi.org/10.1080/13510347.2020.1823970.

[36] Daniëlle Flonk, "Emerging Illiberal Norms: Russia and China as Promoters of Internet Content Control," *International Affairs* 97, no. 6 (2021): pp. 1925–44, https://doi.org/10.1093/ia/iiab146.

[37] For example, see Jevans Nyabiage, "China's Political Party School in Africa Takes First Students from 6 Countries," *South China Morning Post*, June 21, 2022, https://www.scmp.com/news/china/diplomacy/article/3182368/china-party-school-africa-takes-first-students-6-countries; and Yun Sun, "Political Party Training: China's Ideological Push in Africa?," *Brookings Africa in Focus*, July 5, 2016, https://www.brookings.edu/blog/africa-in-focus/2016/07/05/political-party-training-chinas-ideological-push-in-africa/ (accessed February 2, 2022). On party-to-party exchanges organized by the CCP more generally, see Christine Hackenesch and Julia Bader, "The Struggle for Minds and Influence: The Chinese Communist Party's Global Outreach," *International Studies Quarterly* 64, no. 3 (2020): pp. 723–33, https://doi.org/10.1093/isq/sqaa028.

[38] Gregorio Bettiza et al., "Civilizationism and the Ideological Contestation of the Liberal International Order," *International Studies Review* 25, no. 2 (2023): viad006, https://doi.org/10.1093/isr/viad006; David G. Lewis, "Geopolitical Imaginaries in Russian Foreign Policy: The Evolution of 'Greater Eurasia,'" in *The European Union, Russia and the Post-Soviet Space: Shared Neighbourhood, Battleground or Transit*

AUTHORITARIAN RESURGENCE IN THE 2020s   61

and through transnational civil society linkages such as pro-traditional family organizations.[39] And with some success, Russia has justified its war on Ukraine to audiences in the Global South as a conflict against the US-led international order and its hypocritical liberal and Western underpinnings.[40] Moscow's public messaging and Beijing's rise as an anti-liberal global norm-maker are external extensions of their domestic regime legitimation strategies, although many tend to view them as an inevitable outcome of renewed "great power competition."[41]

But how did we get to this world of "offensive authoritarianism," especially given that the United States and its allies forged global governance in their own image, including assigning new technologies and consumerism its liberal norms and values? Crucial changes related to the shift of global power have enabled each one of the pillars of 1990s liberal influence discussed in the previous chapter to be questioned or undermined, profoundly affecting transnational advocacy and the political values embodied in certain areas of global governance. The rise of challengers, aided by the global erosion of liberalism, revealed serious weaknesses in all three of the liberal influence model's assumptions, not only as individual axioms but also as reinforcing one another.

The West Is No Longer Perceived as Best

First, American efficacious authority eroded both because emerging powers broke its monopoly power as a supplier of global goods and

---

Zone on the New Silk Road?, edited by Viktoria Akchurina and Vincent Della Sala (Routledge, 2023), pp. 70–95; Alexander Cooley, "Authoritarianism Goes Global: Countering Democratic Norms," *Journal of Democracy* 26, no. 3 (2015): pp. 49–63, https://doi.org/10.1353/jod.2015.0049.

[39] Kristina Stoeckl, "The Rise of the Russian Christian Right: The Case of the World Congress of Families," *Religion, State and Society* 48, no. 4 (2020): pp. 223–38, https://doi.org/10.1080/09637494.2020.1796172.

[40] See, for example, Maria Repnikova, "Russia's War in Ukraine and the Fractures in Western Soft Power," *Place Branding and Public Diplomacy* 19, no. 2 (2023): pp. 190–94, https://doi.org/10.1057/s41254-022-00282-2.

[41] In reality, the two are intertwined. An international environment that prioritizes understandings of political legitimacy that more closely match a domestic regime can bolster that regime's security and external power. See, for example, Alexander Dukalskis, *Making the World Safe for Dictatorship* (Oxford University Press, 2021); John M. Owen IV, *The Clash of Ideas in World Politics: Transnational Networks, States, and Regime Change, 1510–2010* (Princeton University Press, 2010); and Chris Ogden, *The Authoritarian Century: China's Rise and the Demise of the Liberal International Order* (Bristol University Press, 2022).

standards and because the United States itself no longer was perceived as effective or sometimes even competent. The US-led "hegemonic cartel" in the 1990s was the exclusive provider of global goods and roles in many areas of global governance, including developmental assistance and advice, legal frameworks for managing trade and intellectual property rights, global media, entertainment and information services, and mediator in disputes and conflicts.[42] In other words, the United States was not only perceived as the world's effective "policeman" but also its firefighter, engineer, teacher, journalist, and lead performer.

In the 2000s, emerging authoritarian powers expanded their investments in the provision of global public goods, technologies, and supporting governance structures that would identify them as effective alternative providers. The rise of China's Belt and Road Initiative in the 2010s, with its emphasis on infrastructure and development, provided an alternative global economic model for a great power patron with global ambitions.[43] The establishment of new lending facilities such as the Asian Infrastructure Investment Bank (AIIB) and the New Development Bank of the BRICS provided alternative institutions for developmental lending than the Western-dominated World Bank and IMF. The "Washington Consensus" is no longer prized, and in the 2000s some began to discuss the "Beijing Consensus" as an alternative.[44]

Similarly, authoritarian powers, including China and Russia, also invested in new global media platforms, spending billions of dollars to

---

[42] Alexander Cooley and Daniel Nexon, *Exit from Hegemony: The Unravelling of the American Global Order* (Oxford University Press, 2020).

[43] From the voluminous literature on the Belt and Road and its motivations, see William A. Callahan, "China's 'Asia Dream': The Belt and Road Initiative and the New Regional Order," *Asian Journal of Comparative Politics* 1, no. 3 (2016): pp. 226–43; Lee Jones and Zeng Jinghan, "Understanding China's 'Belt and Road Initiative': Beyond 'Grand Strategy' to a State Transformation Analysis," *Third World Quarterly* 40, no. 8 (2019): pp. 1415–39, https://doi.org/10.1080/01436597.2018.1559046; and Krishna Chaitanya Vadlamannati et al., "Building Bridges or Breaking Bonds? The Belt and Road Initiative and Foreign Aid Competition," *Foreign Policy Analysis* 19, no. 3 (2023): orado15, https://doi.org/10.1093/fpa/orado15. On China's aid and loans abroad generally, see Axel Dreher et al., *Banking on Beijing: The Aims and Impacts of China's Overseas Development Program* (Cambridge University Press, 2022).

[44] For a critical discussion of the Beijing Consensus concept, see Scott Kennedy, "The Myth of the Beijing Consensus," *Journal of Contemporary China* 19, no. 65 (2010): pp. 461–77, https://doi.org/10.1080/10670561003666087.

project their viewpoints globally. Chapter 5 will provide more detail, but Russia spent $70 million on media in the United States alone between 2014 and 2017.[45] China has spent extensively to build its global information apparatus since the 1990s, with an additional infusion of over $6.6 billion in 2009 to expand and improve its external propaganda.[46] The aim is to improve China's soft power, which was explicitly mentioned in the 17th CCP Congress in 2007, challenge the privileged position of Western political ideas, and increase Beijing's "discourse power," or the ability to influence the global discussion.[47] Furthermore, these efforts are built on asymmetric access: With some exceptions, liberal democracies generally do not censor pro-authoritarian voices or platforms, while authoritarian regimes routinely censor liberal democratic ones.[48] The global public sphere now includes dozens of autocracies that have external-facing propaganda outlets, retain public relations firms, and co-opt foreign elites to help tell their story.[49]

---

[45] Dukalskis, *Making the World Safe*, p. 63.

[46] Brady, "China's Foreign Propaganda Machine," p. 54; Wen-Hsuan Tsai, "Enabling China's Voice to Be Heard by the World: Ideas and Operations of the Chinese Communist Party's External Propaganda System," *Problems of Post-Communism* 6, nos. 3–4 (2017): p. 204, https://doi.org/10.1080/10758216.2016.1236667.

[47] Brady, "China's Foreign Propaganda Machine"; Tsai, "Enabling China's Voice"; Jeanne L. Wilson, "Russia and China Respond to Soft Power: Interpretation and Readaptation of a Western Concept," *Politics* 35, nos. 3–4 (2015): pp. 287–300, https://doi.org/10.1111/1467-9256.12095; Kejin Zhao, "China's Rise and Its Discursive Power Strategy," *Chinese Political Science Review* 1, no. 3 (2016): pp. 539–64, https://doi.org/10.1007/s41111-016-0037-8; Nadege Rolland, "China's Vision for a New World Order," National Bureau of Asian Research, Special Report No. 83, January 27, 2020; Maria Repnikova, *Chinese Soft Power* (Cambridge University Press, 2022).

[48] See Alexander Cooley and Daniel H. Nexon, "The Real Crisis of Global Order: Illiberalism on the Rise," *Foreign Affairs* 101, no. 1 (2022): p. 103. One major exception is that in March 2022, the European Union imposed sanctions on RT and Sputnik that included suspended broadcasting and web access. It is worth noting, though, that this came in response to Russia's full-scale invasion of Ukraine, not Russian authoritarianism domestically. See the EU's statement here: https://www .consilium.europa.eu/en/press/press-releases/2022/03/02/eu-imposes-sanctions-on-state-owned-outlets-rt-russia-today-and-sputnik-s-broadcasting-in-the-eu/.

[49] Dukalskis, *Making the World Safe*; Sergei Guriev and Daniel Treisman, *Spin Dictators: The Changing Face of Tyranny in the 21st Century* (Princeton University Press, 2022), pp. 156–63; Adam Scharpf et al., "Dictatorships and Western Public Relations Firms," unpublished manuscript April 3, 2024, https://www.

64 DICTATING THE AGENDA

Likewise, as we will see, the assumptions of liberal primacy in higher education and international sports are also being challenged. Sometimes this comes "from within," as when state legislatures in the United States try to curb academic freedoms on the grounds that curricula are too "liberal" or when athletes like former US National Football League star Colin Kaepernick are allegedly blacklisted from their sports leagues for taking controversial stands. But on a transnational scale, authoritarian states are mounting challenges in these areas. International rankings of universities now feature institutions from China and Singapore near the top that are rooted in contexts subject to illiberal government discipline. In the sporting realm, Saudi Arabian investments have rapidly challenged the commercial dominance of European soccer leagues. In the Olympics sphere, although the United States still regularly tops the Summer Olympics medal count, the 2020 Games saw the US outpace China by a relatively close 112–89 margin.[50] China's General Administration of Sport sets medal count goals and devotes resources to meet them, viewing victory through the lens of national prestige and power.[51]

At the same time as alternative sources of goods and domains of expertise have proliferated, the US suffered a set of self-inflicted blows that seriously eroded its own global standing on what was once assumed to be core areas of authority and competence. Washington's disastrous campaign to enact regime change and promote democracy in Iraq and chaotic withdrawal from Afghanistan in 2021 tarnished an image of military supremacy and the very possibility of external nation-building. The financial crisis of 2008 shook confidence in the US financial system and its lack of regulation and spurred the growth of financial centers in non-Western jurisdictions such as Singapore, Hong Kong, and the UAE. And on January 6, 2021, much of the rest of the world watched in disbelief as supporters of defeated President Donald Trump stormed the US Capitol Building to disrupt the congressional certification of

---

dropbox.com/scl/fi/xk6b6ykobnxv9yiygottn/Dictators_PR_Firms.pdf?rlkey=iq7kx l7z3qwv43u67pnaeqpfn&e=1&dl=0.

[50] In the 2008 Beijing Games, the United States won the medal count 112–100, but China won more golds at 48 to 36, leading to differing reporting of medal count leaders from that year.

[51] Brady, "Beijing Olympics," p. 7.

the vote, irreparably undermining the United States' own image as a guarantor of democratic norms and practices. Even more remarkably, Trump faced no accountability for these actions as the Special Counsel investigations into his role were closed as he returned to the White House four years later.

Market Power Shifts Eastward

In terms of global markets, the American and Western consumer is still important but no longer dominant. Despite its relative underconsumption as an overall proportion of GDP, China's global share of consumer growth over the last decades has been astonishing and its implications profound. Whereas in 1980 China's share of world consumption spending was just 2%, by 2018 it had grown to 12% in dollar terms (and 14% in purchase power).[52]

In the global luxury goods markets especially, once dominated by the West, Chinese middle and upper classes over the last 15 years have turbocharged growth in these sectors. According to the consulting organization McKinsey, the Chinese share of the world luxury market increased from 19% in 2012 ($51b of $252b) to 32% in 2018 ($118b of $368b), with the 2025 share projected to reach 41%.[53] Consider the changing geographic distribution of global sales and retail outlets of the world's leading luxury brand, Moët Hennessy Louis Vuitton, maker of fashion, leather, perfumes, watches, jewelry, and spirits, which in 2021 accounted for $55 billion in sales globally, more than its next three competitors combined.[54] In the year 2000, its Asian sales (excluding Japan) comprised 17% of the company's net global sales, behind the United

---

[52] "China's Consumer Decade," Deutsche Bank, December 1, 2019, https://www.db.com/news/detail/20191201-china-s-consumer-decade?language_id=1.

[53] McKinsey & Company, "Chinese Luxury Report 2019: How Young Chinese Consumers Are Reshaping Global Luxury," April 2019, https://www.mckinsey.com/~/media/mckinsey/featured%20insights/china/how%20young%20chinese%20cons umers%20are%20reshaping%20global%20luxury/mckinsey-china-luxury-report-20 19-how-young-chinese-consumers-are-reshaping-global-luxury.ashx.

[54] Statista, "Luxury Goods Sales of the Leading Luxury Goods Companies Worldwide in 2021," August 29, 2023, https://www.statista.com/statistics/441789/sales-of-the-leading-luxury-goods-companies-worldwide/.

States (28%), France (18%), and the rest of Europe (18%);[55] by 2023 Asian sales (excluding Japan) were the single largest geographic revenue source at 31%, ahead of the United States (25%), France (8%), and the rest of Europe (17%).[56] In terms of the global distribution of retail outlets, in 2000 the 226 Asian (non-Japan) stores accounted for 18% of the company's global network; in 2023 its 2003 Asian (non-Japan) outlets comprised 33% of global outlets, the largest concentration of stores in a single region.[57]

Similar trends unfolded in the global entertainment market, a conveyor belt for US soft power in the 1990s. From 2012 to 2019, box-office revenues in China nearly quadrupled from 17.1 billion to 64.3 billion yuan. As a global share, whereas in 2004 China comprised just 1.1% of global box-office revenues, by 2012 this had grown to 7.8% and in 2021 reached an astonishing 34.3%.[58] As we will explore, increased market share in countries such as China, the UAE, and Russia also recast our understanding over which values and norms were important and which actors held leverage.

Questioning Embedded Autonomy and Cracking Down in Plain Sight

The norms of freedom of expression and embedded autonomy have increasingly become challenged, in part as a direct result of the perceived geopolitical intentions of civil society and its allies. The rights of civil society and other nongovernmental actors to independently exercise their freedom of expression and political advocacy have been eroded on geopolitical grounds precisely because these actors have

---

[55] *Moët Hennessy Louis Vuitton (LVMH) Annual Report 2001*, pp. 5–6, https://ddd.uab.cat/pub/infanu/30082/iaLVMHa2001ieng.pdf (accessed July 15, 2024).

[56] LVMH Annual Report 2023, pp. 16–17, https://lvmh-com.cdn.prismic.io/lvmh-com/Zofmtx5LeNNTwoeG_lvmh_2023-annual-report.pdf (accessed July 15, 2024).

[57] LVMH Annual Report 2001 and LVMH Annual Report 2022.

[58] Statista, "China's Box Office Share in the Global Box Office from 2012 to 2021 with an Estimate for 2022," January 9, 2023, https://www.statista.com/statistics/1046171/china-box-office-share-in-the-global-box-office/. Also see Stephen Fellows, "How Important Is International Box Office to Hollywood?," *Stephen Fellows: Film Data and Education*, May 15, 2017, https://stephenfollows.com/important-international-box-office-hollywood/.

been associated with US-backed politically motivated agendas. The upheaval of the Color Revolutions in the mid-2000s, where street protests against fraudulent elections led to the collapse of governments in the post-communist states of Georgia, Ukraine, and Kyrgyzstan, and the Arab Spring of the early 2010s generated regional and global backlash against civil society actors that helped to foment protests as well as the social media platforms that helped to mobilize them.[59] The Color Revolutions prompted Hu Jintao, Xi Jinping's relatively moderate and mild-mannered predecessor as China's leader, to interpret freedoms in the media and space for dissidents as opening China to destabilizing plots from the United States.[60]

To protect themselves from the effects of liberal political influence, both China and Russia engineered renewed clampdowns on carriers of liberal ideas at home, reframing the post–Cold War norms about media and NGO autonomy and unfettered advocacy as national security threats.[61] About a decade ago, Yulia Kiseleva noted the rise of "a mode of thinking in Russia that increasingly views soft power originating in the West as a threat to the Russian state and its national interests."[62] In China, as mentioned in the introduction chapter, Document Number 9 explicitly identified "Western" ideas about politics, journalism, civil society, economics, and the study of history as threats.[63] Clampdowns

---

[59] On the backlash against civil society, see Leah Gilbert and Payam Mohseni, "NGO Laws After the Colour Revolutions and the Arab Spring: Nondemocratic Regime Strategies in Eastern Europe and the Middle East," *Mediterranean Politics* 25, no. 2 (2020): pp. 182–214, https://doi.org/10.1080/13629395.2018.1537103. On the diffusion-proofing of recent nonviolent revolutions, see Karrie J. Koesel and Valerie J. Bunce, "Diffusion-Proofing: Russian and Chinese Responses to Waves of Popular Mobilizations against Authoritarian Rulers," *Perspectives on Politics* 11, no. 3 (2013): pp. 753–68, https://doi.org/10.1017/S1537592713002107.

[60] Shirk, *Overreach*, p. 158. Shirk also notes that Vladimir Putin reportedly told Hu in that year that George Soros was behind the protests.

[61] Cooley and Nexon, *Exit from Hegemony*, pp. 93–94.

[62] Yulia Kiseleva, "Russia's Soft Power Discourse: Identity, Status and the Attraction of Power," *Politics* 35, nos. 3–4 (2015): p. 323, https://doi.org/10.1111/1467-9256.12100. See also Marcel H. Van Herpen, *Putin's Propaganda Machine: Soft Power and Russian Foreign Policy* (Rowman & Littlefield, 2016), p. 26.

[63] ChinaFile, "Document 9: A ChinaFile Translation," November 8, 2013, https://www.chinafile.com/document-9-chinafile-translation (accessed September 17, 2021). For analysis see Steve Tsang and Olivia Cheung, *The Political Thought of Xi Jinping* (Oxford University Press, 2024), pp. 81–86.

68   DICTATING THE AGENDA

followed in virtually all areas, including media,[64] higher education,[65] and regulations on foreign-linked NGOs.[66] Xi Jinping himself has openly called for renewed ideological battle with the West.[67]

The clampdown extends beyond China and Russia. There has been a diffusion of laws restricting the activities of NGOs, a process of illiberal norm diffusion that often went unnoticed by analysts of international human rights norms.[68] Autocrats curtailed the activities of independent civil society and increased their support for government-organized nongovernmental organizations, including youth groups, anticorruption groups, and women's rights groups that support government initiatives.[69] North Korean authorities regularly produce propaganda warning against the corrosive effects of "anti-socialist" ideas.[70] The Iranian revolutionary government has long positioned itself as an alternative form of government to liberal models and cracked down on influences and movements that push for liberal democratic reforms.[71]

---

[64] Edward Wong, "Xi Jinping's News Alert: Chinese Media Must Serve Party," *New York Times*, February 22, 2016, https://www.nytimes.com/2016/02/23/world/asia/china-media-policy-xi-jinping.html (accessed September 23, 2021).

[65] Carl Minzner, "Intelligentsia in the Crosshairs: Xi Jinping's Ideological Rectification of Higher Education in China," *China Leadership Monitor*, December 1, 2019, https://www.prcleader.org/carl-minzner (accessed July 29, 2021).

[66] ChinaFile, "Fact Sheet on China's Foreign NGO Law," November 1, 2017, https://www.chinafile.com/ngo/latest/fact-sheet-chinas-foreign-ngo-law (accessed September 17, 2021).

[67] Shirk, *Overreach*, pp. 184, 263.

[68] Marlies Glasius et al., "Illiberal Norm Diffusion: How Do Governments Learn to Restrict Nongovernmental Organizations?," *International Studies Quarterly* 64, no. 2 (2020): pp. 453–68, https://doi.org/10.1093/isq/sqaa019.

[69] For an interesting case study, see Stephen G. F. Hall, "Preventing a Colour Revolution: The Belarusian Example as an Illustration for the Kremlin?," *East European Politics* 33, no. 2 (2017): pp. 162–83, https://doi.org/10.1080/21599165.2017.1301435. On recent developments in Belarus's civil society, see Anastasiya Astapova et al., "Authoritarian Cooptation of Civil Society: The Case of Belarus," *Europe-Asia Studies* 74, no. 1 (2022): pp. 1–30, https://doi.org/10.1080/09668136.2021.2009773.

[70] Hyung-min Joo, "Hidden Transcripts in Marketplaces: Politicized Discourses in the North Korean Shadow Economy," *Pacific Review* 27, no. 1 (2014): pp. 53–55, https://doi.org/10.1080/09512748.2013.846931.

[71] Said Amir Arjomand, *The Turban for the Crown: The Islamic Revolution in Iran* (Oxford University Press, 1988); Steven Levitsky and Lucan Way, *Revolution and Dictatorship: The Violent Origins of Durable Authoritarianism* (Princeton University Press, 2022).

AUTHORITARIAN RESURGENCE IN THE 2020s   69

Rwanda under Paul Kagame, in power unofficially since the mid-1990s and officially since 2000, is instructive. While building a single-party regime with deep reach and surveillance over political activities,[72] his government has gone to great lengths to prevent human rights organizations[73] and international media[74] from investigating abuses. Despite a heavy reliance on overseas aid for much of his tenure, he has argued on many occasions that values of democracy and human rights are subjective and should not be foisted on states like Rwanda. At a 2022 press conference upon taking up the chair of the Commonwealth of Nations, for example, Kagame responded to a question from the BBC about Rwanda's human rights and democracy record with a remarkable 26-minute discourse about how the "North" has no monopoly on values and is hypocritical, even addressing the reporter directly, saying:

> I want to assure you: there is nobody in the BBC or anywhere else thereabout who be [*sic*] holding values better than we do, here in Rwanda. Except if you just want to cover up the mistakes of the same people who want to define these values for us. . . . So I just want to let you know that these issues about "upholding values" and so on, as far as I am concerned, as I know, as far as Rwandans are concerned, we don't need any lessons from BBC or from anyone. I tell you this with firm conviction.[75]

---

[72] See, for example, Filip Reyntjens, "Constructing the Truth, Dealing with Dissent, Domesticating the World: Governance in Post-Genocide Rwanda," *African Affairs* 110, no. 438 (2011): pp. 1–34, https://doi.org/10.1093/afraf/adq075; Timothy Longman, *Memory and Justice in Post-Genocide Rwanda* (Cambridge University Press, 2017); and Andrea Purdeková et al., "Militarization of Governance After Conflict: Beyond the Rebel-to-Ruler Frame—the Case of Rwanda," *Third World Quarterly* 39, no. 1 (2018): pp. 158–74.

[73] For example, Human Rights Watch, "Rwanda: Human Rights Watch Researcher Barred," May 16, 2024, https://www.hrw.org/news/2024/05/16/rwanda-human-rights-watch-researcher-barred.

[74] For example, Sally Hayden, "I Have Reported in Rwanda Three Times. On My Fourth Attempt, I Was Not Allowed on the Plane," *Irish Times*, April 21, 2024, https://www.irishtimes.com/opinion/2024/04/20/sally-hayden-i-have-reported-in-rwanda-three-times-i-never-expected-to-be-blocked-from-entering/.

[75] Full video reproduced on *Kigali Today*: https://www.youtube.com/watch?v=fWouunkqOoo (accessed January 18, 2023). Rwandan authorities have tussled with the BBC for years. See below and Filip Reyntjens, "The Struggle over Truth—Rwanda and the BBC," *African Affairs* 114, no. 457 (2015): pp. 637–48, https://doi.org/10.1093/afraf/advo42.

70 DICTATING THE AGENDA

Even in the West, Hungary's Viktor Orbán announced in 2014 his intention to turn his country away from liberal political values, stating, "We have to abandon liberal methods and principles of organizing a society. The new state that we are building is an illiberal state, a non-liberal state."[76] This rhetoric was accompanied by a sweeping program to enact that vision that included dismantling the media, judicial independence, and civil service autonomy.[77] Orbán's institutional dismantling now serves as a model to other populists such as Donald Trump in the United States who view such "deep state" protections as blocking the enactment of an illiberal policy agenda. The latter's successful 2024 campaign promised to root out the "enemy from within" as part of his illiberal vision. Autonomy and independence in critical spheres such as activism, media, and education are no longer reflexively prized as they were in the post–Cold War decade. And as Bush and Hayden have documented, the explosion in international NGOs of the 1990s and 2000s in the United States has given way to a period of institutional stagnation, as rates of INGO growth in the 2010s across all sectors has "declined dramatically."[78]

Countering Liberal Influence Globally

The learning shown by Chinese authorities about how to blunt and counter the spread of liberal values between their two Olympic Games is a microcosm of the learning and diffusion of authoritarian practices at the global level. Just as liberal norms and governance spread globally in the post–Cold War era, authoritarian practices can also diffuse across borders, with effective methods becoming institutionalized at the level of global governance after disparate processes of trial and error.

---

[76] Quoted in Aron Buzogány, "Illiberal Democracy in Hungary: Authoritarian Diffusion or Domestic Causation?," *Democratization* 24, no. 7 (2017): p. 1308, https://doi.org/10.1080/13510347.2017.1328676.

[77] Buzogány, "Illiberal Democracy in Hungary," pp. 1312–14.

[78] Sarah Bush and Jennifer Hadden, "Density and Decline in the Founding of International NGOs in the United States," *International Studies Quarterly* 63, no. 4 (2019): pp. 1133–46, https://doi.org/10.1093/isq/sqz061.

Authoritarian Learning and Emulation

As noted already, the perceived threat of liberal political ideas is not new. For Chinese leaders, for example, concerns about "peaceful evolution"—or the undermining of socialist rule through intentional cultural and political penetration by capitalist powers—have been in evidence since the 1950s.[79] In his history of the PRC's foreign relations, Garver notes at several points how Chinese leaders sought to "inoculate" the population against liberal, "Western," or even specifically "American" political values.[80]

Moreover, we can say with confidence that authoritarian states *will continue* to actively teach one another how to blunt liberal influence. They trade information, methods, policy formulations, and technical know-how to better control liberal ideas and observe and emulate tactics that facilitate extraterritorial illiberal influence. This learning is not necessarily "top down" but can see pro-authoritarian actors network with one another, observe what works, and sometimes swap advice and support.[81] Recent innovations include but are not limited to (self-)censorship resulting from desire to protect market access, libel lawsuits against critics abroad, requirements that citizens abroad return home to renew their passports as a means to control diaspora dissent, and authoritarian influence over global communications platforms or regulatory norms. Here the co-optation of ostensibly liberal institutions like international legal mechanisms, transnational mobility, or

---

[79] Russell Ong, "'Peaceful Evolution,' 'Regime Change' and China's Political Security," *Journal of Contemporary China* 16, no. 53 (2007): pp. 717–27, https://doi.org/10.1080/10670560701562408.

[80] John W. Garver, *China's Quest: The History of the Foreign Relations of the People's Republic of China* (Oxford University Press, 2016), pp. 23, 476, and 481. According to Gewirtz, in the 1980s, as China opened economically, party elites worried about "spiritual pollution," "sugar-coated bullets" of capitalism, and "bourgeois liberalization" and launched propaganda campaigns to counter these perceived threats after the crackdown and aftermath of the pro-democracy Tiananmen Square movement. The device of peaceful evolution "returned to the center of political discourse" and "featured a large cast of villains: American, French, and British officials, and even Hungarian financier George Soros." From Julian Gewirtz, *Never Turn Back: China and the Forbidden History of the 1980s* (Harvard University Press, 2022), pp. 37–63, 250.

[81] Hall, *The Authoritarian International*.

72 DICTATING THE AGENDA

transparency laws sees authoritarian states advance their goals through liberal institutions.[82]

Authoritarian influence can stem from support and guidance offered by ideologically motivated actors, as was the case with the Communist International.[83] In an echo of that period, the CCP has built a school in Tanzania for training of political parties from the region.[84] Sometimes multiple actors network with one another, supported by an authoritarian state, to advance illiberal aims. For example, the World Congress of Families is a transnational network, founded by two Christian-right organizations in the 1990s, that has evolved as an antithetical illiberal mirror to liberal networks such as the Open Society Foundations. With financial backing from Russia and other post-communist funding sources, it brings together anti-liberal advocates from governments, religious institutions, and civic organizations around the world in annual conferences to denounce liberalism and exchange information and tactics about how to advance causes including advocating for the "traditional" family, opposing abortion, integrating state-sponsored religion in public life, and opposing migration.[85]

At other times, adopting authoritarian innovations across borders results from tactical learning from others facing common perceived threats.[86] Autocrats fearful of losing power can emulate tactics from elsewhere that they perceive as effective in shoring up the regime.[87]

---

[82] On authoritarianism and international law, see Tom Ginsburg, "Authoritarian International Law?," *American Journal of International Law* 114, no. 2 (2020): pp. 221–60, https://doi.org/10.1017/ajil.2020.3.

[83] Alexander Vatlin and Stephen A. Smith, "The Comintern," in *The Oxford Handbook of the History of Communism*, edited by Stephen A. Smith (Oxford University Press, 2013), pp. 187–202.

[84] Hackenesch and Bader, "Struggle for Minds"; Yun Sun, "Political Party Training." For a recent report on how this school actively promotes authoritarianism, see Bethany Allen-Ebrahimian, "In Tanzania, Beijing Is Running a Training School for Authoritarianism," Axios, August 20, 2023, https://www.axios.com/chinese-communist-party-training-school-africa.

[85] Stoeckl, "Russian Christian Right."

[86] Hall, *The Authoritarian International.*

[87] Kurt Weyland, *Making Waves: Democratic Contention in Europe and Latin America Since the Revolutions of 1848* (Cambridge University Press, 2014); Kurt Weyland, *Assault on Democracy: Communism, Fascism, and Authoritarianism During the Interwar Years* (Cambridge University Press, 2021).

Sometimes this can be driven by an "authoritarian gravity centre" that acts as a focal point for authoritarian practices within a region.[88] For example, legal mechanisms designed to control dissent have diffused across post-Soviet authoritarian states, with Russia often (but not always) the exemplar.[89] In documenting the diffusion of democracy and authoritarianism in post-communist Europe, for example, Lankina, Libman, and Obydenkova note that "it is well known that Russia has been allocating vast amounts of funding to NGOs, media outlets, and religious groups in post-Soviet states as part of its 'soft power' agenda."[90] Regional diffusion can help provide a rationale for states adopting illiberal measures because it can be packaged as a legitimate response also being undertaken by neighbors facing similar contexts.[91] Learning and emulation can also transcend regions, as Weyland notes how certain fascist techniques that first emerged in Europe were adopted by Latin American dictatorships looking to bolster their conservative autocracies.[92]

Rewiring Global Governance

States can also proactively collaborate to meet the common threat of liberal democracy and advance their priorities, both bilaterally and within the institutions of global governance. In 2021, Russia and China signed an agreement to cooperate in propaganda and news coverage, for example.[93] RT and the *People's Daily* signed a cooperation agreement in

---

[88] Marianne Kneuer and Thomas Demmelhuber, "Gravity Centres of Authoritarian Rule: A Conceptual Approach," *Democratization* 23, no. 5 (2016): p. 788, https://doi.org/10.1080/13510347.2015.1018898.

[89] Edward Lemon and Oleg Antonov, "Authoritarian Legal Harmonization in the Post-Soviet Space," *Democratization* 27, no. 7 (2020): pp. 1221–39, https://doi.org/10.1080/13510347.2020.1778671.

[90] Tomila Lankina et al., "Authoritarian and Democratic Diffusion in Post-Communist Regions," *Comparative Political Studies* 49, no. 12 (2016): p. 1620, https://doi.org/10.1177/0010414016628270.

[91] Glasius et al., "Illiberal Norm Diffusion."

[92] Weyland, *Assault on Democracy*, pp. 243–53, 302–12.

[93] Mara Hvistendahl and Alexey Kovalev, "Hacked Russian Files Reveal Propaganda Agreement with China," *The Intercept*, December 30, 2022, https://theintercept.com/2022/12/30/russia-china-news-media-agreement/ (accessed April 19, 2023).

2014, and in 2015 Xinhua followed suit.[94] The two powers have often amplified similar criticisms of the United States, conspiracy theories, and similar narratives about major events such as Russia's invasion of Ukraine. In the cyberspace regulatory domain, the two states promote information critical of the United States while also advancing similar visions of internet governance to disable dissent.[95]

On the global front, authoritarians have moved to reshape and transform the political values, as embodied in the activities and even staffing, of global governance actors once assumed to be champions of liberal principles. One of the more striking features of global governance over the last 15 years is the proliferation of new international and regional organizations that are led by China, Russia, and other authoritarian countries. In the 1990s and the 2000s scholars and policymakers tended to view regional organizations, through their very act of fostering cooperation or pooling sovereignty, as advancing liberal norms and rules.[96] However, this assumption seems increasingly anachronistic.[97] International organizations comprising autocratic members can help stabilize authoritarian rule within states by lending legitimacy to

---

94 David Bandurski, "China and Russia Are Joining Forces to Spread Disinformation," *Brookings Tech Stream*, March 11, 2022, https://www.brookings.edu/techstream/china-and-russia-are-joining-forces-to-spread-disinformation/ (accessed January 18, 2023).

95 See Flonk, "Emerging Illiberal Norms." For a more general study of the relationship between authoritarian power and the internet, see Oliver Schlumberger et al., "How Authoritarianism Transforms: A Framework for the Study of Digital Dictatorship," *Government and Opposition* 59, no. 3 (20243): pp. 761–83, https://doi.org/10.1017/gov.2023.20.

96 See Jon C. Pevehouse, "With a Little Help from My Friends? Regional Organizations and the Consolidation of Democracy," *American Journal of Political Science* 6, no. 3 (2002): pp. 611–26, https://doi.org/10.2307/3088403; and Jon C. Pevehouse, "Democracy from the Outside-In? International Organizations and Democratization," *International Organization* 56, no. 3 (2002): pp. 515–49, http://www.jstor.org/stable/3078587.

97 There is by now a large literature on how regional organizations can help sustain authoritarian rule. See, for example, Maria J. Debre, "The Dark Side of Regionalism: How Regional Organizations Help Authoritarian Regimes to Boost Survival," *Democratization* 28, no. 2 (2021): pp. 394–413, https://doi.org/10.1080/13510347.2020.1823970; Anastassia V. Obydenkova and Alexander Libman, *Authoritarian Regionalism in the World of International Organizations: Global Perspectives & the Eurasian Enigma* (Oxford University Press, 2019). Beyond regional organizations and on international organizations more generally, see Christina Cottiero and Stephan Haggard,

their leaders, providing funding, and sharing experiences.[98] In the field of election observation, unlike liberal watchdogs that issue critical assessments of elections, regional organizations tend to send observers to validate and support the incumbent governments of authoritarian member states. Development organizations such as the aforementioned Chinese-led AIIB and the BRICS-affiliated New Development Bank provide project finance and development assistance without the explicit liberal norms of counterparts such as the World Bank. Moreover, organizations such as the Shanghai Cooperation Organization and the BRICS have expanded their membership by welcoming authoritarian powers from across Asia, Africa, and the Middle East in a bid to counterbalance the West and the G7.

Of course, authoritarian elites do not always learn the "correct" lessons from their own or others' experiences that would most efficiently entrench their power.[99] While they have more resources at their disposal than average people, they are also not immune to cognitive shortcuts that lead them to misinterpret evidence.[100] However, the ability to watch an innovation designed to disable dissent unfold in a different context and adjust it to one's own needs is a tremendous luxury.

The Internal Demand for Illiberal Alternatives

The supply side of illiberal influence is now also complemented by demand from within many liberal democratic polities. Democratic societies have themselves grappled with a growing backlash against liberal

---

"Stabilizing Authoritarian Rule: The Role of International Organizations," *International Studies Quarterly* 67, no. 2 (2023): sqado31, https://doi.org/10.1093/isq/sqado31.

[98] Obydenkova and Libman, *Authoritarian Regionalism*, p. 49.

[99] Alexander Dukalskis and Christopher D. Raymond, "Failure of Authoritarian Learning: Explaining Burma/Myanmar's Electoral System," *Democratization* 25, no. 3 (2018): pp. 545–63, https://doi.org/10.1080/13510347.2017.1391794; Daniel Treisman, "Democracy by Mistake: How the Errors of Autocrats Trigger Transitions to Freer Government," *American Political Science Review* 114, no. 3 (2020): pp. 792–810, https://doi.org/10.1017/S0003055420000180; Anne Wolf, "How Erroneous Beliefs Trigger Authoritarian Collapse: The Case of Tunisia, January 14, 2011," *Comparative Political Studies* (2024), https://doi.org/10.1177/00104140241252101.

[100] Weyland, *Making Waves*; Weyland, *Assault on Democracy*.

76   DICTATING THE AGENDA

assumptions, values, and activism. Even critics of unipolarity never envisioned the concurrent changes within liberal democratic polities and societies that would precipitate the rise of internal populist movements to challenge liberalism from within. In the wake of the Eurozone economic crisis and dislocations generated by the 2007–8 financial crisis, left-wing parties such as Syriza in Greece and Podemos in Spain rose to prominence alongside right-wing parties such as La Liga in Italy and Marine Le Pen's National Rally to contest the principles of economic liberalism and globalization, as well as, for right-wing parties, migration rights. The dramatic Brexit vote of 2016 and Donald Trump's unexpected election as US president later in the year, and again in 2024 this time with a greater share of the vote, further cemented the belief that liberalism and adherents of "globalism" were now on the back foot in the very core liberal countries of the United Kingdom and United States. Growing political polarization and renewed culture wars across the United States have spread the contestation of liberal values beyond the political system into social institutions such as education, sports, and the public health response to a global pandemic.

As a result, emerging powers not only learn from themselves and one another but have also found like-minded allies and local partners in the West in the form of nationalists and populists who reject liberal values and supporting institutions. Attacks on central bank independence or the independent judiciary and civil service of the "deep state" are not directed by autocrats abroad (although they often fund or platform those voices), but they do assist them. The liberal international order is being contested from "above" and from "within" the West itself, challenging liberal influence and activism at all levels of global politics.[101]

In sum, authoritarian states cooperate with one another, learn from each other, stabilize one another,[102] and gain inspiration from one another in their quest to confront threats, maintain power, and advance their visions.[103] The dramatic rise of China provides support and an enabling environment for other authoritarian states seeking

---

[101] Cooley and Nexon, *Exit from Hegemony*; Adler-Nissen and Zarakol, "Struggles for Recognition."

[102] Oisín Tansey et al., "Ties to the Rest: Autocratic Linkages and Regime Survival," *Comparative Political Studies* 50, no. 9 (2017): pp. 1221–54, https://doi.org/10.1177/0010414016666859.

[103] Weyland, *Making Waves*.

to resist normative pressures.[104] Autocrats also have allies within the liberal democratic house, meaning that innovations that successfully inhibit liberal influence, or even advance iliberal ideas, are likely to diffuse.

The New Authoritarian Offensive: Openly Contesting Liberal Influence

By the 2010s and 2020s authoritarian states had learned and adapted their methods in the ideational arena to a new post–Cold War environment.[105] No longer defensive or even concerned with obfuscating their illiberal values or authoritarian excesses, they had a renewed willingness to change global discourse, elevate their status and exert their own "soft power" influence.[106] Fiercely protective of their sovereignty, they find weak points to exploit in liberal democracy to bolster their global influence and shore up their rule at home.[107]

We now face the reality not only that authoritarian states have effectively neutralized liberal ideas threatening to authoritarians but also that they can reformulate those methods and ideas and inject them back

---

[104] Leif-Eric Easley and Jonathan T. Chow, "Enabling Pariahs: China's Support of Myanmar, North Korea, and Russia for Geopolitical Advantage," *Asian Survey* 64, no. 3 (2024): pp. 396–427, https://doi.org/10.1525/as.2024.2113239.

[105] Guriev and Treisman, *Spin Dictators*.

[106] Christopher Walker, "The Authoritarian Threat: The Hijacking of 'Soft Power,'" *Journal of Democracy* 27, no. 1 (2016): pp. 49–63, https://doi.org/10.1353/jod.2016.0007; Dukalskis, *Making the World Safe*; Peter S. Henne, "What We Talk About When We Talk About Soft Power," *International Studies Perspectives* 23, no. 1 (2022): pp. 94–111, https://ldoi.org/10.1093/isp/ekab007; Repnikova, *Chinese Soft Power*; Julia Gurol, "The Authoritarian Narrator: China's Power Projection and its Reception in the Gulf," *International Affairs* 99, no. 2 (2023), pp. 687–705, https://doi.org/10.1093/ia/iiac266; Camilla Orjuela, "The 'Ideal Citizen' Abroad: Engaging Rwanda's Young Generation Diaspora," *Globalizations* (2023): 1–17, https://doi.org/10.1080/14747731.2023.2275363; Sarah Sunn Bush et al., "International Rewards for Gender Equality Reforms in Autocracies," *American Political Science Review* 118, no. 3 (2024): pp. 1189–203, https://doi.org/10.1017/S0003055423001016; Petra Alderman and Kristin Anabel Eggeling, "Vision Documents, Nation Branding and the Legitimation of Non-Democratic Regimes," *Geopolitics* 29, no. 1 (2024): pp. 288–318, https://doi.org/10.1080/14650045.2023.2165441.

[107] Alexander Cooley et al., "Transnational Uncivil Society Networks: Kleptocracy's Global Fightback Against Liberal Activism," *European Journal of International Relations* 30, no. 2 (2023): p. 20, https://doi.org/10.1177/13540661231186502.

into the global public sphere through several transnational and global channels. Observers are increasingly concerned with the normative and policy dimensions of this reality.[108] And autocrats are not standing still. The next chapter lays out the theoretical framework of the authoritarian snapback to show how authoritarians and their emerging illiberal allies even in the West have responded to and rolled back the advance of once-dominant liberal democratic ideas.

[108] Walker, "The Authoritarian Threat"; Glenn Tiffert, "The Authoritarian Assault on Knowledge," *Journal of Democracy* 31, no. 4 (2020): pp. 28–43, https://doi.org/10.1353/jod.2020.0053; Eva Pils, "Complicity in Democratic Engagement with Autocratic Systems," *Ethics & Global Politics* 14, no. 3 (2021): pp. 142–62, https://doi.org/10.1080/16544951.2021.1958509.

Chapter 4

Authoritarian Snapback Explained

The previous chapters outlined the main features of transnational liberal influence in the 1990s, the latent vulnerabilities in that model, and the authoritarian resurgence. A new phase of democratic advance in the 1990s and early 2000s was perceived as threatening by authoritarian states, but the threat to regime security got amplified along with the capabilities to confront it. With newfound power, and with the confidence and exit options that China especially but also Russia provide, both being global authoritarian powers, autocracies the world over have more latitude to confront liberal democratic influence. This long arc of authoritarian resurgence, learning, and reaction continues to unfold and may go in unexpected directions, but enough time has elapsed that we can discern certain patterns and processes.

This chapter presents a model of how authoritarians respond to the "threat" of liberal democratic influence and advance their own influence in a globalized age. To formulate the model we draw on a diverse range of comparative politics and international relations literature, including on state repression, international order and global governance, human rights, area studies, authoritarian politics, transnational repression, and kleptocracy and transnational networks. If the model is to function as a useful theoretical framework, a healthy dose of simplification is necessary. We take inspiration from the very models of human rights

79

80   DICTATING THE AGENDA

activism and liberal ideational influence that we see authoritarian states attempting to tame and reverse, such as the influential boomerang,[1] norm cascade,[2] and spiral[3] models of human rights change discussed previously.

From Spiraling Toward Liberal Change to Dictating the Agenda?

The desire to resist or reverse liberal influence is long established. As the previous chapter discussed, China has long been concerned with "peaceful evolution." Singapore and others promoted "Asian values" as an alternative to political norms that prioritized the individual vis-à-vis the state.[4] The Color Revolutions and the Arab Spring heightened the sense of threat perceived by autocratic leaders the world over.[5] But the authoritarian resurgence and the availability of illiberal allies within liberal democratic societies has meant that the environment in which to push back is now more promising than it was 30 years ago. Rather than just passively accept or defensively react to external pressures, authoritarians have grown more self-confident and aggressive in confronting external opprobrium, especially that which is rooted in liberal norms or values. Beyond parrying threatening ideas, they have sought to reclaim transnational networks of influence to advance their own political ideas—to dictate the agenda.

---

[1] Margaret E. Keck and Kathryn Sikkink, *Activists Beyond Borders* (Cornell University Press, 1998).

[2] Martha Finnemore and Kathryn Sikkink, "International Norm Dynamics and Political Change," *International Organization* 52, no. 4 (1998): pp. 887–917, https://doi.org/10.1162/002081898550789.

[3] Thomas Risse et al., eds., *The Power of Human Rights: International Norms and Domestic Change* (Cambridge University Press, 1999).

[4] See, for example, Bilahari Kausikan, "Hong Kong, Singapore, and 'Asian Values': Governance That Works," *Journal of Democracy* 8, no. 2 (1997): pp. 24–34, https://doi.org/10.1353/jod.1997.0024.

[5] Evgeny Finkel and Yitzhak M. Brudny, "Russia and the Colour Revolutions," *Democratization* 19, no. 1 (2012): pp. 15–36, https://doi.org/10.1080/13510347.2012.641297; Karrie J. Koesel and Valerie J. Bunce, "Diffusion-Proofing: Russian and Chinese Responses to Waves of Popular Mobilizations Against Authoritarian Rulers," *Perspectives on Politics*, 11, no. 3 (2013): pp. 753–68, https://doi.org/10.1017/S1537592713002107.

No single preconceived master plan undergirds the authoritarian snapback. Rather the authoritarian snapback that we outline in this chapter unfolded over time with improvisational and indeterminant qualities. Contingent decisions in a changing global context meant that the vehicles of liberal influence often became enmeshed with or overseen by illiberal institutions and actors in various ways. Autocrats watched one another's actions and evaluated their own, looking for what worked, and applied what they learned. But importantly, we note that the carriers of transnational liberal influence, such as media outlets, universities, publishing houses, some human rights institutions, and so on, could always be filled with both liberal and illiberal content.[6]

With more capacity and the opportunity to observe and learn what works, we see authoritarian states adopt a series of interlinking tactics illustrated in Figure 4.1. In each of these dimensions, we see the model moving from focusing more on the domestic audience to targeting more international audiences, and from using more defensive measures to deploying more offensive, ambitious, and outward-facing tactics.

First, states *stigmatize* liberal political ideas at home as well as the individuals and institutions associated with them. This is primarily directed at domestic audiences and is mostly defensive insofar as it aims to undermine the resonance of liberal ideas. This works together with and helps prepare the ground for the second step, which is to *shield* the public from liberal political ideas by banning platforms that disseminate them, outlawing certain transnational linkages, and in general deepening control over and surveillance of liberal political discourse. The primary audience is still domestic, but now the backlash has moved beyond rhetoric. The next escalation is for the authoritarian state to, third, *reframe engagement and set new ground rules* for transnational entities, including media, businesses, universities, and entertainment figures. This signals that transnational liberal influence is suspect and that actors should de-politicize themselves or pledge to uphold "local" political values.

---

[6] On global networks and institutions being taken advantage of by illiberal actors, see Alexander Cooley et al., "Transnational Uncivil Society Networks: Kleptocracy's Global Fightback Against Liberal Activism," *European Journal of International Relations* 30, no. 2 (2023): pp. 382–407, https://doi.org/10.1177/13540661231186502.

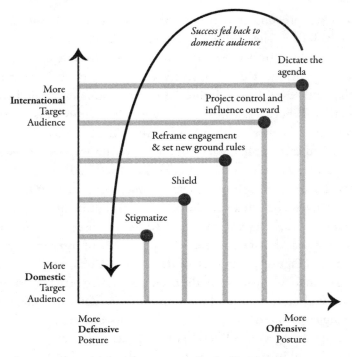

FIGURE 4.1 Authoritarian Snapback Illustrated.

The final two steps entail the external projection of illiberal influence and become markedly more focused on the international audience and characterized by a posture of outward proactivity. This begins with fourth, *projecting control and influence*, often by co-opting or silencing the very institutions that were thought to facilitate the spread of liberal influence in the first place. The process culminates in the most outwardly focused and offensive step, which is, fifth, to *dictate the agenda* by actively denigrating liberal political ideas abroad and advancing illiberal alternatives across a range of domains. This success can then be transmitted back to the domestic audience to highlight the resonance of the state's political ideas abroad, which can be a useful source of domestic legitimacy.

We do not see these components as strictly sequential, but rather we see escalation up the ladder facilitated by regime capacity and ambition. Even the weakest authoritarian regime can rhetorically stigmatize networks of "Western" political influence, but it takes both more power and more ambition to reach the uppermost stages in which liberal influence is reframed, reversed, and *il*liberal influence is projected outward to dictate an agenda. While the elements are not necessarily sequential, we do find that activities in the lower left corner of the figure—stigmatizing and shielding—do help provide foundations for escalation and therefore often appear first. However, a given episode may unfold on different timelines, see movement back and forth between the component parts of the model, or witness overlapping activities.

We hasten to add that we do not claim that authoritarians are 100% successful in their efforts to confront and roll back liberal pressures, just as not all liberal campaigns successfully promoted liberal values in reluctant authoritarian states. Indeed, overstating authoritarian power is often an intentional strategy of authoritarians themselves to reify the image of their power.[7] Nor is movement from each element to the next guaranteed, as some processes may be aborted or fade into irrelevance, or may be advanced by a regime not strong enough to complete the reclamation.

Tactic 1: Stigmatize

To soften up messengers of liberal influence as targets, authoritarians typically portray them in an unfavorable light. Rather than contest or debate the factual substance of the criticism, the immediate tactic of government officials and their agents is often to attack the credibility and authority of the actor who levels the criticism. The most typical forms of stigmatization are to associate messengers with a geopolitical agenda of the West, question the sources of their funding, or associate them with a larger subversive conspiracy involving other delegitimized or criminal actors.[8] A common tactic has been to cast aspersions on the neutrality or independence of messengers, including private actors

---

7 Péter Krekó, "How Authoritarians Inflate Their Image," *Journal of Democracy* 32, no. 3 (2021): pp. 109–23, https://doi.org/10.1353/jod.2021.0037.

8 On domestic delegitimation of opponents framing them as targets for repression, see, for example, Maria Josua, "The Legitimation of Repression in Autocracies," *Oxford Research Encyclopaedia of Politics* (2021), https://doi.org/10.1093/acrefore/9780190228637.013.1988; and Alexander Dukalskis and Christopher Patane, "Justifying Power: When Autocracies Talk About Themselves and Their Opponents," *Contemporary Politics* 25, no. 4 (2019): pp. 457–78, https://doi.org/10.1080/13569775.2019.1570424. Scholarship on stigma in international relations provides insights into the strategies that states take when they are the subject of criticism. See especially Rebecca Adler-Nissen, "Stigma Management in International Relations:

84 DICTATING THE AGENDA

such as media companies, entertainment conglomerates, or academic institutions, and ascribe a malign geopolitical motive or foreign-backed agenda.[9] Authority and autonomy are questioned. In turn, stigmatization primes the domestic audience to be skeptical of external criticisms.

Examples are easy to find. The BBC, for instance, is editorially independent of the British government, yet it is frequently delegitimized as biased and a tool in the box of "the West" to keep other states down.[10] Branches of American universities, while they may receive federal funds, are not arms of Washington in any straightforward way, but they can be framed as a threat to local culture, religion, or political norms.[11] Human Rights Watch, even though it is often critical of US policies in a variety of areas, becomes a US proxy in the conspiracy to hold China down.[12] The Open Society Foundations (OSF) is accused of working closely with the US government to foment the destabilization of regimes in countries where it had foundations, despite its fierce attempts to remain "apolitical . . . and not reflect the opinions or policies of the US government."[13] Networks of liberal

---

Transgressive Identities, Norms, and Order in International Society," *International Organization* 68, no. 1 (2014): pp. 143–76, https://www.jstor.org/stable/43282098. See also Xymena Kurowska and Anatoly Reshetnikov, "Trickstery: Pluralising Stigma in International Society," *European Journal of International* Relations 27, no. 1 (2021): pp. 232–57, https://doi.org/10.1177/1354066120946467.

[9] On this strategy with regard to nongovernmental organizations (NGOs), see Alexander Cooley, "Countering Democratic Norms," *Journal of Democracy* 26, no. 3 (2015): p. 54. See examples from authoritarian responses to the Color Revolutions in Jeanne L. Wilson, "The Legacy of the Color Revolutions for Russian Politics and Foreign Policy," *Problems of Post-Communism* 57, no. 2 (2010): pp. 22–23, https://doi.org/10.2753/PPC1075-8216570202; and Vitali Silitski, "'Survival of the Fittest': Domestic and International Dimensions of the Authoritarian Reaction in the Former Soviet Union Following the Colored Revolutions," *Communist & Post-Communist Studies* 43, no. 4: (2010): p. 342, https://doi.org/10.1016/j.postcomstud.2010.10.007.

[10] For example, in Rwanda see Filip Reyntjens, "The Struggle over Truth—Rwanda and the BBC," *African Affairs* 114, no. 457 (2015): pp. 637–48, https://doi.org/10.1093/afraf/adv042.

[11] Neha Vora, *Teach for Arabia: American Universities, Liberalism, and Transnational Qatar* (Stanford University Press, 2019), pp. 20, 166–67.

[12] Jamie J. Gruffydd-Jones, *Hostile Forces: How the Chinese Communist Party Resists International Pressure on Human Rights* (Oxford University Press, 2022), p. 92.

[13] In recent years, Hungarian leader Viktor Orbán has been most visibly derisive of Soros. See, for example, Shaun Walker, "George Soros: Orbán Turns

influence are often accused of being a conspiracy by Western governments bent on undermining domestic politics—"peaceful evolution" writ large.

Casting doubt on foreign actors or associating threatening political ideas with foreign states is anything but new. Nor is this tendency restricted to fully authoritarian states. But values of freedom of expression, individual rights, and transparency sit at odds with non-democratic rule.[14] Therefore, tarnishing these ideas and their carriers as alien and "Western" is a common tactic that primes domestic audiences to see liberalism as part of a cynical stratagem of nefarious outsiders bent on undermining order and stability.[15] Of course, the ostensible plausibility of this claim is magnified because of the legacy of the Cold War, when intelligence agencies of both sides were involved in supporting (dis)information production and dissemination.[16] That George W. Bush's democracy-promotion agenda became intertwined with the United States' invasion of Iraq in 2003 only elevated the cynicism surrounding liberalism's imperial aspirations.[17] Inherently threatening liberal influence became tied in the authoritarian worldview with government-backed efforts to undermine their regimes.

Stigmatization can serve as a precursor to subsequent crackdowns, which can in turn bolster regime popularity by demonstrating that it is

---

to Familiar Scapegoat as Hungary Rows with EU," *The Guardian*, December 5, 2020, https://www.theguardian.com/world/2020/dec/05/george-soros-orban-turns-to-familiar-scapegoat-as-hungary-rows-with-eu. However, Soros has long been stigmatized by authoritarian governments. In China in the 1980s, for example, see Julian Gewirtz, *Never Turn Back: China and the Forbidden History of the 1980s* (Harvard University Press, 2022), p. 260.

[14] Abel Escribà-Folch, "Repression, Political Threats, and Survival Under Autocracy," *International Political Science Review* 34, no. 5 (2013), pp. 543–60, https://doi.org/10.1177/0192512113488259.

[15] Gruffydd-Jones, *Hostile Forces.*

[16] Frances Stonor Saunders, *The Cultural Cold War: The CIA and the World of Arts and Letters* (New Press, 2013); Melissa Feinberg, *Curtain of Lies: The Battle over Truth in Stalinist Eastern Europe* (Oxford University Press, 2017); Thomas Rid, *Active Measures: The Secret History of Disinformation & Political Warfare* (Profile Books, 2021).

[17] For an astute statement on the contradictions and blind spots of liberal approaches to contemporary global politics, see Patrick Porter, *The False Promise of Liberal Order: Nostalgia, Delusion and the Rise of Trump* (Polity Press, 2020).

targeting "dangerous" groups.[18] For example, before it passed the 2015 law on "Undesirable Organizations" that effectively banned Western nongovernmental organizations (NGOs) and funders, Russia adopted the 2012 Foreign Agent Law, which mandated that all domestic organizations that received funding from foreign sources had to identify themselves as foreign agents and register. Proponents of the law when it first came out presented it as necessary for promoting transparency, but the "foreign agent" label itself recalls Soviet memes of external infiltration and is designed to discourage Russian donors from contributing to such stigmatized organizations.[19] The strategy aims to marginalize threatening ideas and bolster regime popularity all while creating the pretext for subsequent repression.

Similar dynamics apply to the media sphere. China's propaganda apparatus has long denigrated "Western media" as biased and has banned several outlets over the years. But coinciding with China banning broadcasting of BBC Global in China in February 2021, party-owned outlets like Xinhua and the *Global Times* ran several pieces attacking the integrity of the BBC, even mocking its initials as standing for the "Biased Broadcasting Corporation."[20] The BBC Global ban was in response to the United Kingdom banning China's party-owned TV station CGTN for airing forced confessions, a violation of Britain's media regulations. In a separate but related episode, in March 2021 BBC correspondent John Sudworth and his family were forced to leave China under threat from plainclothes thugs after months of stigmatization and attacks on his reporting and reputation.[21]

But it is not just the great authoritarian powers that stigmatize. As noted in the previous chapter, Rwanda, which unlike China or

---

[18] On repression that boosts popularity, see Jean Lachapelle, "Repression Reconsidered: Bystander Effects and Legitimation in Authoritarian Regimes," *Comparative Politics* 54, no. 4 (2022): pp. 695–716.

[19] Human Rights Watch, "Russia: Harsh Toll of 'Foreign Agents' Law: Government Critics Stifled Under Guise of Countering Foreign Influence," June 25, 2013, https://www.hrw.org/news/2013/06/25/russia-harsh-toll-foreign-agents-law.

[20] For example, see "BBC Mocked in China for Misleading Reports, Deceitful Editing Tricks," *Global Times*, February 5, 2021, https://www.globaltimes.cn/page/202102/1215082.shtml.

[21] Emma Graham-Harrison, "BBC Journalist Leaves China After Beijing Criticizes Uighurs Coverage," *The Guardian*, March 31, 2021, https://www.theguardian.com/world/2021/mar/31/bbc-journalist-john-sudworth-leaves-china-amid-criticism-of-networks-coverage.

Russia is small and aid dependent, sees its government aggressively stigmatize foreign critics of Kagame and his Rwandan Patriotic Front (RPF). One of numerous examples occurred after the BBC aired a feature, "Rwanda's Untold Story," in October 2014 that challenged the RPF's preferred version of Rwanda's recent history.[22] The authorities responded quickly multiple times through *The New Times*, an RPF-supporting newspaper, criticizing the show.[23] The government banned the BBC's Kinyarwanda service soon thereafter. The stigmatization continued in telling terms. For example, *The New Times* ran pieces in subsequent years arguing that outrage about the BBC ban was hypocritical because the United Kingdom had accused Russia Today of providing distorted coverage,[24] claiming that the "BBC Kinyarwanda service has been taken over by Rwandan dissidents or it is working to promote their cause,"[25] and likening the BBC opening an East African bureau in Kenya to the British having a soft power "tank" on Rwanda's doorstep.[26] A recent multi-outlet investigative report on Rwanda by the organization Forbidden Stories dubbed "Rwanda Classified"[27] drew a similar reaction from Kigali.[28]

Tactic 2: Shield

To fully inoculate the population against liberal ideas, stigmatization is paired with shielding. Just as authoritarian propaganda aimed

---

[22] Reyntjens, "The Struggle over Truth."

[23] Reyntjens, "The Struggle over Truth," p. 639.

[24] Lonzen Rugira, "Reactions to the BBC's Sanctioning Expose Western Hypocrisy," *New Times*, June 15, 2015, https://www.newtimes.co.rw/section/read/189749.

[25] "BBC at It Again Stoking the Fires," *New Times*, March 31, 2019, https://www.newtimes.co.rw/opinions/bbc-it-again-stoking-fires.

[26] Gatete Nyiringabo Ruhumuliza, "The BCC Has Parked a Tank in Our Front Yard," *New Times*, March 10, 2019, https://www.newtimes.co.rw/opinions/bbc-has-parked-tank-our-front-yard.

[27] See Cécile Andrzejewski et al., "Rwanda Classified: Inside the Repressive Machinery of Paul Kagame's Regime," *Forbidden* Stories, May 28, 2024, https://forbiddenstories.org/rwanda-classified-inside-the-repressive-machinery-of-paul-kagames-regime/.

[28] See Rwanda's official statement here: "Government of Rwanda Statement on *Forbidden Stories* Media Campaign," Republic of Rwanda, May 28, 2024, https://www.gov.rw/blog-detail/government-of-rwanda-statement-on-forbidden-stories-media-campaign.

88   DICTATING THE AGENDA

at a domestic audience is most usefully understood in conjunction with censorship, so stigmatization can work together with shielding to insulate the authorities from external pressure and dampen the domestic and international impact of liberal influence.[29] The former shapes the beliefs of citizens, while the latter deprives them of compelling information or arguments in favor of alternative political visions.[30]

A common technique in the authoritarian repertoire is to curtail or publicly ban the activities of messengers of liberal influence, such as transnational NGOs, advocates, journalists, and lawyers. As mentioned previously, the proliferation of "NGO laws" in authoritarian states makes it more difficult for domestic civil society organizations to work with or take funding from foreign entities.[31] Civil society groups are seen as the "carriers" of liberal influence in issue areas like human rights and are therefore targeted by illiberal leaders.[32] In what appears to be a global trend since the end of the Cold War, at least 130 states have repressed or taken measures to curtail the activities of NGOs.[33] Russia's aforementioned Foreign Agent Law from 2012 and the follow-up Undesirable Organizations Law were designed to undermine and discredit the activities of any domestic organization whose activities conflict with or threaten the perceived regime security of the Russian Federation. In 2021, the scope of the law was broadened to include any foreign or international NGOs that might provide services or transfer money to NGOs with an undesirable status in Russia. Marginalizing liberal

---

[29] Alexander Dukalskis, *The Authoritarian Public Sphere: Legitimation and Autocratic Power in North Korea, Burma, and China* (Routledge, 2017).

[30] For a classic statement of this logic, see Timur Kuran, *Private Truths, Public Lies: The Social Consequences of Preference Falsification* (Harvard University Press, 1997).

[31] Thomas Carothers and Saskia Brechenmacher, *Closing Space: Democracy and Human Rights Support Under Fire* (Carnegie Endowment for International Peace, 2014); Leah Gilbert, "Regulating Society After the Color Revolutions: A Comparative Analysis of NGO Laws in Belarus, Russia, and Armenia," *Demokratizatsiya* 28, no. 2 (2020): pp. 305–32, https://www.muse.jhu.edu/article/754564.

[32] Patricia Bromley et al., "Contentions over World Culture: The Rise of Legal Restrictions on Foreign Funding to NGOs, 1994–2015," *Social Forces* 99, no. 1 (2019): pp. 281–304, https://doi.org/10.1093/sf/soz138.

[33] Suparna Chaudhry, "The Assault on Civil Society: Explaining State Crackdown on NGOs," *International Organization* 76, no. 3 (2022): pp. 549–90, https://doi.org/10.1017/S0020818321000473.

NGOs or civil society groups frees up space to amplify pro-government groups as replacements.[34]

Consistent with this logic, the implementation of anti-NGO laws has been found to be a predictor of subsequent broader repression of civil liberties and physical integrity rights.[35] The repression aims to prevent the organizations from doing their work, thus shielding the population from their findings and the ability to mobilize around them. Anti-liberal NGO laws have the advantage of appearing to mimic similar transparency laws like foreign lobbying registers in democracies. Indeed, supporters of Russia's Foreign Agent Law invoked the parallel explicitly.[36] In reality, key differences exist in terms of their severity, level of restriction, and consequences. Branding a newspaper, NGO, or university a "foreign agent" or asking it to register its foreign contacts in an authoritarian context carries potentially deadly connotations. Ultimately, these laws proved devastating precisely because NGOs that engaged in human rights-related advocacy were actually dependent on foreign funding.[37]

Strikingly, and ironically, Western states did very little to challenge the global legislative backlash against NGOs. Beyond expressions of concern by US or EU officials, Western governments or donors seldom singled out NGOs that were stigmatized or legally challenged, nor did they sanction countries that passed anti-NGO restrictions. In other words, civil society NGOs had the worst of both worlds: They were associated with Western geopolitical ambitions but seldom received the West's actual protection. As authoritarians grew more confident that

---

[34] On repressing civil society to create a pro-government replacement, see Conny Roggeband and Andrea Krizsán, "The Selective Closure of Civic Space," *Global Policy* 12, no. 5 (2021): pp. 23–33, https://doi.org/10.1111/1758-5899.12973.

[35] Suparna Chaudhry and Andrew Heiss, "NGO Repression as a Predictor of Worsening Human Rights Abuses," *Journal of Human Rights* 21, no. 2 (2022): pp. 123–40, https://doi.org/10.1080/14754835.2022.2030205.

[36] Ellen Barry, "Foreign-Funded Nonprofits in Russia Face New Hurdle," *New York Times*, July 2, 2012, https://www.nytimes.com/2012/07/03/world/europe/russia-introduces-law-limiting-aid-for-nonprofits.html (accessed February 2, 2022); Stephen G. F. Hall, *The Authoritarian International: Tracing How Authoritarian Regimes Learn in the Post-Soviet Space* (Cambridge University Press, 2023), p. xii.

[37] James Ron et al., *Taking Root: Human Rights and Public Opinion in the Global South* (Oxford University Press, 2017), pp. 83–113.

90 DICTATING THE AGENDA

targeting NGOs would provoke little more than expressions of concern from foreign embassies, the rollback grew in scope and intensity. For example, the Russian government closed the Moscow office of the OSF in 2003; the organization was declared an "undesirable organization" in 2015 and its activities criminalized.[38] Other authoritarians and illiberal leaders closed down OSF's country-based foundations in Uzbekistan (2004), Azerbaijan (2014), Pakistan (2017), Hungary (2018), and Türkiye (2018). The systematic targeting of NGOs was paralleled by a concerted effort by authoritarians and illiberal leaders to target journalists and independent media outlets, a topic covered in depth in Chapter 5.

Tactic 3: Reframe Engagement and Set New Ground Rules

After casting aspersion on the messenger and clearing away liberal competitors, authoritarians will then translate the influence itself. Messages of liberal influence are reframed and showcased as an affront to all the people of the nation and an attack on the state's sovereignty. Reframing thus broadens the scope of the criticism from narrowly targeting the actions or policy of the authoritarian regime to include the identity and beliefs of the country's citizenry.[39] Powerful social-psychological

---

[38] Human Rights Watch, "Russia: Open Society Foundation Banned. Repeal 'Undesirables' Law," December 1, 2015, https://www.hrw.org/news/2015/12/01/russia-open-society-foundation-banned.

[39] This logic is similar to the familiar "rally around the flag" effect found in studies of economic sanctions and human rights "naming and shaming." This literature suggests that pro-government backlash to external criticism is likely to occur most clearly when the government shapes the narrative and has stronger bases of legitimacy, with the effect playing out differently between audiences. On sanctions see, for example, Julia Grauvogel and Christian von Soest, "Claims to Legitimacy Count: Why Sanctions Fail to Instigate Democratisation in Authoritarian Regimes," *European Journal of Political Research* 53, no. 4 (2014): pp. 635–53, https://doi.org/10.1111/1475-6765.12065; Mikkel Sejersen, "Winnings Hearts and Minds with Economic Sanctions? Evidence from a Survey Experiment in Venezuela," *Foreign Policy Analysis* 17, no. 1 (2021): pp. 1–22, https://doi.org/10.1093/fpa/oraa008; and Masaru Kohno et al., "Foreign Pressure and Public Opinion in Target States," *World Development* 169 (2023): 106305. For a study skeptical of this link, see Timothy Frye, "Economic Sanctions and Public Opinion: Survey Experiments from Russia," *Comparative Political Studies* 52, no. 7 (2019): pp. 967–94, https://doi.org/10.1177/0010414018806530. On human rights naming and shaming, see Gruffydd-Jones,

mechanisms underpin the tendency to see criticisms by outsiders as attacks on one's own group and to therefore fight back against them.[40]

Individuals and organizations must be prepared to make political compromises to access an illiberal environment.[41] But that environment is dynamic. The authoritarian state may change its red lines or influential actors within it may become frustrated with the spread of "foreign" ideas. Domestic laws or regulations that govern domains like higher education, media, technology, or cultural production can change or be newly enforced by fresh personnel. This puts entities associated with liberal influence in a bind by forcing them to choose between abiding by the new rules (and thereby watering down their liberal aims), bucking the new rules (and risking countermeasures), or ceasing operations in the state (thereby forgoing the ability to have any influence).

As liberal influence is ensnared in changing norms, new ground rules are established, and the agendas of actors that remain on the ground are now ripe for co-optation by the authoritarian government. Each successive compromise to self-censor or comply with restrictions makes it more difficult to reverse course and admit that one's initial ambitions have been compromised. The very embeddedness in an illiberal environment that the liberal actor originally sought can become a point of leverage or control *against* that actor, leaving it vulnerable to state strategies that threaten access. Recognizing that choices are often difficult and made under duress,[42] the decision to capitulate to new (or newly stringent) standards of illiberalism becomes bound up with other motives. Over time, an ostensibly liberal actor in an illiberal

---

Hostile Forces; and Brian Greenhill and Dan Reiter, "Naming and Shaming, Government Messaging, and Backlash Effects: Experimental Evidence from the Convention Against Torture," *Journal of Human Rights* 21, no. 4 (2022): pp. 399–418, https://doi.org/10.1080/14754835.2021.2011710.

[40] Gruffydd-Jones, *Hostile Forces*, pp. 17–19; Rochelle Terman, *The Geopolitics of Shaming: When Human Rights Pressure Works—and When It Backfires* (Princeton University Press, 2023).

[41] Eva Pils, "Complicity in Democratic Engagement with Autocratic Systems," *Ethics & Global Politics* 14, no. 3 (2021): pp. 142–62, https://doi.org/10.1080/16544951.2021.1958509.

[42] Pils, "Complicity in Democratic Engagement."

92 DICTATING THE AGENDA

environment becomes more deeply entangled in complex relationships, constituencies, revenue concerns, and risk aversion.

Tactic 4: Project Control and Influence Outward

These mutually reinforcing tactics of stigmatization, shielding, and reframing allow authoritarians to neutralize liberal influence domestically. In turn, they help provide a sturdy base that enables moving beyond defense against liberal influence domestically and toward projecting illiberal influence outward to an international audience. Projecting control and influence outward can take many forms, but three stand out as common: coercion, leveraging market power, and repurposing global governance actors once associated with transmitting liberal norms.

First, methods of authoritarian coercion can be extended beyond borders of the state into transnational spaces to target individual opponents of authoritarian regimes, including exiled dissidents, opposition figures, journalists, and prominent diaspora members.[43] Such transnational repression can range from routine surveillance with technologies such as spyware all the way up to complex operations to

---

[43] Research on "transnational repression" is rapidly expanding and charts the theoretical underpinnings, drivers, and empirical patterns of authoritarian states targeting their citizens abroad for repression. See, among others, David Lewis, "'Illiberal Spaces': Uzbekistan's Extraterritorial Security Practices and the Spatial Politics of Contemporary Authoritarianism," *Nationalities Papers* 43, no. 1 (2015): pp. 140–59, https://doi.org/10.1080/00905992.2014.980796; Dana M. Moss, "Transnational Repression, Diaspora Mobilization, and the Case of the Arab Spring," *Social Problems* 63, no. 4 (2016): pp. 480–98, https://doi.org/10.1093/socpro/spwo19; Gerasimos Tsourapas, "Global Autocracies: Strategies of Transnational Repression, Legitimation, and Co-Optation in World Politics," *International Studies Review* 23, no. 3 (2021): pp. 616–44, https://doi.org/10.1093/isr/viaa061; Saipira Furstenberg et al., "Spatialising State Practices Through Transnational Repression," *European Journal of International Security* 6, no. 3 (2021): pp. 358–78, https://doi.org/10.1017/eis.2021 .10; Dana M. Moss et al., "Going After the Family: Transnational Repression and the Proxy Punishment of Middle Eastern Diasporas," *Global Networks* 22, no. 4 (2022): pp. 735–51, https://doi.org/10.1111/glob.12372; Edward Lemon et al., "Globalizing Minority Persecution: China's Transnational Repression of the Uyghurs," *Globalizations* 20, no. 4 (2023): pp. 564–80, https://doi.org/10.1080/14747731.2022.2135944; and Alexander Dukalskis et al., "The Long Arm and the Iron Fist: Authoritarian Crackdowns and Transnational Repression," *Journal of Conflict Resolution* 68, no. 6 (2024): pp. 1051–79, https://doi.org/10.1177/00220027231188896.

capture or even assassinate people perceived to be political threats. Through transnational repression the authoritarian state attempts to prevent regime critics abroad from raising awareness about human rights abuses or corruption, lobbying external bodies to pressure the state, or networking with domestic activists who may benefit from international linkages, expertise, and resources that exiled dissidents can provide.[44] It is more difficult for states to repress their citizens abroad than at home, but research teams have documented thousands of cases perpetrated by a range of authoritarian states in the post–Cold War era.[45] At times transnational repression is facilitated by cooperation between autocratic governments, while at others it involves authoritarian actors exploiting the openness of liberal democratic societies or the interstices of globalized institutions.[46] The aim is to reduce political threats circulating abroad and eliminate or silence voices who may undermine authoritarian rule at home.

Second, authoritarian states can leverage their market access to induce foreign entities to regulate their political speech or behavior abroad. This approach sees the state threaten to erect barriers to operating in the state unless an actor changes. This tactic will likely become more common if the GDP statistics about more and less liberal democratic states presented in Chapter 1 continue to move in the direction that they have in recent decades.

The international entertainment industry may be particularly prone to these dynamics as "employees" (e.g., athletes or actors) are public-facing figures, while their "employers" (e.g., sports leagues or media

---

[44] Alexander Dukalskis, *Making the World Safe for Dictatorship* (Oxford University Press, 2021).

[45] On transnational repression data, see Alexander Dukalskis et al., "Transnational Repression: Data Advances, Comparisons, and Challenges," *Political Research Exchange* 4, no. 1 (2022): 2104651.

[46] Marcus Michaelsen and Kris Ruijgrok, "Autocracy's Long Reach: Explaining Host Country Influences on Transnational Repression," *Democratization* 31, no. 2 (2023): pp. 290–314, https://doi.org/10.1080/13510347.2023.2267448; Daniel Kremaric, "Nowhere to Hide? Global Policing and the Politics of Extradition," *International Security* 47, no. 2 (2022): pp. 7–47, https://doi.org/10.1162/isec_a_00444; Marlies Glasius, *Authoritarian Practices in a Global Age* (Oxford University Press, 2023).

conglomerates) have economic incentives to not alienate the government in authoritarian states where they may be operating.[47] A critical feature of such public acts is that the punishment is deliberately disproportionate to the original offending act, thus signifying the acute resolve of the government. Whether this involves curtailing market access to a private company and its product, demanding an immediate and public apology, or cutting the broadcast of a popular sporting team in protest, the domestic sacrifice that snapback involves is itself a signal of the government's commitment that it will be uncompromising in its response.[48]

Beyond coercing citizens directly and foreign entities indirectly, authoritarian states deepen their foreign control and influence by co-opting and transforming the agendas of global governance actors.[49] This mode of counterinfluence sees liberal agents and their institutions repurposed for authoritarian goals. In a process that Bettiza and Lewis call "liberal mimicry," authoritarian actors can create entities that adopt "the *form* of liberal discourse and practices, while simultaneously giving these a non-liberal *content*."[50] Institutions with "Western" or liberal appearances can then be used to weaken liberalism. In hindsight it is easy to see that containers of liberal influence could be co-opted. As subsequent chapters of this book will explore in greater detail, this entails adopting forms like global universities, think tanks, media outlets, and sports/celebrity activism while emptying them of their liberal content. The end user may not appreciate the distinction between the form and the content, with pro-authoritarian views entering undetected. The underlying aim is to "discredit aspects of contemporary international architecture—particularly those related to human and

---

47 William D. O'Connell, "Silencing the Crowd: China, the NBA, and Leveraging Market Size to Export Censorship," *Review of International Political Economy* 29, no. 4 (2022): pp. 1112–34, https://doi.org/10.1080/09692290.2021.1905683.

48 One of the most visible recent examples of this dynamic was China's punishment of the National Basketball Association and the Houston Rockets specifically for a pro-democracy tweet about Hong Kong, a topic we discuss in more detail in Chapter 8.

49 Cooley et al., "Transnational Uncivil Society Networks."

50 Gregorio Bettiza and David Lewis, "Authoritarian Powers and Norm Contestation in the Liberal International Order: Theorizing the Power Politics of Ideas and Identity," *Journal of Global Security Studies* 5, no. 4 (2020): p. 567, https://doi.org/10.1093/jogss/ogz075.

political rights."[51] There are two faces to this approach: A new liberal-looking institution can be created, or an existing institution can be influenced from within.

Entities like government-organized nongovernmental organizations (GONGOs) that act as pseudo-civil society organizations, global media arms of authoritarian states, and "zombie" election monitors that rubber stamp authoritarian elections are examples of creating new liberal-looking entities but designing them to support authoritarian regime power.[52] Made possible by increased interconnectivity, these entities undermine liberal values while obscuring authoritarian involvement, thereby reversing the flow of influence originally assumed by the liberal ideational spread. Liberalizing institutions or practices at multiple levels of global governance can be hollowed out and replaced with illiberal content that advances illiberal aims and/or perspectives friendly to authoritarian states.[53]

In addition to creating new entities that look like those associated with liberal influence, the authoritarian snapback can entail changing existing domains from within. When liberal and illiberal entities are entwined, it is entirely plausible that the latter will influence the former rather than the reverse, the common assumption.[54] Pils captures the predicament aptly: "As political communities and systems interact more intensely at a civil society level in today's globalized world, the control exercised by autocrats can be extended to democratic societies and institutions in various ways, potentially undermining the protections of liberal-democratic orders."[55] Here the authoritarian state extends its influence and control abroad by embedding itself in existing entities via channels of engagement originally intended to advance liberal agendas. Attempting to staff United Nations agencies with one's nationals in order to steer that entity toward the state's goals is one

---

[51] Alexander Cooley and Daniel Nexon, *Exit from Hegemony: The Unraveling of the American Global Order* (Oxford University Press, 2020), p. 91.

[52] Christopher Walker, "The Authoritarian Threat: The Hijacking of 'Soft Power,'" *Journal of Democracy* 27, no. 1 (2016): pp. 49–63, https://doi.org/10.1353/jod.2016.0007.

[53] Bettiza and Lewis, "Authoritarian Powers," pp. 569–71.

[54] Glenn Tiffert, "The Authoritarian Assault on Knowledge," *Journal of Democracy* 31, no. 4 (2020): p. 39, https://doi.org/10.1353/jod.2020.0053.

[55] Pils, "Complicity in Democratic Engagement," p. 2.

common tactic, as China has done with regard to the UN Department of Economic and Social Affairs, for example.[56] In an extralegal case, the Qatar-gate scandal revealed how the gulf state infiltrated EU institutions, including bribing individual commissioners and members of the EU Parliament, to dilute EU scrutiny of its labor and human rights practices in the lead-up to the 2022 World Cup and to secure visa-free travel.[57]

Such transformative practices mirror the transnational reputation-laundering networks that illiberal elites and oligarchs have used to deflect scrutiny of their corrupt or otherwise questionable business and governance practices and, instead, to recast themselves as respectable entrepreneurs or global philanthropists.[58] The rise of "uncivil society networks" shows how elites from kleptocracies can engage service providers in liberal democracies—including lawyers, reputation management firms, wealth managers, real estate brokers, and charitable organizations—to ensconce themselves in Western patron networks that support high-profile cultural, artistic, and educational institutions, thereby giving "civil society" currency to them as individuals.

Tactic 5: Dictate the Agenda

The most ambitious and difficult-to-achieve step in the process sees the authoritarian state *dictate the agenda* by actively denigrating or excluding liberal political influence abroad and advancing illiberal alternatives instead. Particularly in their neighborhoods, but in some cases globally, authoritarian states in general "are interested in creating transnational networks in order to disseminate ideas."[59] In addition

---

[56] Courtney J. Fung and Shing-Hon Lam, "Staffing the United Nations: China's Motivations and Prospects," *International Affairs* 97, no. 4 (2021): p. 1145, https://doi.org/10.1093/ia/iiab071.

[57] Eleni Varvitsioti et al., "Inside the 'Qatargate' Graft Scandal Rocking the EU," *Financial Times*, January 29, 2023.

[58] Cooley et al., "Transnational Uncivil Society Networks."

[59] Marianne Kneuer and Thomas Demmelhuber, "Gravity Centres of Authoritarian Rule: A Conceptual Approach," *Democratization* 23, no. 5 (2016): p. 788, https://doi.org/10.1080/13510347.2015.1018898.

to "democracy proofing" their polities against liberal ideas,[60] authoritarians aim to propagate their norms in the global public sphere.[61] With the domestic sphere not only inoculated from liberal influence (tactics 1 and 2) but actively pushing more assertive illiberal alternatives with ostensible public support (tactic 3), and with foreign critics marginalized and co-opted carriers in place (tactic 4), the state is ready to embark on the final step—to dictate the agenda.

Just as the ultimate goal of transnational liberal activists is to socialize authoritarians and their societies into accepting and internalizing liberal norms,[62] for authoritarians the ideal outcome of their multistage pushback is to reframe a priority issue that is accepted at the global level in a manner that is consistent with the regime's interests and preferred narratives. Authoritarian governments even look to change the way actors in democracies formulate the criticism going forward and/or deter other actors from launching similar criticisms.

This final stage of authoritarian snapback represents the opposite of the "socialization" at the end of the liberal diffusion models. In the snapback model, the authoritarian target of criticism intimidates or otherwise induces the sending party to alter or cease its influence agenda or advocacy campaign. Having experienced the public relations crisis or economic consequences that result from the pushback campaign, actors recalculate whether to disavow the criticism, to equivocate or otherwise present "both sides" of an issue, or to engage in self-censorship and not allow political criticism again. The latter, the

---

[60] Laurence Whitehead, "Antidemocracy Promotion: Four Strategies in Search of a Framework," *Taiwan Journal of Democracy* 10, no. 2 (2014): pp. 1–24; Christian von Soest, "Democracy Prevention: The International Collaboration of Authoritarian Regimes," *European Journal of Political Research* 54, no. 4 (2015): pp. 623–38, https://doi.org/10.1111/1475-6765.12100.

[61] Dukalskis, *Making the World Safe.*

[62] On socialization with specific reference to human rights, in addition to the spiral and boomerang models discussed in the previous chapter, see Brian Greenhill, "The Company You Keep: International Socialization and the Diffusion of Human Rights Norms," *International Studies Quarterly* 54, no. 1 (2010): pp. 127–45, https://doi.org/10.1111/j.1468-2478.2009.00580.x; and Ryan Goodman and Derek Jinks, *Socializing States: Promoting Human Rights Through International Law* (Oxford University Press, 2013).

effective depoliticization of politically sensitive issue areas, is especially effective but difficult to measure.

Take the example of the three-decade evolution of the relationship between Hollywood studios and the Chinese government. The former has sought to expand the market for its products, while the latter has increasingly focused on expanding China's cultural power.[63] What becomes clear is that "as China's media market grows, foreign media companies will increasingly need to consider the Chinese market first when developing content."[64] As mentioned previously in the discussion of market leverage, China's share of global box-office revenue has grown dramatically, while the Chinese market is still regulated by a censorship regime. The quasi-state China Film Co-production Corporation acts as a gatekeeper for co-productions by foreign studios with Chinese ones. In turn, this gives it the "potential for broad-reaching global impact because of its relation to content restrictions on global blockbusters."[65] Practically, movies co-produced in China that aim to have a global market must abide by China's film censorship to avoid making two different cuts of the film. Most end users watching the movie outside China therefore will have little idea that they are watching content created to comply with the PRC's censorship regime. Unlike a liberal ideal that might predict that critical or controversial films about China would be screened and debated worldwide, for nearly three decades China has leveraged its real or potential global market power to dictate the agenda and deter such movies from ever being made. This stands in stark contrast to fellow authoritarians like Russia or North Korea, which have regularly served as settings for Hollywood plots and geopolitical thrillers.

But we should not overstate the level of success that this process achieves, and just as complete liberal socialization is an ideal that is rarely achieved, so too is the authoritarian snapback. Nonetheless, routine examples of attempts at authoritarian reclamation can now be found across many domains. Take Western think tanks, for example. The influx of authoritarian funding from countries such as the United

---

[63] Aynne Kokas, *Hollywood Made in China* (University of California Press, 2017), p. 3.

[64] Kokas, *Hollywood Made in China*, p. 163.

[65] Kokas, *Hollywood Made in China*, p. 123.

Arab Emirates or Qatar for programs about "strategic engagement" in US and EU think tanks usually downplays any domestic political concerns about political repression or governance problems and, instead, focuses on the "strategic importance" of the autocracy at hand.[66] Often, authoritarian regimes are abetted by interested corporate or individual donors who maintain business ties in the country. For example, a series of investigative reports on foreign donations to the Atlantic Council revealed how the think tank whitewashed the practices of authoritarian donors, thus compromising the integrity of its programming. This included partnering with Chevron to put on programming about the oil-rich Central Asian state of Kazakhstan that refrained from any criticism of its longtime autocrat Nursultan Nazarbayev and the regime's kleptocratic practices.[67] Thus, authoritarian funding for think tanks in liberal democracies, coupled with the growth of new global networks and partnerships of state-affiliated think tanks supported by governments of China, Russia, Saudi Arabia, and others allows them to use think tanks as instruments of authoritarian "sharp power," not only to silence criticism but to "flood the information landscape with authoritarian talking points."[68]

New transnational actors can also reclaim the dialogue spaces and meeting agendas within international organizations and global institutions that were initially dedicated to promoting transnational liberal dialogues and agendas. Over the 2010s, the Organization for Security and Co-operation in Europe's (OSCE) annual Human Dimension Implementation Meeting (HDIM), established to network liberal activists and human rights defenders across the member countries, was

---

[66] Nadege Rolland, *Commanding Ideas: Think Tanks as Platforms for Authoritarian Influence* (National Endowment for Democracy, 2020), https://www.ned .org/wp-content/uploads/2020/12/Commanding-Ideas-Think-Tanks-as-Platforms-for-Authoritarian-Influence-Rolland-Dec-2020.pdf. See, for example, Casey Michel, *Infiltrating America: How the United Arab Emirates Launched an Unprecedented Political Interference Campaign in the United States* (Human Rights Foundation, 2024), https://hrf.org/wp-content/uploads/2024/05/2024_HRF_UAE-Report_ Final_Web_V1.pdf.

[67] Ken Silverstein and Brooke Williams, "Chuck Hagel's Think Tank, Its Donors and Intellectual Independence," *New Republic*, February 13, 2013, https:// newrepublic.com/article/112398/chuck-hagels-atlantic-council-foreign-donors-and-independence.

[68] Rolland, *Commanding Ideas*, p. 8.

taken over by GONGOs from authoritarian members like Russia and Azerbaijan that seek to advance state positions, sow disinformation, and take up valuable agenda time that would otherwise be used for liberal advocacy.[69] In 2016, the US mission to the OSCE drew attention to these GONGO tactics that sought to undermine the HDIM, including flooding requests for speaking time, booking all side rooms at the venue to prevent adjunct advocacy events and conversations, and teaming up with state media outlets at the venue in a coordinated effort to push official messages and agendas.[70] These tactical innovations are not just about mitigating liberal influence but rather absorb the methods of liberal influence and use them to inject illiberal ideas into the global sphere. They go further than deflecting the agenda and instead aim to dictate it.

Coda: Transmit Success Back to Domestic Audience

How successful the snapback is in any given case will depend on a range of contextual factors, but one thing is clear: Success, whether genuine or manufactured, can be fed back into domestic propaganda streams. A state's ideas being seen as legitimate abroad or a state being an ideational leader can be a source of domestic legitimacy.[71] Illustrating for domestic audiences how illiberal ideas are supported internationally loops back to the beginning of the authoritarian snapback model by further marginalizing liberal ideas. Not only are they unsuitable here at home, the argument goes, but they are even in doubt abroad.

---

[69] Ron Synovitz, "Attack of the GONGOs: Government-Organized NGOs Flood Warsaw Meeting," RFE/RL, September 30, 2019, https://www.rferl.org/a/attack-of-the-gongos-government-organized-ngos-flood-warsaw-meeting/30191944.html.

[70] US Mission to the OSCE, "Mind the GONGOs," September 13, 2016, https://osce.usmission.gov/mind-gongos-government-organized-ngos-troll-europes-largest-human-rights-conference/.

[71] Heike Holbig, "International Dimensions of Legitimacy: Reflections on Western Theories and the Chinese Experience," *Journal of Chinese Political Science* 16, no. 2 (2011): pp. 161–81, https://doi.org/10.1007/s11366-011-9142-6; Bert Hoffmann, "The International Dimension of Authoritarian Regime Legitimation: Insights from the Cuban Case," *Journal of International Relations and Development* 18, no. 4 (2015): pp. 556–74, https://doi.org/10.1057/jird.2014.9; Adele Del Sordi and Emanuela Dalmasso, "The Relation Between External and Internal Legitimation: The Religious Foreign Policy of Morocco and Kazakhstan," *Taiwan Journal of Democracy* 14, no. 1 (2018): pp. 95–116.

Illustrative Example: China and Human Rights

So far, the examples of each tactic have been drawn from a variety of contexts and academic literature to underscore the breadth and spread of this process. In this section we develop a focused example to illustrate how the authoritarian snapback unfolds in one issue area regarding one government. For this we choose China's efforts to reinterpret and repurpose global understandings of human rights. China and global human rights is a "most likely" case for our model because the PRC is powerful and many international human rights are inconsistent with its authoritarian system and are therefore explicitly viewed as threatening.[72]

Tactic 1: Stigmatize

China's approach to human rights relies on stigmatizing them as "Western" with the implication that they are not universally applicable and therefore not necessarily relevant for China. Document Number 9 from 2013 is a good example. Recall that this is a leaked inner-party document detailing ideological threats. The communiqué claims that

> the goal of espousing "universal values" is to claim that the West's value system defies time and space, transcends nation and class, and applies to all humanity. . . . Given Western nations' long-term dominance in the realms of economics, military affairs, science, and technology, these arguments can be confusing and deceptive. The goal [of such slogans] is to obscure the essential differences between the West's value system and the value system we advocate, ultimately using the West's value systems to supplant the core values of Socialism.[73]

Relativizing human rights as "Western" simultaneously "exposes" their foreignness and inapplicability to China, frames them as an attack on

---

[72] To be sure, China is not the only powerful authoritarian state aiming to reshape global understandings of human rights. On Russia, for example, see Marcel H. Van Herpen, *Putin's Propaganda Machine: Soft Power and Russian Foreign Policy* (Rowman & Littlefield, 2016), pp. 143–52.

[73] ChinaFile, "Document 9: A ChinaFile Translation," November 8, 2013, https://www.chinafile.com/document-9-chinafile-translation (accessed September 17, 2021).

the party (and thus the people), and associates them with a geopolitical rival. The stigmatization strategy sees the party propaganda apparatus publicize certain criticisms of China's human rights, especially when they are made by US entities, to "geopoliticize" the issue area and prime audiences to disregard human rights as a genuine value system.[74] The result is that Chinese citizens often see criticism of China's human rights as cynically motivated and subsequently disregard them, or even dig in and view their country as *more* respectful of human rights.[75]

Tactic 2: Shield

Not content to stigmatize them as "Western," the PRC has taken concerted steps to squelch human rights activism. Perhaps most obviously, China's heavily censored internet blocks access to information about human rights in the country and prevents the lateral spread of information and organizational tactics that might catalyze human rights activism. In terms of transnational human rights NGOs, Human Rights Watch does its work without the benefit of an official office in China, while Amnesty International closed its two Hong Kong offices after the 2020 Beijing-imposed National Security Law criminalized a wide range of vaguely characterized activities that the organization could have been seen to violate. In China's crackdowns on domestic NGOs, organizations "with evident pro-liberal inclination, mass mobilization capacities, and/or closer associations with domestic and international 'hostile forces' are . . . most vulnerable to persecution."[76]

Starting in July 2015, Xi Jinping's party-state began a repressive campaign against human rights lawyers domestically, in what became known as the "709" crackdown (so named because it began on July 9, 2015). Human rights law in the PRC arose in the mid-1990s and focused broadly on "organized legal advocacy against arbitrary power

---

[74] Jamie J. Gruffydd-Jones, "Citizens and Condemnation: Strategic Uses of International Human Rights Pressure in Authoritarian States," *Comparative Political Studies* 52, no. 4 (2019): pp. 579–612, https://doi.org/10.1177/0010414018784066.

[75] Gruffydd-Jones, *Hostile Forces*.

[76] Han Zhu and Lu Jun, "The Crackdown on Rights-Advocacy NGOs in Xi's China: Politicizing the Law and Legalizing the Repression," *Journal of Contemporary China* 31, no. 136 (2022): p. 537, https://doi.org/10.1080/10670564.2021.1985829.

for the protection of individual rights and freedoms."[77] While there had been previous campaigns against human rights lawyers in China, the scale of the 709 crackdown differed insofar as hundreds of lawyers were visited by police or detained, with some spending months in detention incommunicado, only later compelled to give forced confessions on TV and/or tried in heavily restricted and skewed proceedings.[78] Consistent with the "shield" logic, information and images about the crackdown itself were filtered and blocked for the wider public on Weibo and WeChat.[79] The propaganda apparatus reported widely but selectively on the crackdown and trials themselves, apparently with the goal of "portraying the defendants as subversive criminals."[80] With human rights as an idea stigmatized in tactic 1 of the snapback, tactic 2 sees information about them restricted and the organizational base on which activism might be built destroyed.

Tactic 3: Reframe Engagement and Set New Ground Rules

In terms of China and human rights, reframing engagement and setting new ground rules involves invoking public opinion and showing broad support for the action. A common rhetorical device to this end in Chinese foreign policy is that an action or statement by a foreigner has "hurt the feelings of the Chinese people."[81] This move elevates the action from a political statement to an attack on the population itself. This is related to the logic that Gruffydd-Jones identifies when discussing the PRC effort to geopoliticize human rights,[82] but it goes even further by

---

77 Hualing Fu, "The July 9th (709) Crackdown on Human Rights Lawyers: Legal Advocacy in an Authoritarian State," *Journal of Contemporary China* 27, no. 112 (2018): p. 555, https://doi.org/10.1080/10670564.2018.1433491.

78 Eva Pils, "The Party's Turn to Public Repression: An Analysis of the '709' Crackdown on Human Rights Lawyers in China," *China Law and Society Review* 3, no. 1 (2018): pp. 1–48, https://doi.org/10.1163/25427466-00301001.

79 Lotus Ruan et al., *We (Can't) Chat: "709" Crackdown Discussions Blocked on Weibo and WeChat* (CitizenLab, 2017), https://tspace.library.utoronto.ca/bitstream/1807/96728/1/Report%2391-709crackdown.pdf (accessed January 18, 2023).

80 Pils, "Party's Turn," p. 17.

81 On this device and its public resonance, see Ric Neo and Chen Xiang, "State Rhetoric, Nationalism, and Public Opinion in China," *International Affairs* 98, no. 4 (2022): pp. 1327–46, https://doi.org/10.1093/ia/iiac105.

82 Gruffydd-Jones, "Citizens and Condemnation."

encouraging the listener not to disregard the criticism but rather to act on it by taking countermeasures. When amplified through state media, such appeals do influence perceptions and attitudes of the public.[83] The result is that the "offending" entity or person now faces not only the authoritarian government but also its public, which is interpreting the situation through a public sphere dominated by the state and shorn of alternative viewpoints.

In the lead-up to the 2008 Beijing Olympics, for example, the phrase was invoked in *China Daily* in response to French protests about China's human rights and criticism from the US House of Representatives about China's Tibet policy.[84] The propaganda outlet *Global Times* claimed that the feelings of the Chinese people were hurt when fashion companies earned money in China but expressed concern about forced labor in Xinjiang.[85] In 2016, Swedish national Peter Dahlin was detained for working with some of the lawyers repressed in the 709 crackdown, and in a televised forced confession was made to say that he "hurt the feelings of the Chinese people."[86] In this way, foreign criticism of China's human rights record gets reframed as an attack on the Chinese people, with the implied new ground rule being to, at minimum, stay silent.

Tactic 4: Project Control and Influence Outward

The PRC is increasingly active in promoting control and influence abroad when it comes to human rights.[87] In terms of coercion, China engages in transnational repression of its citizens frequently, including

---

[83] Neo and Chen, "State Rhetoric."

[84] Amy King, "Hurting the Feelings of the Chinese People: The Origins, First Use, and Logics of That Peculiar Chinese Foreign Policy Phrase," Wilson Center Sources and Methods, February 15, 2017, https://www.wilsoncenter.org/blog-post/hurting-the-feelings-the-chinese-people.

[85] GT Staff Reporters, "'Pure, White Cotton Shouldn't be Tainted!' Chinese Voice Support for Xinjiang," *Global Times*, March 25, 2021, https://www.globaltimes.cn/page/202103/1219499.shtml (accessed January 18, 2023).

[86] Pils, "Party's Turn," p. 16.

[87] Titus C. Chen and Chiahao Hsu, "China's Human Rights Foreign Policy in the Xi Jinping Era: Normative Revisionism Shrouded in Discursive Moderation," *British Journal of Politics and International Relations* 23, no. 2 (2021): pp. 228–47, https://doi.org/10.1177/1369148120957611.

with regard to Xinjiang[88] and other political dissidents.[89] But most germane to this argument, the PRC represses people who are attempting to engage with the UN human rights system, for example by testifying about their experiences.[90] The UN Secretary General in 2021 documented several cases in which the PRC detained citizens domestically who were attempting to work with or access UN human rights bodies, including 14 long-running or repeat cases of repression and threat.[91] For those wishing to testify before the United Nations Human Rights Council, the PRC initially attempts to prevent them from leaving China to do so, but if they are able to attend UN meetings, they are surveilled and intimidated.[92]

Beyond direct transnational repression of its own citizens and exiles, the PRC uses threats to curtail market access to regulate human rights criticism by foreign entities. Chinese authorities have used the threat of market access to regulate statements about China's human rights made by athletes, actors, universities, apparel companies, and publishers, among others.[93] The aim of using economic leverage of this sort is to coerce entities outside China to adopt language and formulations acceptable to Chinese authorities, thereby normalizing Beijing's preferred stances as global consensus.

Liberal mimicry is also useful in the PRC snapback against human rights. The China Society for Human Rights Studies (CSHRS) is one example.[94] The CSHRS has consultative status at the UN as a nongovernmental civil society organization. In that capacity it can

---

[88] Lemon et al., "Globalizing Minority Persecution."

[89] Dukalskis, *Making the World Safe*, pp. 134–37.

[90] Alexander Dukalskis, "A Fox in the Henhouse: China, Normative Change, and the United Nations Human Rights Council," *Journal of Human Rights* 22, no. 3 (2023): pp. 334–50.

[91] OHCHR, "Annual Reports on Reprisals for Cooperation with the UN: OHCHR and Reprisals," https://www.ohchr.org/en/reprisals/annual-reports-reprisals-cooperation-un (accessed June 16, 2022).

[92] Sui-Lee Wee and Stephanie Nebehay, "At U.N., China Uses Intimidation Tactics to Silence Its Critics," Reuters, October 6, 2015, https://www.reuters.com/investigates/special-report/china-softpower-rights/ (accessed March 14, 2022).

[93] Viking Bohman and Hillevi Pårup, *Purchasing with the Party: Chinese Consumer Boycotts of Foreign Companies, 2008–2021*, Swedish National China Centre, Report No. 2, 2022.

[94] This paragraph draws on discussion in Dukalskis, "Fox in the Henhouse," pp. 343–44.

make submissions on human rights issues and engage in proceedings that may influence UN human rights norms. However, since its founding in 1993 the CSHRS has always been headed by a high-level party member and is supervised by the party.[95] Xi Jinping himself stated in remarks published by a theoretical journal of the CCP that "it is necessary to give full play to the roles of the CSHRS and the China Human Rights Development Foundation, and to increase its influence on multilateral human rights institutions such as the United Nations," although the statement appeared only in the Chinese-language version of the remarks, not the English-language summary produced by the journal.[96] Predictably, the CSHRS cheerleads China's policies, reproduces material from other propaganda outlets, lauds Xi Jinping, and does not criticize CCP human rights performance in any meaningful way. A degree of plausible separation between government and society is introduced that may not deceive seasoned observers or human rights diplomats but may work on casual observers who know little about Chinese political institutions.

Tactic 5: Dictate the Agenda

Tactic 5 sees the PRC use the foundations it built in tactics 1–4 to try to change the content of international human rights norms, thus redefining the field. It can mobilize like-minded states to endorse its domestic record.[97] At the United Nations Human Rights Council (HRC), repression in Xinjiang gained attention but saw China mobilize like-minded states to oppose deeper scrutiny or opprobrium.[98] In July 2019, representatives of 18 European states, plus Australia,

---

[95] Titus C. Chen, "A Flamboyant Mandarin in a Declining Liberal Order: China's Revisionist Agenda in Global Human Rights Institutions," *Social Science Research Network*, p. 11, https://ssrn.com/abstract=3403037.

[96] Statement available here: http://www.qstheory.cn/dukan/qs/2022-06/15/c_1128739416.htm (accessed June 17, 2022); English summary: "Xi's Article on China's Human Rights Development to Be Published," *CPC Central Committee Bimonthly Qiushi*, June 15, 2022, http://en.qstheory.cn/2022-06/15/c_771084.htm (accessed June 17, 2022).

[97] Rana Siu Inboden, *China and the International Human Rights Regime, 1982–2017* (Cambridge University Press, 2021).

[98] The following two paragraphs draw on Dukalskis, "Fox in the Henhouse," pp. 341–42.

New Zealand, Japan, and Canada, sent a letter to the UN High Commissioner for Human Rights expressing concern about repression in Xinjiang. Within four days, the PRC mobilized 37 states to send a response decrying the politicization of human rights issues and praising China's human rights record. Nearly all the signatories were representatives of non-democratic states, including Russia, Belarus, North Korea, Iran, Saudi Arabia, and Syria.[99] The Office of the UN High Commissioner for Human Rights, Michelle Bachelet, released a report only minutes before her term was ending. This followed a concerted pressure campaign by China to frustrate the report, including delaying a visit by Bachelet to Xinjiang, which ultimately resulted in highly circumscribed and controversial visit in May 2022.[100] A motion to discuss the final report was rejected by the HRC in October 2022 by a margin of 19 against, 17 for, with 11 abstentions, a result that China presented via Xinhua as a victory against the United States.[101]

---

[99] Full letter available here: "Letter Dated 12 July 2019 from the Representatives of Algeria, Angola, Bahrain, Bangladesh, Belarus, the Plurinational State of Bolivia, Burkina Faso, Burundi, Cambodia, Cameroon, Comoros, the Congo, Cuba, the Democratic People's Republic of Korea, the Democratic Republic of the Congo, Djibouti, Egypt, Equatorial Guinea, Eritrea, Gabon, the Islamic Republic of Iran, Iraq, Kuwait, the Lao People's Democratic Republic, Mozambique, Myanmar, Nepal, Nigeria, Oman, Pakistan, the Philippines, the Russian Federation, Saudi Arabia, Serbia, Somalia, South Sudan, Sri Lanka, the Sudan, the Syrian Arab Republic, Tajikistan, Togo, Turkmenistan, Uganda, the United Arab Emirates, Uzbekistan, the Bolivarian Republic of Venezuela, Yemen, Zambia, Zimbabwe and the State of Palestine to the United Nations Office at Geneva Addressed to the President of the Human Rights Council," United Nations Digital Library, July 12, 2019, https://digitallibrary.un.org/record/3853509?ln=en (accessed January 11, 2023).

[100] Emma Farge, "China Seeks to Stop UN Rights Chief from Releasing Xinjiang Report—Document," Reuters, July 20, 2022, https://www.reuters.com/world/china/exclusive-china-seeks-stop-un-rights-chief-releasing-xinjiang-report-document-2022-07-19/ (accessed November 11, 2022); Austin Ramzy, "U.N. Human Rights Chief Tempers Criticism at End of China Trip," New York Times, May 28, 2022, https://www.nytimes.com/2022/05/28/world/asia/un-human-rights-china.html (accessed June 8, 2022); Yuan Yang, "UN Human Rights Council Blocks Debate on China's Abuses in Xinjiang," Financial Times, October 7, 2022, https://www.ft.com/content/e00c7c4f-f28a-4d6e-b9a4-eb89df8d6d81 (accessed November 11, 2022).

[101] Yang, "UN Human Rights Council." For China's portrayal, see "U.S.-Led Attempts to Use Xinjiang to Contain China's Gravest Violation of Human Rights of All Ethnic Groups in Xinjiang," Xinhua, October 8, 2022, https://english.news.cn/20221008/009060cboedf4e4780cdeb51215a7c44/c.html (accessed November 11, 2022).

Beyond endorsement of its own repression as consistent with human rights, China works to redefine the content of global human rights to be less liberal and more consistent with its own rule. For example, it sponsored a HRC resolution called "Promoting Mutually Beneficial Cooperation in the Field of Human Rights" that weakens the vision of human rights as limiting state power and instead advances a conception of human rights that is built around "dialogue" and state-to-state cooperation.[102] It promotes rights that are more collective or state-led, such as the Right to Development.[103] It supported a resolution on the "Promotion of a Democratic and Equitable International Order" that stipulated that "democracy is not only a political concept, but that it also has economic and social dimensions" and that "attempts to overthrow legitimate Governments by force or other illegal means disrupt the democratic and constitutional order, the legitimate exercise of power and the full enjoyment of human rights."[104] China finds supporters for its views on human rights in the HRC especially from among less democratic states.[105]

Coda: Transmit Success Back to Domestic Audience

China transmits its human rights victories back into the domestic sphere. Xi Jinping has stressed the importance of China's leadership in the human rights field.[106] Successes for the PRC in the United Nations are highlighted and framed as victories for China and defeats for the

---

[102] Human Rights Council, "Promoting Mutually Beneficial Cooperation in the Field of Human Rights," United Nations Digital Library, March 23, 2021, https://digitallibrary.un.org/record/3922298?ln=ru&v=pdf (accessed November 11, 2022).

[103] Inboden, *China and the International Human Rights Regime.* See also Rochelle Terman and Zoltán I. Búzás, "A House Divided: Norm Fragmentation in the International Human Rights Regime," *International Studies Quarterly* 65, no. 2 (2021): pp. 488–99, https://doi.org/10.1093/isq/sqab019.

[104] See documentation at https://www.ohchr.org/en/documents/thematic-reports/a78262-promotion-democratic-and-equitable-international-order.

[105] Inboden, *China.*

[106] 坚定不移走中国人权发展道路 更好推动我国人权事业发展 ("Unswervingly Follow the Path of China's Human Rights Development and Better Promote the Development of Our Country's Human Rights Cause"), *QS Theory*, June 15, 2022, http://www.qstheory.cn/dukan/qs/2022-06/15/c_1128739416.htm (accessed June 17, 2022).

United States.[107] The coda of the China human rights snapback, after scaling the five steps, is to return to basics and feed its anti-liberal victories back to the population to further stigmatize liberal influence and bolster authoritarian norms.

---

[107] "U.S.-Led Attempts to Use Xinjiang to Contain China a Gravest Violation of Human Rights of All Ethnic Groups in Xinjiang," Xinhua. For a Chinese-language version aimed at a domestic audience, see "美国等国'以疆制华'图谋是对新疆各族人民人权的最大侵犯——记中国在联合国人权理事会挫败涉疆决定草案," Xinhua, October 7, 2022, http://www.news.cn/world/2022-10-07/c_1129054482.htm.

Chapter 5

Reconfiguring Global Media Influence

In March 2023 *Wall Street Journal* Russia correspondent Evan Gersch-kovich was detained by the Federal Security Bureau and charged with espionage.[1] After Gerschkovich, an American citizen, was taken from a restaurant in Yekaterinburg, his arrest was broadcast on Russian state television. His legal proceedings were held in secret, with reporters only allowed to see Gerschkovich briefly in the courtroom while he was in a glass box but not to speak with him or observe the proceedings. By the standards of the last 35 years, this case is unusual, as it was the "first time Russia had brought a spy case against an overseas reporter since the Cold War."[2] It followed a raft of new laws and regulations after Russia's full-scale attack on Ukraine in 2022 that severely restricted space for journalists, including foreign correspondents, to operate in the country.[3]

---

[1] See details of the case and Gershkovich's background here: Joe Parkinson and Drew Hinshaw, "Evan Gershkovich Loved Russia, the Country That Turned on Him," *Wall Street Journal*, March 31, 2023, https://www.wsj.com/articles/wsj-reporter-evan-gershkovich-detained-russia-cd03b0f3. Gershkovich was ultimately released in August 2024 in a prisoner exchanged between Russia and several Western states.

[2] Parkinson and Hinshaw, "Evan Gershkovich Loved Russia."

[3] Anton Troianovski and Valeriya Safronova, "Russia Takes Censorship to New Extremes, Stifling War Coverage," *New York Times*, March 4, 2022, https://www.nytimes.com/2022/03/04/world/europe/russia-censorship-media-crackdown.html.

The crackdown within Russia was designed to stifle dissent and prevent foreign and domestic journalists from uncovering critical information about the war and Putin's government. But it was accompanied by renewed attention to Russia's external propaganda and information manipulation. International commentators worried that the country's Russia Today (RT) media brand was gaining traction in shaping views of the conflict, especially among its Spanish-language audience in Latin America.[4] Russia's well-developed infrastructure of online propaganda and disinformation reportedly began to show tangible effects in the politics of some African states.[5] These endeavors did not come out of nowhere, and Russia had long been honing its ability to manipulate information ecosystems beyond its borders, including in the United States and Europe.[6] It is not successful all of the time, but when it is, Russia's external information strategy muddies the waters of public debates, distracts from Russia's shortcomings, elevates useful allies within democratic states, and spotlights negative information and hypocrisy of "the West," positioning Russia as an anti-imperial underdog.

Russia, of course, is not the only player in this game. These two tactics, on the one hand the crackdown on the press within the territorial jurisdiction of the state, and on the other hand the external propagation of pro-authoritarian content, illustrate the two sides of authoritarians' attempts to shape the international information environment. The shifting underlying dynamics of global politics set out in the previous chapters, along with the rise of the internet and the struggles of

---

[4] See, for example, Daniel Rojas Medina, "Growing Audiences and Influence: Russian Media in Latin America," Bertelsmann Foundation, June 9, 2022, https://www.bfna.org/digital-world/growing-audiences-and-influence-russian-media-in-latin-america-7wlrwqpupm/; José Ospina-Valencia, "Russia's Propaganda War in Latin America," *DW*, April 13, 2022, https://www.dw.com/en/how-russia-is-waging-a-successful-propaganda-war-in-latin-america/a-61467050; and Gretel Kahn, "Despite Western Bans, Putin's Propaganda Flourishes in Spanish on TV and Social Media," Reuters Institute, March 30, 2023, https://reutersinstitute.politics.ox.ac.uk/news/despite-western-bans-putins-propaganda-flourishes-spanish-tv-and-social-media.

[5] See, for example, Anndres Schipani et al., "How Russia's Propaganda Machine Is Reshaping the African Narrative," *Financial Times*, February 9, 2023, https://www.ft.com/content/d427c855-c665-4732-9dd1-3ae314464d12.

[6] See, for example, Marcel H. Van Herpen, *Putin's Propaganda Machine: Soft Power and Russian Foreign Policy* (Rowman & Littlefield, 2016); and Peter Pomerantsev, *This Is Not Propaganda: Adventures in the War Against Reality* (PublicAffairs, 2019).

the media industry in liberal democracies, have increased the willingness, ability, and opportunity for authoritarian states to wield media influence beyond their borders.

This chapter traces how authoritarian states are attempting to reshape the global media environment. We explore how autocrats both denigrate and censor independent media while also manipulating it and trying to embed themselves in global media infrastructure in order to dictate the agenda. In the first section, we identify the underpinnings and select tactics of authoritarian media outreach. The chapter then provides data on the dissemination infrastructure available to Russia and China in the form of official bureau- and content-sharing agreements. Third, it discusses commonalities and differences in the content of pro-authoritarian media before discussing, fourth, how authoritarian states learn, adapt, and cooperate in this sphere. The fifth section moves beyond amplification and dissemination to show how authoritarian states restrict the work of foreign journalists, documenting over 1,000 such instances. In presenting the new Authoritarian Restrictions on Foreign Journalists (AFRJ) data set, the chapter illustrates the breadth of actors and the types of measures that authoritarian states use to shield themselves from scrutiny. The picture that emerges from these efforts is one in which amplification and restrictions work together to advance pro-authoritarian narratives and shield them from scrutiny.

Authoritarian Amplification: New Realities of Pro-Authoritarian Media

In the 2000s, authoritarian states openly fretted about their inability to shape global conversations. "Western" media like CNN, the BBC, the Associated Press, Reuters, *New York Times*, and AFP, to name the most prominent, seemed to have powerful agenda-setting capabilities. Outlets like the *Financial Times* and *The Economist* helped shape perceptions of their relatively affluent and elite readers. These outlets, including public broadcasters like BBC, were premised on editorial independence from their host governments even if they reflected the worldviews of their boards, management, and employees.

Crucially though, they were free to cover governments—democracies and autocracies alike—with critical vigor.

Authoritarian states and autocrats lamented that the dominance of "Western" media made it more difficult to get their viewpoints heard and accepted. In a 2006 interview with the *Financial Times*, Vladimir Putin argued that economically powerful countries could manipulate media and project their influence transnationally.[7] The project to undermine "Western" media would become core to the mission of Russia's external propaganda efforts.[8] Starting around the mid-2000s, and with increased frequency from 2008 onward and especially after Xi Jinping took control, Chinese authorities referred to the concept of "discourse power." The idea came to signal that China faced a deficit in its "right to speak" and "right to be heard" internationally because of the hegemony of "Western" media, concepts, and narratives.[9]

Aspiring autocrats in democratic or hybrid political systems often share this perspective. Türkiye's President Recep Tayyip Erdoğan has lamented international media's portrayal of his country, saying, for

---

[7] "Full Text: Vladimir Putin Interview," *Financial Times*, September 10, 2006, https://www.ft.com/content/76e205b2-40e5-11db-827f-0000779e2340. See also Van Herpen, *Putin's Propaganda Machine*, p. 29.

[8] Elswah and Howard note, for example, that when it comes to Russia's RT programming, "The idea that Western media lies is one of the main elements of RT's agenda and significantly shapes the ideological foundation of the channel." See Mona Elswah and Philip N. Howard, "'Anything that Causes Chaos': The Organizational Behavior of Russia Today (RT)," *Journal of Communication* 70, no. 5 (2020): p. 641, https://doi.org/10.1093/joc/jqaa027.

[9] On the origins and conceptualization of "discourse power" see Nadege Rolland, *China's Vision for a New World Order* (National Bureau of Asian Research, 2022); and Kejin Zhao, "China's Rise and Its Discursive Power Strategy," *Chinese Political Science Review* 1, no. 3 (2016): pp. 539–64, https://doi.org/10.1007/s41111-016-0037-8. For helpful online explainers, see Toni Friedman, "Lexicon: 'Discourse Power' or the 'Right to Speak' (话语权, Huàyǔ Quán)", *Digichina*, Stanford Cyber Policy Center, March 17, 2022, https://digichina.stanford.edu/work/lexicon-discourse-power-or-the-right-to-speak-huayu-quan/; and Stella Chen, "Discourse Power," China Media Project, *CMP Dictionary*, May 30, 2022, https://chinamediaproject.org/the_ccp_dictionary/discourse-power/. On China's perceived deficit relative to "Western" political and cultural ideas in the international sphere, see Yiwei Wang, "Public Diplomacy and the Rise of Chinese Soft Power," *Annals of the American Academy of Political and Social Science* 616, no. 1 (2008): pp. 264–65; and Hailong Liu, *Propaganda: Ideas, Discourses and Its Legitimization* (Routledge, 2020), pp. 280–83.

example, after crackdowns on a protest in 2013, that "Turkey is not a country that international media can play games on."[10] When the country's TRT World television station was launched in 2015, the project was positioned as a challenge to the allegedly biased Western media and would present a Turkish viewpoint on global affairs.[11] Hungary's Viktor Orbán, another longtime media critic, told American conservative activists in 2022 that having one's own media is crucial in taking and maintaining power because legacy media was too biased.[12] At the same conservative conference in 2024, El Salvador's president Nayib Bukele—the self-proclaimed "world's coolest dictator"—told his American audience that "the global elites and the media, they work in conjunction. They run some stories and publish them with pictures to reinforce an agenda. You're no strangers to that here in the United States; we deal with that in El Salvador too. That is the free press they talk about? Please."[13]

The 2000s offered new openings for authoritarian states to begin to amplify their media globally. The rise of authoritarian powers is one factor, but developments internal to liberal democracies widened the window of opportunity.[14] Financially, media outlets, especially newspapers, struggled to cope with technological and economic changes that were reconfiguring the news industry. In addition to harming local news coverage, the number of foreign correspondents and bureau in many media outlets declined or even disappeared as it

---

[10] Constanze Letsch and Ian Traylor, "Turkey Unrest: Violent Clashes in Istanbul as Erdoğan Holds Rally," *The Guardian*, June 16, 2013, https://www.theguardian.com/world/2013/jun/16/turkey-unrest-clashes-istanbul-erdoganl.

[11] Mona Elswah and Philip N. Howard, "Where News Could Not Inspire Change: TRT World as a Party Broadcaster," *Journalism* 23, no. 10 (2022): pp. 2079–95, https://doi.org/10.1177/14648849211033444. See reporting from the time at Mehul Srivastava and Henry Mance, "Turkish TV Station Aims to Switch Western Views," *Financial Times*, March 11, 2016, https://www.ft.com/content/cd5d7f46-e77c-11e5-a09b-1f8b0d268c39.

[12] Flora Garamvolgyi, "Viktor Orbán Tells CPAC the Path to Power Is to 'Have Your Own Media,'" *The Guardian*, May 20, 2022, https://www.theguardian.com/us-news/2022/may/20/viktor-orban-cpac-republicans-hungary.

[13] Nayib Bukele, "Discurso Completo CPAC 2024," YouTube, February 24, 2024, https://www.youtube.com/watch?v=hOFErQLbd8k; time 12:28-12:50.

[14] Joshua Kurlantzick, *Beijing's Global Media Offensive: China's Uneven Campaign to Influence Asia and the World* (Oxford University Press, 2023), pp. 140–44.

became prohibitively expensive to maintain full-time staff and support abroad.[15] In the United States between 2005 and 2020, more than 25% of newspapers and half of all journalism jobs disappeared, while between 2018 and 2020 alone 300 newspapers and 6,000 jobs vanished.[16] Politically, the denigration of "mainstream" media by populist leaders and commentators within the West helped sow distrust of legacy media.[17] These developments helped create a void that authoritarian state media could fill and an underlying sentiment of distrust that could be seized upon to discredit reporting critical of authoritarian actors.

Pro-authoritarian state media outlets have seized this opening with aplomb, investing heavily to reconfigure the global media ecosystem. State subsidization means that authoritarian media outlets can take financial losses in pursuit of their work. Media houses from authoritarian states are not transparent, and so we have to look for glimpses into their finances. Even so, the sums are striking. Chinese authorities invested upwards of $6.6 billion starting around 2007 to improve their global propaganda outreach.[18] According to the *New York Times*, the 2017 global budget for Russia's RT was about $323 million.[19]

One keyhole into authoritarian state media financing can be had by examining fillings with the US Department of Justice pursuant to the Foreign Agents Registration Act (FARA). FARA requires that

---

[15] John Maxwell Hamilton and Eric Jenner, "Redefining Foreign Correspondence," *Journalism* 5, no. 3 (2004): pp. 301–21, https://doi.org/10.1177/1464884904044938; Pamela Constable, "Demise of the Foreign Correspondent," *Washington Post*, February 18, 2007, https://www.washingtonpost.com/archive/opinions/2007/02/18/demise-of-the-foreign-correspondent/dfb489f6-2442-4910-b41a-6ff566fd9fdb/.

[16] Penelope Muse Abernathy, *News Deserts and Ghost Newspapers: Will Local News Survive?* (Center for Innovation and Sustainability in Local Media, Hussman School of Media and Journalism, University of North Carolina at Chapel Hill, distributed by the University of North Carolina Press, 2020), https://www.usnewsdeserts.com/wp-content/uploads/2020/06/2020_News_Deserts_and_Ghost_Newspapers.pdf.

[17] Kurlantzick, *Beijing's Global Media Offensive*, p. 141.

[18] Anne-Marie Brady, "China's Foreign Propaganda Machine," *Journal of Democracy* 26, no. 4 (2015): pp. 51–59, https://doi.org/10.1353/jod.2015.0056.

[19] Steven Erlanger, "What Is RT?," *New York Times*, March 8, 2017, https://www.nytimes.com/2017/03/08/world/europe/what-is-rt.html. For further budgetary figures for RT, see Van Herpen, *Putin's Propaganda Machine*, p. 71.

entities doing political work for foreign clients in the United States register and periodically report to the department about their activities and expenditures. FARA filings for China's CGTN showed outlays of nearly $20 million per year to finance the station's American operations.[20] Recent filings for *China Daily*, the CCP's main foreign propaganda newspaper, shows that in the six months prior to April 2023, Beijing subsidized the paper's US operations by $4.3 million.[21] Between 2014 and 2017, Russia's RT spent about $23 million annually in the United States, according to FARA filings.[22] FARA filings for Turkish Radio-Television Corporation, the parent entity of TRT World, showed outlays of $2.7 million for one year from mid-2018 to mid-2019 to finance operating expenses for the channel.[23] And these figures are only a glimpse for the flagship brands of select authoritarian media. They do not include public relations firms that seek favorable coverage for their clients in existing outlets,[24] for example, or wealthy allies of authoritarian leaders buying shares in foreign media outlets. Furthermore, FARA figures are only for the United States, excluding operations in the rest of the world.

Sometimes the FARA filings reveal how states amplify their media but obscure its origins. For example, a 2021 filing showed that Potomac Radio Group, registered in Virginia, received nearly $2.8 million from CGTN in the previous two years to run programming for Beijing on the Washington, DC–area station WCRW.[25] As it happens, this is only

---

[20] Alexander Dukalskis, *Making the World Safe for Dictatorship* (Oxford University Press, 2021), p. 64.

[21] Full filing available here: https://efile.fara.gov/docs/3457-Supplemental-Statement-20230526-38.pdf.

[22] Dukalskis, *Making the World Safe*, p. 63.

[23] Full filing available here: https://efile.fara.gov/docs/6780-Exhibit-AB-20200 312-1.pdf. This was the first period that TRT World was required to register under FARA. Subsequent filings show lower total expenditures. See, for example, the March 2023 filing for the prior six months, which reports an outlay of $420,000 at https://efile.fara.gov/docs/6780-Supplemental-Statement-20230428-6.pdf.

[24] Adam Scharpf et al., "Dictatorships and Western Public Relations Firms," unpublished manuscript, April 3, 2024, https://www.dropbox.com/scl/fi/xk6b6 ykobnxv9yiygottn/Dictators_PR_Firms.pdf?rlkey=iq7kxl7z3qwv43u67pnaeqpfn& e=1&dl=0.

[25] Full filing available here: https://efile.fara.gov/docs/7059-Registration-Stateme nt-20211216-1.pdf. The station has reportedly severed its relationship with CGTN.

one example of a larger global network of radio stations that have run China Radio International content without always being transparent for the listener about who is behind the financing.[26]

Sometimes authoritarian-produced content is laundered via an ostensibly independent funder. In an example of a left-wing anti-liberal ally, American billionaire Neville Roy Singham reportedly funds a global network of pro-China media personalities, think tanks, and civil society groups in close coordination with the Chinese government even though the content appears to be "grassroots."[27] These tactics make it difficult to pin down the exact investment that states like China make in their external influence efforts.

Obscuring authoritarian origins is not only a PRC practice. Russian entities supportive of the Kremlin have penetrated numerous media outlets in its region to amplify pro-Moscow views and denigrate rivals, again without necessarily being transparent about the origins of support.[28] In September 2024, six influential right-wing podcasters in the United States were alleged by the US Department of Justice to have been receiving large sums of money from covert Russian sources.[29] The practice is not new, either. In the 1980s, South Africa's apartheid government ran a multidimensional foreign propaganda campaign that included attempting to purchase an American newspaper through layers of financial intermediaries.[30]

---

[26] Koh Gui Qing and John Shiffman, "Beijing's Covert Radio Network Airs China-Friendly News Across Washington, and the World," Reuters, November 2, 2015, https://www.reuters.com/investigates/special-report/china-radio/#graphic-dc.

[27] Mara Hvistendahl et al., "A Global Web of Chinese Propaganda Leads to a U.S. Tech Mogul," *New York Times*, August 5, 2023, https://www.nytimes.com/2023/08/05/world/europe/neville-roy-singham-china-propaganda.html. Xinhua reported on the *New York Times'* revelations of Singham's network, calling it McCarthyist. See "U.S. Peace Groups Urge to Reject 'New McCarthyism,'" Xinhua, October 8, 2023, https://english.news.cn/20230808/65cfb41170724dd3a74f636c2d58e848/c.html.

[28] Samantha Custer et al., *Winning the Narrative: How China and Russia Wield Strategic Communications to Advance Their Goals* (Gates Global Policy Center, 2011), pp. 29–31, https://docs.aiddata.org/ad4/pdfs/gf1_04_Winning_the_Narrative.pdf.

[29] Alan Suderman and Ali Swenson, "Right-wing Influencers Were Duped to Work for Covert Russian Operation, US Says," Associated Press, September 5, 2024, https://apnews.com/article/russian-interference-presidential-election-influencers-trump-999435273dd39edf7468c6aa34fad5dd

[30] Ron Nixon, *Selling Apartheid: South Africa's Global Propaganda War* (Pluto Books, 2016).

But as a hallmark of the new globalized and enmeshed reality of authoritarian media, content can be shaped by investment practices that are publicly known and legal but not always appreciated by the end viewer. Saudi Arabia stands out as an innovator here. For example, *Vice News*, the youth-oriented outlet known for edgy and gritty reporting on controversial topics, has been criticized for censoring its reporting about Saudi Arabia after striking a deal with its government-controlled MBC group[31] and working through *Vice's* branded content arm to secretly organize a youth festival in the Kingdom.[32] The Penske Media Corporation, owners of *Rolling Stone, Variety*, and a host of other media outlets, received $200 million of investment by the Saudi Research and Media Group (SRMG).[33] As of yet there has not been definitive evidence that the investment has influenced coverage of Saudi Arabia in these outlets, but it is clear that government-controlled Saudi entities have been active in investing and partnering with foreign media since Mohammed Bin Salman's (MBS's) ascent.[34]

In an example of liberal mimicry, the SRMG in 2018 partnered with *The Independent* to set up news sites in Arabic, Urdu, Turkish, and Persian that would feature direct translations of articles from

---

[31] Jim Waterson, "Vice Blocked News Stories That Could Offend Saudi Arabia, Insiders Say," *The Guardian*, August 15, 2023, https://www.theguardian.com/media/2023/aug/15/vice-blocked-news-stories-that-could-offend-saudi-arabia-insiders-say.

[32] Jim Waterson, "Vice Media Secretly Organised $20m Saudi Government Festival," *The Guardian*, February 1, 2022, https://www.theguardian.com/media/2022/feb/01/vice-media-secretly-organised-20m-saudi-government-festival. *Vice* appears to be shutting down as a media outlet. See Maya Yang, "Vice Media to Lay Off Hundreds of Workers and Stop Publishing on Its Site," *The Guardian*, February 22, 2024, https://www.theguardian.com/media/2024/feb/22/vice-media-layoffs-cease-publishing.

[33] Katherine Rosman, "You Don't Know Much About Jay Penske. And He's Fine with That," *New York Times*, March 26, 2022, https://www.nytimes.com/2022/03/26/style/jay-penske.html.

[34] Jim Waterson, "Saudi Arabia Pays UK Firms Millions to Boost Image," *The Guardian*, October 19, 2018, https://www.theguardian.com/world/2018/oct/19/saudi-arabia-pays-uk-firms-millions-to-boost-image; Daniel Thomas and Ivan Levingston, "Saudi-Backed Group Explores Launch of English News Channel to Rival Al Jazeera," *Financial Times*, May 10, 2023, https://www.ft.com/content/2c6f8228-5bcb-46dc-a817-0990727b7d35.

The Independent "alongside content from teams of SRMG journalists" with the four sites to be "owned and operated by SRMG."[35] SRMG is chaired by the Saudi minister of culture.[36] A content analysis of the top headlines returned in the Arabic, Urdu, and Persian editions when searching for the equivalent term "Mohammed bin Salman" reveals stories about MBS's diplomatic visits in the region, positive stories about his policies in Saudi Arabia, and no apparent criticism.[37] The result sees positive news about MBS and Saudi Arabia produced by SRMG circulate internationally under *The Independent*'s name and likeness. The Arabic version of the outlet has reportedly published disinformation about Qatari politics and about Saudi disputes with Qatar before the World Trade Organization.[38] This mimicry functions in addition to Saudi Arabia's many other transnational media ventures that advance pro-Saudi content in Arabic and are amplified by a vast social media operation.[39]

The Visible and Hidden Global Reach of Authoritarian Media: A Closer Look

But even in terms of clearly labeled and above-board expansion of explicitly pro-authoritarian media, the global coverage is impressive. Figure 5.1 depicts the global data we have gathered on the extent of Russian media offices, including RT, TASS, and Sputnik. These are only those that are publicly available and for which a physical presence is noted. In total we can find evidence for the presence of 58 offices combined between all three outlets. There appears to be some overreporting

---

[35] "The Independent Announces Partnership to Create Foreign News Websites," *The Independent*, July 19, 2018, https://www.independent.co.uk/news/media/independent-srmg-saudi-research-marketing-group-urdu-turkish-persian-a8454886.html.

[36] Marc Owen Jones, *Digital Authoritarianism in the Middle East: Deception, Disinformation and Social Media* (Oxford University Press, 2022), p. 78.

[37] The search engine for the Turkish edition was not functional at the time of writing. The search was done in November 2023.

[38] Jones, *Digital Authoritarianism*, pp. 160, 208.

[39] Jones, *Digital Authoritarianism*, pp. 101–20.

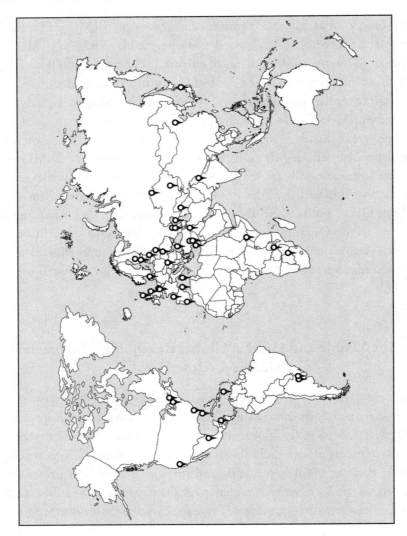

FIGURE 5.1 Offices of Russian State Media Outlets as of 2023.

Note that some European offices of RT and Sputnik were shuttered in 2022 and 2023 due to the invasion of Ukraine, while others were scheduled to open elsewhere

and/or double counting in the outlets' reporting of their own bureau. TASS, for example, lists 57 bureau in 52 countries, but we are only able to find evidence for 14. It is striking though, that the number of total bureaus we can find is a close match for TASS's claimed total, indicating perhaps some correspondents from different outlets share office space or work under multiple labels.

Figure 5.2 shows similar data for China's CGTN and Xinhua.[40] What becomes immediately clear is that the geographical coverage of Chinese media outstrips its Russian counterpart, blanketing virtually every corner of the globe with a physical presence. In total we find evidence for the presence of nearly 200 total offices between the

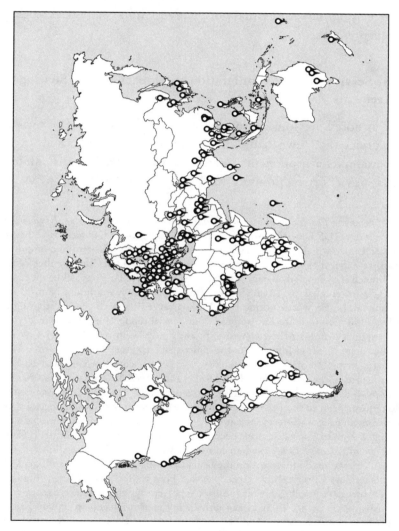

FIGURE 5.2 Offices of Chinese State Media Outlets as of 2023.

---

[40] The data underlying Figures 5.1 and 5.2 are available online as Appendix 5.1 and Appendix 5.2, respectively.

122 DICTATING THE AGENDA

two outlets. A US State Department study of China's global media outreach notes that Xinhua has 181 bureaus, while we are able to find 186, which suggests that we have captured all or nearly all of the offices.[41] Note that this does not include outlets like *China Daily*, *People's Daily*, or the many other state-linked outlets that operate abroad, let alone social media accounts or paid influencers, rendering this an extremely conservative visual portrayal of China's state-backed global media presence.

Wire Services and the Proliferation of Global Content-Sharing Agreements

But, as noted previously, pro-authoritarian media do not always publish under their own name or announce their state-backed origins. For example, a prominent project to expand PRC media influence is China's effort to promote Xinhua as an international news wire

---

[41] *How the People's Republic of China Seeks to Reshape the Global Information Environment* (US Department of State Global Engagement Center, 2023), https://www.state.gov/wp-content/uploads/2023/09/how-the-peoples-republic-of-china-seeks-to-reshape-the-global-information-environment_final.pdf. The number of Xinhua branches is reported on page 7. Our data were gathered in 2023, while the report's data is as of August 2021, which may also explain why we found a handful more bureaus. It is also worth noting that Xinhua serves an intelligence-gathering and analysis function insofar as it produces confidential reports for Chinese leaders. See Kurlantzick, *Beijing's Media Offensive*, p. 49; Emily Weinstein, "Covert Coverage: Xinhua as an Agent of Influence in the United States," Project 2049 Institute, March 7, 2018, https://project2049.net/2018/03/07/covert-coverage-xinhua-as-an-agent-of-influence-in-the-united-states/; and Roger Faligot, *Chinese Spies: From Chairman Mao to Xi Jinping* (Hurst Publishing, 2022), pp. 165, 421. The Xinhua branch in Hong Kong prior to the 1997 handover was used as cover for Chinese special agents, according to Faligot, *Chinese Spies*, pp. 212–13, 224. Other instances of special agents posing as Xinhua journalists have been documented, for example in Faligot, *Chinese Spies*, p. 114. In 2012, a Canadian journalist working for Xinhua alleged that his bureau chief wanted him to spy on the Dalai Lama on the latter's visit to Canada. See "Reporter Says Chinese News Agency Asked Him to Spy," CBC News, August 22, 2012, https://www.cbc.ca/news/politics/reporter-says-chinese-news-agency-asked-him-to-spy-1.1223135. These extra-journalistic functions may help explain Xinhua's impressive global presence. CGTN's website only refers to its three production centers in London, Washington, DC, and Nairobi. We found evidence for 10 bureaus. See "About Us—China Global Television Network," https://www.cgtn.com/about-us.html (accessed November 13, 2023).

service on a par with Associated Press, Reuters, and AFP. Wire services are critical to the flow of news and information, as they help set the agenda and provide the bulk of the infrastructure for the news feed and foreign content for newspapers across the world.[42] Xinhua has expanded globally especially since the 2000s and has done so for political reasons, to amplify China's voice in the world and to gather information about developments abroad, rather than for commercial reasons.[43] Xinhua is explicitly part of China's propaganda apparatus.[44] While the agency has undergone several reforms in the post-Mao era, "A fundamental aspect of Xinhua has remained intact: its political affiliation to the CCP. . . . Throughout 80 years of history, Xinhua has always been under the absolute control and direct supervision of the CCP."[45]

The agency is generously subsidized by the party-state and does not need to make a profit, which means that it can offer Xinhua content for low prices or even for free.[46] This benefits outlets that may not be able to afford subscriptions to private services such as AP, Reuters, or AFP. A 2020 International Federation of Journalists (IFJ) report, for example, noted that dozens of outlets in Afghanistan have signed deals with Xinhua.[47] The same research project found in a survey of journalists from 87 countries that 34% of respondents were aware of Chinese

---

[42] Esperança Bielsa, "The Pivotal Role of News Agencies in the Context of Globalization: A Historical Approach," *Global Networks* 8, no. 3 (2008): pp. 347–66, https://doi.org/10.1111/j.1471-0374.2008.00199.x.

[43] Junhao Hong, "From the World's Largest Propaganda Machine to a Multipurposed Global News Agency: Factors and Implications of Xinhua's Transformation Since 1978," *Political Communication* 28, no. 3 (2011): pp. 377–93, https://doi.org/10.1080/10584609.2011.572487.

[44] Wen-Hsuan Tsai, "Enabling China's Voice to Be Heard by the World: Ideas and Operations of the Chinese Communist Party's External Propaganda System," *Problems of Post-Communism* 64, nos. 3–4 (2017): pp. 203–13, https://doi.org/10.1080/10758216.2016.1236667.

[45] Hong, "World's Largest Propaganda Machine," p. 382.

[46] Kurlantzick, *Beijing's Global Media Offensive*, p. 182.

[47] Louisa Lim and Julia Bergin, *The China Story: Reshaping the World's Media. IFJ Research Report on China and its Impact on Media* (International Federation of Journalists, 2020), p. 8, https://www.ifj.org/fileadmin/user_upload/IFJ_Report_2020_-_The_China_Story.pdf.

content-sharing agreements in their countries.[48] As a result, in terms of number of bureau, countries covered, employees, editors, and outputs, it is competitive with the world's largest newswires.[49] In terms of content, Xinhua offers neutral or positive material about China and more critical content about the United States and the West.[50]

Content-sharing agreements are also important because they can launder the authoritarian state's media through the brand of the partner, much like the Saudi-*Independent* arrangement noted earlier. For example, another IFJ report spotlighted Italy, where ANSA, the country's main news agency, agreed in 2019 to run 50 Xinhua stories per day on its wire.[51] The agreement was apparently ended in 2022 by ANSA, but Xinhua reportedly began working with another smaller news service in Italy, Nova Agency, almost immediately.[52] In these arrangements, the partner effectively becomes a distributor of CCP-approved propaganda. Readers consuming Xinhua content in their own regular news sources may not know what Xinhua is or appreciate that it is controlled by the Chinese party-state. Even when the agreements are just for stock photos and not written material, manipulated or misleading content can be distributed.[53]

Xinhua's rise as a wire service therefore offers China the opportunity to reconfigure the global media ecosystem to be more amenable to the PRC's preferred viewpoints and narratives. But it also helps to set the agenda of the very types of stories that are deemed newsworthy. To be

---

[48] Johan Lindberg et al., "The World According to China: Capturing and Analysing the Global Media Influence Strategies of a Superpower," *Pacific Journalism Review* 29, nos. 1–2 (2023): p. 192, https://doi.org/10.24135/pjr.v29i1and2.1317.

[49] Hong, "World's Largest Propaganda Machine," p. 382.

[50] Samuel Brazys and Alexander Dukalskis, "China's Message Machine," *Journal of Democracy* 31, no. 4 (2020): pp. 59–73, https://doi.org/10.1353/jod.2020.0055.

[51] Louisa Lim et al., *The Covid-19 Story: Unmasking China's Global Strategy* (International Federation of Journalists, 2021), p. 5, https://www.ifj.org/fileadmin/user_upload/210512_IFJ_The_Covid_Story_Report_-_FINAL.pdf.

[52] "How the Italian Media (Silently) Broke with Chinese Outlets," Decode39, August 11, 2022, https://decode39.com/3977/italy-media-broke-china-propaganda-ansa-xinhua/.

[53] For example, see a report by the Taiwan FactCheck Center about a doctored Xinhua photo that was unwittingly circulated by international outlets here: "Chinese Propaganda Campaign Demands More Awareness," Taiwan FactCheck Center, September 19, 2022, https://tfc-taiwan.org.tw/articles/8169 (accessed November 11, 2023).

sure, Xinhua content does not always get picked up,[54] nor does it always succeed in agenda-setting,[55] but in certain contexts it can succeed in amplifying China's preferred content to large audiences who may otherwise remain unexposed.[56] Crucially, as Xinhua content is laundered through the host outlet, consumers may not even know that they are being exposed to PRC propaganda.

Figure 5.3 shows the number of content-sharing agreements we were able to find between Chinese state media, including Xinhua, and foreign entities. In total we were able to find public acknowledgment of 302 content-sharing agreements across the world up to 2023, with the vast majority signed after 2010. Figure 5.3 shows the countries in which these agreements were hosted, with darker colors indicating more agreements with media entities in that country. In these data, Thailand shows up as the most frequent partner for content-sharing agreements with Chinese state media entities, with 19 such agreements. Australia is second with 16, although some of these agreements have ended or appear to be ending due to increased skepticism and scrutiny of China's aims.[57] We stress that this is probably an undercount as not all agreements may be public, or some may be technically public but information about them not readily available.

For comparison, Figure 5.4 shows content-sharing agreements with Russian state media entities up to 2023, with almost all agreed from 2014 onward.[58] In total we were able to find evidence for 99 publicly acknowledged agreements, about one-third the Chinese total. Again, darker colors indicate more agreements in that country. Interestingly, the most frequent destination for Russian content-sharing agreements

---

[54] Dani Madrid-Morales, "Who Set the Narrative? Assessing the Influence of Chinese Global Media on News Coverage of COVID-19 in 30 African Countries," *Global Media and China* 6, no. 2 (2021): pp. 129–51, https://doi.org/10.1177/20594364211013714.

[55] Zhuqing Cheng et al., "The Second-Level Agenda-Building Function of the Xinhua News Agency," *Journalism Practice* 10, no. 6 (2016): pp. 744–62, https://doi.org/10.1080/17512786.2015.1063079.

[56] For example, in Thailand, see Kurlantzick, *Beijing's Global Media Offensive*, pp. 194–99.

[57] Fan Yang, "Beijing's Global Media Influence 2022: Australia," Freedom House, https://freedomhouse.org/country/australia/beijings-global-media-influence/2022 (accessed May 3, 2024).

[58] The data underlying Figures 5.3 and 5.4 are available as Appendix 5.3 and Appendix 5.4, respectively.

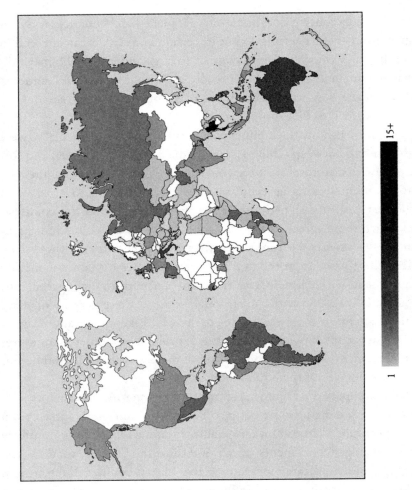

FIGURE 5.3 Content-Sharing Agreements with Chinese State Media (302 total).

is China itself, with 21 such agreements, suggesting not only close media collaboration between the two countries but also Russia's perceived need to maintain a good image in China.

The data show that global spread of authoritarian-backed media is impressive. Authoritarians can disseminate their messages across a range of platforms under a variety of labels. At times they can even find partners willing to help them do it. The reach of authoritarian content is expansive, so it is worth considering what messages they broadcast.

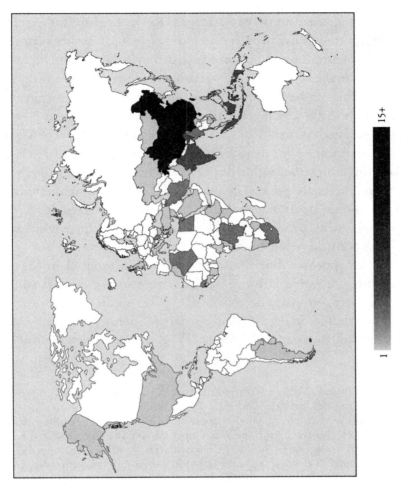

FIGURE 5.4 Content-Sharing Agreements with Russian State Media (99 total).

What Do Authoritarians Say?

In terms of content, authoritarian outlets like RT, CGTN, *China Daily*, TRT World, Egypt's Middle East News Agency, and North Korea's Korea Central News Agency vary in their stylistic output and quality, but they share some commonalities. They rarely, if ever, report on content that undermines their governmental sponsors. As a rule, they laud their leaders uncritically if they report on them and support their state's foreign policy aims.

128   DICTATING THE AGENDA

However, there are some variations. RT in English, for example, rarely reports on Russian politics or Putin as such, at least between 2008 and 2020, instead preferring mostly to denigrate "the West," highlight problems in the United States and Europe, and advance conspiracy theories.[59] This can be seen as part of a broader information strategy to portray Russia as a victim resisting the hegemonic West and protecting its national culture.[60] The strategy is a foundational part of Russia's stated justification for its full-scale invasion of Ukraine in 2022. RT platforms critics from within democracies, including those from the far left interested in opposing US power and from the far right interested in promoting "traditional" values.[61] The aim is to weaken democratic political systems by sowing polarization and distrust, thereby elevating Russia's political system by contrast.

China's approach differs in some respects. The external propaganda platforms are varied in form, but all feature strong message control by the party's propaganda apparatus.[62] PRC media outlets also portray the United States as "poorly governed, plutocratic, racist and a destabilising international influence."[63] Xinhua emphasizes problems

---

[59] Erin Baggott Carter and Brett L. Carter, "Questioning More: RT, Outward-Facing Propaganda, and the Post-West World Order," *Security Studies* 30, no. 1 (2021): pp. 49–78, https://doi.org/10.1080/09636412.2021.1885730; Mona Elswah and Philip N. Howard, "'Anything That Causes Chaos': The Organizational Behavior of Russia Today (RT)," *Journal of Communication* 70, no. 5 (2020): pp. 623–45, https://doi.org/10.1093/joc/jqaa027; Galina Miazhevich, "Nation Branding in the Post-Broadcast Era: The Case of RT," *European Journal of Cultural Studies* 21, no. 5 (2018): pp. 575–93, https://doi.org/10.1177/1367549417751228; Ilya Yablokov, "Conspiracy Theories as a Russian Public Diplomacy Tool: The Case of Russia Today (RT)," *Politics* 35, nos. 3–4 (2015): pp. 301–15, https://doi.org/10.1111/1467-9256.12097.

[60] Yulia Kiseleva, "Russia's Soft Power Discourse: Identity, Status and the Attraction of Power," *Politics* 35, nos. 3–4 (2015): pp. 316–29, https://doi.org/10.1111/1467-9256.12100.

[61] Peter Pomerantsev, "The Kremlin's Information War," *Journal of Democracy* 26, no. 4 (2015), pp. 43–46, https://doi.org/10.1353/jod.2015.0074.

[62] Emeka Umejei, "Chinese Media in Africa: Between Promise and Reality," *African Journalism Studies* 39, no. 2 (2018): pp. 104–20, https://doi.org/10.1080/23743670.2018.1473275; Brazys and Dukalskis, "China's Message Machine."

[63] Thomas Colley and Martin Moore, "News as Geopolitics: China, CGTN and the 2020 US Presidential Election," *Journal of International Communication* 29, no. 1 (2023): pp. 82–103, https://doi.org/10.1080/13216597.2022.2120522.

and shortcomings in Europe and the United States in both its internal and its external content.[64] For example, like its Russian counterpart TASS, Xinhua emphasized themes of US interference and that the United States was at fault in its coverage of 2017–2018 protests in Iran.[65]

However, beyond denigrating rivals, PRC outlets also paint an unremittingly rosy picture of China and its system.[66] According to CCP external propaganda, China is full of rapid economic development, an attractive culture, opportunities to do business, stable global leadership, generosity toward other countries, and so on. Xi Jinping is presented as a uniquely wise and just leader. For example, on the landing page of the English-language website of Xinhua, viewers can see prominently displayed links to dedicated subsites "Xi's Time" and "Xi in My Eyes." Both resemble old-fashioned hagiographic propaganda. The former features quotations, stories, photos, footsteps, and a Xi archive, among others.[67] The latter houses gauzy videos of obsequious foreign commentators sharing how Xi is full of wisdom, always connected to the people and keeping them in his heart, inspiring, a wise philosopher, and so on.[68]

PRC media's positive portrayal of China extends to justifying its own domestic repression. For example, as evidence came to light of Beijing's repression of Uyghurs and other ethnic minorities in Xinjiang, CGTN actively defended its actions, misled audiences about China's true activities, and accused foreign commentators of hypocrisy and bias.[69] Amid international coverage of protests in Hong

---

[64] Brazys and Dukalskis, "China's Message Machine."

[65] Oluseyi Adegbola, Sherice Gearhart, and Janice Cho, "Reporting Bias in Coverage of Iran Protests by Global News Agencies," *International Journal of Press/Politics* 27, no. 1 (2020): pp. 138–57, https://doi.org/10.1177/19401612096694. It should be noted that the evidence for such claims was thin, at best.

[66] Brazys and Dukalskis, "China's Message Machine"; Colley and Moore, "News as Geopolitics."

[67] Full link available here: https://english.news.cn/cnleaders/xistime/ (accessed July 5, 2023).

[68] Full link available here: https://english.news.cn/cnleaders/wyzdxjp/index.htm (accessed July 5, 2023). On June 28, 2023, Xinhua's English-language Twitter account sent a tweet with a video of many of the same foreign personalities extoling the wisdom of Xi Jinping's collected writings as a "modern Chinese masterpiece."

[69] Dukalskis, *Making the World Safe*, pp. 127–34.

Kong, PRC external media portrayed China as a benign and tolerant power being subject to a Western plot to undermine it, amplifying friendly voices supportive of Beijing.[70] It sees criticisms of its policies abroad as emanating from enemies who need to either be tamed or drowned out.[71]

Learning and Adapting to Be More Effective

It is easy to dismiss the effect of authoritarian state media, thinking of it as merely crude propaganda designed to satisfy the bosses back home. Indeed, there are currently real limits to the reach and effectiveness of transnational authoritarian propaganda.[72] Viewership or social media engagement with external propaganda should not be overstated.[73]

But it would be a mistake to entirely disregard the effects of pro-authoritarian propaganda.[74] Exposure can have modest but substantive effects on the public across a range of political contexts[75] and influence

---

[70] Dylan Loh, "Defending China's National Image and 'Defensive Soft Power': The Case of Hong Kong's 'Umbrella Revolution,'" *Journal of Chinese Political Science* 22, no. 1 (2017): pp. 125–29, https://doi.org/10.1007/s11366-016-9419-x.

[71] Tsai, "Enabling China's Voice."

[72] On various limits to China's approach, for example, see Kurlantzick, *Beijing's Global Media Offensive*, pp. 10–12; Zhuqing Cheng et al., "Second-Level Agenda-Building"; Madrid-Morales, "Who Set the Narrative?"; Dani Madrid-Morales and Herman Wasserman, "Chinese Media Engagement in South Africa: What Is Its Impact on Local Journalism?," *Journalism Studies* 19, no. 8 (2018): pp. 1218–35; and Bjorn Jerden and Viking Bohman, *China's Propaganda Campaign in Sweden, 2018–2019* (Swedish Institute of International Affairs, 2019).

[73] Mareike Ohlberg, "Propaganda Beyond the Great Firewall: Chinese Party-State Media on Facebook, Twitter, and YouTube," Mercator Institute for China Studies, 2019, https://www.merics.org/en/china-mapping/propaganda-beyond-the-great-firewall (accessed January 15, 2020).

[74] For a recent review of research on the contours and effects of authoritarian propaganda mostly with a domestic focus, see Bryn Rosenfeld and Jeremy Wallace, "Information Politics and Propaganda in Authoritarian Societies," *Annual Review of Political Science* 27 (2024): pp. 1–19, https://doi.org/10.1146/annurev-polisci-041322-035951.

[75] Daniel Mattingly et al., "Chinese Propaganda Persuades a Global Audience That the 'China Model' Is Superior: Evidence from a 19-Country Experiment," *American Journal of Political Science* (forthcoming, 2024), https://doi.org/10.1111/ajps.12887.

the viewpoints of other media professionals.[76] Studies of Russian outlets have found that respondents are less likely to support US foreign policy after being exposed to RT,[77] that RT's coverage of the 2018 World Cup helped generate positive images of Russia in focus groups and on social media,[78] that RT and Sputnik can help amplify identity grievance narratives and distrust in political institutions among young men and far-right supporters,[79] and that RT and Sputnik have genuine appeal for some segments of liberal democratic polities.[80] In terms of China, a 19-country survey experiment of CGTN content shows that respondents exposed to the treatment have strikingly more positive attitudes toward China's authoritarian political model than the control group.[81] Survey evidence suggests that China's media expansion in six African states between 2007 and 2013 led to modestly more positive views of China.[82] Crucially, authoritarian media actors learn and adapt their media methods and cooperate with one another with the aim of improving over time.[83]

Tentative results like this and the prospect of learning become more important when one considers the ambition of authoritarian media to dictate the agenda. Beyond just pumping out propaganda and promoting content agreements, authoritarian states are attempting to reconfigure and reclaim the global information sphere so that it is

---

[76] Madrid-Morales and Wasserman, "Chinese Media Engagement," p. 1228.

[77] Carter and Carter, "Questioning More."

[78] Rhys Crilley et al., "'Russia Isn't a Country of Putin's!': How RT Bridged the Credibility Gap in Russian Public Diplomacy During the 2018 FIFA World Cup," *British Journal of Politics and International Relations* 24, no. 1 (2022): pp. 136–52, https://doi.org/10.1177/13691481211013713.

[79] Charlotte Wagnsson, "The Paperboys of Russian Messaging: RT/Sputnik Audiences as Vehicles for Malign Information Influence," *Information, Communication & Society* 26, no. 9 (2023): pp. 1849–67, https://doi.org/10.1080/1369118X.2022.2041700.

[80] Charlotte Wagnsson et al., "'Keeping an Eye on the Other Side': RT, Sputnik, and Their Peculiar Appeal in Democratic Societies," *International Journal of Press/Politics* 2023, https://doi.org/10.1177/19401612221147492.

[81] Mattingly et al., "Chinese Propaganda Persuades."

[82] Catie Snow Bailard, "China in Africa: An Analysis of the Effect of Chinese Media Expansion on African Public Opinion," *International Journal of Press/Politics* 21, no. 4 (2016): pp. 446–71, https://doi.org/10.1177/1940161216646733.

[83] Kurlantzick, *Beijing's Global Media Offensive*, pp. 13–15, 95–99.

132   DICTATING THE AGENDA

friendlier to their narratives. With a focus on China, the aforementioned IFJ, one of the largest journalist union and advocacy groups in the world, concluded in a research report and survey of its members that across media types, Beijing is engaged in a sophisticated and "long-term effort to reshape the global news landscape with a China-friendly global narrative."[84]

Sometimes this strategy targets Chinese-speaking populations specifically. A 2018 *Financial Times* investigation revealed over 200 content-sharing agreements between party-affiliated media and Chinese language outlets abroad.[85] Sometimes the strategy is to co-opt the organizational foundations of journalistic activism, as when the corporatist All China Journalists Association (ACJA) signs memoranda of understanding (MOU) with journalist unions abroad.[86] While we have some evidence that this tactic has been deployed on unions in Europe, Asia, and Africa, the MOUs that the ACJA offers generally include nondisclosure agreements, making their content and effects difficult to grasp systematically.[87]

The Importance of Online and Social Media

Efforts like the expansion of Xinhua as a wire service or the promotion of RT or Türkiye's TRT World as a television station or website are efforts to reclaim the traditional media space, but authoritarian media actors also find success in social media and other nontraditional online spaces.[88] RT seized on the rise of YouTube to promote its messages and

---

[84] "The China Story: Reshaping the World's Media," International Federation of Journalists, 2020, p. 8, https://www.ifj.org/fileadmin/user_upload/IFJ_Report_2020_-_The_China_Story.pdf.

[85] Emily Feng, "China and the World: How Beijing Spreads the Message," *Financial Times*, July 12, 2018, https://www.ft.com/content/f5d00a86-3296-11e8-b5bf-23cb17fd1498.

[86] Lindberg et al., "World According to China."

[87] Lindberg et al., "World According to China," p. 192. The MOUs that have become available suggest that there can be substantial variation in the degree of partnership, with some being mostly on paper only and others seeing ACJA provide material support.

[88] The literature on domestic internet controls and practices of authoritarian states is vast. For a book-length study of Chinese internet controls, see Margaret E.

became one of the most viewed news outlets on the platform, far outpacing China's CGTN, for example, and performing particularly well with its Spanish-language content (at least until renewed scrutiny and a European ban on RT after the invasion of Ukraine).[89] Likewise North Korea has learned to use YouTube, including modern influencer strategies, to advance its messages on the platform.[90] Chinese outlets and commentators make frequent use of Twitter, YouTube, and Facebook despite the fact that they are all inaccessible in the PRC itself.[91] Sometimes the origins of this content is deliberately obscured, as when a *New York Times* investigation found that the Chinese propaganda apparatus is often involved in funding, organizing, and supporting pro-CCP

Roberts, *Censored: Distraction and Diversion Inside China's Great Firewall* (Princeton University Press, 2018). For recent comparative studies, see Nils B. Weidmann and Espen Geelmuyden Rød, *The Internet and Political Protest in Autocracies* (Oxford University Press, 2019); and Anita R. Gohdes, *Repression in the Digital Age: Surveillance, Censorship, and the Dynamics of State Violence* (Oxford University Press, 2024). The transnational effects of authoritarian internet control are less studied, but still some important work has been done. On the internet and authoritarian states controlling their diaspora populations and exiles, for example, see Dana M. Moss, "The Ties That Bind: Internet Communication Technologies, Networked Authoritarianism, and 'Voice' in the Syrian Diaspora," *Globalizations* 15, no. 2 (2018): pp. 265–82, https://doi.org/10.1080/14747731.2016.1263079; Marcus Michaelsen, "Far Away, So Close: Transnational Activism, Digital Surveillance and Authoritarian Control in Iran," *Surveillance & Society* 15, nos. 3–4 (2017): pp. 465–70, https://doi.org/10.24908/ss.v15i3/4.6635; and Marcus Michaelsen and Johannes Thumfart, "Drawing a Line: Digital Transnational Repression Against Political Exiles and Host State Sovereignty," *European Journal of International Security* 8, no. 2 (2023): pp. 151–71, https://doi.org/10.1017/eis.2022.27. On the pro-Russian social media sphere extending to migrants in Germany, see Tatiana Golova, "Post-Soviet Migrants in Germany, Transnational Public Spheres and Russian Soft Power," *Journal of Information Technology & Politics* 17, no. 3 (2020): pp. 249–67, https://doi.org/10.1080/19331681.2020.1742265.

[89] On RT's YouTube strategy, see Robert W. Orttung and Elizabeth Nelson, "Russia Today's Strategy and Effectiveness on YouTube," *Post-Soviet Affairs* 35, no. 2 (2019): 77–92, https://doi.org/10.1080/19331681.2020.1742265.

[90] Han Woo Park and Yon Soo Lim, "Do North Korean Social Media Show Signs of Change? An Examination of a YouTube Channel Using Qualitative Tagging and Social Network Analysis," *Journal of Contemporary Eastern Asia* 19, no. 1 (2019): pp. 123–43; Christian Davies, "YouTube Cracks Down on North Korean Vloggers Presenting Regime's 'Likeable' Face," *Financial Times*, June 30, 2023.

[91] Marcel Schliebs et al., "China's Public Diplomacy Operations: Understanding Engagement and Inauthentic Amplifications of PRC Diplomats on Facebook and Twitter," Oxford University, 2021.

foreign YouTube influencers who do not disclose their affiliations to their viewers.[92] Recent reports by Taiwan-based DoubleThink Lab illustrate how pro-CCP social media accounts sought to manipulate online narratives about repression in Hong Kong and Xinjiang.[93] Likewise pro-Russia but apparently nonstate social media influencers in Africa and elsewhere amplify Moscow's justifications for its invasion of Ukraine and interface with pro-Kremlin groups and media outlets.[94] To be sure, pro-authoritarian online content is not always state directed from the top-down,[95] but the increasing power of authoritarian states allows them to amplify those perspectives, reach across borders to target critics, and manipulate global media networks to their advantage.

The global growth of PRC-affiliated or owned apps like TikTok and WeChat along with the information hardware supplied by PRC companies like Huawei constitutes a further step to shape the global media ecosystem. Indeed, even now, WeChat monitors the content for users outside of China to better train its censorship algorithms and censors messages between users inside and outside of China[96] and TikTok

---

[92] Paul Mozur et al., "How Beijing Influences the Influencers," *New York Times*, December 13, 2021.

[93] DoubleThink Lab, *Whitewashing Hong Kong*, 2023; DoubleThink Lab, *Whitewashing East Turkestan*, 2023. Both reports available here: https://medium.com/doublethinklab/reports-whitewashing-hong-kong-and-east-turkistan-c00dfc423dc5.

[94] Grigor Atanesian, "Russia in Africa: How Disinformation Operations Target the Continent," BBC, February 1, 2023, https://www.bbc.com/news/world-africa-64451376; Elian Peltier et al., "How Putin Became a Hero on African TV," *New York Times*, April 13, 2023, https://www.nytimes.com/2023/04/13/world/africa/russia-africa-disinformation.html.

[95] With reference to the Middle East, for example, see Alexei Abrahams and Andrew Leber, "Electronic Armies or Cyber Knights? The Sources of Pro-Authoritarian Discourse on Middle East Twitter," *International Journal of Communication* 15 (2021): pp. 1173–99.

[96] Jeffrey Knockel et al., *We Chat, They Watch: How International Users Unwittingly Build Up WeChat's Chinese Censorship Apparatus* (CitizenLab, 2020), https://tspace.library.utoronto.ca/bitstream/1807/101395/1/Report%23127—wechattheywatch-web.pdf. For a discussion of the implications of algorithms and AI for authoritarian propaganda, see Rosenfeld and Wallace, "Information Politics and Propaganda," pp. 13–14.

appears to dampen the spread of certain topics globally that are at odds with the PRC's viewpoints.[97]

Inauthentic, deliberately obscured, and misleading media content hints at the melding of global authoritarian media's advance and concepts like information warfare. The global information sphere has long been characterized by "active measures" that seek to undermine opponents, sow confusion, mislead publics, and bolster the image of the purveyor.[98] Today debates about influence operations by China and Russia have an information dimension insofar as they aim to manipulate the public spheres of democratic societies for the advantage of the authoritarian state.[99] In his study of China's global media aspirations, for example, Kurlantzick notes the PRC's turn to sharper and more covert methods of influence after its softer "charm offensive" tactics meet their limits.[100]

Authoritarian Learning and Snapback in the Global Media Sphere

The adaptation and blurring of methods are emblematic of the authoritarian learning and cooperation that characterizes the authoritarian snapback. The learning can happen on two levels.[101] First, states can learn and modify based on their own previous experiences.[102] PRC diplomats and state media, for example, may have

---

[97] See "A Tik-Tok-ing Timebomb: How TikTok's Global Platform Anomalies Align with the Chinese Communist Party's Geostrategic Objectives," Network Contagion Research Institute and Rutgers University Miller Center on Policing and Community Resilience, December 21, 2023, https://networkcontagion.us/wp-content/uploads/A-Tik-Tok-ing-Timebomb_12.21.23.pdf.

[98] Thomas Rid, *Active Measures: The Secret History of Disinformation and Political Warfare* (Farrar, Straus, and Giroux, 2020).

[99] See, for example, Martin Kragh and Sebastian Åsberg, "Russia's Strategy for Influence Through Public Diplomacy and Active Measures: The Swedish Case," *Journal of Strategic Studies* 40, no. 6 (2017): pp. 773–816, https://doi.org/10.1080/01402390.2016.1273830; and Alex Joske, *Spies and Lies: How China's Greatest Covert Operations Fooled the World* (Hardie Grant Publishing, 2022).

[100] Kurlantzick, *Beijing's Global Media Offensive*, pp. 69, 75.

[101] For a general version of this two-level-learning argument, see Stephen G. F. Hall, *The Authoritarian International: Tracing How Authoritarian Regimes Learn in the Post-Soviet Space* (Cambridge University Press, 2023).

[102] For example, Kurlantzick, *Beijing's Global Media Offensive*, pp. 13–15.

modified their aggressive "Wolf Warrior" approach to public diplomacy in 2021 in some places after seeing it backfire and damage China's image.[103] On a second level, authoritarian states can learn and adapt methods from one another. As mentioned previously, for example, Moscow and Beijing have taken steps to share knowledge and integrate aspects of their propaganda messaging. Russian and Chinese media entities have signed several agreements over the last 10 years to share content and production and swap tactics with one another at meetings and forums, moves supported by the two countries' leaders.[104]

How do these broad trends presented so far apply to the authoritarian snapback model outlined in the previous chapter? Authoritarian backed media have as one of their core objectives to discredit "Western" media reporting on their countries, thus *stigmatizing* the coverage. The aim is to undermine people's confidence in reporting that may be critical of their state. This theme appears across regime type and geography in authoritarian state and state-linked media as well as the words of their leaders, from Russia[105] to China[106] to Türkiye[107] to Iran[108]

---

[103] Samuel Brazys et al., "Leader of the Pack? Changes in 'Wolf Warrior Diplomacy' After a Politburo Collective Study Session," *China Quarterly* 254 (2023): pp. 484–93, https://doi.org/10.1017/S0305741022001722.

[104] Elena Soboleva, "How Does China Engage with Russia's Media Market?," *The Diplomat*, May 2, 2023, https://thediplomat.com/2023/05/how-does-china-engage-with-russias-media-market/; David Bandurski, "China and Russia Are Joining Forces to Spread Disinformation," Brookings Institution, March 11, 2022, https://www.brookings.edu/articles/china-and-russia-are-joining-forces-to-spread-disinformation/; Maria Repnikova, *China-Russia Strategic Communications: Evolving Visions and Practices* (Background Research Gates Forum 1, 2022), pp. 23–25, https://docs.aiddata.org/ad4/pdfs/gf1_05_China-Russia_Strategic_Communications.pdf; Kurlantzick, *Beijing's Global Media Offensive*, pp. 95–99, 242.

[105] For example, see "Whole World Suffers from Western Propaganda" RT, November 2, 2022, https://www.rt.com/news/565804-western-propaganda-ukraine-conflict/.

[106] For example, see Xia Wenxin, "Western Media Fits Label of Propaganda," *Global Times*, April 29, 2021, https://www.globaltimes.cn/page/202104/1222469.shtml.

[107] For example, see "Biased Western Media Trying to Influence Decision of Turkish Voters," *TRT World*, May 14, 2024, https://www.trtworld.com/turkiye/biased-western-media-trying-to-influence-decision-of-turkish-voters-13196039.

[108] For example, see Mohammed Ghaderi, "Reuters' Tales These Days," Mehr News Agency, July 4, 2018, https://en.mehrnews.com/news/135395/Reuters-tales-these-days.

to Rwanda[109] to Cambodia[110] to Venezuela[111] to North Korea[112] to Myanmar[113] and beyond.

Beyond stigmatizing, many authoritarian states block media outlets from liberal democracies, thus *shielding* their population from alternative voices. In China, media outlets like the *New York Times*, BBC, *The Guardian*, Reuters, *The Economist*, Canadian and Australian Broadcasting Corporations, and many others, as well as platforms like Twitter, YouTube, Facebook, and Google are blocked. Vernacular versions of the BBC have been blocked in Iran, Rwanda, Vietnam, China, North Korea, Afghanistan, Uzbekistan, and others. Sometimes the shielded content is replaced by other pro-authoritarian external media. For example, written evidence in May 2021 to the UK Parliament from the BBC World Service noted that after the February 2021 military coup in Myanmar, "most international TV news channels including BBC World News, CNN and Channel News Asia have been blocked. CGTN in English remains on air."[114]

Engagement is reframed and new ground rules are set as foreign journalists are encouraged to be friendly interlocutors. China's foreign minister, Wang Yi, said in 2019, for example, that the model for foreign journalists should be Edgar Snow, a sympathetic American commentator who lauded Mao and the CCP.[115] To help create more

---

[109] For example, see Patient Kwizera, "Routine Military Overhaul Exposes Western Journalists' Bias on Rwanda," *New Times*, June 13, 2023, https://www .newtimes.co.rw/article/8217/opinions/routine-military-overhaul-exposes-western-journalists-bias-on-rwanda.

[110] For example, see "Military Modernisation Is Obligation, No Foreign Military Base in Cambodia," Agence Kampuchea Press, June 14, 2022, http://www.akp.gov .kh/post/detail/255849.

[111] For example, see https://www.telesurtv.net/analisis/Prensa-hegemonica-censura-a-Maduro-y-legitima-incursion-militar-en-Venezuela-20170823-0059.html.

[112] For example, see "DPRK Is Not Such Country as Described by West: Foreign Visitors," KCNA Watch, August 24, 2013, https://kcnawatch.org/newstream/ 1451895840-557321586/dprk-is-not-such-country-as-described-by-west-foreign-vis itors/.

[113] For example, see "Myanmar Accuses Foreign Media of 'Skyful of Lies,'" Reuters, September 27, 2007, https://www.reuters.com/article/uk-myanmar-media-idUKBKK25444220070927.

[114] Full statement here: https://committees.parliament.uk/writtenevidence/ 36487/pdf/.

[115] See Xu Wei, "Edgar Snow Is Model for Foreign Journalists, Wang Yi Says," *China Daily*, March 7, 2021, https://www.chinadaily.com.cn/a/202103/07/ WS60449ce9a31024adobaad662.html.

sympathetic journalists globally, Beijing has myriad training programs that bring journalists to China, sometimes for up to 10 months, to try to coax more positive coverage about the country.[116] Select journalists or other figures from abroad are brought on officially organized tours to areas like Xinjiang in China[117] or Russia's occupied areas of Ukraine[118] so that they produce stories that align with the state's official viewpoints. For authoritarian states, criticism and perceived bias from those who do not comply with the injunction to be sympathetic are often reframed as an attack on the entire people.[119] Ultimately foreign journalists who persist may face new barriers to their reporting, a topic the next section addresses. The final steps of *projecting control and influence outward* and *dictating the agenda* come as the authoritarian media advance sees pro-authoritarian content spread, platforms repurposed, information laundered through wire services and content-sharing agreements, and norms and infrastructure altered to be friendlier to authoritarianism. The process is facilitated by learning from previous experience and from the activities of other states.

Authoritarian Silencing: Repression of Foreign Journalists

While authoritarian states advance their narratives, they also try to snuff out alternative ones and restrict the space available to

---

[116] Dukalskis, *Making the World Safe*, pp. 123–26; Kurlantzick, *Beijing's Global Media Offensive*, pp. 165–71.

[117] Kate Wong and David Bogi, "How China Uses Muslim Press Trips to Counter Claims of Uighur Abuse," *The Guardian*, August 23, 2020, https://www.theguardian.com/world/2020/aug/23/how-china-uses-muslim-press-trips-to-counter-claims-of-uighur-abuse (accessed May 3, 2024).

[118] "'Press Tours' to Occupied Ukrainian Territories," Estonian Foreign Intelligence Service, https://raport.valisluureamet.ee/2024/en/4-russian-influence-activities/4-1-press-tours-to-occupied-ukrainian-territories/ (accessed May 3, 2024).

[119] For example, in Rwanda, see Sila Cehreli and Gatete Nyiringabo Ruhumilza, "Do Not Mislead: A Rejoinder of Michele Wrong's Book, 'Do Not Disturb,'" *New Times*, April 27, 2021, https://www.newtimes.co.rw/article/185636/Opinions/do-not-mislead-a-rejoinder-of-michela-wrongas-book-ado-not-disturba. For a book-length analysis of this phenomenon in China, see Jamie J. Gruffydd-Jones, *Hostile Forces: How the Chinese Communist Party Resists International Pressure on Human Rights* (Oxford University Press, 2022).

independent outlets to report on their country, including foreign reporters. The global trend appears to be toward more government control and media restrictions. As noted at the outset of this chapter, 2023 saw the first espionage case brought against a foreign journalist in Russia since the Cold War. China from 2018 onward ramped up its expulsion of foreign journalists. In general, authoritarian states censor the press more than their democratic counterparts.[120] But they go beyond this in their outreach abroad, such as when they cooperate with foreign enablers to discredit or sue critics[121] and try to stem the tide of critical information by repressing reporters whose messages may circulate transnationally.

Most violent repression of journalists is meted out against the domestic press, with one data set showing that between 2003 and 2013 "93% of all journalists killed were working locally; only 7% of all journalists killed were working in a foreign country."[122] Often the perpetrator is not the central government but rather local actors fearful of negative coverage for one reason or another.[123] The jailing of journalists appears to have increased since around the mid-2000s.[124] Figure 5.5 presents the global trend in V-Dem's *Harassment of Journalists* variable, in which higher numbers indicate more respect and lower numbers indicate more harassment. Consistent with trends in the jailing of journalists and broader elements of global liberalism, it

---

[120] Sebastian Stier, "Democracy, Autocracy, and the News: The Impact of Regime Type on Media Freedom," *Democratization* 22, no. 7 (2015): pp. 1273–95, https://doi.org/10.1080/13510347.2014.964643.

[121] For a taxonomy of tactics of authoritarian transnational 'spin' tactics, see Sergei Guriev and Daniel Treisman, *Spin Dictators: The Changing Face of Tyranny in the 21st Century* (Princeton University Press, 2022), pp. 147–56.

[122] Anita R. Gohdes and Sabine C. Carey, "Canaries in a Coal-Mine? What the Killings of Journalists Tell Us About Future Repression," *Journal of Peace Research* 54, no. 2 (2017): pp. 157–74, https://doi.org/10.1177/0022343316680859. The IFJ tracks journalist killings annually. For the 2023 report, see IFJ, "Ninety-Four Journalists Killed in 2023, Says IFG," December 8, 2023, https://www.ifj.org/media-centre/news/detail/category/press-releases/article/ninety-four-journalists-killed-in-2023-says-ifj (accessed May 3, 2024).

[123] Anita R. Gohdes and Sabine C. Carey, "Understanding Journalist Killings," *Journal of Politics* 83, no. 4 (2021): pp. 1216–28, https://doi.org/10.1086/715172.

[124] Andrew T. Little and Anne Meng, "Measuring Democratic Backsliding," *PS: Political Science & Politics* 57, no. 2 (2024): p. 8, https://doi.org/10.1017/S104909652300063X.

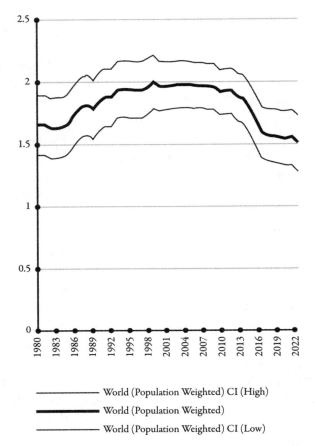

FIGURE 5.5 Trends in Protection of Journalists According to V-Dem.

appears as if there was a plateau in protections for journalists followed by a degradation in recent years.

Beyond harassing or jailing journalists at home, authoritarian states can directly target their exiled journalists abroad, with the assassination of Jamal Khashoggi the most notorious example. In what is surely an underestimate, between 1991 and 2019, at least 163 episodes saw journalists targeted by their home authoritarian states for transnational repression while they were abroad. This includes four assassinations, four additional assassination attempts (including one in which 20 journalists were targeted in Armenia by Iranian secret police in a failed attempt to stage a bus crash), nine abductions, six extraditions, four attacks, and numerous threats, extradition attempts, and threats to the journalist's families remaining in the state.[125]

Authoritarian states or parties can also repress or otherwise silence critical messengers abroad using other methods. Turkish authorities, for example, forced European newspapers critical of the ruling party to shut down after a campaign of intimidation.[126] Chinese officials in Australia have intimidated Chinese-language news outlets there and exerted pressure on advertisers to refrain from supporting critical outlets.[127] Indeed, some evidence suggests that in democracies more trade dependence on China results in a more restricted media space when it comes to China-related issues.[128]

However, one of the most direct methods to influence the narrative about themselves is for authoritarian states to try to frustrate or inhibit the work of foreign journalists.[129] Foreign correspondents and transnational freelancers play a key role in the global media ecosystem in breaking news about authoritarian states. Because domestic journalists in authoritarian states often do not have the latitude to report on issues that may portray the government in a negative light (or be censored if they do), coverage of those stories often is taken up by their foreign colleagues. Foreign journalists play an outsized role in explaining the place they are reporting from to international readers, thereby helping to shape that state's image, including through their social media posts or videos.[130]

Foreign journalists, while not activists per se, often press for greater press freedoms in their host states, for example through foreign correspondents clubs, professional unions, or with the support of advocacy organizations like Reporters Without Borders, Forbidden Stories, or

---

[125] These figures come from the Authoritarian Actions Abroad Database published in Dukalskis, *Making the World Safe.*

[126] Marlies Glasius, *Authoritarian Practices in a Global Age* (Oxford University Press, 2023), pp. 41–45.

[127] Kurlantzick, *Beijing's Global Media Offensive*, pp. 125–26.

[128] Jonas Gamso, "Is China Exporting Media Censorship? China's Rise, Media Freedoms, and Democracy," *European Journal of International Relations* 27, no. 3 (2021): pp. 858–83, https://doi.org/10.1177/13540661211015722.

[129] Dukalskis, *Making the World Safe*, pp. 83–110.

[130] See Dukalskis, *Making the World Safe*, pp. 83–84.

the IFJ. The type of journalism they support and the topics they select therefore often sit at odds with the preferred role for journalism of the authoritarian state. As a result, they often find themselves and their work in the crosshairs of autocratic actors. Although direct violent repression is sometimes used against foreign journalists in authoritarian states, generally the repressive measures meted out against foreign journalists, especially those associated with high-profile outlets from the West, are more subtle and rely on access denial.[131]

In the remainder of this section, we present new data on authoritarian states restricting access to foreign journalists. Consistent with the sequences of authoritarian snapback introduced in the previous chapter, these data illustrate the scope of *shielding* and *reframing engagement and setting new ground rules* undertaken by authoritarian governments between 1999 and 2023 against foreign journalists. Doing so helps *project control and influence outward* by shaping the global narrative about the state. This is bound up with the changing global media landscape described previously, as well as the backlash against advocacy and civil society by authoritarians covered in previous chapters.

The Authoritarian Restrictions on Foreign Journalists (ARFJ) Data Set

We were interested in instances of when authoritarian governments denied or revoked access to foreign reporters using a range of tactics. To compile the data, we began with the group of authoritarian states in the bottom 30% of the V-Dem Liberal Democracy Index for 2021 and looked for events in those states over the entire period. As we found more events in other countries, we included them if they were in the bottom 50% of the index for 2021. We then included a few exceptions, including states that had experienced large improvements in the index

---

[131] This is not to minimize the seriousness of direct repression when it does occur. As discussed in the introduction to this chapter, for example, Evan Gershkovich of the *Wall Street Journal* was arrested in March 2023 in Russia allegedly for espionage and was only released in a prisoner exchange in August 2024. American citizen Jason Rezaian, former bureau chief for *The Washington Post* in Tehran, for example, was arrested and tried by Iranian authorities for espionage, among other alleged crimes and held for nearly two years between 2014 and 2016. Episodes like this are dramatic and are the most extreme manifestation of authoritarian states' repression of foreign journalists.

for 2021 but were near the bottom in previous years, or states that significantly autocratized after 2021. For example, we included events in Burkina Faso after the 2022 coup there even though the country scored well on the LDI for 2021.

These data are presented in Appendix 5.5 as the Authoritarian Restrictions on Foreign Journalists (ARFJ) data set. The ARFJ documents 1,020 instances in which states restricted the activities of journalists between 1999 and 2023. Of course, some authoritarian states, like North Korea, essentially bar access to all foreign journalists except on tightly scripted tours, but these general restrictions are not counted in the ARFJ. Instead, we focus on events in which the country is ostensibly open to foreign journalists but their access is explicitly restricted. We also do not account for spying or surveillance on journalists, an activity that occurs but is difficult to quantify.[132] There are a range of obstacles, both subtle and clumsy, that authoritarian states engineer to frustrate foreign journalists, but we are only able to capture a small sample of them. Accordingly, the ARFJ presents only the tip of the proverbial iceberg of authoritarian harassment of foreign journalists, and there are certainly many instances that are not recorded publicly or not captured here.

Nonetheless, we attempt to record as much as we can. To do so we operate with the following categories of restrictions: *Denied Visa/Accreditation/Entry* captures instances in which the journalist was not able to enter or re-enter the country. Sometimes this occurs when a foreign journalist attempts to enter the country temporarily to cover a specific event such as an election or summit. At other times the denial comes when a foreign correspondent stationed in the country seeks to renew his or her credentials but is denied. In general, a reason is not given for this form of restriction, although it can usually be inferred. *Expelled/Deported/Forced to Flee* captures instances in which the journalist is either officially deported or expelled, or compelled to leave, usually after threats or advice to do so. *Detained for Extended Period* records instances in which the journalist was detained for more than a few hours. Sometimes it is difficult to discern from the public record the length of detention, but if brief detention is followed by the

---

[132] See Dukalskis, *Making the World Safe*, pp. 83–110.

journalist leaving the country, we code it as *Expelled/Deported/Forced to Flee*. However, if the detention is prolonged and/or carries the threat of criminal charges that would see the journalist imprisoned, then we code it as *Detained for Extended Period*. The code *Outlet Disallowed* records instances in which a particular media outlet is no longer allowed to operate or broadcast in the country. Sometimes this occurs simultaneously with revocation of visas or accreditation, but at other times it is unclear.[133] In a few instances the event was difficult to categorize specifically, and so we used a residual category of *Harassed*. Sources for the database come from reputable watchdog groups like Reporters Without Borders and the Committee to Protect Journalists or from media outlets themselves.

To the extent possible we attempt to disaggregate each episode so that it captures one thing happening to one person or entity at one point in time. To qualify for inclusion in the database, the target of the action must be a foreign citizen. This discounts some important cases, as when Myanmar journalists Wa Lone and Kyaw Soe, who worked for Reuters, were jailed for nearly two years after investigating the murder of Rohingya men and boys by the security services in 2017.[134] Also not recorded are restrictions imposed by states about domestic citizens working with foreign journalists, as in China and Belarus, among other places. These are important insofar as they erect barriers between domestic and international journalists, but they are not recorded here, as reliable data on them proved difficult to aggregate.

With these caveats in mind, this data-gathering exercise yielded 1,020 cases of foreign journalists restricted by states in the bottom of V-Dem's Liberal Democracy Index between 1999 and 2023.[135] Figure 5.6 shows the total number of events per year over the entire

---

[133] In four instances China demanded extra information, including about finances, from outlets in order for them to re-register in the country. We coded this as *Extra Restrictions for Accreditation* because we thought it was important although seemingly rare.

[134] See the full story here: Simon Lewis and Shoon Naing, "Two Reuters Reporters Freed in Myanmar After More Than 500 Days in Jail," Reuters, May 7, 2019, https://www.reuters.com/article/us-myanmar-journalists/two-reuters-reporters-freed-in-myanmar-after-more-than-500-days-in-jail-idUSKCN1SD056.

[135] We used the V-Dem list from 2021 to generate our list of states.

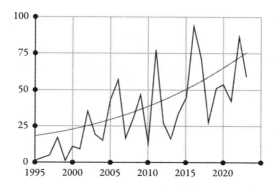

FIGURE 5.6 Yearly Count of Restrictions on Foreign Journalists in ARFJ Data.

timespan. While time trends in such messy data should be taken with a grain of salt, restrictions appear to be becoming more common, which broadly coheres with trends in V-Dem's Harassment of Journalists data and the jailing of journalists discussed previously. The years 2016, 2022, and 2011 were, in that order, the top three for restrictions in the data set by some distance.

Table 5.1 reports the most frequent actions. Clearly, *Denied Visa/Accreditation/Entry* and *Expelled/Deported/Forced to Flee* are the most common tactics to control the ability of foreign journalists to report, accounting together for over 80% of cases. These types of restrictions may not make the headlines as much as more dramatic or violent cases but they appear to constitute the "go to" tools for autocrats wishing to limit the work of foreign journalists.

Table 5.2 shows the 10 countries that most frequently appear in the ARFJ data. As becomes clear from the table, a range of states restrict

Table 5.1 Most Frequent Actions in the ARFJ, 1999–2023

Action	Count	Percentage of Total Cases
Denied Visa/Accreditation/Entry	429	42%
Expelled/Deported/Forced to Flee	403	40%
Detained for Extended Period	99	10%
Outlet Disallowed	66	6%

146 DICTATING THE AGENDA

Table 5.2 Most Frequent Countries in the ARFJ, 1999–2023

Country	Count	% of Total ARFJ Cases	2021 V-Dem Liberal Democracy Index Global Ranking
Russia	138	14%	Bottom 20%
Azerbaijan	70	7%	Bottom 10%
China	56	5%	Bottom 10%
Türkiye	55	5%	Bottom 20%
Burma/Myanmar	48	5%	Bottom 20%
Libya	43	4%	Bottom 30%
Belarus	38	4%	Bottom 10%
Zimbabwe	37	4%	Bottom 30%
Venezuela	35	3%	Bottom 20%
Uzbekistan	25	2%	Bottom 10%

the activities of foreign journalists frequently. By regime type, the list features competitive authoritarian regimes like Türkiye, military ones like Burma/Myanmar, single-party states like China, and personalist regimes like Russia, Azerbaijan, and Belarus. Two monarchies, Qatar and Bahrain, just miss out on the top 10, with 24 and 21 events in the database, respectively. Geographically, states from Europe, Africa, Asia, the Middle East, and Central Asia appear. Journalistic restrictions are a phenomenon of authoritarian politics, not culture or geography. Russia is the clear "leader" on this list, although Azerbaijan, Zimbabwe, Libya, and Belarus stand out as having relatively small populations and likely fewer foreign journalists to restrict in the first place relative to larger and strategically more important states like Türkiye, Russia, and China.

Nevertheless, it is notable that both Russia and China appear so highly on this list. Earlier in this chapter we argued that both states are attempting to reshape the global media environment by expanding the channels through which they can disseminate messages and adapting to new realities. The ARFJ data show that both states pair this effort with measures to clamp down on critical reporting. Not content to broadcast propaganda, both states want to deprive independent reporters and outlets of the information they need to produce stories. While disseminating their messages widely to global audiences and using Western platforms to undermine the West, they shield themselves from the same scrutiny.

The immediate aim of these kinds of restrictions is to *shield* audiences from information or analysis that the government does not want to be broadcast. If a journalist cannot access the country then it is more difficult to reliably report on it. Sources are harder to cultivate, images and colorful details are scarcer, facts are more difficult to verify, and the reliability and authenticity that comes from being "on the ground" are undermined.[136] Not only does this mean that reporters' jobs are harder, but it also leaves them open to accusations of inaccuracy ("How could you possibly know the situation if you're not here?") and bias ("She only reports negatively on our country because she's aggrieved at being denied a visa"). Therefore *engagement is reframed and new ground rules are set*: Report favorably or access will be denied. The resulting information void can be filled with the pro-authoritarian state media discussed in the first part of this chapter.

Conclusion: Reconfiguration and Response

This chapter has provided an overview of the ways in which today's authoritarian states are attempting to reconfigure the global media landscape. The examples cited at the beginning of this chapter, namely the detention of Evan Gershkovich in Russia and the growing influence of RT, illustrate the two sides of the strategy. The reconfiguration of global media to be more friendly to authoritarian states comprises both restrictions on the content that is reported about authoritarian states themselves and the outward reach and amplification of pro-authoritarian

---

[136] Although the effectiveness of these strategies should not be assumed. DeButts and Pan, for example, analyzed select media outlets after their journalists were expelled from China in 2020 and found little discernible difference in coverage, arguing that news outlets adapted to compensate for reduced access. See Matt DeButts and Jennifer Pan, "Reporting After Removal: The Effects of Journalist Expulsion on Foreign News Coverage," *Journal of Communication* (2024): jqae15, https://doi.org/10.1093/joc/jqae015.

media. Much as censorship shields propaganda from scrutiny, the idea is to reduce the amount and quality of information critical of authoritarian governments while simultaneously amplifying pro-government content. All five stages of the snapback model can be seen in the actions described throughout this chapter, with earlier stages corresponding more to restrictions and access denial and the more ambitious steps in the model corresponding to the global authoritarian media advance. The result is a preview of what a global authoritarian public sphere would look like.

However, we are not there yet. Although authoritarians have made great strides in reshaping the global media space, they are not yet completely dictating the agenda. Freedom of the press remains a valued norm worldwide, despite its erosion at the hands of authoritarian states and illiberal movements within the West. A 34-country survey by Pew in 2019 found that about two-thirds of respondents said that press freedom is very important to their country.[137] Legacy media like the *Economist* or *Guardian* are learning to cope with the changed face of the global media industry. Furthermore, the internet has made high-quality specialist information about authoritarian states, such as *NK News*, which focuses on North Korea, available to global audiences more easily and quickly. We will return in more detail to proposed solutions to the problems raised in this book in our conclusion, but when it comes to media, liberal democratic states should preserve their own press freedoms, fund independent public broadcasters appropriately, insulate them from political pressures, and raise media literacy standards for citizens through public information campaigns.

---

[137] Richard Wike and Shannon Schumacher, "Democratic Rights Popular Globally but Commitment to Them Not Always Strong," Pew Research Center, 2020, https://www.pewresearch.org/global/2020/02/27/democratic-rights-popular-globally-but-commitment-to-them-not-always-strong/ (accessed November 13, 2023).

Chapter 6

Repurposing Global Consumer Activism

In 1984 workers at Dunnes Stores, a large grocery and retail outlet in Ireland, refused to handle produce imported from South Africa sold at the stores. The workers were enacting a decision by their union to boycott South Africa's apartheid regime of racist authoritarianism. The Irish public broadcaster RTÉ, in a retrospective about the event, explains how the boycott quickly snowballed into a strike: "When 21-year-old Mary Manning refused to put some fruit through the till, she found herself suspended from work. Nine of her colleagues walked out in support of her, beginning a strike that would last for two years and nine months."[1] The strikers gained notoriety, and the attention was not only domestic.[2] Archbishop Desmond Tutu asked to meet the strikers in London on his way to Oslo to collect his 1984 Nobel Peace Prize, and Nelson Mandela lauded the strikers on his visit to Dublin in 1990. Mary Manning herself went to the Soviet Union in 1985 to try to further publicize the cause and pressure the Irish government to ban the

---

[1] "Striking Out Against Apartheid," RTÉ Archives, https://www.rte.ie/archives/exhibitions/2095-dunnes-strike/ (accessed March 15, 2024).

[2] "This Day 30 Years Ago the Dunnes Stores Anti-Apartheid Strike Began," *The Journal*, July 19, 2014, https://www.thejournal.ie/30-years-dunnes-stores-strike-1579724-Jul2014/ (accessed March 15, 2024).

import of products from apartheid South Africa, eventually succeeding when Dublin did so in 1987.

Of course, this episode is but one example of a much larger and well-known transnational effort to boycott engagement with the apartheid regime to signal disapproval of its racist policies and to pressure it to change its ways. Boycotts are one of the most widely recognized repertoires of collective action to oppose oppression and other perceived injustices. While consumer activism often targets local or domestic actors, transnational boycotts are a quintessential tool of the late 20th and early 21st centuries. However, the political dynamics of transnational consumer activism are changing. With the growing market power of authoritarian states, consumer boycotts in liberal democracies that are contested by authoritarian states are likely to be less effective than in previous decades, when consumers in liberal democracies were dominant. Liberal transnational consumer boycotts can still be effective, but they face changed informational, political, and consumer market contexts than previous efforts. When boycotts touch on issues related to the core interests of a powerful authoritarian state, the market power of that state can now be used to blunt, contest, or even reverse the boycott in ways that were less possible in the 1980s or 1990s.

Drawing upon the authoritarian snapback model, this chapter tells the story of how consumer activism went from a quintessential repertoire concerned with promoting human rights and other liberal causes to one that can be increasingly used to advance authoritarian nationalism. It begins with a review of how consumer activism during the expansion of globalization became a key part of transnational advocacy for advancing human rights. We then present an instructive paired comparison of the anti-sweatshop activism surrounding Nike in the 1990s with anti-forced-labor activism associated with cotton procured from Xinjiang, China, in the 2020s involving H&M. Both featured some tactics of classic liberal advocacy campaigns, but the key difference is that in the latter case the authoritarian state was able to use the cudgel of its consumer market to fire back against overseas companies that initially sided with the activists. The strategy went some way toward taming the power of pro-labor consumer boycotts and persuading many companies to adopt, at most, a quiet approach when it comes to labor standards in China.

Consumer Activism and Transnational Advocacy Movements

In the United States, consumer boycotts have long been a tool for liberal activism and advocacy for the protection and expansion of rights. From the country's foundational Boston Tea Party to the campaigning of labor unions and then civil rights advocacy, most notably the Montgomery bus boycott, consumer activism in the pursuit of social justice or political rights has been a hallmark of American social movements.[3] Some scholars even regard consumer boycotts as the most important activity of American democracy after voting.[4]

Boycotting has also been part of other notable transnational liberal campaigns, including British activism against the global slave trade in the 19th century and the aforementioned international campaign to boycott apartheid South Africa.[5] In their seminal book on human rights activism, Keck and Sikkink note an important case from the 1970s in which activists who were alarmed with food giant Nestlé marketing baby formula irresponsibly to women in the developing world understood that the company was vulnerable to a transnational boycott movement.[6] Here was an instance of activists in several parts of the world using Western-based purchasing power to pressure a Switzerland-based company to change its practices in the developing world.

Patterns of globalization of the 1990s further empowered consumer-oriented advocacy movements with transnational campaigns. The expansion of neoliberal reforms and the global outsourcing of operations by Western-based multinational companies drew attention to comparative labor and environmental standards and the displacement of indigenous peoples, spurring antiglobalization movements and backlash. Importantly, rather than target closed or repressive

---

[3] Laurence Glickman, *Buying Power: A History of Consumer Activism in America* (University of Chicago Press, 2009).

[4] Carline Heldman, *Protest Politics in the Marketplace: Consumer Activism in the Corporate Age* (Cornell University Press, 2017).

[5] Richard A. Hawkins, "Boycotts, Buycotts and Consumer Activism in a Global Context: An Overview," *Management & Organizational History* 5, no. 2 (2010): pp. 123–43, https://doi.org/10.1177/1744935910361644.

[6] Margaret E. Keck and Kathryn Sikkink, *Activists Beyond Borders* (Cornell University Press, 1998), p. 14.

152   DICTATING THE AGENDA

regimes directly, activists targeted Western corporations and their operations. Global marketing and branding further pushed advocates to consider consumer activism as part of a larger campaign against the human rights abuses inflicted by globalization's so-called "race to the bottom."[7]

The global operations of US-based shoe and apparel companies became prime targets in the crosshairs of international media and activists, as manufacturers and subcontractors appeared ever more eager to locate factories to new sites in a bid to keep wages and labor standards low.[8] Scholars attributed the "spotlight" effect of these transnational boycotts and consumer campaigns with exerting enough commercial pressure on sales and downward pressure on stock prices to compel companies to improve their human rights practices.[9]

Such activism is also widely credited with helping to precipitate new governance practices and codes of conduct, including so-called corporate social responsibility (CSR).[10] Throughout the 1990s, multinational corporations (MNCs) adopted new voluntary labor and health standards for workers, accepted some accountability by opening to international monitors, and built corporate brands and marketing campaigns by emphasizing commitments to ethical corporate behavior. In turn, this has led to the embedding of CSR codes within global governance, most notably the United Nations Global Compact.[11] These outcomes represented not only more corporate strategies to brand companies as ethical, but, as Bartley observed, reflected "the negotiated *settlements* and institution-building *projects* that arise out of conflicts

---

7 Jagdish Bhagwati, *In Defense of Globalization: With a New Afterword* (Oxford University Press, 2004).

8 Gay W. Seidman, *Beyond the Boycott: Labor Rights, Human Rights, and Transnational Activism* (Russell Sage Foundation, 2007).

9 Deborah Spar, "The Spotlight and the Bottom Line: How Multinationals Export Human Rights," *Foreign Affairs* 77, no. 2 (1998): pp. 7–12, https://doi.org/10.2307/20048784.

10 Tim Bartley, "Institutional Emergence in an Era of Globalization: The Rise of Transnational Private Regulation of Labor and Environmental Conditions," *American Journal of Sociology* 113, no. 2 (2007): pp. 297–351, https://doi.org/10.1086/518871.

11 Andreas Rasche et al., "The United Nations Global Compact: Retrospect and Prospect," *Business & Society* 52, no. 1 (2013): pp. 6–30, https://doi.org/10.1177/0007650312459999.

involving states, non-governmental organizations (NGOs), and other nonmarket actors, as well as firms."[12]

Snapback Against Liberal Campaigns, New Authoritarian Assertiveness, and Boycotts

This predominant view in the 1990s about how consumer activism had helped to reshape MNCs' behavior and global governance around certain liberal values was not wrong. During the anti-sweatshop campaigns of the 1990s, authoritarian governments of Vietnam, Indonesia, and China remained relatively quiet and passive about the working conditions in their countries, deflecting criticism about their own labor standards and shifting the focus to criticism of the practices of foreign-based companies and their subcontractors. Most important, the most vigorous of these transnational campaigns did appear to prompt changes in the targeted authoritarian governments. For example, Harrison and Scorse found that in response to international pressure from 1989 to 1990 the Indonesian government more than doubled the country's minimum wage; the study also revealed that wages in the textile, apparel, and footwear sector—the sector overwhelmingly targeted by transnational pressure—increased 10%–20% more than other manufacturing sectors.[13] In China, transnational activism in the 1990s was driven by Hong Kong–based civil society groups and activists who leveraged the dominant role of Hong Kong–based capital investments in mainland manufacturing to push for labor rights for mainland workers, specifically for protections for the millions of Chinese migrant laborers who had moved to coastal manufacturing areas like Guangdong.[14] Beijing passed a comprehensive labor relations law in 1995; authorities enacted additional reforms including a new labor contract

---

[12] Bartley, "Institutional Emergence," p. 299.

[13] Ann Harrison and Jason Scorse, "Multinationals and Anti-Sweatshop Activism," *American Economic Review* 100, no. 1 (2010): pp. 247–73, https://doi.org/0.1257/aer.100.1.247.

[14] Yi Xu, "Activism Beyond Borders: The Study of Trans-border Anti-sweatshop Campaigns Across Hong Kong and Mainland China," PhD dissertation, Hong Kong Polytechnic University, 2012, https://theses.lib.polyu.edu.hk/bitstream/200/6759/1/b25302218.pdf. On further applications of the "boomerang pattern" to Hong Kong–based transnational activism, see Yi Xu and Chris King-Chi Chan, "Conductive Activism: Anti-Sweatshop Campaigns Across Hong Kong and Mainland China,"

law that had been debated for years, in the run-up to the 2008 Beijing Olympics campaign.[15]

But the focus on transnational advocacy and CSR did not anticipate that some authoritarian states would grow more assertive in their push-back against such activism and did not foresee that such states, due to their growing market share and consumer power, would launch boy-cotts of their own in response to national directives and grievances highlighted by their governments. In the mid-2000s, even the Chinese government still appeared to be in the shielding stage of the snapback model. For example, when in 2005 a Nike ad featured NBA star Le-bron James beating down Chinese-style cartoons, including mythical dragons, China's State Administration for Radio, Film, and Television accused the ad of insulting China and banned it so as to "protect na-tional honor and traditional Chinese culture."[16] Critically, however, Chinese actions stopped at shielding and did not launch a retaliatory boycott of the company or the NBA.

Chinese government-encouraged consumer campaigns would fun-damentally change in character and voracity beginning in the months prior to the Beijing Summer Games. As discussed earlier, in April 2008, when the Olympic torch relay passed through Paris, a Tibetan protestor grabbed the flame from a Chinese fencer, extinguishing it in the process, and a banner proclaiming "Paris Defends Human Rights Everywhere in the World" was unfurled from Paris City Hall.[17] Outraged Chinese authorities canceled the planned reception at the venue and, soon af-ter, a call to boycott French consumer brands was issued on the largest Chinese Internet Bulletin Board, leading to the immediate targeting of the popular supermarket chain Carrefour and consumer brands that

---

Journal of Contemporary Asia 48, no. 1 (2018): pp. 88–112, https://doi.org/10.1080/00472336.2017.1359651.

[15] "New Labor Law Means Better Image but at a Higher Cost," Xinhua, Decem-ber 31, 2007, https://chinadigitaltimes.net/2007/12/new-labor-law-means-better-image-but-at-higher-cost-wu-zhi/.

[16] Kara Chan et al., "Consumers' Response to Offensive Advertising: A Cross Cul-tural Study," *International Marketing Review* 24, no. 5 (2007): pp. 606–28, https://doi.org/10.1108/02651330710828013.

[17] "Olympic Torch Goes Out, Briefly, in Paris," *New York Times*, April 8, 2008, https://www.nytimes.com/2008/04/08/world/europe/08torch.html.

included Louis Vuitton and Citroën and Peugeot cars. On April 15, 2008, China's Foreign Ministry spokesperson characterized the calls for the boycott as "reasonable and lawful," appearing to mark the first time in the post-Mao era that the Chinese government publicly endorsed a Chinese consumer boycott of particular products of a Western country.[18] The sudden campaign shook the French political establishment to the core, and just a few days later French President Nicholas Sarkozy dispatched a high-level delegation to China, carrying a letter of apology for the torch-related disruptions.[19]

The torch dispute would signal the beginning of a new era of more aggressive pushback and organized consumer campaigns, tacitly or publicly endorsed by Chinese officials, that would take advantage of China's increased market power to counter alleged insults by foreign companies or otherwise remedy grievances. In the late Qing period and in Republican China, nationalistic consumer boycotts did occur and were mostly organized from the bottom up or by interest groups.[20] After the Mao era during which China was isolated, consumer boycotts re-emerged and from around 2008 onward became intertwined with the party's heightened usage of nationalist legitimation.

More recently, Chinese consumers launched boycotts and protests against European luxury brands that were accused of cultural insensitivity and/or racism. These included the French brand Balenciaga in 2018, after the company aired a video showing French men fighting with Chinese customers at the Paris store; the video spurred 20 million social media posts in China with the hashtag "Boycott Balenciaga's racism against Chinese," prompting the company to issue a public

---

[18] Nyiri Pal, "From Starbucks to Carrefour: Consumer Boycotts, Nationalism and Taste in Contemporary China," *Portal: Journal of Multidisciplinary International Studies* 6, no. 2 (2009): pp. 1–25, https://doi.org/10.5130/portal.v6i2.936.

[19] Katrin Bennhold, "France Mounts Diplomatic Charm Offensive to Mollify China," April 21, 2008, *New York Times*, https://www.nytimes.com/2008/04/21/world/europe/21iht-france.4.12200062.html.

[20] Tony Yan and Michael R. Hyman, "Nationalistic Appeals and Consumer Boycotts in China, 1900–1949," *Journal of Historical Research in Marketing* 12, no. 4 (2020): pp. 503–24, https://doi.org/10.1108/JHRM-08-2019-0030.

apology.[21] Boycotts were also launched against other Western luxury brands following accusations of racism, including against Dolce and Gabbana (2018),[22] Lululemon (2020),[23] and Chanel (2021).[24] And in 2022, 50 Chinese students picketed outside of a Dior store in Paris to protest a skirt that resembled a traditional Ming Dynasty garment, with the protest livestreamed to over half a million viewers on the Chinese platforms Weibo and WeChat.[25]

International companies caught in authoritarian-led boycott campaigns can suffer significant financial harm. For example, during a sovereignty dispute with Japan in 2012 not only were there hundreds of anti-Japanese protests in China, but there was also a boycott campaign targeting Japanese brands. The campaign's goal was to pressure the companies so that they would in turn exert pressure on Tokyo to surrender control over disputed islands. Weiss and coauthors demonstrate that the boycotts damaged Japanese brands not only immediately, but even over the longer term, with sales of Japanese cars falling by an estimated 1.1 million during a roughly 15-month period.[26] Fearing financial losses or even being shut out of one of the world's largest markets, companies have powerful incentives to avoid finding themselves in the crosshairs of pro-Beijing boycotts.

---

[21] See "Balenciaga's Racism Enrages Chinese Consumers," *CGTN*, April 4, 2017, https://news.cgtn.com/news/3d3d514d7a49544d77457a6333566d54/share_p.html. Also see Zhiwei Chen, "Alleged 'Racism' Balenciaga and Its Wrathful Chinese Consumers—Analyzed Through the Case Study of 2018 Balenciaga Boycott Event," *Academic Journal of Business & Management* 4, no. 9 (2022): pp. 90–95, https://doi.org/10.25236/AJBM.2022.040913.

[22] Elizabeth Segran, "Why Does Luxury Fashion Hate Chinese Consumers?," Fast Company, December 3, 2018, https://www.fastcompany.com/90273073/why-does-luxury-fashion-hate-chinese-consumers.

[23] Yaling Jiang, "Can Lululemon Be Saved from a PR Crisis in China?," *Jing Daily*, April 21, 2020, https://jingdaily.com/can-lululemon-be-saved-from-a-pr-crisis-in-china/.

[24] Lisa Nan, "Chanel, It's Not Your Apology to Accept," *Jing Daily*, May 5, 2021, https://jingdaily.com/chanel-apology-dj-michel-gaubert/.

[25] Denni Hu, "Hanfu Supporters Protest Dior over Disputed Skirt Design," *Women's Wear Daily*, July 25, 2022, https://wwd.com/fashion-news/fashion-scoops/hanfu-supporters-protest-outside-dior-disputed-skirt-1235261542/.

[26] Jessica Chen Weiss et al., "Commercial Casualties: Political Boycotts and International Disputes," *Journal of East Asian Studies* 23, no. 3 (2023): pp. 387–410, https://doi.org/10.1017/jea.2023.19.

Two Cases of Apparel-Related Transnational Activism and Boycotts

To dig deeper into the shifting politics of transnational boycott campaigns, we engage in a paired-case comparison of two consumer activism and CSR campaigns involving labor rights: Nike and sweatshop labor in the 1990s and forced labor in the Xinjiang cotton industry in the 2020s. The campaigns differ in some respects in terms of specifics, but broadly both involve networks of Western-based activists, labor unions, governments, journalists, and consumers concerned with labor conditions and labor autonomy in East Asia. The main relevant changes between the two cases are the changed underlying power of the target states as well as the time elapsed between the two, affording all actors the opportunity to learn and adjust their methods. The comparison is thus broadly consistent with a "most similar" comparative method in which many factors are similar except key explanatory ones and the outcome.[27] For data we rely on secondary academic sources, journalistic reporting, corporate statements and annual reports, and expert interviews conducted by one of the authors in Stockholm in January 2023 (H&M is a Swedish company headquartered in Stockholm).[28]

Nike and the Anti-Sweatshop Campaigns of the 1990s

Nike is an American company, founded in Eugene, Oregon, in 1965 and named in 1972, founded initially to import athletic shoes from Japan. Under the stewardship of its founder, Phil Knight, by 1990 the company had grown into the largest manufacturer of sports shoes and supplies in the world.[29] Nike's story of growth has become associated with the opportunities and perils associated with the globalization and the outsourcing of manufacturing, as well as becoming an instructive case

---

[27] Jason Seawright and John Gerring, "Case Selection Techniques in Case Study Research," *Political Research Quarterly* 61, no. 2 (2008): p. 304, https://doi.org/10.1177/1065912907313077.

[28] The interview research plan was approved by the University College Dublin's institutional ethics board.

[29] "Nike Profits Increase 84%," *New York Times*, July 10, 1990, https://www.nytimes.com/1990/07/10/business/nike-profits-increase-84.html.

study in how US-based companies responded to human rights-related advocacy campaigns boycotts in the 1990s and 2000s.[30]

Nike's stunning growth in the 1980s was founded upon outsourcing its production of sneakers away from the United States and Japan to locations abroad; by 1982, 86% of Nike's athletic shoes were manufactured in Taiwan or South Korea.[31] But as demand in the 1980s skyrocketed—with athletic shoes surpassing 50% of the footwear market in 1992—wages and costs in these East Asian countries grew more expensive,[32] including as a result of the proliferating labor disputes and unionization of Korean workers as the country democratized.[33]

Nike's South Korean subcontractor relocated production plants to lower-wage markets in the region, most notably Vietnam, Indonesia, and Cambodia. In Indonesia, the company concentrated production in six factories, four of which were owned by its Korean subsidiary, employing over 25,000 workers.[34] NGOs and advocates began reporting on a set of atrocious working conditions and exploitative wages, as the contractors successfully lobbied the Indonesian government led by President Suharto under a "national emergency" clause to pay wages below the minimum wage, which itself was acknowledged to be below subsistence level. Advocacy campaigns included extensive fact-finding and documentation spearheaded by the Asian-American Free Labor Institute (an overseas branch of the AFL-CIO), which fed information about these labor conditions to US lawmakers and media outlets.[35]

---

[30] Richard M. Locke, "The Promise and Peril of Globalization: The Case of Nike," MIT IPC Working Paper 02-008, p. 3, https://web.mit.edu/rlocke/www/documents/Research%20Papers/Locke_Promise%20and%20Perils%20of%20Globalization_Nike.pdf.pdf.

[31] Locke, "Promise and Peril," p. 5.

[32] On Taiwan's rising costs and currency appreciation, see LulLin Cheng, "Sources of Success in Uncertain Markets: The Taiwanese Footwear Industry," *Economic Governance and the Challenge of Flexibility in East Asia* (2001): pp. 33–53.

[33] Jeroen Merk, "Production Beyond the Horizon of Consumption: Spatial Fixes and Anti-Sweatshop Struggles in the Global Athletic Footwear Industry," *Global Society* 25, no. 1 (2011): pp. 83–84, https://doi.org/10.1080/13600826.2010.522984.

[34] Locke, "Promise and Peril," p. 10.

[35] "New Shots Fired in Indonesia Wage War: US Labor is Urging Trade Action Against a Land Where Daily Take Home Pay Is Measured in Cents," *Los Angeles Times*, September 22, 1992, https://www.latimes.com/archives/la-xpm-1992-09-22-wr-1105-story.html.

A 1992 CBS investigation was followed by several articles in current affairs periodicals. However, the response from Nike was to deflect responsibility onto the actions of its subcontractors.[36]

In 1996, within the space of a few weeks, the company was hit with several high-profile media reports and commentaries that severely damaged its reputation. Investigations showed that Nike workers were 75%–80% young women below the age of 24, working 10- to 13-hour shifts earning a daily wage of about $1.60–$2.20.[37] In March 1996, reports emerged that Vietnamese women workers at the Sang Yang factory, a contractor of Nike, had been beaten by supervisors while on the job, prompting further investigations by transnational activists, including those conducted by Thuyen Nguyen, a Vietnamese-born labor activist and founder of the watchdog group Vietnam Labor Monitor.[38] Nguyen toured several factories in Vietnam to document working conditions, with his campaign precipitating the dismissal of a factory manager, which helped put the issue onto the broader US media agenda.[39]

In a now-famous June 1996 column, *New York Times* commentator Bob Herbert accused Nike of operating as a "pyramid of exploitation," in which celebrity perks and the consumption by US youth that drove the company were built on "legions of young Asians, mostly women, who work like slaves to turn out Nike's products."[40] Herbert spotlighted the Indonesian factories, including low wages and horrendous working conditions. Just a few weeks later, this reputational damage was compounded by a *Life* magazine exposé of child labor in

---

[36] Locke, "Promise and Peril," p. 11.

[37] George H. Sage, "Justice Do It! The Nike Transnational Advocacy Network: Organization, Collective Actions, and Outcomes," *Sociology of Sport Journal* 16, no. 3 (1999): p. 209, https://doi.org/10.1123/ssj.16.3.206.

[38] Verena Dobnik, "Activist Finds Abuses at Vietnam Nike Plants," *Washington Post*, March 27, 1997, https://www.washingtonpost.com/archive/business/1997/03/28/activist-finds-abuses-at-vietnam-nike-plants/17fb810d-97ca-430b-8e91-3e16bd50ab3c/.

[39] "Nike Suspends a Vietnam Boss," *New York Times*, March 28, 1997, https://www.nytimes.com/1997/03/28/business/nike-suspends-a-vietnam-boss.html.

[40] Bob Herbert, "In America, Nike's Pyramid Scheme," *New York Times*, June 10, 1996, https://www.nytimes.com/1996/06/10/opinion/in-america-nike-s-pyramid-scheme.html.

160   DICTATING THE AGENDA

Pakistan—entitled "Six Cents an Hour"—that prominently featured a photo of a child stitching together a football with the Nike logo. Another high-profile embarrassment hit the company in 1997 after a devastating audit undertaken by Ernst & Young of a factory in Vietnam that detailed numerous egregious health and safety concerns was leaked to NGOs and the *New York Times*.[41]

These episodes, among others, spurred international NGOs to target Nike as a symbol of globalization and "race to the bottom" labor practices. Locke shows how various NGOs and activists, including Oxfam Clean Clothes Campaign and Press for Change, launched websites dedicated to highlighting Nike's labor conditions. These groups led pickets and protests at factories and Nike headquarters and mobilized universities into a boycott of Nike products, as their online coordination and networking was singled out as a new era of effective youth-driven "global identity politics" and antiglobalization activism.[42] At US college and university campuses, protests supported by the anti-Nike network targeted the multibillion-dollar collegiate licensing business; by 1999, over 60 universities had established network chapters.

Collectively, these actions damaged the company's reputation and earnings: In early 1998, Nike's profits plummeted by 69%, its share price was halved, and the company announced plans to lay off 1,600 workers.[43] The same year, CEO Phil Knight acknowledged the scale of the reputational damage when he admitted that "the Nike product has become synonymous with slave wages, forced overtime and arbitrary abuse" and announced that the company would agree to raise wages of its employees and allow members of international watchdogs and NGOs to inspect its factories alongside international auditors.[44] The company also launched a high-profile CSR campaign, committing

---

[41] Steven Greenhouse, "Nike Shoeplant in Vietnam Is Called Unsafe for Workers," *New York Times*, November 7, 1997, https://www.nytimes.com/1997/11/08/business/nike-shoe-plant-in-vietnam-is-called-unsafe-for-workers.html.

[42] Victoria Carty, "The Internet and Grassroots Politics: Nike, the Athletic Apparel Industry and the Anti-Sweatshop Campaign," *Tamara: Journal for Critical Organization Inquiry* 1, no. 2 (2001): p. 38.

[43] Liam McCall, "Nike Announces Profit Drop, Layoffs," Associated Press, March 18, 1998, https://apnews.com/article/aa1307ecb21f06f6966fca828ea7d38e/.

[44] John H. Cushman, "Nike Pledges to End Child Labor and Apply U.S. Rules Abroad," *New York Times*, May 13, 1998, https://www.nytimes.com/1998/05/13/business/international-business-nike-pledges-to-end-child-labor-and-apply-us-rules-abroad.html.

the company to a number of new standards that would be displayed across all its factories and enforced by external safety committee and supervisors.[45] However, even that became controversial when the company was sued in California courts for allegedly misrepresenting its CSR record and its social impact in its public communications; the case actually reached the US Supreme Court before it was ultimately settled without a ruling on constitutional issues.[46]

In general, authoritarian government responses to the transnational anti-Nike campaigns of the 1990s were tepid and notably nonconfrontational. In Vietnam, analysis at the time highlighted that the Vietnamese government was intent on securing political support for a free-trade deal with the United States (signed soon after in 2000) that was being vocally opposed by US labor organizations like the AFL-CIO.[47] In fact, in response to these US court cases authorities in Vietnam actually defended the company and publicly praised Nike for raising its labor standards.[48] In Indonesia, the controversy over Nike, waged in the mid-1990s, soon gave way to the East Asian financial crisis of 1997 that decimated the economy and swept the Suharto regime from power.

In China, central authorities in the 1990s remained relatively passive and silent, despite the official count of annual labor disputes increasing 10-fold from 1994 to 2003 (from 19,098 to 800,000).[49] Regional governments, tasked with enforcing labor codes, would regularly side

---

[45] Kristen Bell DeTienne and Lee W. Lewis, "The Pragmatic and Ethical Barriers to Corporate Social Responsibility Disclosure: The Nike Case," *Journal of Business Ethics* 60 (2005): p. 363, https://doi.org/10.1007/s10551-005-0869-x.

[46] See Don Mayer, "Kasky v. Nike and the Quarrelsome Question of Corporate Free Speech," *Business Ethics Quarterly* 17, no. 1 (2007): 65–96, https://doi.org/10.2307/27673158.

[47] "Vietnam Labour Body Defense Nike after Court Ruling," Reuters, May 3, 2002.

[48] Seth Mydans, "Vietnam: Communist Defends Capitalist Giant," *New York Times*, May 4, 2002, https://www.nytimes.com/2002/05/04/world/world-briefing-asia-vietnam-communist-defends-capitalist-giant.html.

[49] Joseph Yu-shek Cheng et al., "Multinational Corporations, Global Civil Society and Chinese Labour: Workers' Solidarity in China in the Era of Globalization," *Economic and Industrial Democracy* 33, no. 3 (2012): pp. 384–85, https://doi.org/10.1177/0143831X11411325. Furthermore, according to the authors, despite these labor protests Chinese trade union membership actually declined 26% from 1995 to 1999 and it was not until the early 2000s that the corporatist All-China Federation of Trade Unions aggressively pushed to increase trade union membership in the 2000s, pushing MNCs that had routinely ignored Chinese labor laws in the 1990s to tolerate unionization.

with corporate suppliers, such as in the case of authorities in Dongguan consistently supporting production giant Yue Yuen, Nike's main Chinese contractor, despite regular labor unrest and persistent reports alleging unpaid wages and environmentally unsafe working conditions.[50] Most tellingly, in China, not only did Nike avoid public criticism from Beijing, but it also established itself as the dominant domestic apparel sponsor and consumer name by sponsoring the players and teams in the inaugural Chinese professional basketball league in 1995 and lending its name to high school basketball leagues throughout the country.[51] Ironically, Nike's status China in the 1990s was such that its sales in the country grew at over 60% throughout the decade, even as the company's bottom line was rocked by campaigns in the United States.

Activism and Snapback, 2017–2022: Repression in Xinjiang, Cotton Standards, and H&M

With the consumer boycotts and activism about Nike's labor standards in the 1990s as a backdrop, this section describes contemporary developments involving cotton certification standards, H&M, and labor standards in cotton supply chains. What becomes clear is that the authoritarian snapback has in important respects reshaped the field of consumer activism when it comes to powerful authoritarian states. The latter, in this case China, are more willing and able to use market power and mobilized nationalism to respond directly without necessarily making concessions.

Background: Repression in Xinjiang and Activist Campaigns

Based largely in the Xinjiang Uyghur Autonomous Region (XUAR) of China, Uyghurs as an ethnic group have a distinct cultural identity

---

[50] Jeroen Merk, "Restructuring and Conflict in the Global Athletic Footwear Industry," in *Global Economy Contested: Power and Conflict across the International Division of Labour*, edited by Marcus Taylor (Routledge, 2008), pp. 150–52, 155–57.

[51] Matthew Forney et al., "Marketing: How Nike Figured Out China," *Time*, October 24, 2004, https://time.com/archive/6739750/marketing-how-nike-figured-out-china/.

from the Han majority in China, including using a different language and often practicing Islam. Uyghurs have long faced discrimination and repression by the PRC, and this has often stoked contention.[52] Xinjiang has often been viewed through a securitized lens by Chinese authorities with separatism a persistent concern, but repression began to accelerate after a militarized clampdown in 2009 following a cycle of protests and riots.[53]

In 2014, Chinese leader Xi Jinping began to promote a comprehensive policy package to repress Uyghur identity and autonomous networks with the rationale of preventing separatism and terrorism.[54] The party-state ramped up its surveillance of the Uyghur population, looking for signs of "extremism" that could include simple acts like attending mosque too much or having a beard, with officials ultimately categorizing people by their levels of trustworthiness.[55]

Starting in 2017, the campaign evolved into a program of mass internment. The numbers are disputed, but perhaps up to one million people (out of a Uyghur population in Xinjiang of about 10 million) were incarcerated in prison-like re-education camps.[56] Prisoners were kept under constant surveillance and were required to study party ideology and profess loyalty to the CCP.[57] Documents suggest that a points system was used to reward signs of loyalty to the party-state and

---

[52] Gardner Bovingdon, *The Uyghurs: Strangers in Their Own Land* (Columbia University Press, 2010).

[53] David Tobin, *Securing China's Northwest Frontier: Identity and Insecurity in Xinjiang* (Cambridge University Press, 2020).

[54] Austin Ramzy and Chris Buckley, "'Absolutely No Mercy': Leaked Files Expose How China Organized Mass Detentions of Muslims," *New York Times*, November 16, 2019, https://www.nytimes.com/interactive/2019/11/16/world/asia/china-xinjiang-documents.html (accessed January 10, 2023).

[55] Joanne Smith-Finley, "Securitization, Insecurity and Conflict in Contemporary Xinjiang: Has PRC Counter-Terrorism Evolved into State Terror?," *Central Asian Survey* 38, no. 1 (2019): pp. 1–26, https://doi.org/10.1080/02634937.2019.1586348; James Leibold, "Surveillance in China's Xinjiang Region: Ethnic Sorting, Coercion, and Inducement," *Journal of Contemporary China* 29, no. 121 (2020): pp. 46–60, https://doi.org/10.1080/10670564.2019.1621529.

[56] Adrian Zenz, "'Thoroughly Reforming Them Towards a Healthy Heart Attitude': China's Political Re-Education Campaign in Xinjiang," *Central Asian Survey* 38, no. 1 (2019): pp. 102–28, https://doi.org/10.1080/02634937.2018.1507997.

[57] Darren Byler, *In the Camps: China's High-Tech Penal Colony* (Columbia University Press, 2021).

164 DICTATING THE AGENDA

proficiency in Mandarin with being able to contact family or to ultimately be released.[58] Even before detention or after release, Uyghurs faced a form of "digital enclosure" in which high-tech methods were used to control the movements, activities, and access to information of the Uyghur population.[59] Low-tech methods like visits and even extended homestays by party-state civil servants in Uyghur households deepened the government's apparatus of control.[60] From these granular measures in the home all the way up to global transnational repression and persecution of Uyghurs abroad,[61] the PRC has sought to exert thorough dominance over Uyghurs to preclude the possibility of opposition.

These policies had profound effects on catalyzing attention and activism outside China about the Uyghur cause. Global media attention on Xinjiang intensified particularly in the autumn of 2019 with two major leaks of internal Chinese documents to the *New York Times* and International Consortium of Investigative Journalists that provided details of the repressive campaign and the inner workings of the reeducation camps. Groups like the World Uyghur Congress and the Uyghur Human Rights Project gained new prominence and supporters for their work opposing the crackdown. In a classic "boomerang" pattern, Uyghur activism, repressed in the PRC itself, gained support from major international NGOs like Human Rights Watch (HRW),

---

[58] Bethany Allen-Ebrahimian, "Exposed: China's Operating Manuals for Mass Internment and Arrest by Algorithm," International Consortium of Investigative Journalists, November 24, 2019, https://www.icij.org/investigations/china-cables/exposed-chinas-operating-manuals-for-mass-internment-and-arrest-by-algorithm/ (accessed January 10, 2023).

[59] Byler, *In the Camps*. See also Josh Chin and Liza Lin, *Surveillance State: Inside China's Quest to Launch a New Era of Social Control* (St. Martin's Press, 2022); and Adrian Zenz, "The Xinjiang Police Files: Re-Education Camp Security and Political Paranoia in the Xinjiang Uyghur Autonomous Region," *Journal of the European Association for Chinese Studies* 3 (2022): pp. 263–311, https://doi.org/10.25365/jeacs.2022.3.zenz.

[60] See, for example, Darren Byler, "China's Government Has Ordered a Million Citizens to Occupy Iughur homes. Here's What They Think They're Doing," *China File*, October 23, 2018, https://www.chinafile.com/reporting-opinion/postcard/million-citizens-occupy-uighur-homes-xinjiang.

[61] Edward Lemon et al., "Globalizing Minority Persecution: China's Transnational Repression of the Uyghurs," *Globalizations* 20, no. 4 (2023): pp. 564–80, https://doi.org/10.1080/14747731.2022.2135944.

Amnesty International, PEN America, and Scholars at Risk, as well as local diaspora groups, who in turn brought further attention to the cause and pressure on democratic governments and companies to act.[62]

This media attention, research, and activism led to responses by some governments and intergovernmental organizations, but also to aggressive pushback by the PRC. The US government, under both the first Trump and Biden administrations, imposed economic sanctions on several officials and companies involved with the repression. In July 2020, the PRC responded to sanctions on officials responsible for repression in Xinjiang with countersanctions on some high-profile US politicians who had been vocal about the issue.[63] Similar dynamics unfolded in Europe. In March 2021, the European Union sanctioned four PRC officials who were involved with the re-education camps with asset freezes and travel bans.[64] These measures were met with a furious response by China, with Beijing imposing countersanctions on several European politicians as well as some European researchers and think tanks who study Xinjiang or China more generally.[65]

Over time, it became clear that the re-education camps were only part of the story, with programs of government-led labor transfer also operating amid this coercive environment.[66] Labor transfer schemes

---

[62] Henryk Szadziewski, "The Push for a Uyghur Human Rights Policy Act in the United States: Recent Developments in Uyghur Activism," *Asian Ethnicity* 21, no. 2 (2020): pp. 211–22, https://doi.org/10.1080/14631369.2019.1605497; Lina Lenberg, "Uyghur Diaspora Activism in the Face of Genocide," *International Journal of Human Rights Education* 6, no, 1 (2022): pp. 1–18.

[63] Don Weinland and Demetri Sevastopulo, "China Imposes Sanctions on US Lawmakers in Retaliation for Xinjiang Measures," *Financial Times*, July 13, 2020, https://www.ft.com/content/4674a6b6-cb67-44c5-9360-b2a4b9cff bbe (accessed January 11, 2023).

[64] Stuart Lau and Jacopo Barigazzi, "EU Imposes Sanctions on Four Chinese Officials," *Politico*, March 22, 2021, https://www.politico.eu/article/eu-imposes-sanctions-on-four-chinese-officials/ (accessed January 10, 2023).

[65] See a briefing by the parliament here: Matthew Parry, "Chinese Counter Sanctions on EU Targets," European Parliament, May 2021, https://www.europarl.europa.eu/RegData/etudes/ATAG/2021/690617/EPRS_ATA(2021) 690617_EN.pdf (accessed January 13, 2023).

[66] Darren Byler, "The Camp Fix: Infrastructural Power and the 'Re-Education Labour Regime' in Turkic Muslim Industrial Parks in North-West China," *China Quarterly* 255 (2023): pp. 628–43, https://doi.org/10.1017/S0305741022001618. On the various complex, sometimes overlapping but sometimes separate systems of

meant Uyghurs could be sent to factories in Xinjiang or to other areas in China far from their communities.[67] Leaked internal studies and the PRC's own propaganda apparatus effectively admit that these programs are coerced and have the intention of weakening Uyghur culture.[68]

Given its importance to Xinjiang's economy, cotton-harvesting and labor standards in the textile industry became especially relevant. In 2018, the Chinese government itself reported that 450,000 new Turkic Muslim workers were employed in the cotton and textile industries as part of new labor regimes.[69] Such numbers reflect a system in which local officials use their deepening reach into ethnic minority villages and households to mobilize people to harvest cotton or engage in other labor, often for months at a time far from their homes.[70] This system of coerced cotton harvesting, which is distinct from the re-education camp system, not only sees government officials mobilize and transfer populations for labor, but also entails political monitoring, political

---

labor transfer and forced labor with regard to Xinjiang, see Adrian Zenz, "The Conceptual Evolution of Poverty Alleviation through Labour Transfer in the Xinjiang Uyghur Autonomous Region," *Central Asian Survey* 42, no. 4 (2023): pp. 649–73, https://doi.org/10.1080/02634937.2023.2227225.

[67] "'Break Their Lineage, Break Their Roots': China's Crimes Against Humanity Targeting Uyghurs and Other Turkic Muslims," Human Rights Watch, April 19, 2021, https://www.hrw.org/report/2021/04/19/break-their-lineage-break-their-roots/chinas-crimes-against-humanity-targeting#_ftn189 (accessed January 10, 2023).

[68] John Sudworth, "'If the Others Go I'll Go': Inside China's Scheme to Transfer Uighurs into Work," *BBC*, March 2, 2021, https://www.bbc.com/news/world-asia-china-56250915 (accessed January 10, 2023).

[69] For a typology of the pathways into the various involuntary labor programs relevant to Xinjiang, see Adrian Zenz, "Beyond the Camps: Beijing's Grand Scheme of Coercive Labor, Poverty Alleviation and Social Control in Xinjiang," Congressional-Executive Commission on China Hearing Testimony, October 17, 2019, https://www.cecc.gov/sites/chinacommission.house.gov/files/documents/Beyond%20the%20Camps%20CECC%20testimony%20version%20%28Zenz%20Oct%202019%29.pdf (accessed June 10, 2024). See also Human Rights Watch, "'Break Their Lineage, Break Their Roots.'"

[70] Adrian Zenz, "Coercive Labor in Xinjiang: Labor Transfer and the Mobilization of Ethnic Minorities to Pick Cotton, New Lines Institute for Strategy and Policy, December 14, 2020, https://newlinesinstitute.org/china/coercive-labor-in-xinjiang-labor-transfer-and-the-mobilization-of-ethnic-minorities-to-pick-cotton/ (accessed January 11, 2023).

education sessions, and sometimes separating of parents from their children, with the latter put into public care with accompanying political education.[71]

While these programs unfold out of sight of most casual observers due to media restrictions in China generally and Xinjiang even more stringently, these are by no means small schemes. Roughly 85% of China's cotton is produced in Xinjiang, accounting for about 20% of global supply.[72] The scale of production helps explain the large numbers of laborers cited previously, with Zenz estimating approximately 570,000 people mobilized for these programs in 2018 based on official and quasi-official Chinese sources.[73]

Beyond harvesting cotton, the manufacturing process itself has been subject to regimes of labor coercion. HRW notes that the post-2014 crackdown on Uyghurs coincided with the "vertical integration of China's garment manufacturing sector" that saw textile factories move to Xinjiang, closer to both the source of China's cotton and to laborers who could work in them.[74] With state support "Since 2017, factories have flocked to take advantage of the newly built industrial parks of the re-education camp system and the cheap labour and subsidies that accompany them."[75] Former detainees and mobilized rural laborers can be sent to factories to work for low wages in rigid conditions, with refusal regarded as a sign of suspicion that can put the person in the crosshairs of the very coercive system that feeds detainees into the camps in the first place.[76]

The development of this system gave transnational actors a lever they could use to try to influence China's repressive policies in this area. For example, the Coalition to End Forced Labour in the Uyghur Region, an umbrella organization that includes several high-profile NGOs, Uyghur groups, and labor unions, began issuing statements in 2020,

---

[71] Zenz, "Coercive Labor in Xinjiang"; Zenz, "Conceptual Evolution."

[72] Alix Kroeger, "Xinjiang Cotton: How Do I Know If It's in My Jeans?," BBC News, March 26, 2021, https://www.bbc.com/news/world-asia-china-56535822 (accessed January 11, 2023).

[73] Zenz, "Coercive Labor in Xinjiang."

[74] Human Rights Watch, "Break Their Lineage."

[75] Byler, "The Camp Fix," p. 633.

[76] Byler, "The Camp Fix," p. 634; Zenz, "Conceptual Evolution"; Zenz, "Beyond the Camps."

sending letters to political leaders, and pressuring corporations and asset managers to change their practices.[77] The Clean Clothes Campaign, a Netherlands-based NGO and member of the coalition, engages in lobbying and advocacy around forced labor in the Xinjiang cotton industry.[78] HRW calls on governments that have not yet done so to enact legislation in response to forced labor in Xinjiang.[79] The International Trade Union Confederation, representing a membership of over 200 million, presented evidence to the International Labour Organization about Uyghur forced labor.[80] The Inter-Parliamentary Alliance on China, a transnational group of legislators, has made statements on forced labor in Xinjiang.[81]

In line with the boomerang model, advocacy and attention to forced labor in Xinjiang appeared to meet with some initial tactical success. In December 2021, US President Joe Biden signed into law the Uyghur Forced Labor Prevention Act with near-unanimous bipartisan support in Congress. The law effectively creates the presumption that goods from Xinjiang are made with forced labor insofar as it bans all imports from Xinjiang unless it can be determined that they were not produced with forced labor.[82] The legislation followed a series of regulatory

---

[77] End Uyghur Forced Labor, "About Our Coalition," https://endu yghurforcedlabour.org/about/ (accessed January 11, 2023).

[78] "End Uygur Forced Labour," Clean Clothes Campaign, https://cleanclothes .org/campaigns/end-uyghur-forced-labour (accessed January 11, 2023).

[79] Human Rights Watch, "Australia: Act on China's Abuses in Xinjiang," September 13, 2022, https://www.hrw.org/news/2022/09/13/australia-act-chinas-abuses-xinjiang (accessed January 11, 2023).

[80] Emma Farge, "China's Labour Policies in Xinjiang Are Discriminatory, ILO Body Says," Reuters, February 11, 2022, https://www.reuters.com/world/ilo-seeks-changes-chinas-discriminatory-labour-policies-xinjiang-2022-02-11/ (accessed January 11, 2023).

[81] For example, see "IPAC Highlights Uyghur Labor Abuse," IPAC statement, May 10, 2023, https://www.ipac.global/news/ipac-highlights-uyghur-labor-abuse (accessed June 17, 2024).

[82] Felicia Sonmez, "Biden Signs Uyghur Forced Labor Prevention Act Into Law," *Washington Post*, December 23, 2021, https://www.washingtonpost.com/politics/biden-uyghur-labor-law/2021/12/23/99e8d048-6412-11ec-a7e8-3a8455b71fad_sto ry.html (accessed January 11, 2023). The US Customs and Border Protection agency explains that this "rebuttable presumption" applies to "any goods, wares, articles, and merchandise mined, produced, or manufactured wholly or in part in" Xinjiang, listing cotton as one of the high-priority goods for the ban. See "Uyghur Forced

orders by the Trump administration banning the import of certain categories of goods originating in Xinjiang, including cotton and tomato products.[83] Across the Atlantic, the European Commission unveiled in September 2022 proposed rules that would ban the import of products made with forced labor, although the measures are not as strict or robust as some advocates had hoped. The proposals do not mention Xinjiang or China specifically, but, off the record, "The consensus among most EU lawmakers is that the ban is meant largely to target China."[84] The European Parliament approved the measures in April 2024.[85]

Cotton Standards, Activism, and Corporate Self-Regulation

Industry also took measures at self-regulation. Among these was the Better Cotton Initiative (BCI), which is an industry-led nonprofit organization to which farmers, producers, suppliers, retailers, brands, and civil society groups can pay to join. As of 2023, annual fees ranged from €100 to €45,000 depending on the entity's category and income.[86] The organization had more than 2,500 members in January 2023, including well-known companies like H&M, Amazon, Gap, Levi Strauss, Walmart, Adidas, Hugo Boss, Puma, Urban Outfitters, and so on. Among the organization's members were 489 based in China.[87] Of those 489,

---

Labor Prevention Act," U.S. Customs and Border Protection, https://www.cbp.gov/trade/forced-labor/UFLPA (accessed January 11, 2023); "UFLPA Frequently Asked Questions," Department of Homeland Security, https://www.dhs.gov/uflpa-frequently-asked-questions (accessed January 11, 2023).

[83] Jeanne Whalen and Eva Dou, "Trump Administration Bans Imports of Cotton and Tomatoes from China's Xinjiang Region, Citing Forced Labor," *Washington Post*, January 13, 2021, https://www.washingtonpost.com/us-policy/2021/01/13/us-ban-xinjiang-cotton-tomatoes/ (accessed January 11, 2023).

[84] Sarah Anne Aarup et al., "5 Things to Know About EU Plan to Ban Imports Made with Forced Labor," *Politico*, September 12, 2022, https://www.politico.eu/article/5-things-to-know-about-eu-plan-to-ban-imports-made-with-forced-labor/ (accessed January 11, 2023).

[85] "EU Parliament Approves Ban of Products Made with Forced Labour," Reuters, April 23, 2024, https://www.reuters.com/world/europe/eu-parliament-approves-ban-products-made-with-forced-labour-2024-04-23/ (accessed June 17, 2024).

[86] https://bettercotton.org/wp-content/uploads/2020/07/BCI-Membership-Fees-2017-2021-All-Categories-as-of-June2020.pdf (accessed July 9, 2024).

[87] "Find Members," Better Cotton, https://bettercotton.org/membership/find-members/ (accessed January 11, 2023).

129 first became members in 2021 or 2022. One member since 2019 was Xinjiang Dongchunxing Textile Company, which was featured in a 2020 *China Daily* propaganda piece describing the very processes of coerced Uyghur labor outlined previously.[88]

The BCI has a Better Cotton Standard System, which focuses on environmental, social, and economic sustainability.[89] In BCI parlance, China is defined as a "Better Cotton Standard Country," which it defines as "Countries where the Better Cotton Standard System is directly implemented by BCI's on-the-ground Implementing Partners."[90] The four implementing partners in China were listed as of 2023 as: CottonConnect China, Huangmei County Huinong Scientific and Technology Planting and Breeding Cooperative, Shandong Binzhou Nongxi Cotton Professional Cooperative, and Songzi Nanwuchang Grain Cotton Oil Specialised Cooperative.[91] It had previously worked with the Xinjiang Production and Construction Corps, which is now an entity sanctioned by the United States for human rights abuses.[92] On October 21, 2020, the BCI issued a statement on its website (since removed) stating that it is halting all "field-level activities" in Xinjiang due to "sustained allegations of forced labour and other human rights abuses" in the region, and noting that since March 2020 it had "suspended licensing and assurance activities in XUAR."[93]

As mentioned previously, in March 2021, the United States, EU, the United Kingdom, and Canada coordinated an announcement of

---

[88] Zhou Mo, "Dongguan Companies Giving Boost to Xinjiang Economy," *China Daily*, December 25, 2020, https://global.chinadaily.com.cn/a/202012/25/WS5fe5917da31024adoba9e931.html (accessed January 11, 2023).

[89] "What We Do," Better Cotton, https://bettercotton.org/what-we-do/ (accessed January 11, 2023).

[90] Better Cotton, "Better Cotton in China," https://bettercotton.org/where-is-better-cotton-grown/better-cotton-in-china/ (accessed January 11, 2023).

[91] Better Cotton, "Better Cotton in China."

[92] Nithin Costa, "China Labour Watchdogs Face Touch Tradeoffs to Keep Access Alive," Al Jazeera, August 10, 2022, https://www.aljazeera.com/economy/2022/8/10/in-china-labour-watchdogs-face-comprises-tough-choices-to-stay#:~:text=Tokyo%2C%20Japan%20%E2%80%93%20When%20the%20Better, history%20of%20human%20rights%20abuses (accessed January 12, 2023).

[93] Bethany Allen-Ebrahimian, "Xinjiang Statement Removed from Cotton Watchdog Website," Axios, April 13, 2021, https://www.axios.com/2021/04/13/xinjiang-cotton-watchdog (accessed January 11, 2023).

a series of sanctions on entities responsible for human rights violations in Xinjiang. Only days after these sanctions were announced, the China office of the BCI issued a statement saying: "Since 2012, the Xinjiang project site has performed second-party credibility audits and third-party verifications over the years, and has never found a single case related to incidents of forced labor."[94] The statement was reproduced by China's Ministry of Foreign Affairs and various PRC consulates and media outlets.[95] Indeed, the day of BCI China's statement that it found no forced labor in Xinjiang, March 25, 2021, the CCP-owned *Global Times* ran a story on the subject, also citing a statement the BCI office apparently gave to the outlet in January of that year saying that its investigations revealed no forced labor and that the allegations were made by the central BCI office, not the Chinese branch.[96] Only four hours later the *Global Times* posted another lengthy and detailed story challenging BBC reporting, profiling several farmers in Xinjiang, quoting industry insiders, and blaming foreigners for starting false narratives about Xinjiang.[97] Two days later it followed up with an article blaming "anti-China forces in the US and the West."[98] Several other

---

[94] "China Branch of Cotton Trade Body Finds No Forced Labour in Xinjiang," Reuters, March 26, 2021, https://www.reuters.com/article/us-bci-cotton-xinjiang-idUSKBN2BI1KH (accessed January 11, 2023).

[95] For example, see "Consulate General Denounces Article About Xinjiang Lies," *China Daily*, May 31, 2021, https://global.chinadaily.com.cn/a/202105/31/WS60b442daa31024adobac27c4.html (accessed January 11, 2023); and Spokesperson 发言人办公室 Twitter/X account, "#BCI Shanghai Representative Office Stated," https://twitter.com/MFA_China/status/1376884629190311940?s=20 (accessed January 11, 2023). For an example catering to a domestic audience, see "休想抹黑!关于新疆棉花的6个事实," *People's Daily*, March 26, 2021, http://world.people.com.cn/n1/2021/0326/c1002-32062128.html (accessed March 12, 2024). Based on interviews with informants in Sweden, many conclude that the local office of the BCI was door-knocked by state media, with the former having little choice but to issue a statement along these lines.

[96] Li Xin et al., "BCI's China Office Says No 'Forced Labor' Found in Xinjiang in Past 8 Years," *Global Times*, March 25, 2021, https://www.globaltimes.cn/page/202103/1219417.shtml (accessed January 12, 2023).

[97] Li Xin et al., "Exclusive: Stories Behind BCI Ceasing Sourcing Cotton from China's Xinjiang Over Forced Labor Rumors," *Global Times*, March 25, 2021, https://www.globaltimes.cn/page/202103/1219475.shtml (accessed January 12, 2023).

[98] Li Xin et al., "Exclusive: How US Forced 'Xinjiang Forced Labor' Narrative on Enterprises, Industry Agencies," *Global Times*, March 27, 2021, https://www.globaltimes.cn/page/202103/1219582.shtml (accessed January 12, 2023).

external party-state outlets ran content on the topic as well, including Xinhua[99] and CCTV.[100] The news was aired domestically on state TV on March 27, 2021.[101] The quick succession of the articles and the timing of the announcement raises the possibility that the response was coordinated, at least in its amplification.

However, many aspects of BCI's halt to its Xinjiang operations and the fallout remain unknown. Following its statement, it has not explained what happened, and it routinely declines media inquiries on the subject.[102] Its 2021 annual report says that it had 11 full-time employees in China (out of 141 globally) and an office in Shanghai since 2012. Otherwise, the annual report says little about its work in China except that the council approved the 2020 financial statements, which included "a €325,000 adjustment, which was a provision to restructure our operational activity in China," and nothing about its debacle in China that year.[103] Its 2022–23 annual report also does not mention specifics but does note that "the majority of staff in China are employed by Mian Feng Da, a separate legal entity,"[104] an apparently new arrangement that was not present

---

[99] "Xinhua Commentary: BCI's Cotton Boycott Against China Is Hasty and Doomed to Fail," Xinhua, March 30, 2021, http://www.xinhuanet.com/english/2021-03/30/c_139846876.htm (accessed January 12, 2023).

[100] CCTV Twitter/X account, "No Forced Labor Was Ever Found in #Xinjiang," https://twitter.com/cctvasiapacific/status/1375403601925865474?lang=fr (accessed January 12, 2023).

[101] Mimi Lau, "Chinese Branch of Better Cotton Initiative Challenges Headquarters and Says It Has Found No Evidence of Xinjiang Forced Labour," South China Morning Post, March 29, 2021, https://www.scmp.com/news/china/politics/article/3127501/chinese-branch-better-cotton-initiative-challenges-headquarters (accessed January 12, 2023).

[102] Finbarr Bermingham, "Better Cotton Initiative's Fall a Cautionary Tale of Trying to Be All Things to All People," South China Morning Post, April 12, 2021, https://www.scmp.com/news/china/diplomacy/article/3129087/bcis-fall-cautionary-tale-trying-be-all-things-all-people?module=perpetual_scroll_0&pgtype=article&campaign=3129087 (accessed January 12, 2023); Allen-Ebrahimian, "Xinjiang Statement"; Costa, "China Labour Watchdogs."

[103] "2021 Annual Report," Better Cotton, p. 23, https://bettercotton.org/wp-content/uploads/2022/06/Better-Cotton-2021-Annual-Report.pdf (accessed January 12, 2023).

[104] "2022–23 Annual Report," Better Cotton, p. 22, https://bettercotton.org/wp-content/uploads/2023/10/2022-23-Annual-Report-1.pdf (accessed June 28, 2024).

in the 2021 report. Other watchdog groups and supply chain reviewers have faced detention, surveillance, harassment, and denial of access.[105]

Although the BCI was effectively tamed by April 2021 when it came to Xinjiang,[106] as if to complete the authoritarian snapback process by preparing to dictate the agenda, China in June 2021 launched its own cotton initiative, the Cotton China Sustainable Development Program.[107] The program is managed by the China Cotton Association (CCA), which is a federation of growers, companies, and cooperatives that is supervised by the Ministry of Civil Affairs. A summary of minutes from the CCA's April 2022 annual council meeting showed that the group resolved to set up an administrative committee in part "as an initiative to protect Xinjiang cotton."[108] The *Global Times* described efforts to set up a "homegrown independent sustainable standard and certification system" as such:

> The move marks a milestone in overhauling the global cotton rule-making system, which is currently monopolized by the Better Cotton Initiative (BCI), a West-led industry body that has apparently been manipulated by some anti-China forces in their slandering against China and its policies in Northwest China's Xinjiang Uygur Autonomous Region.[109]

The "homegrown" standards were released in March 2022.[110] Chinese regulators announced in October 2023 that the new standards would

---

[105] Costa, "China Labour Watchdogs."

[106] Bermingham, "Better Cotton Initiative's Fall."

[107] Li Xuanmin, "Chinese Cotton Industry Launches Program, to Counter Western Crackdown on Xinjiang Exports," *Global Times*, June 17, 2021, https://www.globaltimes.cn/page/202106/1226394.shtml (accessed January 12, 2023).

[108] "Takeaways of 2022 CCA Annual Council Meeting," American Cotton Shippers Association, https://acsa-cotton.org/wp-content/uploads/2022/04/Takeaways-of-2022-CCA-Annual-Council-Meeting.pdf (accessed January 12, 2023).

[109] Xuanmin, "Chinese Cotton Industry."

[110] Full standards (in Chinese) available here: https://www.business-human rights.org/documents/37416/%E4%B8%AD%E5%9B%BD%E6%A3%89%E8%8A %B1%E5%8F%AF%E6%8C%81%E7%BB%AD%E7%94%9F%E4%BA%A7_COTT ON_CHINA_Sustainable_Production.docx (accessed January 12, 2023).

apply beginning in September 2024.[111] For the *Global Times*, they were explicitly framed as a counter to the BCI:

> The CCSD was launched by the CCA in June 2021, aiming to build a homegrown independent sustainable standard and certification system to counter the current standard system, which is monopolized by the Better Cotton Initiative (BCI), a West-led industry body.[112]

Not content to levy countersanctions, neuter existing standards, and proffer new standards, the PRC has also reached to the United Nations to reframe sanctions for repression of human rights, including in Xinjiang, as themselves as a violation. In May 2024, the UN Special Rapporteur on the negative impact of the unilateral coercive measures on the enjoyment of human rights undertook a 12-day visit to China. The rapporteur position was created by the UN Human Rights Council in 2014 and is charged with investigating and reporting on how sanctions degrade human rights.[113] The rapporteur in May 2024, Belarussian national Alena Douhan, visited Xinjiang on her trip and claimed that sanctions on cotton producers, among other entities, were undermining poverty reduction efforts there.[114] The visit was encouraged by the Chinese state and widely trumpeted in its external propaganda, framed as a "UN expert" finding the sanctions illegal and calling for their removal rather than ending the forced labor itself.[115]

---

[111] "新版棉花强制性国标发布", October 21, 2023, Xinhua, http://www.news.cn/fortune/2023-10/21/c_1129929999.htm (accessed March 12, 2024).

[112] Xuanmin, "Chinese Cotton Industry."

[113] See the full mandate here: Special Rapporteur on Unilateral Coercive Measures, "Mandate of the Special Rapporteur," OHCHR, https://www.ohchr.org/en/special-procedures/sr-unilateral-coercive-measures/mandate-special-rapporteur (accessed May 27, 2024).

[114] See the press release here: "China: UN Expert Says Unilateral Sanctions Must Not Be Used as Foreign Policy Tool and Means of Economic Coercion," OHCHR, May 17, 2024, https://www.ohchr.org/en/press-releases/2024/05/china-un-expert-says-unilateral-sanctions-must-not-be-used-foreign-policy.

[115] For example, see Liu Xin and Ni Hongzhang, "Unilateral Sanctions Against China Do Not Conform with a Broad Number of International Legal Norms: UN Expert," *Global Times*, May 17, 2024, https://www.globaltimes.cn/page/202405/1312519.shtml (accessed May 27, 2024); and "UN Expert Calls to Remove

H&M and Party-Supported Consumer Backlash

The Xinjiang cotton snapback also targeted individual brands and is worth a closer look for the different aspects of the model that it highlights. The BCI is relatively unknown to the average apparel consumer, and it has nothing as such for consumers to boycott beyond the brands that are constituent members. But highly recognizable brands were also caught up in the cross-pressures and had to confront the reality that China was not just a place to source materials or labor, but also an increasingly important *consumer* market for their products. This fundamental difference from the 1990s apparel boycotts helped shape different processes and outcomes in the episodes.

Swedish fashion giant H&M is one such company. H&M is certainly not the only company targeted by China-based consumer boycotts due to Xinjiang. Bohman and Pårup find evidence of at least 90 boycotts in the PRC of foreign brands between 2008 and 2021.[116] Of those 90, 11 were triggered by company or employee statements or actions about Xinjiang. These included not only H&M, but also Walmart, Adidas, Puma, Hugo Boss, Arsenal Football Club, Intel, Nike, Asics, Zara, and Burberry. All 11 took place in 2021 except Arsenal, which is discussed more in Chapter 8. Of the 11, three issued apologies for their alleged transgressions: Intel, Hugo Boss, and Asics. Zara did not issue an apology but removed a statement from its website that had expressed concern at human rights violations in Xinjiang.

But the H&M case stands out. The company had been relatively vocal about Xinjiang as early as 2019 and had been among the most important and active BCI members.[117] Furthermore, H&M is

---

Unilateral Sanctions Against China Citing 'Illegality,'" *CGTN*, May 18, 2024, https://news.cgtn.com/news/2024-05-18/UN-expert-calls-to-remove-sanctions-aga inst-China-citing-illegality--1tHAMtfxLhu/p.html (accessed May 27, 2024).

[116] Viking Bohman and Hillevi Pårup, *Purchasing with the Party: Chinese Consumer Boycotts of Foreign Companies, 2008–2021* (Swedish National China Centre, 2022), https://kinacentrum.se/wp-content/uploads/2022/07/purchasing-with-the-party-chinese-consumer-boycotts-of-foreign-companies-20082021-3.pdf (accessed September 9, 2022).

[117] Bohman and Pårup, *Purchasing with the Party*.

176 DICTATING THE AGENDA

headquartered in Sweden and in the years leading up to the 2021 H&M boycott the more general Sweden-China relationship was contentious for several reasons, including human rights issues, conflicts over 5G, and China's 2015 capture and rendition of Gui Minhai, a Swedish citizen of Chinese origin who had published books critical of the Chinese leadership while living in Hong Kong.[118] China's ambassador to Sweden from 2017 to 2021 was Gui Congyou, widely regarded "as one of the fiercest Wolf Warrior diplomats not only in Europe, but within China's entire diplomatic system."[119]

The timeline is instructive.[120] A May 2019 *Wall Street Journal* investigative report identified a large cotton mill as part of the region's forced labor systems and indicated that the company supplied yarn to suppliers for H&M T-shirts.[121] In response to request for comment, H&M told the reporters, somewhat ambiguously, that it did not plan to get new suppliers in the region. A March 2020 report by the Australian Strategic Policy Institute identified H&M as a customer of the same company profiled in the *Wall Street Journal* report, the Huafu group, and noted that Uyghur workers were taken to work in the company's facilities in 2017 and 2018.[122]

---

[118] Bohman and Pårup, *Purchasing with the Party*.

[119] Stuart Lau, "China's Top 5 Wolf Warrior Diplomats Sinking Their Fangs into Europe," *Politico*, August 11, 2022, https://www.politico.eu/article/chinas-top-5-wolf-warrior-diplomats-sinking-their-fangs-into-europe/ (accessed January 13, 2023). On "wolf warrior diplomacy" generally, see Peter Martin, *China's Civilian Army: The Making of Wolf Warrior Diplomacy* (Oxford University Press, 2021).

[120] "Timeline: H&M's China Sales Hit as Boycott Bites," Reuters, July 2, 2021, https://www.reuters.com/article/us-h-m-results-china-timeline-idCAKCN2E81DV (accessed January 13, 2023).

[121] Eva Dou and Chao Deng, "Western Companies Get Tangled in China's Muslim Clampdown," *Wall Street Journal*, May 16, 2019, https://www.wsj.com/articles/western-companies-get-tangled-in-chinas-muslim-clampdown-11558017472 (accessed January 13, 2023).

[122] Vicky Xiuzhong Xu et al., *Uyghurs for Sale: "Re-Education", Forced Labour and Surveillance Beyond Xinjiang* (Australian Strategic Policy Institute Policy Brief, 2020), p. 33, https://ad-aspi.s3.ap-southeast-2.amazonaws.com/2022-10/Uyghurs_for_sale-11OCT2022.pdf?VersionId=N2JQOako7S4OTiSb6L7kKE5nY2d_LD25 (accessed January 13, 2023).

In September 2020, H&M issued a statement on due diligence and Xinjiang specifically.[123] The statement explained the company's concern about forced labor and discrimination of minorities in Xinjiang. Offering further detail, it stated:

> We do not work with any garment manufacturing factories located in XUAR, and we do not source products from this region. . . . XUAR is China's largest cotton growing area, and up until now, our suppliers have sourced cotton from farms connected to Better Cotton Initiative (BCI) in the region. As it has become increasingly difficult to conduct credible due diligence in the region, BCI has decided to suspend licensing of BCI cotton in XUAR. This means that cotton for our production will no longer be sourced from there.

The September 2020 statement and H&M's actions apparently garnered little public attention in China until six months later in March 2021.[124] Indeed, according to a China luxury fashion trade website, in February 2021 H&M announced that it planned a new collaboration with a Chinese streetwear brand.[125] On March 11, 2021, an online sales launch for an H&M collaboration with Irish designer Simone Rocha that had been advertised widely by Chinese fashion influencers was apparently so popular that it crashed the sales portal.[126] In short, the statement itself appeared not to influence H&M's business in China for several months.

---

[123] Full statement available here: H&M Group, "H&M Group Statement on Due Diligence," https://hmgroup.com/sustainability/fair-and-equal/human-rights/h-m-group-statement-on-due-diligence/ (accessed January 13, 2023).

[124] Bohman and Pårup, *Purchasing with the Party*, p. 16.

[125] Gemma A. Williams, "H&M Collaborates with Pronounce," *Jing Daily*, February 23, 2021, https://jingdaily.com/hm-pronounce-collaboration-chinese-designers/ (accessed January 13, 2023).

[126] Gemma A. Williams, "Fairytale Ending for Simone Rocha's H&M Collab," *Jing Daily*, March 11, 2021, https://jingdaily.com/hm-simone-rocha-collaboration-china-crash/ (accessed January 13, 2023).

178 DICTATING THE AGENDA

This all changed in late March 2021.[127] On March 23, 2021, the day after sanctions were imposed on officials involved in human rights abuses in Xinjiang, a Weibo user posted screenshots of H&M's September 2020 statement, with commentary critical of the company. One day later the Communist Youth League shared on Weibo the statement along with the (subsequently deleted) BCI statement, resulting in hundreds of thousands of "likes" and "shares." The same day, March 24, H&M products were unavailable on major e-commerce platforms and disappeared from online mapping and location services in China. Xinhua released a satirical cartoon of H&M on the same day. One day later, on March 25, the main state television station, CCTV, ran a story highly critical of H&M. Ministry of Foreign Affairs spokespersons defended the online discourse as legitimate, influencers stopped working with H&M, and the *People's Daily* ran content lambasting the company. The fact that the September 2020 statement remained dormant for so long only to be suddenly the subject of instantaneous outrage across several different platforms strongly suggests a level of coordination, or at least party-state cheerleading of nationalist sentiment.[128]

About a week after the boycott started H&M's CEO indicated that the episode resulted in about 20 stores closing in China.[129] But the company did not apologize. It issued a relatively anodyne statement on March 31, 2021, saying: "We are working together with our colleagues in China to do everything we can to manage the current challenges and find a way forward" and explaining that China is an important market

---

[127] Events in this paragraph are summarized from Bohman and Pårup, *Purchasing with the Party*, pp. 16–18.

[128] Bohman and Pårup, *Purchasing with the Party*, p. 16. See also Raymond Zhong and Paul Mozur, "How China's Outrage Machine Kicked Up a Storm Over H&M," *New York Times*, March 19, 2021, https://www.nytimes.com/2021/03/29/business/china-xinjiang-cotton-hm.html. Shirk argues that the boycott was "government mobilized." See Susan Shirk, *Overreach: How China Derailed Its Peaceful Rise* (Oxford University Press, 2023), p. 235.

[129] "Timeline: H&M's China Sales Hit as Boycott Bites," Reuters.

and supplier and that the company wants to act in a responsible and respectful way.[130]

Within six months of the boycott China went from H&M's fourth largest consumer market to outside its top 10.[131] In August 2022, H&M returned to Alibaba's e-commerce platform Tmall, although its return on many other apps, including mapping services, was not in evidence.[132] Many online commentators pledged to continue to boycott the brand, and while H&M has launched other labels for the Chinese market, it is not clear what will happen if consumers discover that these are H&M brands.[133] H&M has said little else about the episode.

Xinjiang, Forced Labor, and the Authoritarian Snapback

Overall, the forced labor, cotton standards, and advocacy episode that unfolded over about a five-year period from 2017 to 2022 reveals the authoritarian snapback process at play. Liberal activism was in some measure effective when it came to forced labor in the cotton industry in Xinjiang, even getting companies like H&M on board.

However, the episode shows how the PRC *stigmatized* efforts by activists to highlight forced labor. Activists were tarnished as "anti-China forces" or personally insulted or even sued, as is the case with Adrian Zenz, a researcher on these issues sanctioned by the PRC on March 22,

---

[130] Full statement available here: H&M Group, "Statement on H&M in China," March 31, 2021, https://hmgroup.com/news/statement_hm_china/ (accessed January 13, 2023).

[131] Hillevi Pårup, "Chinese Consumer Boycotts May Have Abated but the Ripple Effects Are Still Being Felt," China Observers in Central and Eastern Europe, October 20, 2022, https://chinaobservers.eu/chinese-consumer-boycotts-may-have-abated-but-the-ripple-effects-are-still-being-felt%EF%BF%BC/ (accessed January 13, 2023).

[132] Clarence Leong, "H&M Returns to China's Internet After a 16-Month Disappearance," *Wall Street Journal*, August 16, 2022, https://www.wsj.com/articles/h-m-returns-to-chinas-internet-after-a-16-month-disappearance-11660653643 (accessed January 13, 2023).

[133] Pårup, "Chinese Consumer Boycotts."

2021.[134] Even the BCI, a relatively friendly engagement partner with China over the years, was attacked in the PRC press. Companies like H&M perceived to be insufficiently respectful of Chinese consumers were stigmatized through state media.[135] Likewise "the West" and advocates for fair labor in Xinjiang can be cast as hypocritical, as when the Chinese propaganda apparatus pointed out the United States' and Europe's own history of using slavery in the cotton industry.[136] Domestic audiences were *shielded* from the truth about repression or forced labor in Xinjiang by China's propaganda and censorship systems.

In the face of criticism about Xinjiang cotton, the PRC *reframed engagement and set new ground rules* by mobilizing and amplifying nationalistic voices that cast doing business in China as accepting China's terms, including those that governed the Xinjiang cotton industry. The consumer boycott of H&M sought to force it to abide by Chinese cotton labor standards if it wanted to be a viable consumer brand in the Chinese market. The ire of a nationalistic public was used as a cudgel to enforce the new rules of engagement, and technological fixes to take the company off the Chinese internet were designed to squeeze the brand's bottom line.

In this case H&M can be seen as an example, or a signal to other companies for the state to *project control and influence outward*. The penalties that H&M faced are likely intended for other companies contemplating similar activism—however tame—about Xinjiang cotton or any other human rights issue to preemptively toe the line. This has been supplemented by regulatory measures, such as investigating Western companies that do not use Xinjiang cotton on the

---

[134] On the lawsuit, see Eva Dou, "Academic Faces Chinese Lawsuit for Exposing Human Rights Abuses in Xinjiang," *Washington Post*, March 10, 2021, https://www.washingtonpost.com/world/asia_pacific/china-sanctions-uighurs-xinjiang/2021/03/10/dd57f8c8-814a-11eb-be22-32d331d87530_story.html (accessed June 17, 2024).

[135] For example, see Global Times WeChat account, "嘴上说不要新疆棉花,美国身体很诚实" https://mp.weixin.qq.com/s/JtZfUGAl3lKuHD-OShrk7g (accessed March 12, 2024).

[136] Zhong and Mozur, "China's Outrage Machine."

grounds that they are discriminating against Xinjiang cotton companies, thereby signaling enforcement of the new ground rules.[137] Likewise the PRC sought to tame the BCI while still letting it exist in China under the ground rules set by the state. Even the heads of the BCI appear to remain hesitant to speak about Xinjiang, and the organization's original statement is no longer on its website. Sanctions to combat forced labor were framed by a China-friendly UN special rapporteur as themselves a violation of human rights, thus granting the imprimatur of UN legitimacy to China's human rights violations.[138]

Finally, China sought to *dictate the agenda* by setting up new "home-grown" cotton standards with the aim of legitimizing Xinjiang's cotton industry and the problematic labor regime that sustains it. On the consumer side, dictating the agenda comes through companies actively supporting Xinjiang cotton or being replaced. This may look like Hugo Boss's initial apology, which extolled the quality of Xinjiang cotton and noted that the company would still use it, although that apology was subsequently retracted.[139] Or it may be that H&M is replaced in the Chinese market by other local brands, which Bohman and Pårup posit as a potential reason that it was selected as a target.[140] Shein, a Chinese fast-fashion giant, reportedly tells US lawmakers and regulators privately that it does not use Xinjiang cotton while remaining publicly silent on Xinjiang.[141] Regardless, H&M's experience with the authoritarian snapback would be different had it been operating in the 1990s with a relatively less powerful Chinese consumer market. Successes are

---

[137] Natalie Sherman, "China Probes Calvin Klein over Xinjiang Cotton," BBC, September 25, 2024, https://www.bbc.com/news/articles/c2opxwwqqzwo.

[138] On China's approach to special procedures and rapporteurs in the UN human rights system, see Rana Siu Inboden, "China, Power and the United Nations Special Procedures: Emerging Threats to the 'Crown Jewels' of the International Human Rights System," *Global Policy* 15 (2024): pp. 74–84, https://doi.org/10.1111/1758-5899.13275.

[139] Bohman and Pårup, *Purchasing with the Party*.

[140] Bohman and Pårup, *Purchasing with the Party*.

[141] Eleanor Olcott et al., "Shein Sought to Reassure US Over China Supply Chain Ahead of IPO," *Financial Times*, June 20, 2024, https://www.ft.com/content/25105b73-f073-4b9d-bf0f-59099d0ee1eb.

182   DICTATING THE AGENDA

fed back to domestic audiences and amplified via state media as they occur, including regarding the BCI and cotton standards[142] and the UN special rapporteur's comments.[143]

Conclusion: Pro-Authoritarian Consumer Activism

What becomes clear from this analysis is that the landscape for consumer boycotts, corporate activism, and international organization monitoring when it comes to labor activism has changed. In the years between the 1990s and 2020s the revived market power of authoritarian China could be used in ways that were more impactful. Escalation up the authoritarian snapback model in the 2020s was facilitated by China's power but also by the PRC's ability to watch and learn in the intervening years how to handle foreign boycotts and where to find leverage points. The fact that the Xinjiang issue touches on China's perceived insecurity when it comes to sovereign control amplified the response and made the snapback more apparent and visible.

For certain, transnational companies are still influenced by naming-and-shaming tactics and the stigmatization of certain authoritarian regimes and their social practices. The withdrawal of over a thousand of Western companies from the Russian market in 2022, with some suspending operations and others withdrawing permanently, following Russia's invasion of Ukraine demonstrated a collective stigmatization of a regime by companies arguably not seen since apartheid

---

[142] For example, see "U.S.-Led Attempts to Use Xinjiang to Contain China a Gravest Violation of Human Rights of All Ethnic Groups in Xinjiang," Xinhua, October 8, 2022, https://english.news.cn/20221008/009060cb0edf4e4780cdeb51215a7c44/c.html (accessed November 11, 2022); "独家揭秘:美国如何操纵'强迫劳动'议题打压中国棉花企业," Xinhua, March 28, 2021, http://www.xinhuanet.com/world/2021-03/28/c_1211087051.htm (accessed March 12, 2024); "就是为了阻碍中国发展"—起底美国涉疆人权谎言," Xinhua, October 26, 2023, http://www.news.cn/world/2023-10/26/c_1212294102.htm (accessed March 12, 2024); "嘴上说不要新疆棉花,美国身体很诚实," Global Times WeChat Account, https://mp.weixin.qq.com/s/JtZfUGAl3lKuHD-OShrk7g (accessed March 12, 2024).

[143] For example, see "和评理 | 滥施单边制裁不得人心 美国应迷途知返", May 20, 2024, http://www.chinanews.com.cn/gj/2024/05-20/10220376.shtml (accessed May 27, 2024).

South Africa.[144] However, the mostly Western corporate boycott is not shared by non-Western companies,[145] while nominal US allies, including Türkiye and the UAE, have welcomed sanctioned oligarchs and seemingly facilitated re-export. At the very least, the politics of consumer contestation that once projected predominantly liberal values and agendas has become contested globally, including within the UN human rights system itself. A more maximalist possibility is that consumer boycotts can be used to enforce pro-authoritarian values and practices transnationally.

[144] For a running list of Western companies that boycotted or suspended operations in Russia, see Yale School of Management, "Over 1000 Companies Have Curtailed Operations in Russia—but Some Remain," November 27, 2023, https://som.yale.edu/story/2022/over-1000-companies-have-curtailed-operations-russia-some-remain.

[145] Alexander Cooley and Brooke Harrington, "The Power of Stigma: Shaming Russian Elites Has Helped Weaken Putin," *Foreign Affairs*, October 27, 2022, https://www.foreignaffairs.com/russian-federation/power-stigma-shaming-russia-elites-weaken-putin.

Chapter 7

Harnessing Global Higher Education

In July 2023, scholar-activist Gubad Ibadoghlu, then a visiting fellow at the London School of Economics (LSE), was arrested while visiting his native Azerbaijan.[1] Ibadoghlu has been critical of high-level elite corruption in Azerbaijan and involved in opposition politics, so his arrest on possessing extremist material and currency counterfeiting was widely seen as politically motivated. Many organizations issued statements condemning the arrest and calling for his release, including the LSE[2] and TU Dresden, where he was due to take up a new post in autumn 2023.[3] Curiously, though, the Oxford University student newspaper *Cherwell* reported that Oxford's Nizami Ganjavi Centre for the Study of the History, Languages, and Cultures of Azerbaijan, the Caucasus and Central Asia hadn't said a word. The paper reported that the center was funded by an anonymous £10 million donation, the

---

[1] For background on the case, see Geneva Abdul, "Health of LSE Academic Detained in Azerbaijan at Risk, Say Family," *The Guardian*, September 14, 2023, https://www.theguardian.com/world/2023/sep/14/health-of-lse-academic-detained-in-azerbaijan-at-risk-say-family (accessed June 24, 2024).

[2] LSENews Twitter/X account, "Our Statement on Dr Gubad Ibadoghlu," https://x.com/LSEnews/status/1684555182170832899 (accessed June 24, 2024)

[3] TU Dresden, "Visiting Scholar Dr. Gubad Ibadoghlu Released into House Arrest," April 24, 2024, https://tu-dresden.de/tu-dresden/universitaetskultur/news/dr-gubad-ibadoghlu-in-den-hausarrest-entlassen-1?set_language=en (accessed June 24, 2024)

details of which Oxford was not forthcoming about, and featured as a board member Nargiz Pashayeva, sister-in-law of Azerbaijan's ruler for the last 21 years, Ilham Aliyev.[4] It seemed odd that a well-funded research center at one of the United Kingdom's most prestigious universities stayed silent about an arrested academic in the country of the research center's focus.[5] The authoritarian snapback appeared to be complete with Ibadoghlu removed from the center's agenda. However, following the *Cherwell* story in December 2023 a group of academics were able to organize a seminar on the political economy of Azerbaijan in honor of Ibadoghlu, including securing funding from the center. The small event is memorialized on the center's website, but the board has still not made a collective statement.[6] The donor to the center remains anonymous. As it happens, in October 2024 Ibadoghlu was shortlisted for the prestigious Sakharov Prize for Freedom of Thought by the European Parliament.

Episodes like this illustrate ongoing contestation about human rights and liberal values at the heart of international higher education, showing both the expanding scope of authoritarian influence in the sector and the agency that remains to push back against it. This chapter examines the contours of the emerging global snapback against liberal higher education's models, values, and initiatives. Though higher education is often overlooked by international relations experts and policymakers, its post–Cold War trajectory offers important insights into the rapid spread of Western soft power as well as the subsequent drivers of its waning influence and the global erosion of related liberal values such as academic freedom and the right to protest on campus.

---

[4] Suzanne Antelme, "Oxford Centre with Mystery £10M Donor and Family Links to Autocratic Ruler Silent on Regime's Imprisonment of LSE Academic," Cherwell, October 16, 2023, https://cherwell.org/2023/10/16/oxford-centre-mystery-10m-donor-family-links-to-autocratic-ruler-silent-on-imprisonment-lse-academic/ (accessed June 24,2024). In fact, the Aliyevs have ruled the country for decades, as Aliyev's father was Azerbaijan's Communist Party secretary from 1969 to 1982 and president from 1993 to 2003.

[5] A detailed account of the episode is provided in John Heathershaw et al., *Indulging Kleptocracy: British Service Providers, Communist Elites and the Enabling of Corruption* (Oxford University Press, forthcoming 2025), chapter 10.

[6] Oxford Nizami Ganjavi Centre, "The Political Economy of Modern Azerbaijan," https://www.ongc.ox.ac.uk/article/the-political-economy-of-modern-azerbaijan-a-seminar-in-honour-of-dr-gubad-ibadoghlu. Individual board members have spoken out.

DICTATING THE AGENDA

Similar to other global domains, in the 1990s and 2000s, US and Western universities, both private universities and public institutions, were widely perceived as leaders in scientific and technical innovation, research, and academic excellence across most fields. They also provided a model for liberal arts education and publicly maintained a commitment to safeguarding academic freedom for faculty and students.[7] The post–Cold War drive toward internationalization and spread of US global higher education both mirrored and was enabled by key features of globalization, including the legal harmonization promoted by the World Trade Organization (WTO) and regional trade agreements, greater population mobility, and the marketization of higher education and related efforts by universities to expand their revenue base.

At the same time, universities throughout the world are viewed as potential sites of activism, social mobilization, and political protest. For example, US university campuses served as the major sites of anti–Vietnam War protests. More recently they have become lightning rods for civil rights and social justice-related protest and/or campaigns advocating for university divestment from certain countries (South Africa, Israel) or associations such as maintaining endowment investments in fossil fuels.[8] Many of the pro-Palestinian campus demonstrations and encampments that swept across US and European universities in spring 2024 openly referenced these earlier waves of campus activism.[9]

At first glance, the global authoritarian snapback against liberal education appears less severe than in the realms of human

---

[7] On the evolution of the US university on these dimensions, see Steven Brint, *Two Cheers for Higher Education: Why American Universities Are Stronger Than Ever—and How to Meet the Challenges They Face* (Princeton University Press, 2020).

[8] Roderick A. Ferguson, *We Demand: The University and Student Protests* (University of California Press, 2017). Over recent years, many of America's leading institutions have themselves sought to uncover and come to terms with their own complicity with practices such as slavery, land appropriation, and systemic discrimination, even as they have encouraged critical research and liberal campus activism. See, for example, Craig Steven Wilder, *Ebony and Ivy: Race, Slavery, and the Troubled History of America's Universities* (Bloomsbury Publishing USA, 2013).

[9] "A Look at the Protests of the War in Gaza That Have Emerged at US Colleges," Associated Press, April 30, 2024, https://apnews.com/article/gaza-war-campus-protests-966eb531279f8e4381883fc5d79d5466.

rights nongovernmental organizations (NGOs), foreign journalism, or consumer activism. After all, many universities in liberal democracies in the United States, United Kingdom, and other liberal democracies are still widely recognized as global leaders, while their internationalization efforts continue to spur global demand for their degrees, research collaboration, and formal institutional partnerships. However, a closer examination suggests that the internationalization that occurred almost exclusively on liberal terms in the 1990s and early 2000s has peaked; universities in non-democracies capture an increasing share of the global higher-education market, while dozens of transnational branch campuses established by universities in partnerships with authoritarian hosts such as China, Singapore, and the Gulf region that were supposed to spread liberal higher education globally have revised the initial liberal terms of their partnerships or folded. Moreover, nationalist and illiberal regimes in the European education space, and in certain US states, are now actively suppressing liberal education, co-opting it, or, as in the cases of Hungary and Türkiye, a combination of both.[10] And higher-education partnerships are increasingly implicated in intensifying geopolitical rivalries, most notably growing US competitive tensions with China and intense scrutiny and new national security-related legislation in both countries that have curtailed international educational partnerships and collaborations.[11]

The next section briefly overviews some of the major trends in the globalization and internationalization of US, UK, and Australian higher education over the last three decades, focusing on student mobility, foreign funding, and global university rankings. We then scrutinize a particular form of global partnership that has emerged from this internationalization era: the transnational campus where a university in one country has opened a degree-granting campus overseas, usually in partnership or with the financial support of a host country. It explores how interactions between the liberal democratic offshore campus with its authoritarian hosts have reframed the liberal educational mission and

---

[10] Evan Schofer et al., "Illiberal Reactions to Higher Education," *Minerva* 60, no. 4 (2022): pp. 509–34, https://doi.org/10.1007/s11024-022-09472-x.

[11] John Aubrey Douglass, ed., *Neo-Nationalism and Universities: Populists, Autocrats and the Future of Higher Education* (Johns Hopkins University Press, 2021).

redefined the boundaries of academic freedom. The following section then recounts the rise and decline of the Central European University (CEU) in Budapest, Hungary, and shows how a flagship project of liberal education within a former communist country was stigmatized, politically attacked, expelled, and arguably replaced because of its perceived liberal mission and activism. We conclude by identifying other trends in the global contestation of liberal higher education, including the spread of authoritarian models abroad and the backlash against liberal education within the West itself, particularly in the United States.

The Ascendence of the Liberal Model in Global Higher Education

The post–Cold War period saw the dramatic globalization of higher education, principally led by the internationalization efforts of US and Western universities. Valued at $24 billion in 1995,[12] the higher-education sector rapidly grew as a result of the expansion of global services facilitated by the WTO and its General Agreement on Trade in Services.[13] By 2019, one market research firm estimated total international higher-education expenditure at $196 billion, expecting it to reach $433 billion by 2030, an 18-fold increase since 1995.[14] Internationalization has also become strategic priority for most tertiary institutions. Another study of over 500 universities worldwide finds that more than 95% of universities in the United States, United Kingdom, and Australia now have institutionalized offices that focus on internationalization and development, most headed by senior-level

---

[12] Vik Naidoo, "Transnational Higher Education: A Stock Take of Current Activity," *Journal of Studies in International Education* 13, no. 3 (2009): p. 311, dio:10.1177/1028315308317938.

[13] Philip G. Altbach and Jane Knight, "The Internationalization of Higher Education: Motivations and Realities," *Journal of Studies in International Education* 11, nos. 3–4 (2007): p. 291, https://doi.org/10.1177/1028315307303542.

[14] "$196B International Education Market Set to Reach $433B by 2030," *HolonIQ*, February 9, 2022, https://www.holoniq.com/notes/196b-international-education-market-set-to-reach-433b-by-2030.

administrative officers.[15] According to UNESCO, the number of global students enrolled in higher education has increased from 82 million in 1995 to 235 million in 2022.[16]

Internationalization also has profoundly impacted the institutional development of higher-education sectors, as US and Western principles and practices have been privileged, disseminated, and emulated. For example, the Bologna Process, created out of the European Union's push to harmonize and reform European higher education in the late 1990s, standardized degrees and credit hours, delineated graduate and undergraduate courses of study, promoted student and researcher mobility, and stipulated accreditation standards and periodic quality assurance reviews.[17] These reforms have directly influenced countries of the post-communist region and have formed the basis of intraregional cooperation in higher education. Some authors even identified the Bologna Process as the backbone of an emerging "international regime" in global higher education, coordinating expectations around these reform principles as a basis for international collaboration.[18] Increased student mobility, standardization, accreditation, and research collaborations are all distinguishing features of US as well as European internationalization efforts; at the same time, such internationalization has also been criticized as driving the commodification of education, commercialization, and market-based competition.[19]

---

[15] Seungah S. Lee and Francisco O. Ramirez, "Globalization of Universities as Organizational Actors?," in *University Collegiality and the Erosion of Faculty Authority* (Emerald Publishing, 2023), pp. 94–95, https://doi.org/10.1108/S0733-558X20230000086004.

[16] "What You Need to Know About Higher Education," UNESCO, April 20, 2023, https://www.unesco.org/en/higher-education/need-know.

[17] Jeroen Huisman et al., "Europe's Bologna Process and Its Impact on Global Higher Education," in *The Sage Handbook of International Higher Education*, edited by Darla K. Deardorff, Hans de Wit, John D. Heyl, and Tony Adams (Sage Publications, 2012), pp. 83–84, https://doi.org/10.4135/9781452218397.n5.

[18] Hila Zahavi and Yoav Friedman, "The Bologna Process: An International Higher Education Regime," in *The Bologna Process and its Global Strategy* (Routledge, 2020), pp. 22–38.

[19] See John K. Hudzik and Michael Stohl, "Comprehensive and Strategic Internationalization of US Higher Education," in *The Sage Handbook of International Higher Education*, edited by Darla K. Deardorff, Hans de Wit, John D. Heyl, and Tony Adams (Sage Publications, 2012), pp. 61–80, https://doi.org/10.4135/9781452218397.n4;

Indicators of Global Influence: People, Donations, and Rankings

Internationalization captures a range of processes and global flows, but three indicators seem especially relevant for illustrating the outsized global position of leadership of private and public universities in liberal democracies: student mobility, foreign donations, and global university rankings.

In the immediate post–Cold War era, US universities became magnets for international students, including from China and the Global South. According to the Open Doors report published by the International Institute for Education, international students in the United States, totaling 400,000 in 1990, surpassed one million in 2018–19.[20] A large percentage of this population appears to be accounted for by the meteoric growth in students from China. For example, during the 2001–2 academic year just under 60,000 students from mainland China attended US universities; that number more than doubled to 157,600 in 2010–11, and peaked at 372,500 in 2019–20, before falling off because of the Covid-19 global pandemic.[21] In the United Kingdom, and despite fears of a post-Brexit slump, international students have continued to increase, totaling 555,000 in 2021, 143,800 of which were from China and 55,000 from India.[22] This increase in enrollment of international students has been critical in compensating for budget shortfalls and cuts in public sector funding in the United States and United Kingdom. One study estimated that international students annually contributed over $22 billion in revenues to US state economies, more than the gaming or the music and movie industries combined.[23]

---

and John K. Hudzik, *Comprehensive Internationalization: Institutional Pathways to Success* (Routledge, 2014), pp. 7–25.

[20] "Enrollment Trends," OpenDoors Data, https://opendoorsdata.org/data/international-students/enrollment-trends/.

[21] Laura Silver, "Amid Pandemic, International Student Enrollment at U.S. Universities Fell 15% in the 2020–21 School Year," Pew Research Center, December 6, 2021, https://www.pewresearch.org/short-reads/2021/12/06/amid-pandemic-international-student-enrollment-at-u-s-universities-fell-15-in-the-2020-21-school-year/.

[22] "Global Flow of Tertiary-Level Students," UNESCO Institute for Statistics, https://uis.unesco.org/en/uis-student-flow.

[23] Niall Hegarty, "Where We Are Now—the Presence and Importance of International Students to Universities in the United States," *Journal of International Students* 4, no. 3 (2014): p. 227, https://doi.org/10.32674/jis.v4i3.462.

Along with student mobility, foreign funding and donations to US and UK universities have surged over the last decade. According to the US Department of Education, between 2013 and 2019, the reported total of foreign donations to US universities exceeded $4 billion, with Hong Kong, the United Kingdom, Canada, China, India, and Saudi Arabia the reported leading foreign donors.[24] These official data almost certainly underreport the inflow of foreign funds given that they are complicated by the fact that US-registered branches of foreign organizations, such as the Qatar Foundation, which has donated over $1 billion to US universities, are not identified as "foreign" for reporting purposes, while certain high-profile major donors who hold multiple citizenships are regarded as domestic donors.[25] In addition, research collaborations involving universities, governments, and the private sector are increasingly common as forms of international partnerships and a key part of the evolution of internationalization.[26]

In turn, such internationalization efforts have helped to establish and reinforce the reputations of the elite universities of the West as global leaders, as captured in a series of prominent global higher-education rankings. Strikingly, in 2003 not a single non-Western university was included in the top 100 institutions of the inaugural Academic Ranking of World Universities (ARWU) or "Shanghai Rankings" compiled and published by Shanghai Jiao Tong University.[27] The rankings themselves

---

[24] US Department of Education, "Section 17 of the Higher Education Act of 1965," https://www2.ed.gov/policy/highered/leg/foreign-gifts.html (accessed June 6, 2023); Office of the General Counsel, US Department of Education, "Institutional Compliance with Section 117 of the Higher Education Act of 1965," October 2020, https://www2.ed.gov/policy/highered/leg/institutional-compliance-section-117.pdf.

[25] For example, Ronnie Chan made a $350 million donation to Harvard University in 2014 (at the time a record gift) as a dual US and Hong Kong citizen. See Alexander Cooley et al., "Foreign Donations in the Higher Education Sector of the United States and the United Kingdom: Pathways for Reputation Laundering," *Journal of Comparative and International Higher Education* 14, no. 5 (2022): pp. 43–79, https://doi.org/10.32674/jcihe.v14i5.4625.

[26] Manuel Heitor, "How University Global Partnerships May Facilitate a New Era of International Affairs and Foster Political and Economic Relations," *Technological Forecasting and Social Change* 95, nos. 3–4 (2015): pp. 276–93, https://doi.org/10.1016/j.techfore.2015.01.005.

[27] 2023 Academic Ranking of World Universities, https://www.shanghairanking.com/rankings/arwu/2003. Interestingly, the rankings themselves were initially funded by the Chinese government as an attempt to discern the gap in performance and resources between leading universities and Western counterparts.

192 DICTATING THE AGENDA

have become a controversial topic in global higher education, with the methods allegedly favoring the legacies, endowments, and research missions and outputs of long-established institutions.[28] And despite the overall trend undermining liberal norms and standards in other areas of global governance, both the Chinese and Russian governments have largely accepted the authority of the major rankings systems. They routinely report these rankings in state media and use them as geopolitical benchmarks and confirmations of global status for their own educational systems.[29] The first university from an authoritarian state to enter the ARWU top 100 was Russia's Moscow State University in 2007, while in 2016 Tsinghua University became the first Chinese university to enter the rankings.

Internationalization Evolving on Whose Terms?

But along all three of these dimensions of internationalization, namely student mobility, foreign donations, and global rankings, we see signs that the hegemonic status and global influence of Western universities has peaked, as well as some reversals and internal scrutiny of the liberal model. In the realm of student mobility, according to the International Institute for Education, the total number of international students coming to the United States appears to have peaked in 2019 at 1,095,299;[30] the number of Chinese students reached 369,548 in 2019, dropping to 289,526 in 2023 (out of a total of 1,057,188).[31]

---

[28] See Ellen Hazelkorn, "Rankings and the Global Reputation Race," *New Directions for Higher Education*, no. 168 (2014): pp. 13–26, https://doi.org/10.1002/he.20110.

[29] See, for instance, Zou Shuo, "Chinese Universities Climb World Rankings," *China Daily*, November 14, 2022, https://www.chinadaily.com.cn/a/202211/14/WS637180a4a310491754329692.html. On Russia, see Larisa Taradina and Maria Yudkevich, "Russia: Ranking Fever—Do We Know the Remedy?," in *Global Rankings and the Geopolitics of Higher Education*, edited by Ellen Hazelkorn (Routledge, 2016), pp. 168–85.

[30] Data obtained from International Institute for Education's Project Atlas, https://www.iie.org/research-initiatives/project-atlas/explore-data/united-states-2/ (accessed July 9, 2024).

[31] International Institute for Education, Project Atlas, based on Chinese official statistics, https://www.iie.org/research-initiatives/project-atlas/explore-data/china-2/ (accessed July 9, 2024).

Over the same time, international enrollments in Chinese and Russian universities have dramatically increased. From 2013 to 2019 the number of international students attending universities in China grew from 524,672 to over 718,558, but, of those, the number of US-based students in the country during that same period fell from 24,625 to just 20,996.[32] In Russia, inflows of international students increased from 282,921 in 2016 to 351,127 in 2022, despite Western sanctions and travel restrictions placed on Russia following its invasion of Ukraine in February 2022.[33] Interestingly, according to UN data, while democracies (led by South Korea, but including Japan and the United States in the top five) are among the leading sending countries to China, in Russia the leading sending countries both before and after the war have been authoritarian Kazakhstan, China, Uzbekistan, and Turkmenistan.[34]

The political roles and influences that inform these sizable student populations, especially from China, also appear more complicated. Whereas many have assumed that foreign students would inevitably be socialized and inculcated with liberal norms as a result of their liberal education abroad, recent reports, such as a Human Rights Watch (HRW) study on the 160,000 Chinese students studying in Australia, show that authoritarian states routinely maintain surveillance and a network of informants on students abroad, while emboldening students to object and even protest against curricular content or events that are critical of politically sensitive national issues.[35]

Much like the episode at Oxford recounted at the beginning of this chapter, the flow of foreign donations to the United States, once left

---

[32] International Institute for Education, Project Atlas, https://www.iie.org/research-initiatives/project-atlas/explore-data/china-2/ (accessed July 9, 2024).

[33] International Institute for Education, Project Atlas, https://www.iie.org/research-initiatives/project-atlas/explore-data/russia-2/ (accessed July 9, 2024)

[34] "Global Flow of Tertiary-Level Students," UNESCO Institute for Statistics, https://uis.unesco.org/en/uis-student-flow.

[35] Sophie McNeill, "They Don't Understand the Fear We Have," Human Rights Watch, June 31, 2021, https://www.hrw.org/report/2021/06/30/they-dont-understand-fear-we-have/how-chinas-long-reach-repression-undermines; Yan Xiaojun and Mohammed Alsudairi, "Guarding Against the Threat of a Westernising Education: A Comparative Study of Chinese and Saudi Cultural Security Discourses and Practices Towards Overseas Study," *Journal of Contemporary China* 30, no. 131 (2021): pp. 803–19, https://doi.org/10.1080/10670564.2021.1884962.

unscrutinized, has also generated political controversy and calls for more transparency in reporting by universities. A 2019 US Department of Justice investigation into foreign funding, especially by China, Russia, and Middle Eastern countries, accused some of the most prestigious universities in the United States of failing to report billions of dollars in foreign donations from authoritarian-linked donors and sources.[36] A further review of these initial reporting documents by the *Wall Street Journal* estimated that these universities failed to disclose about $6.5 billion in donations, many accepted anonymously, from these countries of concern.[37] The question of whether this inflow of foreign funding compromises research integrity or academic freedom has also become more pressing, as politically exposed individuals seek to launder their reputations through gifts to prestigious foreign universities and authoritarian state donors seek to set more positive research agendas in Western institutions.[38] Illustrative of the *projecting control and influence outward* and *dictating the agenda* steps of the authoritarian snapback model, a growing sense of self-censorship of academics involved in foreign-funded research projects and centers is also concerning.[39] For example, a comparison of research projects and events hosted by UK-based Middle Eastern research centers that were funded by Gulf countries versus those that were not found that Gulf-funded centers were less likely to sponsor research on human rights, democracy, and gender equality.[40]

---

[36] Office of the General Counsel, US Department of Education, "Institutional Compliance with Section 117 of the Higher Education Act of 1965," October 2020, p. 13, https://www2.ed.gov/policy/highered/leg/institutional-compliance-section-117.pdf. Foreign donations over $250,000 are meant to be reported.

[37] Kate O'Keeffe, "Education Department Investigating Harvard, Yale over Foreign Funding," *Wall Street Journal*, February 13, 2020, https://www.wsj.com/articles/education-department-investigating-harvard-yale-over-foreign-funding-115 81539042.

[38] Alexander Cooley et al., "Foreign Donations in the Higher Education Sector of the United States and the United Kingdom: Pathways for Reputation Laundering," *Journal of Comparative & International Higher Education* 14, no. 5 (2022): pp. 43–79, https://doi.org/10.32674/jcihe.v14i5.4625.

[39] Tena Prelec et al., "Is Academic Freedom at Risk from Internationalisation? Results from a 2020 Survey of UK Social Scientists," *International Journal of Human Rights* 26, no. 10 (2022): pp. 1698–722, https://doi.org/10.1080/13642987.2021.2021398.

[40] Jonas Bergan Draege and Martin Lestra, "Gulf-Funding of British Universities and the Focus on Human Development," *Middle East Law and Governance* 7, no. 1 (2015): pp. 25–49, https://doi.org/:10.1163/18763375-00701005.

In terms of emerging positioning in global rankings, universities in democracies continue to dominate the most influential lists, but universities from China and Singapore have made significant inroads in recent years. In the 2023 edition of the Shanghai rankings, China placed 10 institutions in the top 100, along with two from Singapore, and an additional 13 institutions between the 101st to 150th spots.[41] These moves are the results of Beijing's efforts to elevate a selection of universities in the global standings through increased funding via Project 985, mandating more courses be taught in English, and launching its own international recruiting campaign for researchers and scholars.[42] Interestingly, and in line with disputing the authority of other international rankings, three major Chinese universities announced in 2022 that they would be withdrawing from global university rankings.[43] In sum, while Western universities, especially from the United States and United Kingdom, remain major players in internationalization, the flows and ecology of internationalization may no longer be as conducive to liberal models and values as they once were.

The Rise of the Transnational Campus

Perhaps the most distinctive organizational form to emerge from this era of globalization of higher education and the rise of transnational education is the "offshore campus," also referred to as a "microcampus."[44] According to the Cross-Border Education Research Team (C-BERT), a transnational or "offshore campus" is one in which "an entity that is owned, at least in part, by a foreign higher-education provider; operated in the name of the foreign education provider; and provides an entire academic program, substantially on site, leading to a degree awarded

---

[41] "2023 Academic Ranking," Shanghai Ranking.

[42] Xiaohua Zong and Wei Zhang, "Establishing World-Class Universities in China: Deploying a Quasi-Experimental Design to Evaluate the Net Effects of Project 985," *Studies in Higher Education* 44, no. 3 (2019): pp. 417–31, https://doi.org/10 .1080/03075079.2017.1368475; Nicola Galloway et al., "The Internationalisation,' or 'Englishisation,' of Higher Education in East Asia," *Higher Education* 80, no. 3 (2020): pp. 395–414, https://doi.org/10.1007/s10734-019-00486-1.

[43] Yojana Sharma, "Three Major Universities Quit International Rankings," *University World News*, May 11, 2022, https://www.universityworldnews.com/post .php?story=20220511170923665#.

[44] See Kyle Long, *The Emergence of the American University Abroad* (Brill, 2020).

by the foreign education provider."[45] Some type of degree conferral, as opposed to maintaining a physical location or even facilitating student exchanges or providing limited classes, is the key criterion for inclusion.

The Rise of the Democratic-Authoritarian Transnational Campus

In terms of ongoing transnational educational cooperation by regime type, as of March 2023 according to C-BERT data, four of the five largest exporters of transnational campuses ("sending institutions") in active partnerships were democracies, with Russia the exception: United States (84), United Kingdom (46), France (38), Russia (39), Australia (20). But long-standing autocracies comprised four of the five largest importers (or "host institutions") of transnational campuses, with Malaysia the exception: China (47), UAE (30), Singapore (16), Malaysia (15), and Qatar (15). Breaking down the C-BERT data by regime type suggests that universities from both democratic and authoritarian hosts appear to partner with like and opposite regime types roughly equally, with 136 current partnerships between democratic sending countries and authoritarian hosts and 133 current branch campuses of democracies in other democracies.[46]

To gain a more comprehensive picture of the range, history, and political dynamics specifically informing transnational partnerships involving democratic sending countries and authoritarian hosts, we integrated the data from C-BERT with data compiled by Global American Higher Education and our own research into now-discontinued transnational partnerships.[47] Our resulting database of

---

45 "International Campuses," C-Bert, https://www.cbert.org/intl-campus. Long and his collaborators use the term "microcampus" as distinct from an international joint-campus, though both confer degrees. See "About," Global American Higher Education, https://www.globalamericanhighereducation.org/about.html.

46 Breaking down all global historical transnational partnerships by regime dyads (sending-hosting), gives us a count of 136 in Democracies-Autocracies, 133 in Democracies-Democracies, 28 in Autocracies-Democracies, and 25 in Autocracies-Autocracies.

47 Global American Higher Education, Institutional database, January 2023 (data originally collected by Kyle Long et al.), https://www.globalamericanhighereducation .org. We include Malaysia as an authoritarian host country in Figure 7.1 because all of the agreements were made before a dramatic political liberalization in 2018.

democratic sending-authoritarian host country dyads identifies 222 individual transnational partnerships, 190 which remain active, which are visually represented in Figure 7.1 by the location of the host country.

The lion's share of these transnational democratic partnerships with authoritarian hosts such as China, UAE, Qatar, and Singapore have been established after 2000, appearing or negotiated during the global liberal plateau. Overall, 12 of the 15 transnational US partnerships with China were established after 2000, with nine of them after 2010.[48] NYU–Abu Dhabi opened to much publicity in 2010, joining the Rochester Institute for Technology (2008) and eight UK

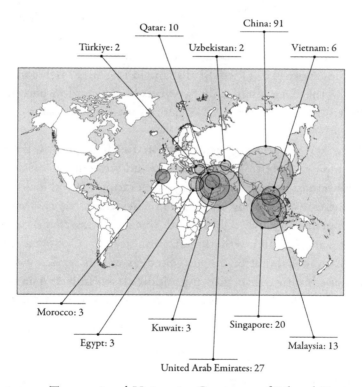

FIGURE 7.1 Transnational University Campuses of Liberal Democratic Sending Countries in Authoritarian Host Countries, as of 2023

---

[48] Per Panangipalli, of the 72 US universities in China established since 1949, 45 are cooperative programs, 21 are joint universities, and five are branch campuses.

campuses. US partnerships with Qatar are hosted in what is now known as Education City near Doha; the first was established in 1998 in partnership with Virginia Commonwealth University, with additional partnerships added with Weill Cornell Medicine (2001–), Texas A&M (2003–24), Carnegie Mellon (2004–), Georgetown University (2005–), and Northwestern University (2008), as well as HEC Paris (2010–) and University College London (2010–). Northwestern University-Qatar (NU-Q) operates a degree program specifically focused on journalism, despite the lack of a media freedom law in the country and systemic government censorship of the media.[49] Three US campuses currently continue to operate in Singapore, including the Culinary Institute (2011) and Digipen (2008). However, in this same time frame, several transnational US campuses were established and subsequently disbanded: NYU's Tisch School of the Arts in Singapore (2007) was closed in 2015, while Yale's partnership with National University Singapore (2011) will be disbanded in 2025; Michigan State's campus in the UAE lasted only two years because of low enrollments (2008–10),[50] while Texas A&M's campus was abruptly shut down in 2024.

Several key factors have been mentioned as driving this wave of offshore campuses. On the "supply side," US and Western universities have sought internationalization as a way of elevating their global prestige and reputations, either by creating branches or, in the case of NYU (which opened in UAE, China, and Singapore), as part of a global network central to an internationalization strategy. Opportunities for research and collaboration are also cited, as well as servicing demand for higher education from growing middle classes in East Asia and the Middle East. On the "demand side," collaborations with prestigious

---

See Sainsha Panaangipalli, "Research Brief: China," Global American Higher Education, January 2023, https://www.globalamericanhighereducation.org/uploads/8/1/3/2/81324196/gahe-research-brief-china-january2023.pdf.

[49] Neetu Arnold, *Outsourced to Qatar: A Case Study of Northwestern University-Qatar* (National Association of Scholars, 2022), https://www.nas.org/storage/app/media/Reports/Middle%20East%20Studies%20Centers/Outsourced%20to%20Qatar.pdf.

[50] Spencer Witte, "When Partnerships Fail: Lessons from the United Arab Emirates and Singapore," in *Global Opportunities and Challenges for Higher Education Leaders: Briefs on Key Themes*, edited by L. E. Rumbley, R. M. Helms, P. M. Peterson, and P. G. Altbach (Brill, 2014), https://doi.org/10.1007/978-94-6209-863-3_1045-49.

foreign partners appear to be part of new national state-building and developmental strategies. For example, Singapore prioritized international collaborations as a core of its Global Schoolhouse initiative of 2002, designed to make the small state a regional hub for international students and research centers,[51] while the Gulf countries have cited investing in educational partnerships as a key part of moving away from hydrocarbon-dependent rentier economies to more sustainable knowledge-based economies.[52]

But the most important single driving factor appears to be financial. In the Gulf, both Qatar and the UAE have covered hundreds of millions of dollars in expenses of foreign partners, including construction costs and operating costs, and scholarships at Western levels of tuition. The financial terms of the agreements are often secret, but one investigation based on university tax documents estimated that the annual outlay for all six Western branches in Qatar is over $320 million. The one public budget has been VCU's, under the terms of its second 10-year contract (2012–21), and details an annual operating budget of $39.5 million, of which more than $30 million is covered by the Qatar Foundation and the rest by tuition and fees.[53]

Beyond covering the construction and operating expenses of their offshore campuses, Gulf governments also have been among the most significant foreign donors to the home campuses of their partners. According to the US Department for Education's Foreign Gifts and Contracts Report databases, Qatar, Saudi Arabia, and the UAE account for the lion's share of foreign donations. In the case of Qatar, since the establishment of their Qatar Education City campuses (through May 2023), US universities have received billions in payments in the forms of gifts and contracts from Qatari sources: Carnegie Mellon

---

[51] Kyna Rubin, "Singapore's Push for Foreign Students," *International Educator* 17, no. 1 (2008): pp. 56–59.

[52] For critical discussions, see Neha Vora, *Teach for Arabia: American Universities, Liberalism, and Transnational Qatar* (Stanford University Press, 2018), chapter 1; and Christopher Davidson, "US University Campuses in the Gulf Monarchies," in *The Political Economy of Education in the Arab World*, edited by Hicham Alaoui and Robert Springborg (Lynne Rienner Publishers, 2021), pp. 125–46.

[53] Nick Anderson, "In Qatar Education City, U.S. Colleges Are Building an Academic Oasis," *Washington Post*, December 6, 2015, https://www.washingtonpost.com/local/education/in-qatars-education-city-us-colleges-are-building-an-academic-oasis/2015/12/06/6b538702-8e01-11e5-ae1f-af46b7df8483_story.html.

$491.3 million, Cornell $599 million, Georgetown $358.9 million, Northwestern $343.6 million, Texas A&M $546.7 million; and Virginia Commonwealth $165.1 million.[54] Notably, since the establishment of NYU–Abu Dhabi, NYU has received $111.7 million from various Emirati entities.

Whose Norms and Sovereignty Are Influencing Whose?

The influx of these massive revenues has brought even more scrutiny to the question of whether US liberal higher-educational norms, including academic freedom, freedom of expression, and government noninterference, will be maintained on what have been presented as fully integrated campuses and programs.

While acknowledging some of the challenges in partnering with authoritarian hosts, at the outset US administrators insisted publicly that they were interested in acting as agents of liberal social transformation in the partnering authoritarian host country. At the opening ceremony of NU-Q, Northwestern President Henry Bienen stated, "We are honored to be part of Qatar's commitment to progressive social change and excited about this momentous new chapter in Northwestern's history,"[55] while Everette Dennis, CEO and dean of NU-Q ambitiously commented, "What we're doing here has the potential to transform a whole society. It is a tremendous challenge in a place where freedom of expression abuts tradition and religion at every corner."[56]

Certainly, these campuses have promoted certain liberal norms in their Gulf hosts. Perhaps the most important of them for Qatari

---

[54] Authors' calculations from https://sites.ed.gov/foreigngifts/. We added the tallies from the new online reporting system (2020–23) to the existing totals for each of these schools reported in Davidson, "US University Campuses in the Gulf Monarchies." Note that the amount for Cornell University was accumulated from 2020 to 2023.

[55] "Opening Ceremonies Held for Northwestern University Campus in Qatar," Targeted News Service, Mar 23, 2009, http://ezproxy.cul.columbia.edu/login?url=https://www.proquest.com/wire-feeds/opening-ceremonies-held-northwestern-university/docview/468135497/se-2.

[56] Radi Letzter, "In Focus: Forging a Free Press at Northwestern's Qatar Campus," Daily Northwestern, May 13, 2013, https://dailynorthwestern.com/2013/05/13/top-stories/forging-a-free-press-at-northwesterns-qatar-campus/.

authorities is the high percentages of women among the student body and faculty; as of 2023 62% of the Education City students and over 70% of faculty and teachers were women;[57] also notably, women comprised 45% of Texas A&M's engineering program, a better gender ratio than other engineering programs in the United States.[58] A wide range of liberal arts classes are taught at these campuses, including Georgetown's signature introductory religion class. Students are encouraged to join a selection of clubs and groups and organize activities, as they would on a campus in a democracy. More unintentionally, Vora has shown how certain liberal educational norms and practices at Education City have raised political consciousness among South Asian migrant students about local issues, such as Qatar's restrictive citizenship laws and strict migration practices.[59]

Transnational Challenges

But if the publicly stated goal of these partnerships really was to help bring about social transformation and liberalization in these hosts through academic engagement, the record indicates iffy results. On V-Dem's Academic Freedom Index, Qatar, the UAE, Singapore, and China—the four largest importers of branch campuses—all show similar or, in China especially, degraded respect for academic freedom in 2023 compared to 20 years prior.[60]

It is difficult and unfair to expect universities to act as drivers of change in the face of broader forces strengthening authoritarianism. But we can assess the evolution and records of these partnerships on their own terms as transnational conduits of liberal education and values. After more than a decade of these collaborations, two major

---

[57] "Education City Stadium to Become a Sporting Hub for Girls," Qatar Foundation, February 21, 2023, https://www.qf.org.qa/stories/education-city-stadium-to-become-sporting-hub-for-women-and-girls.

[58] "Why Is Qatar's Percentage of Engineering Students Double That of the US," Qatar Foundation, July 21, 2018, https://www.qf.org.qa/stories/why-is-qatar's-percentage-of-female-engineering-students-double-that-of-the.

[59] Neha Vora, "Between Global Citizenship and Qatarization: Negotiating Qatar's New Knowledge Economy Within American Branch Campuses," *Ethnic and Racial Studies* 37, no. 12 (2014): pp. 2243–60, https://doi.org/10.1080/01419870.2014.934257.

[60] See V-Dem's graphing tool here: https://v-dem.net/data_analysis/VariableGraph/.

challenges to liberal norms have emerged at these offshore campuses: the close monitoring of academic research on topics with local political sensitivity and the restrictions on using the campus as a space for organizing and activism. The transnational campus is not a seamless space that safeguards liberal academic ideals; instead, there is selective deployment of legal geography within and across these collaborations. In fact, national law is invoked by both host authorities and US administrators in certain situations to justify censorship and the imposition of social restrictions.

The compromising of academic freedom has included both overt and self-censorship, usually on topics that are particularly sensitive to local authorities. In China, the extent of formal censorship on foreign educational partnerships is not known precisely, but joint university partnerships are increasingly subject to new security laws and intrusive mandates. For example in 2017, the Chinese government informed foreign university branches that they must have party secretaries serving as vice chancellors and on their boards.[61] Beyond such formal measures, self-censorship among students and faculty who refrain from discussing or researching sensitive political and historical topics appears to be the norm.[62]

In the Gulf hosts, reports have documented how researchers have refrained from delving into sensitive topics such as the region's migration system and migrant rights, domestic corruption, dynastic politics, prostitution, and sexuality.[63] In a set of high-profile cases involving NYU–Abu Dhabi, in 2015 UAE authorities denied entry to the country to an NYU faculty member researching migrant rights;[64] a couple of years later, after two home-campus-based NYU faculty of Shiite background

---

[61] Emily Feng, "Beijing Vies for Greater Control of Foreign Universities in China," *Financial Times*, November 19, 2017, https://www.ft.com/content/09ecaae2-ccdo-11e7-b781-794ce08b24dc.

[62] See *Obstacles to Excellence: Academic Freedom and China's Quest for World Class Universities* (Scholars at Risk, 2019), pp. 73–74, https://www.scholarsatrisk.org/wp-content/uploads/2019/09/Scholars-at-Risk-Obstacles-to-Excellence_EN.pdf.

[63] Michael H. Romanowski and Ramzi Nasser, "Identity Issues: Expatriate Professors Teaching and Researching in Qatar," *Higher Education* 69 (2015): pp. 653–71, https://doi.org/10.1007/s10734-014-9795-0; Vora, "Between Global Citizenship and Qatarization."

[64] Stephanie Saul, "NYU Professor Is Barred by United Arab Emirates," *New York Times*, March 16, 2015, https://www.nytimes.com/2015/03/17/nyregion/nyu-professor-is-barred-from-the-united-arab-emirates.html.

were denied entry, NYU's journalism institute voted to cut ties with NYU–Abu Dhabi.[65] In Qatar, a novel authored by a VCU English professor, who was also the founder of the Doha Writers' Workshop, and set in Qatar was banned from sale.[66] Questions of academic freedom at NU-Q were raised when an academic survey in 2015, conducted across several Arab countries by the school, had its Qatari answers to the question "Is your country headed in the right direction" removed upon publication.[67]

In addition to overt censorship and self-censorship, the mission of the transnational university campus has been reframed as one that does not include political organizing, on-campus advocacy, or the freedom to host events of a politically sensitive nature. Events headlining LGBTQ artists and performers have been canceled on security pretexts, and overt political organizing is highly monitored and restricted. The legal precarity of the transnational campus has included complaints among students at NU-Q that they are discriminated against by a home campus leadership that is not committed to upholding their rights of assembly, their rights as student workers at the university, and the proper consideration of Title IX complaints.[68]

At Yale-NUS, restrictions on political organizing and content came to a head in 2019 when the college canceled a planned weeklong course, Dialogue and Dissent in Singapore, led by the Singaporean playwright Alfan Bin Sa'at.[69] In response to criticisms leveled by human rights organizations, Yale-NUS President Tan Tai Yong maintained that the college retained a "thriving culture of open discussion," but Singapore's

---

[65] Sarah Maslin Nir, "NYU Journalism Faculty Boycotts Abu Dhabi Campus," *New York Times*, November 7, 2017, https://www.nytimes.com/2017/11/07/nyregion/nyu-journalism-professors-abu-dhabi-campus.html.

[66] Karen Kapsidelis, "Qatar Censors Have Banned VCU Professor's New Novel," *Richmond Times-Dispatch*, March 16, 2014, https://richmond.com/qatar-censors-have-banned-vcu-professors-new-novel/article_cfa37265-6097-57e1-9aa3-9d2b9533dc34.html.

[67] Arnold, *Outsourced to Qatar*, p. 9.

[68] See Danya Al-Saleh and Neha Vora, "Contestations of Imperial Citizenship: Student Protest and Organizing in Qatar's Education City," *International Journal of Middle East Studies* 52, no. 4 (2020): pp. 733–39, https://doi.org/10.1017/S0020743820001026.

[69] Martin Abbugao, "Yale in Academic Censorship Row in Singapore," AFP International Text Wire in English, October 28, 2019.

education minister, Ong Ye Kung, supported the cancellation and underscored the government's right to intervene in political events on campus, noting that "academic freedom cannot be carte blanch for anyone to misuse an academic institution for political advocacy."[70] A subsequent investigation conducted by Yale's vice president and vice provost for global strategy, Pericles Lewis, into the circumstances surrounding the course's cancellation found that the decision to cancel the course was the result of internal processes and "mostly administrative" errors and not due to government interference;[71] however, the report also cited as justifications the Curricular Committee's concerns that the course "would expose international students to sanctions for illegal participation in off-campus protests" and that senior leadership believed that it "did not include a range of political perspectives."[72]

In his testimony at a subsequent parliamentary session, Ong Ye Kung actually justified the Singaporean government's support for the cancellation, noting that the course included watching films about foreign dissidents, making protest placards, and conducting "partisan political activities."[73] He further noted that the foreign students participating in such activities would have violated Singaporean law because "only Singaporean citizens and permanent residents are allowed to protest in the designated corner," and stressed that "educational institutions must not deviate from their missions to advance education and maintain high academic standards, and that although Singapore retained avenues for political parties and activists to champion their causes and exercise rights, educational institutions, and especially the formal curriculum, are not the platforms to do this."[74]

---

[70] Rei Kurochi, "Yale-NUS Saga: Academic Freedom Can't Be Carte Blanche for Misusing Academic Institutions for Political Advocacy, Says Ong Ye Kung," *Straits Times*, August 21, 2021, https://www.straitstimes.com/politics/parliament-academic-freedom-cant-be-carte-blanche-for-misusing-academic-institutions-for.

[71] Office of the Vice President for Global Strategy, "Report on the Cancellation of Lab Module on 'Dialogue and Dissent,'" Yale University, September 28, 2019, https://news.yale.edu/sites/default/files/files/Pericles-Lewis-Yale-NUS-report.pdf.

[72] Office of the Vice President for Global Strategy, "Cancellation of Lab Module," pp. 8–9.

[73] "Singapore: Yale-NUS College's (YNC) Withdrawal of a Project," *Singapore Government News*, October 7, 2019.

[74] Speech as reported in "Why Yale-NUS Course on Dissent Was Scrapped: Ong Ye Kung," *Straits Times*, October 7, 2019, https://www.straitstimes.com/politics/ong-ye-kung-on-cancelled-yale-nus-module-and-academic-freedom.

In other words, the public role of the university as a center of organizing and political expression was not welcomed, legal, or a legitimate part of the campus's mandate. In August 2021, Yale-NUS abruptly announced the termination of the high-profile college, effective in 2025; external coverage of the decision emphasized that the institution, despite its extreme selectivity, had failed to meet fundraising goals, but also drew attention to ongoing tensions over the university's academic freedom and autonomy in governance.[75] Interestingly, one of the reasons given by Singapore in severing the partnership was to expand and "democratize" liberal arts education in Singapore.[76] However, in 2022 it was announced that NUS college, the anointed successor to Yale-NUS, would not actually offer any liberal arts courses in its core curriculum.[77]

The Fate of Transnational Partnerships: Finances and Academic Freedom

The demise of the Yale-NUS partnership is one of 34 partnerships of transnational higher-education campuses involving a liberal democratic sending country and an authoritarian host that have folded since their post–Cold War establishment (see Appendix 7.1). Fourteen of these closures occurred prior to 2016 and 20 afterward, with the median lifespan of a transnational campus in the group at nine years. The largest single cause of closures was financial,

---

[75] Karen Fischer, "A 'Flabbergasting' Decision: Abrupt End of Yale-NUS Partnership Offers Lessons to Colleges Seeking Global Re-Engagement," *Chronicle of Higher Education*, September 21, 2021, https://www.chronicle.com/article/a-flabbergasting-decision; for an insightful essay about academic controls in Singapore, see Cherian George, "From Scandal to Business as Usual: Normalising Controls over Academia," June 11, 2024, https://knowledgepraxis.academia.sg/blog/2024/06/11/cherian-george/.

[76] Sandra Davie, "Yale-NUS to Stop Taking in Students, NUS Plans to Set Up New Liberal Arts College," *Straits Times*, January 24, 2022, https://www.straitstimes.com/singapore/parenting-education/yale-nus-plans-to-drop-liberal-arts-subjects-from-core-curriculum-as-nus-college-takes-shape.

[77] Ng Wei Kai, "Yale-NUS Successor NUS College Will Not Feature Liberal Arts Subjects in Core Curriculum," *Straits Times*, September 1, 2021, https://www.straitstimes.com/singapore/parenting-education/yale-nus-to-stop-taking-in-new-students-as-part-of-nus-plans-for-a-new. We thank Kirsten Han for alerting us to this development.

with at least half of these closures citing financial difficulties or lack of enrollment in their programs. However, concerns about academic freedom or other political compromises played an important role in at least 10 of these closures, with publicly cited or reported reasons including forced gender segregation (Houston Community College in Qatar), politically motivated conferral of honorary degrees to host country officials (University of South Wales in Dubai), and reputational concerns over a country's human rights abuses (University of Liverpool in Egypt; Stockholm University of Economics in St. Petersburg and Moscow following Russia's invasion of Ukraine).

Our point here is not just that compromises to academic freedom have been made in these authoritarian states. Rather, it is that almost immediately after establishing these lucrative partnerships on the prestige derived from the university brand, both sending campus university administrators and host country officials narrowed their terms of engagement in a manner more consistent with the policies and public messaging of these regimes rather than the liberal mission of the university. Reflecting on whether Georgetown Qatar compromised the university's educational values, Georgetown President John J. DeGioia responded in an interview, "Being engaged is better than not . . . we are contributing, I think, to building a common good in the region." However, such debates about whether engagement yields net local or regional positive impacts are themselves far-flung benchmarks from those identified at the outset of these academic collaborations.[78]

Furthermore, the process of treating practices and university functions normally regarded as core to academic freedoms and university governance on home campuses as lying *beyond* the core "academic mission" of the offshore institution has itself reverberated *within* the home campus itself. One example is the acceptance and normalization that academic freedoms can be contextualized and conditioned by the law of the more restrictive branch host. In a telling debate among the university faculty in the Northwestern Faculty Senate in 2021 over adopting a new faculty handbook, several faculty objected to updated language, proposed by university administrators, that may have circumscribed

---

[78] Quoted in Anderson, "In Qatar Education City."

academic freedom for faculty in overseas branches "to the extent that applicable laws allow."[79] After further faculty discussion and senate deliberation, this language was changed, instead, to note, "While academic freedom essentially coexists with established legal frameworks, on rare occasions the two may be in conflict."[80] Interestingly, the university's experiences in the Gulf appear to have launched a debate about the legal parameters surrounding the concept of academic freedom.[81]

Dictating the Educational Agenda: The Rise and Decline of the Central European University

The final section of this chapter examines the fate of the Central European University, the largest single investment in a new liberal educational project made in a former communist state. Founded in 1991, shortly after the fall of communism in Eastern Europe, CEU was established by the Hungarian hedge fund manager and philanthropist George Soros, who envisioned that the university would become a hub for promoting a "new form of social organization" based on open society concepts such as critical thinking, democratic values, and public

---

[79] Sarah MacLaughlin, "Northwestern Faculty Debate Academic Freedom Abroad amid Changes to Faculty Handbook," Fire.org, August 25, 2021, https://www.thefire.org/news/northwestern-faculty-debate-academic-freedom-abroad-amid-changes-faculty-handbook. An even more substantial change to home campus academic freedom standards was proposed but ultimately withdrawn after faculty outcry, at University College Dublin, one of the authors' home institutions. See Jack Power, "Concern over Proposed Changes to UCD's Academic Freedom," *Irish Times*, April 9, 2020, https://www.irishtimes.com/news/education/concern-over-proposed-changes-to-ucd-s-academic-freedom-1.4225393. The changes were explicitly justified as a way to foster internationalization. Coincidentally or not, the change was proposed to faculty the same month that UCD received approval from the Chinese Ministry of Education to open two new joint ventures in China. See "UCD Announces Two New International Colleges in China," University College Dublin, April 30, 2020, https://www.ucd.ie/newsandopinion/news/2020/april/31/ucdannouncestwonewinternationalcollegesinchina/.

[80] "Northwestern University Faculty Handbook," Northwestern University, August 5, 2021, https://www.northwestern.edu/provost/docs/faculty_handbook_aug2021.pdf.

[81] "Minutes of the Faculty Senate," Northwestern University, July 14, 2021, https://www.northwestern.edu/faculty-senate/documents/2018-current/minutes_fs_7.14.21.pdf.

208   DICTATING THE AGENDA

policymaking.[82] Initially established in Prague before relocating the same year to Budapest, Soros directly supported the university with annual $20 million donations until 2001, when he made a $250 million contribution to endow the university, the largest single gift made to a European institution of higher education.[83] Over two decades, the university rapidly became a global magnet for students and international faculty, boasting nearly 17,000 alumni with an extensive global network of national alumni chapters and activities.[84] However, once the Fidesz Party, led by prime minister Viktor Orbán, returned to power in 2010, CEU faced an escalating set of challenges and authoritarian tactics roughly congruent with the stages of authoritarian snapback.

A Liberal Education Paradigm for Central Europe

Founded initially as a provider of graduate programs and professional studies in the era of the post-communist transition, CEU built its reputation as a regional and international leader in the social sciences, with highly ranked departments in economics, political science, law, history, philosophy, and environmental policy. CEU added an important university press in 1993 and a distinct School of Public Policy in 2012.

The university's charter and accreditation was provided by the State of New York, while it was regarded as a private university in Hungary. From its founding, the CEU promoted a clear vision that sought to anchor higher education and public policy training in liberal values as well as to facilitate connections for its community to the West itself. Its first public board statement now reads as a manifesto that epitomizes the strength of the soft power of Western education models in the immediate post–Cold War period.[85] It observed: "Everyone in

---

[82] See George Soros, *Soros on Soros: Staying Ahead of the Curve* (John Wiley & Sons, 1995), chapter 6. Soros deliberately sought to support those social sciences that had been suppressed during communism.

[83] Tamar Lewin, "Soros Gives $250 Million to University in Europe," *New York Times*, October 14, 2001, https://www.nytimes.com/2001/10/14/world/soros-gives-250-million-to-university-in-europe.html.

[84] Alumni page, Central European University, https://alumni.ceu.edu.

[85] Zbigniew Pelczynsky, "The Central European University," *International Sociology* 7, no. 1 (1992): pp. 115–17, https://doi.org/10.1177/026858092007001010.

Europe today wants a high-quality Western-style education. The CEU will provide for the region the equivalent of the best Western education, and thereby attract the best students of the highest calibre," and listed the university's four primary objectives as to introduce a Western-style curriculum both at CEU and across other universities, educate a new corps of East European leaders, raise standards and methods of teaching and learning throughout the region, and foster cooperation and understanding among citizens of different countries of the region.[86]

The Escalating Stages of Authoritarian Snapback: Orbánism and the CEU

Despite CEU's early successes and seismic impact on the Central European educational and policy landscape, as early as 1992 some Hungarian politicians were openly critical of Soros and the liberal and cosmopolitan values he was promoting through his foundation and the university.[87] But the investments made by CEU propelled the university to elite status within just a few years, while its civic mission and liberal values aligned with attempts by successive Hungarian governments to introduce the reforms necessary to prepare Hungary for accession to NATO and the European Union.

Following the financial crisis of 2008, the re-election of Viktor Orbán and his nationalist Fidesz Party in 2010 set the stage for an escalating battle with the university over its mission and political purpose. Orbán and his party became open champions of illiberalism and critical of Hungary's Western orientation.[88] With a parliamentary supermajority, Orbán and his allies began to dismantle democratic institutions, including amending the constitution, establishing a media oversight board, appointing political supporters to the country's Supreme Court,

---

[86] Pelczynsky, "The Central European University," p. 115.

[87] Soros himself published an op-ed in 1992 in the *New York Times* appealing to certain Hungarian parliamentarians not to regard him and his sponsored activities as "anti-Hungarian." See George Soros, "Parliamentary Paranoia in Hungary," *New York Times*, October 5, 1992, https://www.nytimes.com/1992/10/05/opinion/parliamentary-paranoia-in-hungary.html?searchResultPosition=1.

[88] János Kornai, "Hungary's U-Turn: Retreating from Democracy," *Journal of Democracy* 26, no. 3 (2015): pp. 34–48, https://doi.org/10.1353/jod.2015.0046.

and redrawing electoral districts in a way that favored his party.[89] In classic populist fashion, Orbán launched a high-profile campaign against migrants and EU policies of resettlement, while dialing up the stigmatization of NGOs and other groups advocating for migrant rights.[90] As Jenne et al. have shown, official state media at the time pumped out false stories that advanced a conspiracy, rife with anti-Semitic tropes and xenophobia, that Soros and his allies were determined to resettle millions of Syrian refugees in the country.[91] In 2018, the parliament passed further anti-NGO legislation that also targeted the university by making it a criminal offense for any Hungarian organization (including a university) to help migrants or asylum seekers, a move that precipitated a decline in Hungary's democracy rankings. The same year in August, Hungary's Ministry for Human Capacities announced that it was immediately revoking licenses and accreditation from CEU and one other university for their master's in gender studies, citing lack of demand in the labor market and an incompatibility of the course of studies with Christianity and Christian values.[92]

The anti-migrant, anti-gender, and anti-Soros agendas were explicitly used to stigmatize the CEU's faculty, mission, and programming and reframe the institution as beholden to the scheming of its benefactor.[93] In 2017, state media published a large exposé, complete

[89] Miklós Bánkuti et al., "Hungary's Illiberal Turn: Disabling the Constitution," *Journal of Democracy* 23, no. 3 (2012): pp. 138–46, https://doi.org/10.1515/9786155225550-006; Petra Bárd and Laurent Pech, "How to Build and Consolidate a Partly Free Pseudo Democracy by Constitutional Means in Three Steps: The 'Hungarian Model,'" *SSRN Electronic Journal* (2019), https://doi.org/10.2139/ssrn.3608784.

[90] On migration and the mobilization of anti-EU sentiment by Orbán and other East European leaders, see Ivan Krastev, *After Europe* (University of Pennsylvania Press, 2017).

[91] Erin K. Jenne et al., "Antisemitic Tropes, Fifth-Columnism, and 'Soros-Bashing,'" in *Enemies Within: The Global Politics of Fifth Columns*, edited by Harris Mylonas and Scott Radnitz (Oxford University Press, 2022), p. 45.

[92] Andrea Pető, "Feminist Stories from an Illiberal State: Revoking the License to Teach Gender Studies in Hungary at a University in Exile (CEU)," in *Gender and Power in Eastern Europe: Changing Concepts of Femininity and Masculinity in Power Relations*, edited by Katharina Bluhm, Gertrud Pickhan, Justyna Stypińska, and Agnieszka Wierzcholska (Springer, 2021): pp. 35–44.

[93] Jan-Werner Muller, "Hungary: The War on Education," *New York Review of Books*, May 20, 2017, https://www.nybooks.com/online/2017/05/20/hungary-the-war-on-education-ceu/.

with pictured profiles of individual professors, of CEU faculty who were ostensibly serving Soros's allegedly anti-family, globalist agenda. The same year, the Hungarian parliament passed a law, just one week after its introduction, mandating that foreign-accredited universities in the country must have an established foreign branch. This ostensibly technical requirement seemed aimed directly at the CEU as the New York–accredited university lacked a US-based home campus.[94] After the government failed to ratify a proposed agreement that would bring CEU in compliance with the 2017 law, the university announced on December 3, 2018, that it had been "forced out of Hungary" and that it would be moving its main campus and center of operations to Vienna.[95]

External Reactions: Liberal Outrage and Illiberal Allies

Reactions to CEUs persecution generated some predictable reactions within the EU, but also revealed that Orbán's decision had both tacit and overt support. The leader of the European People's Party, the parliamentary coalition of right-wing parties in the European Parliament that included Fidesz, expressed disappointment with the decision but recommended no action, aside from encouraging an expedited review of the case by the European Court of Justice.[96] However, by the time the court ruled in October 2020 that the registration legislation introduced by the Hungarian government, as expected, had violated EU law, it was too little, too late. The ruling had little practical consequence given that the expensive relocation to Vienna was almost completed.[97]

---

[94] Gabor Simonovits and Jan Zilinsky, "This Is Why Hungary Is Trying to Close George Soros's Prestigious University," *Washington Post*, April 7, 2017, https://www .washingtonpost.com/news/monkey-cage/wp/2017/04/07/why-is-hungary-trying-to-close-george-soross-prestigious-university/.

[95] Central European University, "CEU Forced Out of Budapest: To Launch U.S. Degree Programs in Vienna in September 2019," December 3, 2018.

[96] "Europe's Conservatives Shrug as Soros' University Exits Hungary," *Politico Europe*, December 3, 2018, https://www.politico.eu/article/europes-conservatives-shrug-as-soros-university-exits-hungary/.

[97] Benjamin Novak, "E.U. Court Rules Against Hungary Law Targeting Soros-Funded University," *New York Times*, October 6, 2020, https://www.nytimes.com/ 2020/10/06/world/europe/hungary-soros-university-court.html.

Illustrating how illiberal allies can assist the authoritarian snapback, David Cornstein, the US ambassador appointed by the Trump administration, who had initially stated that his priority upon arriving in Hungary was to keep the university open, in a subsequent interview appeared to blame CEU and Soros for having an "adversarial relationship" with the Hungarian government and prime minister.[98] Orbán's actions were backed by right-wing advisers and US media commentators including Steve Bannon and Tucker Carlson. Indeed, for some, they were presented as a blueprint for how other governments should fight back against institutionalized liberalism.[99]

And as if to punctuate Hungary's illiberal turn within higher education, in 2021, just a couple of years after CEU's exit, the Hungarian government announced plans for the construction of a satellite campus of China's prestigious Fudan University in Budapest under a $1.8 billion deal financed by a loan from China Development Bank, potentially making the Shanghai-based school the first Chinese university in the European Union.[100] Despite protests, Beijing and Budapest remained committed to the project. Hungarian opposition parties were able to gather 470,000 signatures, almost 5% of Hungary's population, to hold a referendum on the issue but a court later ruled such a vote unconstitutional.[101] In sharp contrast to CEU, the Fudan-Hungary agreement lays out a version of higher education as a technical, developmental endeavor; absent are any liberal value commitments.[102] Some observers note that it gives Fudan access to EU research funding,

---

[98] Interviewed and quoted in "American University CEU Kicked Out of Hungary, Says It Will Move to Vienna," NPR, https://www.npr.org/2018/12/06/674310948/american-university-ces-kicked-out-of-hungary-says-it-will-move-to-vienna.

[99] Benjamin Wallace-Wells, "What American Conservatives See in Hungary's Leader," *New Yorker*, September 13, 2021, https://www.newyorker.com/news/annals-of-inquiry/what-rod-dreher-sees-in-viktor-orban.

[100] "What's Next for China's Fudan Campus in Hungary?," RFE/RL, June 8, 2022, https://www.rferl.org/a/hungary-orban-china-fudan-budapest/31888800.html; for analysis and details of proposed funding arrangements, see Szabolcs Panyi, "Huge Chinese Loan to Cover the Construction of Fudan University in Budapest," Direkt36, April 6, 2021, https://www.direkt36.hu/en/kinai-hitelbol-keszul-a-magyar-felsooktatas-oriasberuhazasa-a-kormany-mar-oda-is-igerte-egy-kinai-cegnek/.

[101] "Hungary Opposition Cheered by 'Symbolic Victory' on Referendum," *Balkan Insight*, January 21, 2022, https://balkaninsight.com/2022/01/21/hungary-opposition-cheered-by-symbolic-victory-on-referendum/.

[102] See "Strategic Cooperation Agreement Between the Government of Hungary and Fudan University," https://cdn.kormany.hu/uploads/document/f/fo/fof/foffa411cded441997e44cafeaa381db9ebc0356.pdf (accessed March 13, 2024).

Chinese students a way to study in Europe in a familiar environment, and if successful may constitute a new model of transnational higher-education cooperation, allowing authoritarian-backed higher education a better platform from which to dictate the agenda.[103]

The Global Erosion of the Liberal Education Model

Like other areas where US and Western soft power and liberal advocacy once appeared dominant, the internationalization of liberal education appears to have reached its limits and its main tenets are being contested in a variety of settings. Universities based in democracies remain prestigious and desirable partners for authoritarian countries, but international engagement appears to be transforming and reframing liberal norms of higher education, rather than simply disseminating them globally. The rapid rise of the transnational campus set in authoritarian hosts has modified the mission of the liberal university, most notably by negating its functional role as a site for political organizing and has forced home-country administrators to reframe and contextualize what was once assumed to be a universal or globalizing project.

The establishment and exit of the CEU in Hungary illustrate how the stages of authoritarian snapback apply to liberal higher education and reveals just how quickly and successfully the authoritarian playbook can be wielded in this area once assumed to be relatively autonomous and uncontested. The systematic delegitimization and closure of CEU is paralleled by other similar episodes of stigmatization, state media attacks, and administrative measures taken by authoritarian and populist governments against higher-education institutions; for example, in August 2021 the Russian government closed Smolny College, the 25-year-old liberal arts college in St. Petersburg that was operated with Bard College, after declaring it an "undesirable organization."[104]

---

[103] Bence Nemeth, "What China's New Campus in Europe Means for Its Ambitions to Compete in Global Higher Education," King's College London, June 3, 2021, https://www.kcl.ac.uk/what-chinas-new-campus-in-europe-means-for-its-ambitions-to-compete-in-global-higher-education (accessed March 13, 2024).

[104] Stephanie Saul, "Russia Bans Bard College, and Other Universities Ask What's Next," *New York Times*, August 5, 2021, https://www.nytimes.com/2021/08/05/us/bard-college-russia-ban-undesirable.html.

At the same time, as illustrated in the Fudan-Hungary partnership, authoritarian countries are also increasing their influence through their own transnational educational projects. Chief among them is China which, through its Confucius Institutes, have been increasingly scrutinized, especially in the United States.[105] We are only starting to understand the scope and actual soft power influence of some of these institutions and initiatives.[106] For example, Brazys and Dukalskis have found that, globally, over time, the presence of Confucius Institutes improves the tone of local media coverage about China and events relevant to China.[107] A 2021 HRW report on Chinese students studying in Australia found broad self-censorship as a result of the Chinese government monitoring student activities while pro-democracy students reported widespread fear of harassment, intimidation, and informants.[108]

Perhaps most alarming is that on top of this global backlash and reframing of the purpose and scope of higher education, a growing illiberal challenge within liberal democracies to core long-standing principles appears to be gaining momentum. In March 2024, the Board of Regents of Texas A&M announced suddenly that it was canceling its contract with Qatar and closing down its campus, following a concerted campaign by right-wing groups and Texas legislators to uncover ties between the transnational campus and Islamic extremists.[109] Within the United States, 16 legislatures have introduced bills

---

[105] "China's Impact on the US Education System," United States Permanent Subcommitee on Investigations, https://www.hsgac.senate.gov/wp-content/uploads/imo/media/doc/PSI%20Report%20China's%20Impact%20on%20the%20US%20Education%20System.pdf.

[106] See, for example, Alexander Dukalskis, "Higher Education Partnerships with China: US and European Responses to a Changing Context," *PS: Political Science & Politics* 57, no. 1 (2024): pp. 137–41, https://doi.org/10.1017/S1049096523000616.

[107] Samuel Brazys and Alexander Dukalskis, "Rising Powers and Grassroots Image Management: Confucius Institutes and China in the Media," *Chinese Journal of International Politics* 12, no. 4 (2019): pp. 557–84, https://doi.org/10.1093/cjip/poz012.

[108] McNeill, "They Don't Understand."

[109] Gary Wasserman, "An American University Retreats from Qatar to Texas," Gulf International Forum, March 17, 2024, https://gulfif.org/an-american-university-retreats-from-qatar-to-texas/.

limiting the teachings of "critical race theory" and other concepts relating to social justice, while the issue has also been wielded to dismantle tenure and other institutions respecting academic freedom at public universities.[110] In April 2022, the Republican governor of Florida, Ron DeSantis, signed a bill severely limiting tenure at public universities as a measure intended to prevent faculty from perpetuating "intellectual orthodoxy" in the classroom.[111] Similarly, in Texas, Lt. Governor Dan Patrick in February 2022 declared that ending university tenure would be a "top priority" after a group of faculty reaffirmed their right to teach critical race theory and courses about racial justice.[112]

The outbreak of war in Gaza following the October 7, 2023, attacks by Hamas unleashed a further wave of protest and scrutiny of university governance and the precarity of academic freedom on US campuses. Following weeks of on-campus demonstrations by student organizations in response to the Israel-Hamas conflict in Gaza, Columbia University in New York suspended two pro-Palestinian student organizations.[113] In April 2024, the university invited the New York Police Department to forcibly remove a pro-Palestinian encampment and then, two weeks later, to remove dozens of students who had barricaded themselves into Hamilton Hall, arresting 300 individuals on

---

[110] Colleen Flaherty, "Legislating Against Critical Race Theory," *Inside Higher Ed*, June 8, 2021, https://www.insidehighered.com/news/2021/06/09/legislating-against-critical-race-theory-curricular-implications-some-states.

[111] Divya Kumar, "DeSantis Signs Bill Limiting Tenure at Florida Public Universities," *Tampa Bay Times*, April 19, 2022, https://www.tampabay.com/news/education/2022/04/19/desantis-signs-bill-limiting-tenure-at-florida-public-universities/.

[112] Aaron Sullivan, "Dan Patrick's Plan to End Tenure Has yet to Come to Fruition, but Some Texas Lawmakers Are Targeting the Curriculum," *Daily Texan*, February 12, 2023, https://thedailytexan.com/2023/02/12/dan-patricks-plan-to-end-tenure-has-yet-to-come-to-fruition-but-some-texas-lawmakers-are-targeting-cla ss-curriculum/.

[113] Liset Cruz and Claire Fahy, "Columbia Faces Protests after Banning Pro-Palestinian Groups," *New York Times*, November 15, 2023, https://www.nytimes .com/2023/11/15/nyregion/columbia-university-ban-student-groups-israel-hamas-war.html. On the protests and questions of academic freedom in Middle East studies, see Alexander Cooley, "The Uprisings of Gaza: How Geopolitical Crises Have Reshaped Academic Communities from Tahrir to Kyiv," *Political Science Quarterly* (2024): qqae006, https://doi.org/10.1093/psquar/qqae006.

campus over the course of the operation.[114] Columbia's experience spawned other pro-Palestinian university demonstrations and encampments around the country, which accounted for at least 2,950 arrests across 61 campuses.[115] Statements of concern among higher-education watchdogs and external observers expressed alarm at the limits of academic freedom, the influence of university donors and the role of protest and free expression on the contemporary university.[116] The tools and techniques of authoritarian snapback are now openly borrowed and used within the US academy, showing how certain liberal values are squeezed between illiberal forces in democracies and the rise of powerful and adaptive authoritarian states.

---

[114] Ayana Archie, "New York Police Arrest 300 as They Clear Hamilton Hall at Columbia University," NPR, May 1, 2024, https://www.npr.org/2024/05/01/1248401802/columbia-university-protests-new-york.

[115] April Rubin et al., "Mapped: Where Pro-Palestinian Student Protesters Have Been Arrested," Axios, May 10, 2024, https://www.axios.com/2024/04/27/palestinian-college-protest-arrest-encampment.

[116] Ryan Quinn, "Will Academic Freedom and Campus Free Speech Survive?," Inside Higher Ed, May 10, 2024, https://www.insidehighered.com/news/faculty-issues/academic-freedom/2024/05/03/will-academic-freedom-and-campus-free-speech. See, for example, the letter of concern by the American Civil Liberties Union here: Anthony Romero and David Cole, "Open Letter to College and University Presidents on Student Protests," ACLU, April 26, 2024, https://www.aclu.org/news/free-speech/open-letter-to-college-and-university-presidents-on-student-protests.

Chapter 8

Rewriting the Playbook: Global Sports

In October 2023, just hours before the Fédération Internationale de Football Association's (FIFA) deadline for potential hosts to bid for the 2034 World Cup, Football Australia announced that it would not be bidding for the tournament, effectively leaving Saudi Arabia as the sole candidate to host the world's most watched event.[1] A contemporary newspaper account explained: "With little hope of countering the Saudis' influence and support, the Australian federation announced it was dropping out and would instead pursue other events."[2] Saudi investments, growing star power, ownership of foreign clubs, and the reportedly close personal ties between FIFA President Gianni Infantino and Saudi ruler Mohammed Bin Salman (MBS) all appear to have contributed to Saudi Arabia's advantageous bidding position.[3]

---

[1] Michael Roppolo, "Saudi Arabia Becomes Sole Bidder for 2034 World Cup After Australia Drops Out," CBS News, October 31, 2023, https://www.cbsnews.com/news/saudi-arabia-world-cup-bids-2034/.

[2] Tariq Panja, "Saudi Arabia Confirmed as Sole Bidder for 2034 World Cup," *New York Times*, October 31, 2023, https://www.nytimes.com/2023/10/31/world/middleeast/saudi-arabia-world-cup-2034.html.

[3] Graham Dunbar, "Saudi Arabia Formally Informs FIFA of Its Wish to Host the 2034 World Cup as the Favorite to Win," Associated Press, October 9, 2023, https://apnews.com/article/saudi-arabia-2034-world-cup-fifa-9615e4fe6275666b3bfc5d88315ea4ef.

218   DICTATING THE AGENDA

Like global media, higher education, and consumer boycotts, international sports, in both major club competitions and international tournaments, is a realm whose governance and immediate post–Cold War trajectory were heavily influenced by the dominance of Western soft power, consumerism, liberal principles, and activism. The internationalization of major professional sports leagues in the United States and Europe generated lucrative new markets, media rights, and licensing deals globally, while attracting leading international players to their clubs. Signature global mega-sporting events such as the Olympics, as we discussed earlier, now seemingly free of Cold War rivalries, grew as global spectacles and became opportunities for transnational advocacy for liberal causes like democratization and human rights. The relationship between sports and political influence appeared to flow in a one-way expansion of Western culture, consumerism, and liberal politics to these new frontier settings and markets.

But, as with other global realms, by the mid-2010s the liberal trajectory of international sport had halted and then began to reverse. Flagship global events, now hosted by authoritarian governments, staged competitions that sought to promote their own rising power status, normalize their domestic control, and marginalize foreign critics. Political expression and protest by athletes on social and political issues, once tolerated if not guaranteed at both the national and professional club levels, have been increasingly restricted. Rather than confront authoritarian hosts about prior public commitments to upholding values such as freedom of expression and anti-discrimination, sporting federations, leagues, and corporate sponsors now openly court their sponsorship and have themselves adjusted their public justifications for these partnerships. Authoritarians have ensconced themselves in these global commercial and political networks, with liberal values and successful human rights activism among the casualties.

This chapter tells the story of how global sports went from being globalized but dominated by Western sports leagues and democratic host countries of major events in the 1990s and early 2000s to changing in the 2010s and 2020s as new authoritarian actors penetrated global sports markets and increasingly hosted sports mega-events. That evolution entailed sports morphing from a site of liberal political acculturation to one in which authoritarian political red lines were being drawn and policed transnationally. While previous chapters of this book juxtaposed the 2008 and 2022 Beijing Olympics, this chapter draws on a broader range of cases across many contexts, including the National Basketball Association (NBA), English Premier League, Formula One, the rise of "sportswashing" through the hosting of mega-events such as the World Cup and Olympics, and the dramatic entrance of Saudi Arabia in the 2020s as a major patron of international sport in areas such as LIV Golf and world football.

Globalization and the Internationalization of Sport

During the Cold War, international sporting competitions were arenas for superpower rivalry. The Soviet Union attempted to outcompete the West by demonstrating its superiority in the Olympic medal count tables, World Cup competitions, and other international championships.[4] It was rare for athletes from the communist bloc to play in the professional leagues of the West as they would have had to defect to do so. Likewise, Western athletes did not go the other direction as there were no professional sports leagues in the USSR. The collapse of the Soviet bloc in the early 1990s brought the financial allure of potentially joining Western sports leagues and living in the West, while major sporting events, along with their growing global corporate sponsorships, were awarded almost exclusively to democratic hosts. These twin developments left major authoritarian states bereft of their star athletes and ensnared in transnational political projects that they either were unable or unwilling to successfully influence.

The 1990s and 2000s were pivotal decades for Western soft power that saw the internationalization and expansion of major sporting club competitions. US and European professional leagues and domestic competitions attracted the world's best players, while expanding marketing and viewership rights globally. During the 1990s, North American sports leagues such as the National Hockey League and Major League Baseball expanded and attracted an unprecedented

---

[4] On various aspects of sports and the Cold War, see the collection of essays in Stephen Wagg and David L. Andrews, *East Plays West: Sport and the Cold War* (Routledge, 2007).

international pool of players.[5] Starting in the late 1980s amid Gorbachev's reforms, communist bloc athletes began to flock to the United States, although several bureaucratic, political, and financial hurdles had to be overcome to do so, sometimes including defection.[6] Within a few years, the "Russian Five" group of former Soviet hockey players, including three future Hockey Hall of Famers, formed the core of the Detroit Red Wings Stanley Cup–winning teams in 1997 and 1998. The mid-1990s also saw major soccer leagues in Europe, including the United Kingdom, Germany, and France, dramatically internationalize their player pools, in part bolstered by a 1995 European Court ruling that made it easier for European players to play outside of their home country. By the 2017–18 season in the United Kingdom's Premier League, the most valuable sports league in the world, foreign players made up over 60% of the league.[7]

The NBA also made a decisive global leap. Having sent a team of NBA superstars such as Michael Jordan, Larry Bird, Magic Johnson,

---

[5] According to Baseball Almanac, in 1980 there were 80 non-US-born players in Major League Baseball (MLB) (8.9% of the total). In 1990, there were 107 (10.7%). In 2000, there were 246 (20.7%). In 2010, there were 307 (25.2%), and in 2023, 371 (25.9%). See "MLB Players by Birthplace During the 2022 Season," Baseball Almanac, https://www.baseball-almanac.com/players/birthplace.php?y=2022. These numbers exclude Puerto Rico, but when included, the overall trend does not substantively change. Because players coming to the league mostly do so from relatively democratic states, MLB has largely avoided many of the authoritarian-generated political controversies that have emerged in some other sports. The main exceptions are Venezuela, which briefly was subject to sanctions in 2019 that prevented Venezuelan MLB players from participating in the Venezuelan winter league, and Cuba, which has a long and complex relationship with the MLB. Cuban players generally must defect from the island in order to play in the MLB. On the Venezuelan sanctions episode, which remained in place for two government-affiliated teams, see "U.S. Exempts Local Baseball League from Venezuela Sanctions: Document," Reuters, December 3, 2019. On the history of the MLB-Cuba relationship, see Thomas F. Carter and John Sugden, "The USA and Sporting Diplomacy: Comparing and Contrasting the Cases of Table Tennis with China and Baseball with Cuba in the 1970s," *International Relations* 26, no. 1 (2011): pp. 101–21, https://doi.org/10.1177/0047117811411741.

[6] For a contemporaneous report, see Brian Friedman, "Soviet Invasion: Spring Thaw for USSR Athletes Looking West," *Los Angeles Times*, April 30, 1989, https://www.latimes.com/archives/la-xpm-1989-04-30-sp-3073-story.html.

[7] Gregor Aisch et al., "Where Athletes in the Premier League, the N.B.A. and Other Sports Leagues Come from, in 15 Charts," *New York Times*, December 29, 2017, https://www.nytimes.com/interactive/2017/12/29/upshot/internationalization-of-pro-sports-leagues-premier-league.html.

and Charles Barkley, known as the "Dream Team," to dominate the 1992 Summer Olympic Men's Basketball Tournament in Barcelona, NBA executives soon rolled out a number of initiatives to develop global interest in the league and the game. The NBA established overseas initiatives, including the NBA Global Games and Basketball Without Borders, but also sought to scout and attract international players to the league.[8] It worked. At the open of the 2023–24 season, the NBA boasted a record 125 international players from 40 countries, including stars like Giannis Antetokounmpo (Greece), Luka Dončić (Slovenia), Joel Embiid (Cameroon), Nikola Jokić (Serbia), Kristaps Porzingis (Latvia), and Victor Wembanyama (France).[9]

The NBA Goes to China: But Who Changed Whom?

The single most important growth market for the NBA was China. Basketball had long had a following in the country, but the Cultural Revolution put a halt to the sport. In January 1979 Deng Xiaoping famously attended—and appeared to enjoy—a Harlem Globetrotters game on his crucial visit to the United States as China was opening to the world after Mao's death. This gave permission domestically to not treat basketball as an ideological threat.[10] The NBA first played exhibition games with teams from the People's Liberation Army in 1979,[11] and an NBA China Friendship Tour in 1985 saw the Chinese national basketball team travel to United States and get training from top coaches.[12] When David Stern became NBA commissioner in 1984, he launched a globalization plan that included China.

---

[8] See the oral histories from international players compiled by *Sports Illustrated* at Andrew Sharp, "Coming to America," *Sports Illustrated*, https://www.si.com/longform/2018/nba-international-oral-history/index.html.

[9] "NBA Rosters Feature Record 125 International Players from 40 Countries," https://www.nba.com/news/nba-international-players-2023-24.

[10] Fuhua Huang, "Glocalisation of Sport: The NBA's Diffusion in China," *International Journal of the History of Sport* 30, no. 3 (2013): p. 270, https://doi.org/20.1080/09523367.2012.760997.

[11] Jay Mathews, "Bullets on the 'Zou' in Peking," *Washington Post*, August 26, 1979, p. M1.

[12] Ed Badger, "Coach of Chinese Discovers Basketball Translates Easily," *New York Times*, October 20, 1985.

Crucially, major corporations including Nike underpinned this engagement as they sponsored athletes to go to China to popularize basketball and its associated athletes and apparel.[13] By 1994 party-owned CCTV was broadcasting the NBA Finals between the New York Knicks and the Houston Rockets live nationwide, while the league itself opened its first office in Hong Kong in 1992 and by 2004 was playing preseason games in China.[14]

Interest exploded in 2002 after Chinese star Yao Ming was drafted first overall by the Houston Rockets in 2002. During his first season Chinese television viewership for NBA games was typically 15 times larger per game than US audiences (15 million vs. 1 million) and up to 30 times larger when Yao was playing.[15] Beyond skyrocketing viewership, Yao's emergence is credited for the NBA opening an office in Beijing and launching its Chinese-language website.[16] Yao was also China's figurehead at the 2008 Beijing Summer Olympics and widely credited with becoming a role model and catalyst for the league's expansion across the country. The Houston Rockets' president, George Postolos, summarized, "Yao is a dream for David Stern and the NBA. He takes globalization to a new level."[17]

By 2019–20, the viewership of the NBA in China was estimated at a stunning 500 million compared with 15–20 million in the United States.[18] In 2019, the league's total revenue from China was estimated to be at least $500 million, with the league having signed a five-year $1.5 billion digital rights contract with China's Tencent in July 2017. On

---

[13] Huang, "Glocalisation of Sport."

[14] Jeff Zillgate and Mark Medina, "As Impasse over Pro-Hong Kong Tweet Simmers, What's at Stake for the NBA in China?," *USA Today*, October 9, 2019, https://www.usatoday.com/story/sports/nba/2019/10/09/nba-china-hong-kong-whats-at-stake/3912447002/.

[15] Brook Larmer, *Operation Yao Ming: The Chinese Sports Empire, American Big Business, and the Making of an NBA Super Star* (Penguin, 2005), chapter 18, Kindle location 5452 of 7381.

[16] Larmer, *Operation Yao Ming*, 5544.

[17] Brook Larmer, "The Center of the World," *Foreign Policy*, October 20, 2009, https://foreignpolicy.com/2009/10/20/the-center-of-the-world/.

[18] Sam Amico, "Nearly 500 Million in China Watched NBA Programming in 2018-19," *Sports Illustrated*, July 10, 2020, https://www.si.com/nba/cavaliers/nba/cavaliers/nba-amico/china-basketball-season-resume-orlando.

the marketing front, the NBA launched its first store in 2008 but soon had over 200 official NBA merchandise stores, including, according to Xinhua, the world's largest in Guangzhou.[19] In 2022 ESPN estimated NBA China's total worth at $5 billion.[20]

Tellingly, contemporaneous American accounts of Yao Ming's rise as an NBA superstar usually frame the story as one where the expansion of the NBA, its marketing affiliates, and US sports culture would amalgamate a global superstar from an emerging authoritarian power.[21] Yao in his first year signed seven-figure sponsorship deals with corporate giants including Apple, Visa, Gatorade, and Pepsi and launched a fierce shoe sponsorship bidding competition that landed him a deal with Reebok worth $60 million a year and included equity in the Reebok China division, which likely took his net proceeds to over $100 million per year.[22] American fans were fascinated by Yao, as marketers portrayed him as subtle, humorous, and almost entirely apolitical, while "the US media overall . . . delivered one valentine after another, conveying appealing representations of a hard-working, earnest, funny and self-effacing yet confident young man, a fast learner with a good attitude, adjusting nicely to the strangeness of American life."[23] And yet, while Yao was an American corporate marketer's dream come true, to the Chinese government he also "was an ideal spokesperson because of his emphasis on teamwork, his loyalty to the nation, and his rigorous work ethic" who "perfectly fitted the idea of 'harmonious citizenship'"

---

[19] "World's Largest NBA Flagship Store Opens in China," Xinhua, November 10, 2020, http://www.xinhuanet.com/english/2020-11/10/c_139506432.htm.

[20] Mark Fainaru-Wada and Steve Fainaru, "NBA Owners, Mum on China Relationship, Have More Than $10 Billion Invested There," ESPN, May 19, 2022, https://www.espn.com/nba/story/_/id/33938932/nba-owners-mum-china-relationship-more-10-billion-invested-there.

[21] For example, one contemporaneous article interviewed Rockets owner Les Alexander, who predicted that "Yao will be 'bigger than Michael Jordan in the world; not in the U.S. but in the world.' He added, 'There are so many Asians, he'll be the biggest athlete of all time.'" Jere Longman, "Yao's Success Speeds NBA's Plans for China," *New York Times*, December 15, 2002, https://www.nytimes.com/2002/12/15/sports/pro-basketball-yao-s-success-speeds-nba-s-plans-for-china.html.

[22] Larmer, *Operation Yao Ming*, location 5650.

[23] Thomas Oates and Judy Polumbaum, "Agile Big Man: The Flexible Marketing of Yao Ming," *Pacific Affairs* 77, no. 2 (2004): p. 199, https://doi.org/10.2307/40022498.

224   DICTATING THE AGENDA

and could help in "efforts to reshape the perception of China as a cold, harsh, Communist country that has been ever-present in popular and political depictions in American society."[24]

After he retired in 2011, Yao returned to China, first as owner of the Shanghai Sharks and then as chairman of the Chinese Basketball Association. While he maintained an apolitical image in the United States during his playing career, since retirement he has been a delegate to the Chinese People's Political Consultative Conference, a mostly powerless advisory and consultative body in the CCP's United Front system of political control.[25] He was a spokesperson for Beijing's 2022 Winter Olympics bid and helped project an apolitical image for the Games abroad, deflecting from questions about repression in Xinjiang or the condition of Chinese women's tennis star Peng Shuai, who had apparently been held in some form of detention by authorities after accusing a top party official of sexual abuse.[26]

Yao's own remarkable story and the NBA's marketing machine in China paved the way for additional lucrative endorsement deals from Chinese companies for a number of NBA stars. Apparel and sneaker companies including Anta, Li-Ning, and PEAK have signed sponsorship deals with NBA players on a par with their US deals. For example, superstar Dwyane Wade signed an initial $10 million deal with Li-Ning before extending to a lifetime deal;[27] Golden State Warriors star Klay Thompson in 2016 signed a 10-year extension with Anta reportedly worth $80 million in what the player hoped would make him "the Michael Jordan one day of Anta."[28] Engagements like this seemed

---

[24] Haozhou Pu, "Mediating the Giants: Yao Ming, NBA and the Cultural Politics of Sino-American Relations," *Asia Pacific Journal of Sport and Social Science* 5, no. 2 (2016): p. 90, https://doi.org/10.1080/21640599.2016.1191703.

[25] Anthony Kuhn, "China's Legislative Session: Many Stars, but Little Power," NPR, March 15, 2016, https://www.npr.org/sections/parallels/2016/03/15/470533082/chinas-legislative-session-many-stars-but-little-power.

[26] Ken Moritsugu, "Former NBA Great Yao Ming Addresses Peng Shuai, Olympics," Associated Press, January 17, 2022, https://apnews.com/article/coronavirus-pandemic-novak-djokovic-winter-olympics-nba-sports-e573831da689216245067ef7f7242c0c.

[27] Bryan Kalbrosky, "These Are The NBA Players Under Contract with Chinese Sneaker Brands," HoopsHype, October 8, 2019, https://hoopshype.com/2019/10/08/houston-rockets-daryl-morey-china-li-ning-anta-peak/.

[28] Jack Maloney, "Klay Thompson Signs $80M Deal with Anta, Aims to Be the M.J. of Chinese Shoe Brand," *CBS Sports*, June 30, 2017, https://www.cbssports.com/

unimaginable to marketers and NBA fans of the early 2000s. We pick up the story of the NBA and China later in this chapter.

International Mega-Events and Liberal Projections

Chapter 2 noted the liberal norms that seemed to inform international press and IOC scrutiny of Beijing's Summer Games in 2008, while Chapter 3 contrasted those with the more systematic pushback asserted by Beijing when it hosted the 2022 Winter Games. It is worth reflecting on the fact that between 1990 and 2007, every Olympiad and men's World Cup was hosted by a consolidated democratic country (or countries in the case of the joint 2002 World Cup held jointly in Japan and South Korea), a remarkable run of 14 straight competitions.

Koch theorizes the "event ethnography" of large gatherings such as sporting events, observing that "events are important sites of analysis not *despite* the fact that they are temporary, but *because* they are temporary."[29] They bring together not only athletes and their supporting networks but also a range of prevailing transnational actors, materials, and narratives that engage with the event space in formal and informal ways.[30] During this run of democratic hosts, the international press routinely emphasized liberal narratives surrounding a host country's history, local politics, and social trends. For example, just prior to 1990, Seoul's hosting of the 1988 Summer Olympics was celebrated for pushing forward South Korea's ongoing democratic transition from decades of military dictatorship,[31] while Barcelona's 1992 Games projected an

---

nba/news/klay-thompson-signs-80m-deal-with-anta-aims-to-be-the-m-j-of-chinese-shoe-brand/.

[29] Natalie Koch, "Event Ethnography: Studying Power and Politics Through Events," *Geography Compass* 17, no. 2 (2023): p. 2, https://doi.org/10.1111/gec3.12729.

[30] Koch, "Event Ethnography," pp. 3–4.

[31] International Olympic Committee, "Seoul 1988: South Korea Opens Up to the World," https://olympics.com/ioc/legacy/living-legacy/seoul-1988. Although the Seoul Olympics are now viewed as both a showcase and catalyst of Korean democratization, it is important to note that the games were awarded in 1981, when the country was ruled by authoritarian President Chun Doo Hwan who viewed the games as an opportunity to bolster his international image and legitimacy. Chun stepped down months before the games in 1988. See David Black and Shona Bezanson, "The Olympic Games, Human Rights and Democratisation: Lessons from Seoul and Implications for Beijing," *Third World Quarterly* 25, no. 7 (2004): pp. 1245–61, https://

image of a modern, democratic, and European country that left behind dictatorial rule and reconciled anticipated tensions between Catalan nationalists and central authorities.[32]

In the case of European and world football, commercial growth in the 2000s appeared premised upon promoting a message of diversity, social equality, and inclusion, themes that would appeal to new countries, markets, and corporate partners. The Union of European Football Associations (UEFA) and FIFA began their much-publicized antiracism campaigns in the mid-2000s, promoted at the 2004 European Championships and 2006 World Cup in Germany, though substantively these campaigns by football bodies would be criticized for their lack of rigor and systemic engagement with promoting change. For example, the FIFA Task Force Against Racism and Discrimination, founded by FIFA's president, Sepp Blatter, in 2013 was disbanded in 2016, two years before the World Cup in Russia, with the justification that it had addressed all major issues and "completely fulfilled its mission."[33]

Host country officials of mega-events strategically deployed liberal values and storylines emphasizing democratic progress and social justice, also helping drive media coverage.[34] Take South Africa's hosting of the 2010 FIFA World Cup. The country was awarded the World Cup in 2003, beating out Morocco, and was celebrated as the first African host of the tournament. As part of the bid, South African officials stressed

---

doi.org/10.1080/014365904200281258. See also Victor D. Cha, *Beyond the Final Score: The Politics of Sport in Asia* (Columbia University Press, 2009), pp. 123–28. Cha writes, "The Games brought the desired change to the country but also brought world attention to the internal forces of democratization," p. 127.

[32] John Hargreaves and Manuel Garcia Ferrando, "Public Opinion, National Integration and National Identity in Spain: The Case of the Barcelona Olympic Games," *Nations and Nationalism* 3, no. 1 (1997): pp. 65–87, https://doi.org/10.1111/j.1354-5078.1997.00065.x.

[33] "FIFA Disbands Racism Task Force, Says Job Done," *The Telegraph*, September 26, 2016, https://www.telegraph.co.uk/football/2016/09/26/fifa-disbands-racism-task-force-says-job-done/; "Fifa Disbands Its Anti-Racism Taskforce Declaring that the Job Is Done," *The Guardian*, September 25, 2016, https://www.theguardian.com/football/2016/sep/25/fifa-anti-racism-task-force-russia-2018-world-cup.

[34] Some argue that the liberal bias extends to reporting on the competitions themselves, with one study finding that coverage of the Olympics highlights the successes of democracies disproportionately when measured against medal counts. See Rogelio Alicor L. Panao and Adrian Justin L. Gache, "Level Field? Sports, Soft Power and the Liberal Democratic Bias," *International Journal of Sports Policy and Politics* (2024), https://doi.org/10.1080/19406940.2024.2356590.

South Africa's own political reforms since the apartheid era and its successful staging of the Rugby World Cup in 1995, when President Nelson Mandela had triumphantly celebrated the country's return to the international sporting stage after decades of isolation, presenting the event as an opportunity for national unity and political reconciliation.[35] Indeed, President Mbeki in the opening ceremony of the 2010 World Cup finals emphasized both African humanism and liberal values, including freedom from oppression and democracy, as some of the important values that South Africa, as the representative of Africa, shared with the world.[36]

Authoritarian Emergence and the New Sportswashing

As the power of authoritarian states rebounded in the 2010s, the sports world and authoritarian politics became re-enmeshed. Individually, ascendant authoritarian regimes have deployed sport, and successful engagement in global sport, as a form of nation-building designed to legitimize regime rule.[37]

But there are important differences between the current authoritarian resurgence and Cold War–era sporting rivalries. If Cold War sports politics was about the competition for medals as a geopolitical proxy battle between different political ideologies, the new authoritarian politics appears more intent to co-opt and transform the institutions and events that comprise the very international and club competitions once associated with the West. As with the example of the NBA courting the Chinese market in the 1990s and 2000s, Western and international sporting committees and federations initially justified many of these new engagements as vehicles for integrating authoritarian hosts into the global community, implicitly or explicitly championing the power of international sport to promote open values.

---

[35] Lynette Steenveld and Larry Strelitz, "The 1995 Rugby World Cup and the Politics of Nation-Building in South Africa," *Media, Culture & Society* 20, no. 4 (1998): pp. 609–29, https://doi.org/10.1177/016344398020000400.

[36] David Smith, "World Cup 2010 Embraces Triumph and Disaster at the Same Time," *The Guardian*, June 19, 2010, https://www.theguardian.com/football/2010/jun/19/world-cup-2010-south-africa.

[37] See Koch's discussion of Kazakhstan's "soft-authoritarian" nation-building in Natalie Koch, "Sport and Soft Authoritarian Nation-Building," *Political Geography* 32 (2013): pp. 41–52.

228   DICTATING THE AGENDA

By the 2010s, however, a discernible shift was underway in the venues chosen to host international mega-events, as sites in liberal democracies gave way to emerging powers hosting the world's most watched competitions.[38] While from 1990 through 2007 all Olympics and World Cups were held in consolidated democratic states, 5 out of the 12 of these major sporting events between 2008 and 2022 were held in consolidated *authoritarian* regimes (Russia twice, China twice, Qatar once).[39] Prior public optimism about the potential transformative value of international sport gave way to a new widespread scrutiny that authoritarians were strategically using the international attention brought by hosting major global events in order to whitewash their political repression and human rights records, marginalize international criticism, and secure international legitimacy.[40]

During the 2010s, these practices came to be referred to as "sportwashing."[41] The term gained media prominence in reference to Azerbaijan's use of the inaugural 2015 European Games to burnish its image as a modernizing European country and downplay its abysmal

---

[38] Jonathan Grix and Donna Lee, "Soft Power, Sports Mega-Events and Emerging States: The Lure of the Politics of Attraction," *Global Society* 27, no. 4 (2013): pp. 521–36, https://doi.org/10.1080/13600826.2013.827632.

[39] Although, it is worth noting that in addition to France hosting the 2024 Summer Olympics, pending hosts for the games are Italy, the United States, and Australia, and for the World Cup joint hosts are scheduled for 2026 Canada / United States / Mexico and 2030 Spain/Portugal/Morocco, with Saudi Arabia due to host in 2034.

[40] On Russia's domestic political and foreign policy goals in hosting the 2014 Sochi Winter Olympics and the 2018 FIFA Men's World Cup, for example, see Owen Gibson, "Sochi Games Held Up as a Symbol of Olympic Extravagance and Waste," *The Guardian*, February 5, 2014, https://www.theguardian.com/sport/2014/feb/05/sochi-games-olympic-extravagence-cost-winter-russia; and Andrey Makarychev, "From Sochi—2014 to FIFA—2018: The Crisis of Sovereignty and the Challenges of Globalization," in *Mega Events in Post-Soviet Eurasia: Shifting Borderlines of Inclusion and Exclusion*, edited by Andrey Makarychev and Alexandra Yatsyk (Palgrave Macmillan, 2016): pp. 195–213. We note that the empirical evidence on the effectiveness of "sportswashing" is mixed, at best. For an effort to systematically assess the effects of Qatar's 2022 tournament on public opinion in Germany, see Christian Gläßel et al., "Does Sportswashing Work? First Insights from the 2022 World Cup in Qatar," *Journal of Politics* (forthcoming, 2024), https://doi.org/10.1086/730728; see also Johannes Gerschewski, Heiko Giebler, Sebastian Hellmeier, Eda Keremoğlu, and Michael Zürn (2024) "The Limits of Sportswashing. How the 2022 FIFA World Cup Affected Attitudes About Qatar." *PloS one* 19, no. 8: e0308702.

[41] We hasten to add that this is not necessarily new, as the trade-off between major sports events as an image-booster and a scrutiny-enhancer has long been known. See Cha, *Beyond the Final Score*; and Adam Scharpf et al., "International Sports Events

human rights record.[42] In the year before the event, the government visibly increased its repression, imprisoning 13 high-profile journalists and activists on various criminal charges.[43] And in the days prior to the opening ceremony, the Baku government barred accreditation to several foreign journalists and prevented Amnesty International from releasing a critical report in Baku.[44] Just a couple of years later, a major investigation revealed that between 2012 and 2014 the Azeri government had funneled $2.9 billion through four related UK-registered shell companies in a scheme designed to buy influence among Europe's politicians, lobbyists, and consultants.[45]

New Authoritarian Markets, New Authoritarian Partners

Sportswashing may be part of the story, but the reality of authoritarian enmeshment in global sport goes deeper. In both international

---

and Repression in Autocracies: Evidence from the 1978 FIFA World Cup," *American Political Science Review* 117, no. 3 (2023): pp. 909–26, https://doi.org/10.1017/S0003055422000958. However, we argue that the renewal of authoritarian power and its embeddedness in the transnational networks that would drive change are helping catalyze important shifts in that trade off. The academic literature on "sportswashing" as a distinct form of authoritarian soft power is substantial and growing. See Jules Boykoff, "Toward a Theory of Sportswashing: Mega-Events, Soft Power, and Political Conflict," *Sociology of Sport Journal* 39, no. 4 (2022): pp. 342–51, https://doi.org/10.1123/ssj.2022-0095; Sarath Ganji, "The Authoritarian's Guide to Football," *Journal of International Affairs* 74, no. 2 (2022): pp. 37–64; Michael Skey, "Sportswashing: Media Headline or Analytic Concept?," *International Review for the Sociology of Sport* 58, no. 5 (2023): pp. 749–64, https://doi.org/10.1177/10126902221136086; and Sven Daniel Wolfe, "'For the Benefit of Our Nation': Unstable Soft Power in the 2018 Men's World Cup in Russia," *International Journal of Sport Policy and Politics* 12, no. 4 (2020): pp. 545–61, https://doi.org/10.1080/19406940.2020.1839532; Gläßel et al., "Does Sportswashing Work?"

[42] Jane Buchanan, "Azerbaijan's European Games: Giving Sport a Bad Name," Human Rights Watch, June 16, 2015, https://www.hrw.org/news/2015/06/16/azerbaijans-european-games-giving-sport-bad-name.

[43] Caroline Christie, "Human Rights Abuses and the European Games in Azerbaijan," Vice, June 15, 2015, https://www.vice.com/en/article/gv77m7/human-rights-abuses-and-the-european-games-in-azerbaijan.

[44] Amnesty International, "Amnesty International Barred from Baku Ahead of European Games," June 10, 2015, https://www.amnesty.org/en/latest/news/2015/06/amnesty-international-barred-from-baku-ahead-of-european-games/.

[45] Luke Harding et al., "Everything You Need to Know about the Azerbaijani Laundromat," *The Guardian*, September 7, 2017, https://www.theguardian.com/world/2017/sep/04/everything-you-need-to-know-about-the-azerbaijani-laundromat.

competitions and global club sport, authoritarian states learned to use their financial leverage and political power to play the West's game. In European club football, the entry of authoritarian owners, investors, and sponsors has helped to fuel the global growth of top leagues, such as the English Premiership and Spain's La Liga, and the rapid expansion of the UEFA Champions League (UCL), Europe's premier annual club competition.

First, authoritarians, both in the form of state-affiliated companies and individual owners, have openly acquired a number of European football's most prized clubs. In June 2003, Chelsea Football Club announced that longtime owner Ken Bates had sold the club for £140 million to the Russian billionaire Roman Abramovich, a major shareholder of one of Russia's largest oil companies and reported ally of the Kremlin.[46] Abramovich vigorously denied having purchased the club at the request of Russian president Vladimir Putin, and in 2019 settled a defamation case with a British journalist on the subject.[47] The club's competitive successes under Abramovich's ownership were undeniable. Chelsea proceeded to go on a massive spending spree to acquire leading players, winning its first Premier League title in 2004–5 and four times thereafter, as well as the prestigious UCL in 2011 and 2021.

The Russian oligarch's success paved the way for other similar acquisitions shortly after. Most notably in 2008 the Abu Dhabi–based City Football Group (owned by Abu Dhabi Group, which was the investment group of Sheikh Mansur bin Zayed and the UAE ruling family) acquired Manchester City and proceeded to win eight Premiership titles, reportedly spending over £2.5 billion in the process.[48] As of 2024, five teams in the Deloitte's "Money League," its ranking of the 20 richest world football clubs by annual revenue, were currently or recently owned by foreign owners from authoritarian countries

---

[46] "Russian Businessman Buys Chelsea," BBC, July 2, 2003, http://news.bbc.co.uk/2/hi/3036838.stm.

[47] "Catherine Belton, Journalist and Author of 'Putin's People: How the KGB Took Back Russia and Then Took on the West,'" Foreign Policy Centre, February 15, 2023, https://fpc.org.uk/catherine-belton-journalist-and-author-of-putins-people-how-the-kgb-took-back-russia-and-then-took-on-the-west/.

[48] Andy Restrepo, "Who Is Man City Owner Sheikh Mansour and What's His Net Worth?," as.com, June 7, 2023, https://en.as.com/soccer/who-is-man-city-owner-sheikh-mansour-and-whats-his-net-worth-n-2/.

(Table 8.1).[49] On balance fans of these clubs welcomed the significant investments made by their new owners and chose to ignore the politics. Tellingly, after Abramovich was forced to sell Chelsea by the UK government following Russia's invasion of Ukraine in February 2022, Chelsea fans disrupted the minute of applause dedicated to showing support for Ukraine to chant the name of the Russian former owner.[50] In addition to these five, reports indicate that Russian-Uzbek billionaire Alisher Usmanov, who owned a stake in Arsenal Football

Table 8.1 Authoritarian Ownership in Highest Revenue-Generating Football Clubs, as Valued by Deloitte Football Money League 2024

Club (Country)	Buyer/ Stakeholder (Associated Authoritarian Country)	Date of Acquisition	Cost ($US); percentage stake	Reported Revenue Generation in 2024 (€)*
Manchester City (UK)	Abu Dhabi United Group (UAE)	2008	$247 mn; 100%	825.9 mn
Paris Saint-Germain (France)	Qatar Sports Investment (Qatar)	2011; 2012	$74.5 mn; 70% $30 mn; 30%	801.8 mn
Chelsea (UK)	Roman Abramovich (Russia)	2003-2022	$233 mm, 100%; resold in 2022 for $5.3 bn	589.4 mn
Inter Milan (Italy)	Suning Commerce Group (China)	2016-2024	$307 mn; 68.6%	378.9 mn
Newcastle (UK)	Public Investment Fund (Saudi Arabia)	2021	$326 mn; 80%	287.8 m

Source: Deloitte Football Money League 2024, https://www.deloitte.com/uk/en/services/financial-advisory/analysis/deloitte-football-money-league.html.

---

[49] "Deloitte Football Money League 2024," Deloitte, https://www2.deloitte.com/uk/en/pages/sports-business-group/articles/deloitte-football-money-league.html.

[50] Robert Summerscales, "Chelsea Fans Disrupt Minute's Applause for Ukraine with Roman Abramovich Chant," *Sports Illustrated*, March 5, 2022, https://www.si.com/fannation/soccer/futbol/video/chelsea-fans-hijack-ukraine-tribute-with-roman-abramovich-chant.

Club from 2007 until 2018, funded Everton Football Club while he was barred from entering the United Kingdom in 2021;[51] Usmanov, and his financial networks, have been sanctioned multiple times by Western governments following Russia's invasion of Ukraine.[52]

A second source of authoritarian funding has come from the vast revenues generated from the growth in media and broadcasting rights for Europe's leading football leagues. Overall, during the 2022/23 season, broadcasting rights constituted 42% of the revenue stream of the worlds' 20 richest clubs, compared with 41% from corporate sponsorships and 18% from gameday sales.[53] UEFA's total revenue from media rights and commercial rights increased from €647 million in 2005 to €2.1 billion in 2016 and €5.7 billion in 2020/21;[54] By 2023 total revenues from global sponsorship for the UCL alone had reached $603 million.[55] As with the NBA, growth in international broadcasting rights has been led by China, which for the period from 2019 to 2022 were worth £535 million for the Premier League, more than a 12-fold increase and the highest of any single market of the league's overall £4.35 billion overseas broadcasting rights in 2019.[56]

Also notable in the global sports media landscape is the rise of Qatar-based BeIN Media. Founded by the Al Jazeera media

---

[51] Simon Goodley, "Oligarch Funded Everton Football Club While Barred from UK," *The Guardian*, May 3, 2023, https://www.theguardian.com/business/2023/may/03/oligarch-funded-everton-football-club-while-barred-from-uk-alisher-usmanov.

[52] Aamer Madhani, "US, UK Aim Sanctions at Russian Oligarchs' Finance Networks," Associated Press, April 12, 2023, https://apnews.com/article/russian-oligarch-alisher-usmanov-treasury-sanctions-putin-24cd2d7557bc7c45b9ecb38591537643.

[53] "Deloitte Football Money League 2024," Deloitte, https://www2.deloitte.com/uk/en/pages/sports-business-group/articles/deloitte-football-money-league.html.

[54] Statista, "Total Revenue of UEFA from 2005/06 to 2021/22," https://www.statista.com/statistics/279056/revenue-of-the-uefa/; UEFA, "UEFA Financial Report 2021/22 Annex," June 30, 2022, https://editorial.uefa.com/resources/0280-17b3db253a76-5a377185eae6-1000/uefa_financial_report_annex_2021-22_en.pdf.

[55] "UEFA Champions League Generates $606.3 Million Sponsorship Revenue for 2023 Season, Reveals GlobalData," GlobalData, August 3, 2023, https://www.globaldata.com/media/sport/uefa-champions-league-generates-606-3-million-sponsorship-revenue-2023-season-reveals-globaldata/.

[56] Tim Wigmore, "Premier League 'Big Six' Cash In as Overseas TV Rights Rise 35 Per Cent," *The Telegraph*, August 3, 2019, https://www.telegraph.co.uk/football/2019/08/03/premier-league-big-six-cash-overseas-tv-rights-rise-35-per-cent/.

network in 2012 after the Gulf state in 2010 was awarded the 2022 World Cup, the group acquired the Australia-based Setanta group and then signed strategic discovery agreements with an assortment of Western media outlets, including Turner Broadcasting. It acquired the exclusive rights to broadcast a number of prestigious club and signature international events to the Middle East and North Africa, including the UEFA Champions League ($600 million deal in 2021), the Premier League ($500 million in 2020), as well as the Olympics ($250 million through 2024) and 2022 FIFA World Cup.[57]

The third source of revenues come from the growth of corporate sponsorships from companies that are owned by or associated with authoritarian states. These deals began mid-decade after the turn of the century, have grown in value and importance, and have been led by the airline sector. As Appendix 8.1 details, we identified 62 individual sponsorship deals since 2006 by airlines from authoritarian countries, including Aeroflot (Russia), Emirates and Etihad Airways (UAE), Qatar Airways, and, since 2023, Saudi-based airlines. The most lucrative of these are the shirt sponsorships for the mega European football clubs including Manchester City (Etihad Airways; $80 mn annually), Real Madrid (Etihad Airways; $70 mn annually), Arsenal (Emirates; $56 mn annually), and AS Roma (Qatar Airways; $48 mn annually).[58] Other categories of sponsors include state-affiliated tourism boards, among

---

[57] Tom Bassam, "Uefa Secures US$600m Deal from BeIN for MENA Champions Leagues Rights," Sportspro, June 10, 2021, https://www.sportspromedia .com/news/uefa-tv-rights-bein-sport-mena-champions-league-2021/?zephr_sso_ott =Jm25d9; Rohith Nair, "BeIN Sports Secures Premier League Rights Till 2025 in $500m Deal," Reuters, December 17, 2020, https://www.reuters.com/article/soccer-england-premierleague-int/bein-sports-secures-premier-league-rights-till-2025-in-500m-deal-idUSKBN28R2B8.

[58] Adam Crafton, "Manchester City's Sponsors, the Links to Abu Dhabi and What It Means for Newcastle United," The Athletic, February 17, 2022, https:// theathletic.com/3120837/2022/02/17/special-report-manchester-citys-sponsors-the-links-to-abu-dhabi-and-what-it-means-for-newcastle-united/; Rory Jones, "Real Madrid Check in '€70m a Year' Emirates Extension," Sportspro, October 17, 2022, https://www.sportspromedia.com/news/real-madrid-emirates-shirt-sponsor-2026-laliga-worth/#:~:text=While%20terms%20of%20the%20new,%2468.28%Emirates Extensio20million)%20annually%20to%20Real; "AS Roma, Qatar Airway [sic] Multi-Year Shirt Sponsorship Worth 40 Million Euros-Source," Reuters, April 23, 2018, https://www.reuters.com/article/soccer-italy-as-roma-qatar-airways/as-roma -qatar-airway-multi-year-shirt-spnsorship-worth-40-mln-euros-source-idUSI6N1R

234 DICTATING THE AGENDA

them Visit Abu Dhabi, the Rwandan Development Board and Visit Rwanda, Visit Saudi, and the Qatar Tourism Authority, and some well-known state energy companies, such as Russia's Gazprom, sponsor of a number of European football tournaments, and Azerbaijan's State Oil Company. Increasingly, authoritarian states have learned to use their financial leverage and political power to sponsor and play the world's game.

Formula One Expands Its Frontiers

Soccer is not alone in experiencing these shifts. In 2004 as part of a campaign to expand its global reach, the Formula One (F1) motor race, which takes place throughout the year over a series of different country circuits, hosted the sport's first ever races in China and Bahrain. As with the realm of higher education, the expansion of these races to these emerging authoritarian markets at the height of globalization in the 2000s was covered as a symbol of these countries' internationalization and importance as expanding markets.[59] The 2004 Chinese Grand Prix held in Shanghai underscored the city's status as a global cultural and commercial hub and was held there every year until 2019, when it was suspended due to Covid-19. The most salient political concern surrounding the 2004 inaugural Bahrain Grand Prix, the first F1 race to be held in the entire Middle East, was that of event security and the fear of terrorism, not authoritarian politics.[60] The race has been run every year since, except for 2011 when the Bahraini government cracked down on

---

OooW; Zahraa Alkhaisi, "Emirates Hands Arsenal $280 Million in Record Sponsorship Deal," CNN, February 19, 2018, https://money.cnn.com/2018/02/19/news/companies/emirates-arsenal-record-sponsorship-deal/index.html.

[59] Mure Dickie and Francesco Guerrera, "Shanghai Gears Up for China's Maiden Grand Prix," *Financial Times*, September 24, 2004. A contemporary *New York Times* opinion piece chastised the city for its authoritarian corruption and "vast waste of public funds," observing that "as a city it seems unwilling to face up to how much it owes both to the central government and its own exclusivist city-state policies, which would be unthinkable in freer countries, like India or Indonesia." See Philip Bowery, "Grand Prix: For the Teal Shanghai, Look Under the Hood," *New York Times*, September 28, 2004, https://www.nytimes.com/2004/09/28/opinion/grand-prix-for-the-real-shanghai-look-under-the-hood.html.

[60] Stephen Wade, "Bahrain Revved Up for Inaugural F1 Race," *Toronto Star*, April 3, 2004.

protestors.[61] Within a few years of these races, the International Automobile Federation (FIA), the motor sport's governing body, added an array of authoritarian hosts including Singapore, run every year since 2008, Abu Dhabi (UAE) (since 2009), Azerbaijan (since 2016), Russia (2014–21), and, since 2021, the Saudi Arabian Grand Prix and Qatar Grand Prix. Whereas in 2003 all 14 F1 race hosts countries were democracies, in 2023, seven of 23 hosts were non-democratic.[62]

International human rights groups have consistently criticized the FIA for awarding these races, while FIA officials have maintained that its engagement with these countries is a force for promoting good and global standard-setting. In 2022, in the wake of F1 signing a new 15-year deal with Bahrain to continue racing though 2036, a coalition of human rights groups sent a letter to FIA executive director Stefano Domenicali accusing F1 of a "failure to engage with civil society and acknowledge rights abuse in Bahrain" and observing that such sportswashing overlooked "institutionalized repression" in the country.[63] F1 responded by claiming, "For decades Formula One has worked hard to be a positive force everywhere it races, including economic, social, and cultural benefits."[64] In prior years, drivers of F1 questioned the human rights practices of authoritarian hosts. Most prominently, Lewis Hamilton, a seven-time world champion, issued blistering critiques in 2021 of new hosts Qatar and Saudi Arabia's human rights records, having previously criticized Bahrain, to which Domenicali responded, "It is important to make clear that Formula 1 is not a cross-border

---

[61] "Formula One Accused by Humanitarian Groups of Ignoring Human Rights Abuse in Bahrain," ESPN, March 15, 2022, https://www.espn.com/f1/story/_/id/33508287/formula-one-accused-ignoring-human-rights-abuse-bahrain-humanitarian-groups.

[62] "2023 FIA Formula 1 World Championship," GP Archive, https://gparchive.com/formula-1/formula-1-seasons/2023-formula-1-season/.

[63] Reproduced in MENA Rights Group, "Rights Groups Condemn F1's 'Double Standard' for Racing in Bahrain Amidst 'Continued Institutional Repression,'" March 17, 2022, http://menarights.org/en/articles/rights-groups-condemn-f1s-double-standard-racing-bahrain-amidst-continued.

[64] "Formula One Accused by Humanitarian Groups of Ignoring Human Rights Abuse in Bahrain," ESPN, March 15, 2022, https://www.espn.com/f1/story/_/id/33508287/formula-one-accused-ignoring-human-rights-abuse-bahrain-humanitarian-groups.

236   DICTATING THE AGENDA

investigatory organization."[65] In December 2022, the FIA announced that it had updated its International Sporting Code and that its drivers would have to secure written permission from the FIA, starting in the 2023–24 season, before making "political statements," a measure designed to preserve "the general principle of neutrality."[66]

From Speaking Out to Remaining Neutral: Voice and Protest in Global Sport

The FIA controversy over political speech, and the governing body's new formal restrictions on drivers, spotlights another area in global sport where liberal norms have shifted: that of guaranteeing athletes the freedom of political expression and protest. The Olympics are a useful example to consider. Officially, the IOC has long adhered to a formal policy, designated in Rule 50 of the Olympic Charter, of opposing religious, political, and ethnic demonstrations by athletes during the Games.

Historically, however, the Olympics has regularly been associated with political controversy and protest.[67] From Nazi Germany's use of the 1936 Summer Olympics for regime propaganda to the late Cold War boycotts of the 1980 Moscow and 1984 Los Angeles Summer Games, the Olympics has been a site for political expression. The most iconic act of individual protest occurred in the 1968 Mexico City Summer Olympics when two African American athletes, Tommie Smith and John Carlos, raised their fists in a Black Power salute during the playing of the US national anthem at the medal ceremony to protest racial injustice in the United States. Smith and Carlos were immediately

---

[65] Giles Richards, "Lewis Hamilton Puts F1 on Notice Over Human Rights Before Bahrain GP," *The Guardian*, March 25, 2021, https://www.theguardian.com/sport/2021/mar/25/lewis-hamilton-speaks-out-on-human-rights-before-bahrain-gr and-prix. Domenicali continued, "We are a sports rightsholder that has the important job of promoting our sport across the world in line with the policies I have set out. Unlike governments and other bodies we are not able to undertake the actions you request, and it would not be appropriate for us to pretend we can."

[66] "Formula 1 Drivers to Require Permission to Make Political Statements at Races," ABC, December 20, 2022, https://www.abc.net.au/news/2022-12-21/formula-1-drives-to-require-permission-to-protest/101796162.

[67] Jules Boykoff, "Protest, Activism, and the Olympic Games: An Overview of Key Issues and Iconic Moments," *International Journal of the History of Sport* 34, nos. 3–4 (2017): pp. 162–83, https://doi.org/10.1080/09523367.2017.1356822.

suspended from the US Olympic team and expelled from the Olympic Village by the IOC, but their actions became a symbol of civil rights protest, with the duo publicly rehabilitated in the lead up to the 1984 Los Angeles Games.[68]

In one study of protests at the Olympics, Cottrell and Nelson find that, through the 2008 Beijing Games, the number of protest activities at the Olympics actually had increased significantly over the century, and even more sharply since the end of the Cold War.[69] Although Rule 50 has remained in effect in the post–Cold War era, transnational activists increasingly targeted the Olympics as a site for advocacy for liberal causes related to social justice, environmental activism, democratic representation, and the rights of indigenous communities.[70] Strikingly, the authors found that, in the face of increasing protests, both the IOC and host states maintained their resistance to protests and curtailed spaces for them.[71] Post-2008, Olympic hosts Russia (2014) and China (2022) severely restricted protests, while the IOC has sought to preempt and restrict political expression on domestically sensitive topics altogether. In early 2021, in anticipation of athletes taking knees at the Tokyo Olympics (2020 Summer Games, rescheduled for summer 2021), the IOC reaffirmed Rule 50, which kept the protest ban in place for arenas of competition and medal ceremonies, but allowed athletes to "express their views" either by wearing an article of clothing or making a symbolic gesture before the start of a competition.[72]

---

[68] Simon Henderson, "'Nasty Demonstrations by Negroes': The Place of the Smith–Carlos Podium Salute in the Civil Rights Movement," *Bulletin of Latin American Research* 29 (2010): pp. 78–92, https://doi.org/10.1111/j.1470-9856.2009.00339.x.

[69] Patrick M. Cottrell and Travis Nelson, "Not Just the Games? Power, Protest and Politics at the Olympics," *European Journal of International Relations* 17, no. 4 (2011): pp. 729–53, https://doi.org/10.1177/1354066110380965.

[70] Most notably, at the 2000 Summer Games in Sydney, gold medalist Cathy Freeman ran a victory lap holding both the Australian and Aboriginal flags, a technical breach of Rule 50 that ignited a debate within the host country but which brought no punitive sanctions.

[71] Cottrell and Nelson, "Not Just the Games?," pp. 740–41.

[72] Andrew Keh, "Olympics Allows Protests, but Not During Events or on Medals Stand," *New York Times*, July 2, 2021, https://www.nytimes.com/2021/07/02/sports/olympics/olympics-protests-tokyo.html. See the IOC's guidance here: "IOC Extends Opportunities for Athlete Expression During the Olympic Games Tokyo 2020," Olympics, July 2, 2021, https://olympics.com/ioc/news/ioc-extends-opportunities-for-athlete-expression-during-the-olympic-games-tokyo-2020.

The IOC justified this reaffirmation of the policy by citing the results of a large survey that it administered to over 3,500 athletes from 185 countries participating in 41 different events.[73] The survey found that 42% of respondents deemed it "appropriate" for athletes to "demonstrate or express individual views" in the media, 38% in press conferences, and 36% in the mixed zones, while only 16% deemed it appropriate for individual views to be expressed on the medal podium, 14% on the field of play, and 14% at the opening ceremony.[74] The report underscored that "a clear majority of athletes believe that it is *not* appropriate for athletes to demonstrate or express their views in these three places—67% deem the podium 'not appropriate'... and 70% think the same for the Opening Ceremony and for the field of play."[75] However, disaggregating the survey's own data by national origin of athletes shows that those surveyed from China and Russia were considerably more likely to disapprove of protest and individual expression irrespective of venue and context. For example, only a majority of athletes from China and Russia deemed it "not appropriate" for athletes to express their views on political issues in the media (85% and 56%) or at press conferences (87% and 56%), considerably higher than the 40% average and smaller percentages from the United States (27%), Great Britain (27%), Canada (18%), and Germany (18%).[76]

More broadly, nuanced attempts to navigate the support for the universal ideals like anti-discrimination publicly espoused by sporting federations have increasingly been overrun by authoritarian host nations openly invoking domestic law and asserting their sovereign right to be free of external, and especially Western, criticism. The issue is not just that authoritarian hosts have increased in their self-confidence. International stakeholders also have been increasingly reluctant to publicly oppose restrictions on political expression or reconcile seeming

---

[73] IOC Athletes' Commission Report, *Athlete Expression Consultation*, https://olympics.com/athlete365/app/uploads/2021/04/IOC_AC_Consultation_Report-Athlete_Expression_21.04.2021.pdf.

[74] IOC Athletes' Commission Report, *Athlete Expression Consultation*, p. 2.

[75] IOC Athletes' Commission Report, *Athlete Expression C*onsultation, p. 20.

[76] Publicis, "Athlete Expression Consultation: Quantitative Results," https://olympics.com/athlete365/app/uploads/2021/04/21042021-Athlete-Expression-Consultation-PSE-1.pdf., pp. 11–12.

contradictions between a host country and the sporting body's own statements that promote freedom of expression, inclusion, and/or anti-discrimination. The NBA and English Premier League's clashes with Chinese authorities over critical comments on social media and FIFA's staunch support of World Cup host Qatar's ban on symbols of pro-LGBTQ tolerance and activism suggest that the space for sports as an arena to promote fundamental liberal principles has shrunk markedly. We discuss each in turn.

Protesting Beijing's Crackdowns: Snapback Against the NBA and Premier League

The nexus of sports and politics in China became a global story in 2019, with a confrontation between China and the NBA highlighting the new era of authoritarian backlash.[77] On October 4, 2019, Houston Rockets general manager Daryl Morey tweeted a graphic with the slogan "Fight for Freedom, Stand with Hong Kong," which was deleted shortly after.[78] The following day, Rockets owner Tilman Feritta responded on Twitter that "@dmorey does NOT speak for the @HoustonRockets . . . we are NOT a political organization." However on October 6 the Chinese Basketball Association, led by Yao Ming, announced that it would suspend all cooperation with the team and CCTV 5, the sports channel of China's leading state broadcaster, and suspended broadcasting of Rockets games. Stores pulled Rockets merchandise from shelves, and sponsors, including sportswear company Li-Ning and the Shanghai Pudong Development Bank, announced they would cancel their contracts.[79] Eleven of the NBA's 13 official

---

[77] Victor Cha and Andy Lim, "Flagrant Foul: China's Predatory Liberalism and the NBA," *Washington Quarterly* 42, no. 4 (2019): pp. 23–42, https://doi.org/10.1080/0163660X.2019.1694265; William D. O'Connell, "Silencing the Crowd: China, the NBA, and Leveraging Market Size to Export Censorship," *Review of International Political Economy* 29, no. 4 (2022): pp. 1112–34, https://doi.org/10.1080/09692290.2021.1905683.

[78] Jordan Valinsky, "How One Tweet Snowballed into the NBA's Worst Nightmare," CNN, October 11, 2019, https://www.cnn.com/2019/10/09/business/nba-china-hong-kong-explainer/index.html.

[79] Laura He, "China Suspends Business Ties with NBA's Houston Rockets over Hong Kong Tweet," CNN, October 7, 2023, https://www.cnn.com/2019/10/07/business/houston-rockets-nba-china-daryl-morey/index.html.

Chinese partners immediately suspended ties with the league.[80] One report estimated the "negative impact" from the controversy at $200 million.[81] When Morey switched jobs to be the general manager of the Philadelphia 76ers in 2020, Sixers games were blocked for the season in China.[82]

But while the Chinese response was swift and unequivocal, NBA officials soon found themselves issuing contradictory statements that waffled between containing the damaging fallout of his comments and defending Morey's freedom of expression.[83] The league's initial response on October 6 recognized that Morey's views had "deeply offended many of our friends and fans in China, which is regrettable" and noted, "We have great respect for the history and culture of China and hope that sports and the NBA can be used as a unifying force to bridge cultural divides and bring people together."[84] But within the United States, political pressure on the NBA mounted when a bipartisan group of US lawmakers, including Ted Cruz and Alexandria Ocasio-Cortez, co-signed a letter urging the NBA to suspend its activities in China until Beijing halted its boycott of the Rockets.[85] Anticipating this backlash, on October 8 the NBA commissioner released yet another statement affirming the importance of freedom of expression but acknowledging the different systems and beliefs between the two countries and the

---

[80] Amelia Lucas and Lian Wu, "Nearly All of the NBA's Chinese Partners Have Cut Ties with the League," CNBC, October 9, 2019, https://www.cnbc.com/2019/10/09/nearly-all-of-the-nbas-chinese-partners-have-cut-ties-with-the-league.html.

[81] Adrian Wojnarowski and Zach Lowe, "NBA Revenue for 2019–20 Season Dropped 10% to $8.3 Billion, Sources Say," ESPN, October 28, 2020, https://www.espn.com/nba/story/_/id/30211678/nba-revenue-2019-20-season-dropped-10-83-billion-sources-say; O'Connell, "Silencing the Crowd."

[82] "China Drops Philadelphia 76ers Broadcasts as Hong Kong Row Continues," *The Guardian*, December 30, 2020, https://www.theguardian.com/sport/2020/dec/30/china-drops-76ers-broadcasts-daryl-morey.

[83] Cindy Boren, "The NBA's China-Daryl Morey Backlash, Explained," *Washington Post*, October 7, 2019, https://www.washingtonpost.com/sports/2019/10/07/nba-china-tweet-daryl-morey/#.

[84] "NBA Statement," NBA Communications, October 6, 2019, https://pr.nba.com/nba-statement/.

[85] Jason Owens, "Ted Cruz, Alexandria Ocasio-Cortez Co-Sign Congressional Request That NBA Suspend Its Activities in China," *Yahoo News*, October 9, 2019, https://sports.yahoo.com/ted-cruz-alexandria-ocasio-cortez-cosign-congressional-request-that-nba-suspend-activities-in-china-021745024.html?guccounter=1.

existence of different viewpoints on various issues.[86] Days later, Silver publicly revealed that the Chinese government had asked the NBA to fire Morey, a claim that the Chinese Ministry of Foreign Affairs denied.[87] In response, CCTV accused Silver of defaming China to "please American politicians" and warned that he would face "retribution."[88] During this time, a number of individual NBA players who maintained individual endorsement deals or business interests in China, including Rockets star player James Harden and league superstar Lebron James, issued public apologies as the commercial incentives of various actors associated with the league became a point of leverage for Beijing.[89]

As events unfolded, US news coverage emphasized the NBA's dependence on the Chinese market and vulnerability to Chinese reprisals, while Chinese news outlets emphasized how the incident had harmed business relations between the NBA and its Chinese partners, including partners of the Rockets that had already invested so much with the team.[90] On social media, discussions inside the PRC emphasized territorial integrity and Western hypocrisy, while those outside China

---

[86] Sopan Deb, "Adam Silver Commits to Free Speech as Chinese Companies Cut Ties with the NBA," *New York Times*, October 8, 2019, https://www.nytimes.com/2019/10/08/sports/adam-silver-nba-china-hong-kong.html.

[87] Jenna West, "Adam Silver: Chinese Government Asked NBA to Fire and Discipline Daryl Morey," *Sports Illustrated*, October 17, 2018, https://www.si.com/nba/2019/10/17/chinese-government-asked-nba-fire-daryl-morey.

[88] Catherine Wong, "NBA Commissioner Adam Silver Will Face 'Retribution' for Defaming China, State Media Says," *South China Morning Post*, October 19, 2019, https://www.scmp.com/news/china/diplomacy/article/3033707/nba-commissioner-adam-silver-will-face-retribution-defaming.

[89] Tyler J. Tedford et al., "Hong Kong Hardball," *International Journal of Sport Policy and Politics* 13, no. 4 (2021): pp. 733–39, https://doi.org/10.1080/19406940.2021.1915850. See also Wojnarowski and Lowe, "NBA Revenue." Harden reportedly said, "We apologize. You know, we love China. We love playing there." Quoted in Michael McCann, "How China Could Inflict 'Retribution' Against Adam Silver, NBA," *Sports Illustrated*, October 20, 2019, https://www.si.com/nba/2019/10/20/adam-silver-nba-face-retribution-china.

[90] Hui Zhao and Chiara Valentini, "Navigating Turbulent Political Waters: From Corporate Political Advocacy to Scansis in the Case of NBA-China Crisis," *Journal of Public Relations Research* 34, nos. 1–2 (2022): pp. 64–87, https://doi.org/10.1080/1062726X.2022.2064288. Perhaps not surprisingly, the authors show that US and Western media outlets framed the protests in Hong Kong in relation to liberal political values such as freedom and democracy, while Chinese newspapers emphasized the issue of sovereignty and the protestors as inciting separatism.

stressed themes of authoritarianism and free speech.[91] And, in an inconvenient stateside complication for the league's position as a defender of free expression, Joe Tsai, the Taiwanese-born billionaire owner of the Brooklyn Nets, referred to the Hong Kong protests as "separatists" and said that Morey's post was "damaging to the relationship with our fans in China."[92] Highlighting the connections between the NBA and Chinese market, Tsai is the cofounder with CCP member Jack Ma of the Chinese e-commerce giant Alibaba, where he remains on the board and a significant individual shareholder.

A few months after the NBA story broke, the English Premier League had its own, lesser publicized, spat with China regarding a different political stand related to China's forced re-education camps in Xinjiang. In December 2019, Mesut Özil, a German-Turkish World Cup–winning football star for the prestigious Arsenal Football Club posted a message on his Instagram and Twitter accounts that criticized Beijing's repressive policies toward Uyghurs. Özil, a practicing Muslim, accused China of shutting down mosques and madrasas, burning Qurans, killing religious scholars, and sending Uyghurs to mass detention camps. He referred to the Xinjiang region as "East Turkestan," a label to which the Chinese authorities object. Özil had reportedly been advised of the commercial risk in sending the message, including losing access to his 6 million Weibo followers, forgoing sponsorship deals, and being seen as a liability in the transfer market for clubs with real or aspirational business ties to China.[93] In Istanbul, the post helped spur demonstrations in solidarity with Uyghurs and support for Özil.[94]

China reacted swiftly to the post, removing Arsenal's next match against Manchester City from the state broadcaster's CCTV schedule

---

[91] Xu Jian et al., "Sports in the Transnational Public Sphere: Findings from the Case of Daryl Morey's Hong Kong Tweet," *International Journal of the History of Sport* 37, no. 12 (2020): pp. 1139–58, https://doi.org/10.1080/09523367.2020.1769070.

[92] Sopan Deb and Li Yuan, "Nets Owner Joe Tsai Didn't Seem Political. Until Now," *New York Times*, October 7, 2019, https://www.nytimes.com/2019/10/07/sports/joe-tsai-nba-china.html.

[93] Rory Smith and Tariq Panja, "The Erasure of Mesut Özil," *New York Times*, October 26, 2020, https://www.nytimes.com/2020/10/26/sports/soccer/mesut-ozil-arsenal-china.html.

[94] "Turkish Protesters March in Support of Uighurs After Ozil Comments," Reuters, December 20, 2019, https://www.reuters.com/article/world/turkish-protesters-march-in-support-of-uighurs-after-ozil-comments-idUSKBN1YO2C6/.

and removing Özil altogether from China's version of the 2020 Evolution Pro Soccer video game.[95] When Arsenal matches did return to a privately owned streaming service, commentators reportedly refused to say Özil's name.[96] Ostensibly to distance themselves from the views expressed by their player, Arsenal released a statement on the Chinese social media platform Weibo a few days later stating that "the content he expressed is entirely Özil's personal opinion" and that "Arsenal is always apolitical as an organization."[97] The club also reportedly urged the player to avoid political statements and removed Özil from a merchandise campaign for the Lunar New Year.[98] Özil's exclusion from the team for most of the season afterward and subsequent transfer to Turkish club Fenerbahçe in January 2021 was interpreted by some outlets as a commercial decision born out of fear of further Chinese reprisals, though the club officials insisted the move was strictly performance related.[99]

Perhaps most striking of all was the contrasting stance taken by both the NBA and Premier League and their clubs toward issues of racial discrimination, police brutality, and social justice following the Black Lives Matter protests of 2020. Both leagues offered official statements affirming racial equality and supported player gestures of support, including kneeling during the national anthem (NBA) or before match opening kick-offs (Premiership). Just two months before Özil's tweet and the club's claim to be nonpolitical, Arsenal sent a tweet of support for Nigerian fans who were protesting against police brutality.[100] The NBA allowed players to wear slogans such as "Equality" or "Justice Now" on the back of their jerseys, while the Premier League also allowed teams to wear "Black Lives Matter" shorts for the first 12 matches of the restarted 2019–20 season. NBA commissioner Adam Silver expressed support for players using their standing as professional

---

[95] Shamoon Hafez, "Mesut Ozil: Is China a Factor in Midfielder's Exile from Arsenal Squad," BBC, October 23, 2020, https://www.bbc.com/sport/football/54623161.

[96] Smith and Panja, "Erasure of Mesut Özil."

[97] "Mesut Ozil: Arsenal Distance Club from Player's Social Media Post," BBC, December 14, 2019, https://www.bbc.com/sport/football/50795173.

[98] Smith and Panja, "Erasure of Mesut Özil."

[99] Simon Stone, "Mesut Ozil: Arsenal Chief Denies Commercial Decision Behind Response to Uighurs Comments," BBC, February 18, 2021, https://www.bbc.com/sport/football/56108677.

[100] Smith and Panja, "Erasure of Mesut Özil."

244 DICTATING THE AGENDA

athletes for activism, and the league would establish a new charity, the NBA Foundation, which would contribute $300 million over the next decade to empowering Black communities through economic development and education.[101] The contrast between the two reactions was not lost on some athletes. Senegalese footballer and former Chelsea player Demba Ba in an interview in 2020 lamented the considerable pressure for players to be silent on discrimination and repression of Uyghurs, despite the renewed awareness of social equality and justice that had been activated by BLM movement.[102] When asked about what issues and campaigns the league would support, Premier League CEO Richard Masters said "Politics—no. Moral causes—yes, when agreed."[103]

The Qatar World Cup and LGBTQ Advocacy

The question of the scope and reach of transitional liberal activism also became an issue during the 2022 FIFA World Cup in Qatar, when the host's policies regarding LGBTQ communities became a flashpoint. Although a number of transnational actors undertook a classic transnational activist campaign, Qatari authorities not only remained firm on their insistence on restricting expressions of support for LGBTQ rights but were also supported by FIFA officials who exerted pressure on individual athletes and teams to drop their own public demonstrations of support.

In the months leading up to the World Cup, transnational activists mounted a classic naming-and-shaming campaign by spotlighting the Qatari government's discriminatory policies and leveraging the international media spotlight afforded by the event. Human Rights Watch released a report documenting cases of the Gulf country's

---

[101] Isabel Togoh, "The NBA Is Donating $300 Million Over the Next Decade to Black Empowerment," *Forbes*, August 6, 2020, https://www.forbes.com/sites/isabeltogoh/2020/08/06/the-nba-is-donating-300-million-over-the-next-decade-to-black-empowerment/?sh=1e8d51161af4.

[102] "Demba Ba Calls for Uighur Solidarity Protest over Treatment by China," BBC, August 19, 2020, https://www.bbc.com/sport/football/53801271. Ba observed that "Arsenal talked about Black Lives Matter but when it was about Uighur lives Arsenal didn't want to talk about it because of the pressure and economic impact."

[103] Laura Scott, "Richard Masters: Premier League Chief on Liverpool, Newcastle Takeover and More," BBC, June 30, 2020, https://www.bbc.com/sport/football/53234324.

security services arbitrarily arresting LGBTQ people and abusing them in detention.[104] The report provided documentation and eyewitness testimony of incidents of the violations and drew attention to the fact that FIFA in 2016 signed the United Nations Guiding Principles on Business and Rights, which obligated the international body to "avoid infringing on the human rights of others and address adverse human rights impacts."

But the most potent activist campaign involved 10 of the participating European teams that had committed to wearing supportive armbands at the tournament, in defiance of Qatari law. The effort, which had been spawned earlier in the season by the Dutch government and football association and supported by the top leagues in the Netherlands, was referred to as the OneLove initiative and had steadily built momentum throughout the course of the summer and fall run-up to the tournament. Having worn them in the September 2022 European Nations League matches, these European national teams planned to wear rainbow OneLove armbands during their World Cup matches.

FIFA's response to the campaign became increasingly antagonistic and punitive. After having threatened to fine participating national teams, FIFA officials, a few hours before the start of the competition, warned that any player wearing an armband would be issued a yellow card caution, thereby jeopardizing their actual performance on the field.[105] FIFA encouraged participating countries to, instead, join its "No Discrimination" campaign, which did not single out LGBTQ communities as entitled to protections.[106] A statement released by the federations said, "We are very frustrated by the FIFA decision, which we believe is unprecedented."[107]

---

[104] Human Rights Watch, "Qatar: Security Forces Arrest, Abuse LGBT People," October 24, 2022, https://www.hrw.org/news/2022/10/24/qatar-security-forces-arrest-abuse-lgbt-people.

[105] "England, Wales & Other Nations Will Not Wear OneLove Armbands," BBC, November 22, 2022, https://www.bbc.com/sport/football/63699477.

[106] "FIFA Launches New Armbands but England and Wales Still Show Support for OneLove," BBC, November 19, 2022, https://www.bbc.com/sport/football/63687774; Tariq Panja, "Germany Protests FIFA Decision That Blocked Rainbow Armbands," New York Times, November 23, 2022, https://www.nytimes.com/2022/11/23/sports/soccer/german-player-protest-armbands-world-cup.html.

[107] "England, Wales," BBC.

Rather than downplaying their restrictive laws, Qatari officials addressed and dismissed the advocacy campaign head-on.[108] The country spent a fortune on Western PR firms and spin doctors, as well as legal firms that sent letters to British journalists who have reported critically on Qatar.[109] The country's World Cup ambassador, Khalid Salman, told a German interviewer that LGBTQ people attending the tournament should "accept our rules" and remarked that homosexuality was "damage to the mind."[110] FIFA itself appeared to grow increasingly supportive of the Qatari government's pushback. Just months before, in June 2022, the organization had marked Pride Month by flying a rainbow flag over its headquarters in Zurich, while publicly communicating that it would work with organizers to ensure that the World Cup would be inclusive.[111] Yet when the tournament came, not only did FIFA threaten the organizers of the OneLove campaign with on-field sanctions, but in an extraordinary news conference held the day before the opening match, FIFA President Infantino accused the West and European countries of "hypocrisy" in reporting on the human rights situation in Qatar and defended the Gulf country's social policies and progress on migrant labor standards.[112] The apparent capitulation of FIFA leadership to Doha was accentuated by multiple news reports of security guards at stadiums forcing traveling fans to discard rainbow T-shirts flags and any other visible signs of LGBTQ advocacy.[113] In

---

[108] Ellen Iones, "Qatar's Anti-LGBTQ Policies Explained," Vox, December 3, 2022, https://www.vox.com/2022/12/3/23477966/qatar-anti-lgbtq-fifa-world-cup.

[109] Jim Waterson, "A Fortune's Coming Home: How British PR Firms Won Big Representing Qatar," The Guardian, December 16, 2022, https://www.theguardian.com/football/2022/dec/16/how-british-pr-firms-won-big-representing-qatar-2022-world-cup.

[110] "Qatar Ambassador Comments on Homosexuality 'Harmful and Unacceptable,'" BBC, November 8, 2022, https://www.bbc.com/sport/football/63561340.

[111] FIFA, "FIFA Celebrates Pride Month," June 1, 2022, https://www.fifa.com/news/fifa-celebrates-pride-month.

[112] Shamoon Hafez and Emma Sanders, "Fifa President Infantino Accuses the West of 'Hypocrisy,'" BBC, November 19, 2022, https://www.bbc.com/sport/football/63687412.

[113] Ben Church, "World Cup Soccer Fans Stopped by Security Officials for Wearing Rainbow-Colored Items," CNN, November 28, 2022, https://www.cnn.com/2022/11/26/football/german-soccer-fans-rainbow-colors-qatar-2022-world-cup-spt-intl/index.html.

the final days of the actual tournament, the issue faded from coverage, even as Belgian police in Brussels raided a number of European parliamentarians in the course of an investigation into their complicitly in a Qatar reputation-laundering and influence campaign that had targeted the EU.[114]

Saudi Arabia Enters the Global Arena

At around the same time, Qatar's Gulf neighbor made a dramatic entrance onto the international sporting landscape. After decades of showing little interest in global sport and entertainment, in 2021 Saudi Arabia's sovereign wealth fund, the Public Investment Fund (PIF), began to shake up a number of international competitions and leagues by announcing a raft of substantial investments. The roots of this new "sports diplomacy" date back to 2015 and the rise of MBS, but the effects have become dramatic in a short span of time and its targets more visible and prestigious.[115] Framed as part of its effort to diversify its economy, provide more entertainment opportunities for its domestic population, and rebrand its political image,[116] the PIF, along with other major state sponsors such as Aramco, have sought to host a number of international sporting and sports entertainment competitions in Saudi Arabia (including the America's Cup yachting race, World Wrestling Entertainment, and Italian and Spanish Supercup soccer competitions), increase funding and promotion for existing initiatives like the Saudi Cup horse race (now the world's richest), F1 and the Saudi professional

---

[114] The federal prosecutor's office claimed "that third parties in political and/or strategic positions within the European parliament were paid large sums of money or offered substantial gifts to influence parliament's decision" on granting visa-free travel between the European Union and Doha. See Valentina Pop et al., "European Parliament Shaken by Scandal," *Financial Times*, December 11, 2022, https://www.ft.com/content/1023d8aa-1fa4-4e6f-abbb-68ef101ccb72.

[115] Aaron Ettinger, "Saudi Arabia, Sports Diplomacy, and Authoritarian Capitalism in World Politics," *International Journal of Sport Policy and Politics* 15, no. 3 (2023): pp. 531–47, https://doi.org/10.1080/19406940.2023.2206402.

[116] Rick Maese, "The Middle East Play to Rule Global Sports," *Washington Post*, November 7, 2023, https://www.washingtonpost.com/sports/interactive/2023/middle-east-sports-investment/?itid=sf_sports_top-table_poo1_foo1.

soccer league, and launch new alternatives to existing global sporting initiatives. In a matter of a couple of years, the Gulf kingdom had upended the global sports landscape and secured its greatest prize: the right to host the 2034 World Cup.

Beyond these highly visible efforts, we have identified and compiled 323 active Saudi sponsorships in global sport in 2023 (Appendix 8.2). Figure 8.1 displays these individual active Saudi sponsorships in 2023,

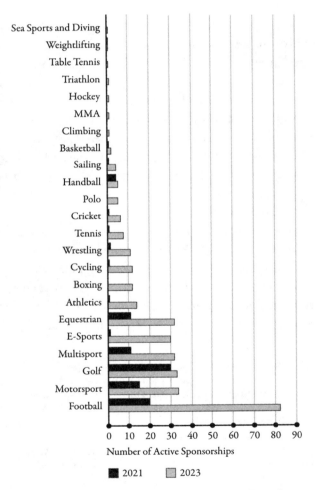

FIGURE 8.1 Saudi Arabian Sports Sponsorships Active in 2021 and 2023.

compared with 2021, across several different sports. Football has received a lion's share of Saudi support, but significant investments have also been made in motorsport, golf, and e-sports. These initiatives have ignited a debate in the West about how to distinguish between a strategic economic decision and a renewed attempt to sportswash and exert transnational authoritarian influence on an unprecedented scale.[117]

The interventions in the world of soccer are a case in point. The PIF and other state-controlled financial entities have reshaped the European-dominated landscape in short order. Not only did PIF buy Newcastle United Football Club in 2021 but it also took over four Saudi domestic teams. This financial injection allowed the Saudi Pro League to become a major player in the international transfer market for football talent. In the 2023 summer transfer window, Saudi Pro League teams spent nearly €1 billion on transfer fees alone (excluding salaries), placing it ahead of the German, French, Spanish, and Italian leagues, and behind only the English Premier League in terms of spending.[118] Global stars like Cristiano Ronaldo, Karim Benzema, Neymar Jr., N'Golo Kante, Sadio Mane, Jordan Henderson, Roberto Firmino, Riyad Mahrez, and many others moved to ply their trade in the kingdom. The PIF's financial heft has drawn top soccer talent away from European leagues on a scale not seen before. Not coincidentally, several of these players, including Benzema, Mahrez, and Henderson, publicly supported Saudi Arabia's bid to host the 2034 World Cup, the latter despite his previously vocal support for LGBTQ inclusion when he was a Liverpool player. The world's greatest player, Argentina World Cup winner Lionel Messi, reportedly turned down a massive $400 million contract to play in the league to play at Miami instead, although he did sign a three-year contract with Saudi's Tourism Authority to be a tourism ambassador.[119]

---

[117] Maese, "Middle East Play."

[118] "Saudi Clubs Spent Almost $1 Billion in Transfer Window, Trailing Only Premier League," Reuters, September 8, 2023, https://www.reuters.com/sports/soccer/saudi-spending-transfer-window-second-only-premier-league-2023-09-08/.

[119] Karim Zidan, "Lionel Messi Chose to Play in MLS. But He's Still Saudi Arabia's 25$ Million Pitch Man," *The Guardian*, August 15, 2023, https://www.theguardian.com/football/2023/aug/15/lionel-messi-saudi-arabia-tourism-deal-mls-inter-miami.

The Unfolding LIV-PGA Partnership

In October 2021, just weeks after PIF's acquisition of Newcastle, former professional golfer Greg Norman announced that he would be joining LIV Golf Investments as commissioner in an effort to create and promote "new opportunities across professional golf."[120] The ambitious scale of the LIV proposals shook up professional golf as the Saudi-backed group launched not just additional events, but unfurled plans for a new professional competition that sought to attract leading players from the Professional Golf Association's (PGA) tour. Investing over $2 billion in the effort, LIV Golf promoted the tour as a "player-focused" alternative to the PGA, with players guaranteed prize money, appearance fees, and signing bonuses.[121] For example, PGA stars Phil Mickelson and Dustin Johnson were paid $200 million and $150 million respectively just to join the new tour. The initiative launched a firestorm among golfers, especially after the PGA suspended 17 golfers for participating in LIV's inaugural event in June 2022.[122]

The unprecedented investment in LIV, coupled with the PIF's other contemporaneous sports acquisitions, fueled criticism that the state investment fund's primary motivation was sportswashing and using the new league primarily to distract from criticism of Saudi Arabia's poor human rights record.[123] An investigative report by the *New York Times* found documents from global consulting giant McKinsey, an adviser to the project, that characterized the financials of the project as a "high-risk high-reward endeavor" and warned that the league would lose

---

[120] Bill Pennington, "Greg Norman Takes Aim at PGA Tour with New Saudi-Backed Gold League," *New York Times*, October 29, 2021, https://www.nytimes.com/2021/10/29/sports/golf/greg-norman-pga-saudi-arabia.html.

[121] Alan Blinder et al., "What Is LIV Golf? It Depends Who You Ask," *New York Times*, May 22, 2023, https://www.nytimes.com/article/liv-golf-saudi-arabia-pga.html.

[122] Scooby Axson and Cail Clinton, "PGA Suspends LIV Golf Series Participants as a Saudi-Backed League Gets Underway," *USA Today*, June 9, 2022, https://www.usatoday.com/story/sports/golf/2022/06/09/liv-golf-serie-participants-suspended-pga-tour/7561580001/.

[123] For example, see Human Rights Watch, "Saudi Arabia: Pro Golf Merger 'Sportswashes' Abuses," June 7, 2023, https://www.hrw.org/news/2023/06/07/saudi-arabia-pro-golf-merger-sportswashes-abuses.

hundreds of millions of dollars if it could not successfully attract the world's top players and acquire media rights.[124] During the course of its litigation, a US federal judge ruled that the Saudi wealth fund's role was well beyond that of a mere investor, finding that PIF was "the moving force behind the founding, funding, oversight and operation of LIV" and that Yasir Al-Rumayyan, the governor of the fund, was personally involved in the planning and developing of LIV.[125]

In June 2023, in a stunning twist of events, the PGA and LIV announced that they planned to merge, halting all pending litigation, in a "landmark agreement to unify the game of golf, on a global basis."[126] At a US Senate hearing on the proposed merger in the summer of 2023, Senator Richard Blumenthal, chair of the Senate Permanent Subcommittee on Investigations, pointedly stated at its opening, "Today's hearing is about much more than the game of golf. It is about how a brutal, repressive regime can buy influence—indeed even take over—a cherished American institution simply to cleanse its public image."[127] He and other senators expressed apprehension at the control over the game that was being given to the Saudi side.[128] Of particular concern was a non-disparagement clause, identified in supporting documents obtained by the Senate, that "appears to prevent the PGA tour from

---

[124] Alan Blinder and Sarah Hurtes, "Confidential Records Show That a Saudi Golf Tour Built on Farfetched Assumptions," *New York Times*, December 11, 2022, https://www.nytimes.com/2022/12/11/sports/golf/liv-saudi-pga.html.

[125] Alan Blinder, "PGA Tour Can Depose Saudi Wealth Fund's Leader, Judge Rules," *New York Times*, February 17, 2023, https://www.nytimes.com/2023/02/17/sports/golf/liv-pga-saudi-influence.html.

[126] Lilian Rizzo, "PGA Tour Agrees to Merge with Saudi-Backed LIV Golf," CBNC, June 6, 2023, https://www.cnbc.com/2023/06/06/pga-tour-agrees-to-merge-with-saudi-backed-rival-liv-golf.html.

[127] "US Senate Panel Rips into Saudi Involvement in PGA Tour-LIV Tie-Up," Reuters, July 12, 2023, https://www.reuters.com/sports/golf/pga-tour-official-defend-saudi-backed-liv-tie-up-before-us-senate-panel-2023-07-11/.

[128] Senator Blumenthal commented, "There is something that stinks about this path that you're on right now . . . because it is a surrender and it is all about the money. And that's the reason for the backlash that you've seen. The equity ownership interest that the Saudis will have—and that's a term from this agreement—gives them financial dominance. They control the purse strings." See Rick Maese, "PGA Tour Defends Saudi Deal in Senate as Emails Show Plan's Origins," *Washington Post*, July 11, 2023, https://www.washingtonpost.com/sports/2023/07/11/pga-tour-liv-hearing-senate/.

criticizing Saudi Arabia."[129] Although as of spring 2024 the two sides were still negotiating details of the merger, it seems clear that the PGA is likely to be reshaped and the game transformed by the Saudi-backed intervention. Quintessential of the globalized but authoritarian-friendly contemporary world of sports, US-based consultancy firms helped facilitate Saudi Arabia's objectives.[130]

For his part, Saudi leader MBS has publicly dismissed accusations of "sportswashing." In a September 2023 interview he said, "If sportswashing (is) going to increase my GDP by 1%, then we'll continue doing sportswashing."[131] To be sure, Saudi Arabia's motives for its interventions in the sports world are multifaceted and include economic factors. But the easy dismissal of liberal sportswashing advocacy in this way illustrates the ability of a powerful authoritarian state to project its influence outward and (re)claim and depoliticize a domain with stunning rapidity. The entanglements and dependencies that Saudi investments in sports create among foreign leagues, athletes, advertisers, investors, and international governing associations help to align the interests of those actors with the interests of the kingdom.[132] Liberal values become a casualty.[133]

Conclusion

As with global media, consumer boycotts, and higher education, the prominence of liberal norms in the governance of international sport has shifted since the West's initial global dominance in the 1990s

---

[129] Richard Blumenthal, "Blumenthal Delivers Opening Statement at Hearing on Proposed PGA Tour-LIV Golf Agreement," July 11, 2023, https://www.blumenthal. senate.gov/newsroom/press/release/blumenthal-delivers-opening-statement-at-hea ring-on-proposed-pga-tour-liv-golf-agreement.

[130] Stephanie Kirchgaessner, "Top US Consultancies Face Scrutiny over Role in Saudi Arabia's Sports Push," *Irish Times*, February 6, 2024, https://www.irishtimes .com/sport/2024/02/06/top-us-consultancies-face-scrutiny-over-role-in-saudi-arabias-sports-push/.

[131] "Saudi Crown Prince Says He Does Not Care About 'Sportswashing' Claims," Reuters, September 22, 2023, https://www.reuters.com/world/middle-east/saudi-crown-prince-says-he-does-not-care-about-sportswashing-claims-2023-09-22/.

[132] Ettinger, "Saudi Arabia," pp. 541–42.

[133] Ettinger, "Saudi Arabia," pp. 543–44.

and early 2000s. Non-democracies are increasingly hosting the most prominent international sporting events such as the football World Cup and the Olympic Games, usually as platforms for promoting their country in the international spotlight. Accusations that regimes in countries such as Azerbaijan, China, Russia, Qatar, and Saudi Arabia are engaging in "sportswashing" are routinely ignored and dismissed, with accusations of Western hypocrisy routinely leveled back at critics of these mega-events.

Two trends, consistent with the themes of this book, are striking: First, the shift in market power from Western markets to non-Western centers has added significant new sources of revenue in international team and club sports, including from broadcasting rights and team and league sponsorships. It is hardly surprising that the governance and public image of these sporting events and teams have increasingly adopted the priorities, images, and values of their new sponsors. Second, these shifts in market and governance power are eroding the freedom of expression for athletes to offer liberal criticism of the human rights and governance practices of these new hosts and sponsors. FIFA's crackdown on World Cup–related LGBTQ activism or the formal restrictions placed by federations like the FIA on their athletes' speech and criticism of host country practices in the name of ensuring political neutrality mirrors the erosion of the freedom of expression across other governance spheres. In this respect, international sport appears to be subject to the same market and geopolitical trends as other areas of global governance, with actors enmeshed in relationships that are changing their incentives.

Chapter 9

Conclusion

It is sometimes difficult to appreciate how much has changed when viewing world events from an incremental perspective. Small changes can seem minor at the time, but a few years later they may have accumulated into something significant. Taking a longer perspective can throw into relief how much has changed and why. Consider four contrasting episodes—two involving Russia and two involving China—that illustrate how differently the world of transnational information, advocacy, consumerism, and political influence operates in an era of authoritarian resurgence than it did in an age of liberal democratic dominance.

Let's start in Russia. In 1998, former Soviet leader Mikhail Gorbachev famously starred in a commercial for Pizza Hut, the American fast-food chain that opened its first store in Russia in 1990. Gorbachev walks into Pizza Hut to find a father and adult son, a few tables over, debating the leader's legacy. The father associates him with instability and confusion, the son with freedom and hope. The mother smooths things over by proclaiming, "Because of him we have many things, like Pizza Hut!" Here was a man who once controlled the fate of a global empire advertising pizza from his former geopolitical rival while the weighty political debates that defined his leadership were subsumed to Western consumer culture.[1] As Musgrave notes in his insightful essay on the episode, Western consultants and PR specialists produced the ad, which ultimately aired on broadcast television during the 1998 Rose Bowl, an iconic American football game.[2] To add insult to injury, Gorbachev's motivation for taking the gig appeared to be his need for money, a potent symbol of the decimation of the Soviet system.[3] Russia appeared weak, poor, and ensnared in a US-led hegemony that equated consumerism with liberal values and illustrated the dominance of Western technical expertise and political models.

Fast-forward 26 years. In February 2024, nearly exactly two years after Russia launched a devastating full-scale invasion of Ukraine, American right-wing media personality Tucker Carlson traveled to Moscow to meet Russian dictator Vladimir Putin. Putin, as should be clear by now, is a five-term autocrat who has not only invaded Russia's neighbors but also cracked down domestically on political challengers, the media, civil society, LGBTQ rights, and much else. Carlson admires Putin's style of anti-liberal politics as well as that of Hungarian illiberal leader Viktor Orbán, a quintessential witting ally of right-wing illiberalism from within a liberal democracy. During a two-hour-long interview, the only one Putin had granted to a Western interviewer since the war, the Russian leader gave long historical diatribes and toyed with the overmatched but amenable interviewer.[4] During the same trip, Carlson aired a video of himself celebrating all of the substitute food stuffs and consumer goods available at a Russian supermarket despite Western sanctions and the pullout from the country of many large foreign companies.

Here was Russia engaging with Western media and technical consultants but on its terms. Of course, interviewing authoritarian leaders and visiting their countries is not new, nor is it very controversial

---

[1] Paul Musgrave, "Mikhail Gorbachev's Pizza Hut Thanksgiving Miracle," *Foreign Policy*, November 28, 2019, https://foreignpolicy.com/2019/11/28/mikhail-gorbachev-pizza-hut-ad-thanksgiving-miracle/.

[2] Musgrave, "Mikhail Gorbachev's Pizza Hut."

[3] Musgrave, "Mikhail Gorbachev's Pizza Hut."

[4] See, for example, Adam Gabbatt and Andrew Roth, "Putin Tells Tucker Carlson the US 'Needs to Stop Supplying Weapons' to Ukraine," *The Guardian*, February 9, 2024, https://www.theguardian.com/world/2024/feb/08/vladimir-putin-tucker-carlson-interview.

256 DICTATING THE AGENDA

on its own. But here was an American media personality using his sizable platform and notoriety to uncritically amplify the views of an illiberal autocrat and celebrate the consumer welfare of a country sanctioned by the West. The interview itself was disseminated to the world on Western-owned social media platforms including X (formerly Twitter) and YouTube, where English- and Russian-language versions are housed on the Kremlin's official channel.[5] While Putin put journalists in jail and designated civil society activists as "foreign agents" or "undesirable organizations" at home, he was happy to use the allies, technologies, and information platforms of the West, not to mention its press freedoms, in an attempt to project his influence outward.

Let's rewind again and look to China. US President Bill Clinton gave a speech in March 2000 supporting China's accession to the World Trade Organization and permanent normal trade relations with the PRC. In his effort to rally congressional support, Clinton made the case that thicker trade and economic interactions with China would increase the chances that its leaders would liberalize politically. Greater economic freedom, Clinton argued, would ultimately result in Chinese people demanding more political accountability. It was a common argument at the time, and Clinton made it persuasively, but it was his comments about the internet that have ensured the speech's legacy. In highlighting the information technology tariffs that would be lifted by 2005, Clinton quipped, "Now there's no question China has been trying to crack down on the Internet. (Chuckles.) Good luck! (Laughter.) That's sort of like trying to nail jello to the wall. (Laughter.)"[6]

Fast-forward to today. China did not crack down on the internet in the sense of banning it. But it did learn how to control it and use it for its own ends, developing a sophisticated system not only to censor

---

[5] In English: https://www.youtube.com/watch?v=hYfByTcY49k and in Russian: https://www.youtube.com/watch?v=ncPW2pyOzJU. The Russian version has nearly double the number of views (accessed March 13, 2024).

[6] Full text available here: "Full Text of Clinton's Speech on China Trade Bill," *New York Times*, March 9, 2000, https://archive.nytimes.com/www.nytimes.com/library/world/asia/030900clinton-china-text.html.

political content and foreign news and social media platforms,[7] but also to use digital technologies for surveillance,[8] repression,[9] and propaganda.[10] Not content to control things at home, Chinese authorities reach abroad. They allow or facilitate distributed denial of service attacks on websites hosted abroad to which they object, which has the effect of disabling the site for users anywhere in the world.[11] The PRC uses Western tech platforms, and the free speech protections that undergird their operation, to spread its messages.[12] Chinese authorities have also reached abroad to police their own citizens using social media platforms while overseas, for example reportedly arresting and charging (but later apparently dropping the charges) a Chinese student who tweeted about Xi Jinping while he was studying at the University of Minnesota.[13]

---

[7] Margaret E. Roberts, *Censored: Distraction and Diversion Inside China's Great Firewall* (Princeton University Press, 2018); Gary King et al., "How Censorship in China Allows Government Criticism but Silences Collective Expression," *American Political Science Review* 107, no. 2 (2013): pp. 326–43, https://doi.org/10.1017/S0003055413000014.

[8] Josh Chin and Liza Lin, *Surveillance State: Inside China's Quest to Launch a New Era of Social Control* (St. Martin's Press, 2022); Darren Byler, *In the Camps: China's High-Tech Penal Colony* (Columbia University Press, 2021).

[9] Xu, Xu, "To Repress or to Co-Opt? Authoritarian Control in the Age of Digital Surveillance," *American Journal of Political Science* 65, no. 2 (2021): pp. 309–25, https://doi.org/10.1111/ajps.12514.

[10] Rongbin Han, "Manufacturing Consent in Cyberspace: China's 'Fifty-Cent Army,'" *Journal of Current Chinese Affairs* 44, no. 2 (2015): pp. 105–34, https://doi.org/10.1177/186810261504400205.

[11] For an example, see Anita R. Gohdes, *Repression in the Digital Age: Surveillance, Censorship, and the Dynamics of State Violence* (Oxford University Press, 2024), pp. 25–26.

[12] Yingjie Fan et al., "Strategies of Chinese State Media on Twitter," *Political Communication* 41, no. 1 (2024): pp. 4–25, https://doi.org/10.1080/10584609.2023.2233911.

[13] Bethany Allen-Ebrahimian, "University of Minnesota Student Jailed in China over Tweets," Axios, January 22, 2020, https://www.axios.com/2020/01/23/china-arrests-university-minnesota-twitter. Users tweeting from within China have reportedly been jailed. See Chun Han Wong, "China Is Now Sending Twitter Users to Prison for Posts Most Chinese Can't See," *Wall Street Journal*, January 29, 2011, https://www.wsj.com/articles/china-is-now-sending-twitter-users-to-prison-for-posts-most-chinese-cant-see-1161932917. This is not to say that content on Western social media platforms does not ever influence political conversation in China. On the crossover, see Yingdan Lu et al., "How Information Flows from the World to China," *International Journal of Press/Politics* 29, no. 2 (2022): pp. 305–27, https://doi.org/10.1177/19401612221117470.

Even more than taming the potential liberal influence of the internet while using it for repression and propaganda, China has sought to project its control and influence outward and dictate the agenda. Each year the Cyberspace Administration of China and Zhejiang Provincial People's Government organize the World Internet Conference in partnership with three United Nations entities: the UN Department of Economic and Social Affairs, the International Telecommunication Union, and the World Intellectual Property Organization.[14] The conference not only brings together many leading regulators, lobbyists, and political and industry leaders, but now also brands itself as a permanent international organization to spread its vision for internet governance globally. The founding of the organization in 2022 featured a congratulatory message from Xi Jinping as well as statements by the head of the UN Department of Economic and Social Affairs, Chinese national and Communist Party member Liu Zhenmin.[15] Not content to stigmatize and shield Chinese citizens from liberal influences on the internet or to project influence outward, Chinese authorities are trying to dictate the agenda of digital infrastructure and regulation and set standards that the rest of the world will, ideally, follow.

The triumph inherent in the first vignettes involving Gorbachev and Clinton now seems almost quaint. The idea that efforts by authoritarians to maintain power would be overrun by the appeal of liberalism or consumerism or eroded by the decentralizing forces of new technologies, all of which were being advanced by states that were much more powerful than their own, has clearly not played out the way many observers had predicted or hoped. Neither consumerism nor digital technologies are inherently laden with liberal or democratic values, yet the overwhelming assumption among analysts and scholars from the late 1980s to the early 2000s, was that they were part of an irreversibly expanding infrastructure of liberal global influence. Activists operating in this permissive environment could meet with success in advancing liberal goals. This was not a wholly unreasonable argument at the time,

---

[14] See https://www.wuzhenwic.org/ (accessed March 13, 2024).
[15] See https://www.wuzhenwic.org/2022-07/14/c_788696.htm (accessed March 13, 2024).

and of course today we have the luxury of viewing these assumptions with decades of hindsight and information unavailable to actors at the time. But, as we have explored throughout this book, transnational linkages in areas such as media, consumer activism, higher education, and sports are less conducive to transmitting liberal influence and, in some cases, have enabled the very depoliticization and even transformation of those liberal actors themselves.

The authoritarian resurgence captured by the second vignettes involving Putin and Xi are characteristic of the political world we now inhabit. Rather than summarizing our arguments and contributions made thus far, the remainder of this conclusion addresses two central questions: Where are we going and what should be done? We begin by thinking about where we are going in three emerging issue areas, projecting how they may play out given the arguments of this book.

Applying the Argument to Emerging Global Issues

The authoritarian snapback against democrats and human rights activists is a characteristic of today's international politics. In this book we have sought to go farther and expand our understanding of the scope of global issue domains where the prevalence of once-dominant liberal actors and values has given way to authoritarian competition or, as in the case of global sport, the redefinition of the domains as apolitical or even as "beyond politics." In this era of "great power competition," analysts and policymakers have argued that liberal democracies must do all they can to ensure that they can promote the liberal values of an "open world" for new global domains and challenges that require international cooperation.[16] Our arguments about the repurposing of global governance have cautionary implications for how we understand the unfolding dynamics of activism and global governance in these emerging issue areas. In this section we spotlight three: climate change, gender politics, and artificial intelligence.

---

[16] See Rebecca Lissner and Mira Rapp-Hooper, *An Open World* (Yale University Press, 2020).

The Emerging Politics of Greenwashing

Consider the politics and networks informing the governance of international cooperation on addressing the global climate crisis, arguably the greatest challenge of our times. Policymakers and international relations scholars frequently make the argument that "great power competition" should be set aside to promote pragmatic interstate cooperation when dealing with issues of common global concern such as climate change. Though such calls may be understandable, our research suggests that authoritarians are already well on the way to repurpose and exploit global governance networks that outwardly appear responsive to liberal advocacy for their own autocratic purposes.

Similar to the term "sportswashing," the term "greenwashing" is defined by the United Nations as "misleading the public to believe that a company or other entity is doing more to protect the environment than it is" and promoting "false solutions to the climate crisis that distract from and delay concrete and credible actions."[17] Such tactics may include falsely claiming a plan to reduce emissions to "net zero," implying that a minor improvement has had a major impact, or claiming leadership in the climate domain through the branding of a particular global event.[18]

Authoritarians often try to use the global spotlight from other events, such as sporting mega-events, to burnish their green credentials. For example, a Swiss regulator found that the Qatari government's claims that the 2022 FIFA World Cup would be the "first carbon neutral World Cup" were misleading "commercial communication" and that the government's actual offsetting measures had failed to comply with international standards.[19] Similarly, Beijing's public claims that the 2022 Olympics would be "carbon-neutral" and "green" were

---

[17] United Nations, "Greenwashing—the Deceptive Tactics Behind Environmental Claims," https://www.un.org/en/climatechange/science/climate-issues/greenwashing#:~:text=By%20misleading%20the%20public%20to,some%20more%20obvious%20than%20others.

[18] United Nations, "Greenwashing."

[19] "Fifa Misled Fans by Claiming the Qatar World Cup Would Be Carbon Neutral, a Swiss Regulator Found," *The Guardian*, June 3, 2023, https://www.theguardian.com/football/2023/jun/07/fifa-carbon-neutral-qatar-world-cup-misled-fans-swiss-regulator#:~:text=The%20message%20that%20Qatar%20would,2%20than%20any%20previous%20event.

CONCLUSION   261

undermined by preparatory practices such as deforestation and relying on chemical-heavy artificial snow.[20] Although authoritarian hosts of the Olympics have touted their green credentials, an environmental study of all the Winter and Summer Games from 1992 to 2020 found steady overall declines in ecological and social sustainability practices, despite the IOC's adoption of a sustainability agenda in the 1990s.[21]

Authoritarians have also proven eager to host the world's main UN-endorsed conferences on climate change (COP), hosting three high-profile conferences in Egypt (2022), the UAE (2023), and Azerbaijan (2024), leading to reports that the conferences themselves became forums repurposed to advance the agendas of energy-producing countries and fossil fuel companies. Months before hosting COP28, ADNOC, the UAE state-owned company headed by Sultan Al Jaber, who was also appointed the COP28 head of summit, announced a major five-year $150 billion expansion plan, involving increasing oil-producing capacity to five million barrels per day by 2025 and a major expansion of the country's biggest oil field.[22] COP28 was itself scrutinized for taking greenwashing tactics to new levels. The lead-up to the conference featured a disinformation campaign in which fake Twitter accounts promoted the UAE's environmental record and tweeted in support of Sultan Al Jaber, while a circle of advisers reportedly edited Wikipedia pages that had spotlighted his role as CEO of the Abu Dhabi National Oil Company.[23] A BBC investigation, using leaked documents prepared for Sultan Al Jaber, revealed that the UAE positioned its role

---

[20] Christian Shepherd, "In Parched Beijing, Claims of a 'Green' Olympics May Not Hold Water," *Washington Post*, January 20, 2022, https://www.washingtonpost.com/sports/olympics/2022/01/20/china-winter-olympics-snow-pollution/.

[21] Martin Müller et al., "An Evaluation of the Sustainability of the Olympic Games," *Nature Sustainability* 4, no. 4 (2021): pp. 340–48, https://doi.org/10.1038/s41893-021-00696-5.

[22] Anthony D. Paola, "UAE Plans Global Energy Push with $150 Billion in Spending," Bloomberg, November 28, 2022, https://www.bloomberg.com/news/articles/2022-11-28/uae-plans-global-energy-push-with-adnoc-s-150-billion-spending.

[23] Ivana Kottasova, "Fake Twitter Profiles, Wikipedia Editing and PR Battles: Inside the Push to Greenwash the COP28 Climate Summit," CNN, July 18, 2023, https://www.cnn.com/2023/07/18/middleeast/cop-28-dubai-greenwashing-climate/index.html; Ben Stockton, "COP28 President's Team Accused of 'Greenwashing,'" *The Guardian*, May 30, 2023, https://www.theguardian.com/environment/2023/may/30/cop28-president-team-accused-of-wikipedia-greenwashing-sultan-al-jaber.

as the host of UN climate talks as an opportunity to strike oil and gas deals.[24]

More broadly, autocratic regimes now seem comfortable extending the scope of their repression of civil society into environmental advocacy, while deflecting any resulting international criticism through engaging in climate diplomacy with democracies. One study of Vietnam suggests that after working relatively unencumbered for over a decade, the Vietnamese government arrested four prominent environmental leaders in civil society, just after the country had secured funding commitments from G7 countries at the 2022 COP27 summit in Egypt.[25] Cambodia has jailed members of a prominent youth environmental group for allegedly plotting against the government.[26] As in other issue domains where autocrats attempt to dictate the agenda, public statements of concern in large democracies about the government crackdown were offset by prominent diplomatic meetings, including with US Special Envoy John Kerry, who visited Hanoi the same year.[27] And while democracies internally debate whether such political concerns about authoritarian countries should be "compartmentalized" in the name of securing global cooperation on common challenges like the climate crisis, authoritarians are not only actively neutering transnational activists and their networks but also successfully using climate diplomacy as a political strategy to bolster their autocratic regimes on the international stage.

Genderwashing

The rise of greenwashing as a strategy for securing international legitimacy is paralleled by the rise of "genderwashing." According to

---

[24] Justin Rowlatt, "UAE Planned to Use COP28 Climate Talks to Make Oil Deals," BBC, November 27, 2023, https://www.bbc.com/news/science-environment-67508331.

[25] Kirk Herbertson, "Climate Change Diplomacy Has an Authoritarianism Problem," JustSecurity, November 2, 2022, https://www.justsecurity.org/83887/climate-change-diplomacy-has-an-authoritarianism-problem.

[26] Rebecca Ratcliffe, "Cambodia Jails 10 Environmentalists in 'Crushing Blow to Civil Society,'" *The Guardian*, July 2, 2024, https://www.theguardian.com/world/article/2024/jul/02/cambodia-jails-10-environmentalists-in-crushing-blow-to-civil-society.

[27] Herbertson, "Climate Change Diplomacy."

CONCLUSION 263

Bjarnegård and Zetterberg, authoritarian genderwashing refers to the "promotion of gender equality *with ulterior motives*," including taking credit for gender advances within the political system in order to deflect attention away from persistent non-democratic practices by a regime.[28] Prominent genderwashing tactics include adopting formal gender-based quotas for female participation in legislatures and/or the judiciary, establishing ministries or national agencies dedicated to promoting gender equality, or publicly conferring certain selective rights, despite maintaining widespread inequality in other domains. The use of gender quotas to bolster the liberal democratic credentials of a regime can itself be traced back to 1995 Beijing Declaration and Platform for Action, widely regarded as the most progressive international agreement for advancing women's rights, where 189 countries unanimously signed a declaration committing to promoting the equality of women, including the institutional representation of women.[29] Not surprisingly, Beijing is usually viewed as an iconic case study and turning point in the global women's rights movement and is included in Keck and Sikkink's influential 1998 book on the rise of liberal transnational networks.[30]

However, years later, of the 75 countries that have adopted gender quotas since Beijing, 51 are authoritarian.[31] Often these quotas appear to be adopted for the purpose of deflecting attention away from other democratic shortcomings. One of the most widely cited examples is how Rwanda, often portrayed as a global leader in women's political participation since its introduction of a gender quota law in 2003,[32] has strategically used the country's increasing female representation (which hit 61% following the 2018 election) to divert attention from the regime's escalation of domestic repression and more

---

[28] Elin Bjarnegård and Pär Zetterberg, "How Autocrats Weaponize Women's Rights," *Journal of Democracy* 33, no. 2 (2022): pp. 60–75, https://doi.org/ https://doi.org/10.1353/jod.2022.0018/.

[29] Fourth World Conference on Women, 4–15 September 1995, Beijing, China," United Nations, https://www.un.org/en/conferences/women/beijing1995.

[30] Margaret E. Keck and Kathryn Sikkink, *Activists Beyond Borders* (Cornell University Press, 1998), chapter 5.

[31] Bjarnegård and Zetterberg, "How Autocrats Weaponize Women's Rights," p. 60.

[32] Jennie E. Burnet, "Rwanda: Women's Political Representation and Its Consequences," in *The Palgrave Handbook of Women's Political Rights*, edited by Susan Franceschet, Mona Lena Krook, and Netina Tan (Palgrave, 2019), pp. 563–76.

assertive transnational repression against exiled political dissidents and journalists.[33]

Autocratic genderwashing is particularly effective as it plays upon the liberal order's association of women's rights with democracy. International recognition that governments have made progress on women's rights can bring benefits such as increased foreign aid, positive media attention, and even international prizes and recognitions. Accordingly, autocrats have important incentives to publicly improve some indicators of women's rights without making progress on issues like media freedom and repression of civil society or introducing genuine political competition.[34] Research on such prestige-based strategies by autocrats suggests that they are effective in attracting international donors. For example, a survey experiment conducted by Bush and Zetterberg in the United States and Sweden revealed that publics in donor countries perceive that autocracies with increasing women's political representation are more democratic, and respondents are more willing to support giving these countries foreign aid.[35] Professionals in the development and democracy-promotion domains also perceive autocracies that adopt certain women's rights policies as more democratic and more likely to support aiding them.[36]

Ultimately, genderwashing appears to be growing in popularity as an autocratic form of countering liberal activism precisely because it deploys certain liberal values to both offset more widespread authoritarian practices and mollifies international criticism of democratic shortcomings. Domestically, however, the use of gender quotas by embattled autocrats is itself creating a wider backlash, in countries like Algeria, to

---

[33] Yarik Turianskyi and Matebe Chisiza, "Lessons from Rwanda: Female Political Representation and Women's Rights," South African Institute for International Affairs Occasional Paper 253 (2017), https://saiia.org.za/wp-content/uploads/2017/03/Occasional-Paper-253.pdf; Bjarnegård and Zetterberg, "How Autocrats Weaponize Women's Rights."

[34] Daniela Donno et al., "International Incentives for Women's Rights in Dictatorships," *Comparative Political Studies* 55, no. 3 (2022): pp. 451–92, https://doi.org/10.1177/00104140211024306.

[35] Sarah Sunn Bush and Pär Zetterberg, "Gender Quotas and International Reputation," *American Journal of Political Science* 65, no. 2 (2021): pp. 326–41, https://doi.org/10.1111/ajps.12557.

[36] Sarah Sunn Bush et al., "International Rewards for Gender Equality Reforms in Autocracies," *American Political Science Review* 118, no. 3 (2024): pp. 1189–203.

women's empowerment.[37] At the same, the rise of "genderbashing"—the erosion of women's rights in the name of upholding traditional and/or family values—is also a widely deployed strategy, especially among governments openly embracing critiques of social and political liberalism, including in Russia and Hungary.[38] However, what both genderwashing and genderbashing have in common is the attempt to transform transnational and global networks that traditionally have promoted liberal values into new relations and terms of engagement that preserve authoritarian autonomy and international legitimacy.

Governing AI

Our analysis also has cautionary implications for understanding the challenges associated with governing artificial intelligence (AI) as a global public policy area. The rise of AI as an urgent issue requiring governance rules and safety standards has been spurred by the wide dissemination, since 2022, of new large-language models such as ChatGPT, released by Open AI. On the one hand, AI-based tools have the potential to dramatically enhance governance across fields like education, healthcare, and labor. At the same time, the meteoric spread of AI has heightened concerns about how best to stem disinformation, safeguard rights such as data privacy, security, and access, and determine at what scale AI-related regulations should be implemented.

Initial attempts to create a global regulatory framework for AI appear to have been driven by liberal democratic states, also reflecting the center of gravity of this emerging technology. According to the Stanford University's AI Index Report, in 2023 the United States led in the global production of notable AI models with 61, followed by 21 in the European Union and 15 in China. Initially, the world's liberal

---

[37] Yuree Noh et al., "Regime Support and Gender Quotas in Autocracies," *American Political Science Review* 118, no. 2 (2024): pp. 706–23, https://doi.org/10.1017/S000305542300059X.

[38] Bjarnegård and Zetterberg, "How Autocrats Weaponize Women's Rights"; "Genderwashing or Genderbashing? Reconciling the Different Faces of Modern Autocrats," *The Loop*, ECPR's political science blog, https://theloop.ecpr.eu/genderwashing-or-genderbashing-reconciling-the-different-faces-of-modern-autocrats/.

democratic countries also appear to be at the forefront of international efforts to create new regulatory standards to ensure that the emerging global governance of AI also protects core individual rights in line with liberal democratic values.

Most notably, at the beginning of November 2023, the United Kingdom hosted the first inaugural AI Safety Summit, which brought together governments, leading AI companies, civil society groups, and industry experts to discuss how AI risks can be mitigated through setting common standards and internationally coordinated action.[39] The conference's resulting "Bletchley Declaration" articulated principles that should inform global cooperation and regulatory efforts on AI, tying them into support for the UN Sustainable Developments Goals as well as the need to protect a number of rights and principles, including "human rights, transparency and explainability, fairness, accountability, regulation, safety, appropriate human oversight, ethics, bias mitigation, privacy, and data protection."[40]

A few months later, the EU made headlines when in March 2024 it adopted the EU Artificial Intelligence Act, creating the world's first comprehensive framework for AI regulation that adopted a risk-based approach, designating AI systems as "unacceptable," "high," "limited," and "minimal." These provisions build upon and complement the EU's globally impactful General Data Protection Regulation, leading EU lawmakers to express hope that this foundational legislation will help drive global standards and embed the ethical use of AI in a manner that upholds democracy, individual rights, and safety, while still encouraging innovation and efficiency gains.[41] The same month, the United Nations General Assembly unanimously adopted its first AI resolution,

---

[39] "AI Safety Summit 2023," Gov.uk, https://www.gov.uk/government/topical-events/ai-safety-summit-2023.

[40] "The Bletchley Declaration by Countries Attending the AI Safety Summit 1–2 November 2023," Gov.uk, November 1, 2023, https://www.gov.uk/government/publications/ai-safety-summit-2023-the-bletchley-declaration/the-bletchley-declaration-by-countries-attending-the-ai-safety-summit-1-2-november-2023.

[41] Kelvin Chan, "Europe Agreed on World-Leading AI Rules. How Do They Work and Will They Affect People Everywhere?," AP, December 11, 2023, https://apnews.com/article/eu-ai-act-artificial-intelligence-regulation-0283a10a891a24703068edca e3d60deb.

cosponsored by the United States and China, that encouraged countries to "safeguard human rights, protect data and monitor AI against risks."[42]

Yet despite the invocation of de-risking and liberal values, this early global normative consensus appears more performative than substantive, with the exceptions to these liberal rules significant and actual cooperation seemingly sparse. China's participation in the Bletchley safety summit seemed symbolic, given that it routinely uses AI in its surveillance systems and its own national regulatory frameworks "clearly appear intended to strengthen China's system of authoritarian government."[43] Beijing's emerging rules on issues like bias appear targeted at its private developers, not as restrictions or guidelines for government agencies, with no mention of rules for AI use by law enforcement and domestic security services.[44] And although present at Bletchley, China is not a member of other international AI cooperative initiatives, including the G7-backed Global Partnership on Artificial Intelligence, nor are Chinese companies currently included in the Partnership on AI, a tech industry initiative designed to inform international standards setting on AI with good governance principles and inputs drawn from academia and civil society.[45]

In fact, the Bletchley Declaration itself papered over the inability of signatories to achieve consensus on what form global AI regulations should take, which actors should be responsible for drafting them, or where a testing hub should be established.[46] Global surveys suggest

---

[42] Alexandra Alper, "UN Adopts First Artificial Intelligence Global Resolution," *Reuters*, March 21, 2024, https://www.reuters.com/technology/cybersecurity/un-adopts-first-global-artificial-intelligence-resolution-2024-03-21/.

[43] Matt O'Shaugnessy, "What a Chinese Regulation Proposal Reveals About AI and Democratic Values," May 16, 2023, https://carnegieendowment.org/posts/2023/05/what-a-chinese-regulation-proposal-reveals-about-ai-and-democratic-values?lang=en.

[44] O'Shaugnessy, "Chinese Regulation Proposal."

[45] Huw Roberts et al., "Global AI Governance: Barriers and Pathways Forward," *International Affairs* 100, no. 3 (2024): pp. 1277–81, https://doi.org/10.2139/ssrn.4588040.

[46] Kiran Stacey and Dan Milmo, "UK, US, EU and China Sign Declaration of AI's 'Catastrophic' Danger," *The Guardian*, November 1, 2023, https://www.theguardian.com/technology/2023/nov/01/uk-us-eu-and-china-sign-declaration-of-ais-catastrophic-danger.

268 DICTATING THE AGENDA

that public awareness about ChatGPT in adopting countries across the Global South is actually growing at a higher pace than in producing countries.[47] And although liberal democratic countries have hailed their own initial regulatory efforts, the much-publicized EU regulation has itself been criticized for exempting AI tools developed for the military, defense, or protection of national security.[48] The accelerating militarization of AI, now fueled by great power competition, makes the importance of establishing new norms over human control over technologies like autonomous weapons systems all the more urgent.[49]

Regardless, authoritarian powers are not standing still. In February 2022, Russia and China announced that the two countries "attach great importance to the issues of governance in the field of artificial intelligence,"[50] and in May 2024 they reaffirmed their cooperation in the area.[51] In summer 2024, intelligence officials from the United States, Canada, and the Netherlands confirmed that Russia in new international influence operations was using an AI-enhanced software package to spread propaganda via thousands of rapidly generated social media accounts with the aim of "undermining support for Ukraine and stoking internal political divisions."[52]

---

[47] According to the 2024 Stanford AI Index, a higher percentage of the public in Kenya (81%), Pakistan (76%), South Africa (69%), India (82%), and Indonesia (76%) were aware of ChatGPT than in France (60%), Germany (60%), the United States (55%), and United Kingdom (61%). See *Artificial Intelligence Index Report* (Stanford University Human-Centered Artificial Intelligence, 2024), https://aiindex.stanford .edu/report/#individual-chapters.

[48] Dan Milmo and Alex Hern, "What Will the EU's Proposed Act to Regulate AI Mean for Consumers?," *The Guardian*, March 14, 2024, https://www .theguardian.com/technology/2024/mar/14/what-will-eu-proposed-regulation-ai-mean-consumers.

[49] Denise Garcia, *The AI Military Race: Common Good Governance in the Age of Artificial Intelligence* (Oxford University Press, 2024), pp. 1–13.

[50] See President of Russia, "Joint Statement of the Russian Federation and the People's Republic of China on the International Relations Entering a New Era and the Global Sustainable Development," February 4, 2022, http://en.kremlin.ru/supplement/5770 (accessed May 27, 2024).

[51] "What Is Putin and Xi's 'New Era' Strategic Partnership?," Reuters, May 16, 2024, https://www.reuters.com/world/what-is-putin-xis-new-era-strategic-partnership-2024-05-16/ (accessed May 27, 2024).

[52] Steven Lee Myers and Julian E. Barnes, "U.S. and Allies Take Aim at Covert Russian Information Campaign," *New York Times*, July 9, 2024.

CONCLUSION   269

Where Are We Going? Liberalism, Geopolitics, and Multipolarity

Throughout this book, we have looked at how the authoritarian resurgence has targeted transnational liberal influence and sought to transform the appeal and dominance of liberal values across several areas of global governance. However, some scholars and analysts view some of the current normative and political shifts covered in this book not in terms of authoritarian resurgence, but as either the natural outcome of an increasingly multipolar world or the result of the broader global rise of populist or nationalist rulers, across both the West and non-West.[53] Our own chapters have spotlighted the illiberal backlash within the West across issues such as education, media, and sports. We agree that the crisis of liberalism coincides with, and at times is fueled by, geopolitical shifts and the authoritarian resurgence globally.

Our arguments both support and clarify dynamics of both of these parallel trends. Geopolitically, the ongoing shift away from the US-led liberal international order to a world characterized by multipolarity and the increasing importance of non-democratic powers, institutions, and values is evident and accelerating. In areas such as alignment with the United States and the West on United Nations votes, the leadership of prominent global institutions and the rise of alternative regional organizations as sources of ordering, it is clear that the democratic powers no longer set governance agendas and rules as they did in the immediate post–Cold War era.[54]

Understandably, many of the critiques of transnational liberalism are also leveled at US foreign policy writ large. Championing political rights abroad is criticized as undermining a country's sovereignty; the West's own double standards of supporting authoritarian allies or

---

[53] Alexander Cooley and Daniel H. Nexon, "The Real Crisis of Global Order: Illiberalism on the Rise," *Foreign Affairs* 101, no. 1 (2022): pp. 103–18.

[54] Amitav Acharya, *The End of American World Order* (Oxford University Press, 2015); Alexander Cooley and Daniel Nexon, *Exit from Hegemony: The Unraveling of the American Global Order* (Oxford University Press, 2020). On UN General Assembly voting patterns and shifts away from alignment with the West by emerging powers, see Martin Binder and Autumn Lockwood Payton, "With Frenemies Like These: Rising Power Voting Behaviour in the UN General Assembly," *British Journal of Political Science* 52, no. 1 (2022): pp. 381–98, https://doi.org/10.1017/S0007123420000538.

friends despite their illiberal actions is criticized as "hypocrisy"; seemingly capricious Western decisions to intervene abroad are equated with neo-imperialism; and sanctions are viewed as forms of hegemonic economic warfare. Yet, importantly, global authoritarians now readily wield these themes strategically to justify and deflect from their own democratic shortcomings and acts of aggression, helping to crystallize the increasingly prevalent view that the non-democratic world either rejects or is incompatible with liberal norms and practices that it has previously supported. Just as the "liberal international order" is sometimes invoked to mask Western dominance, so is a "multipolar world," with its connotations of equality and respect, sometimes deployed cynically to advance geopolitical aims and justify autocratic rule.

For example, in a public speech delivered in September 2022, just after Russia's unliteral annexation of four eastern Ukrainian territories, Vladimir Putin decried US "double" and "even triple standards" and US imperialism, accused the United States of testing biological weapons on human subjects in Ukraine, and railed against the evils of gender reassignment surgery.[55] The latter's inclusion in a speech about annexation reveals Putin's own fixation with presenting Russia's war in Ukraine as the front line in a global fight against the alleged social and cultural incursion of liberal values. Accordingly, the question is not why countries are contesting liberal values or US leadership of the world order, but why authoritarians now so frequently justify their own international aggression and violation of international commitments as post-Western power shifts. Publicly advocating for or aligning with a multipolar world is a globally appealing way of avoiding international scrutiny and accountability.

As we have made clear throughout this book, the crisis of liberalism is also playing out within the West, and especially within the United States, in addition to stemming from an increasingly assertive authoritarian world. The rise of self-styled nationalists or populists include Donald Trump and Victor Orbán in the West, as well as President Recep Tayyip Erdoğan in Türkiye and Prime Minister Narendra in India,

---

[55] Vladimir Putin, "Signing of Treaties on Accession of Donetsk and Lugansk People's Republics and Zaporozhye and Kherson Regions to Russia," The Kremlin, September 30, 2022, http://en.kremlin.ru/events/president/news/69465.

CONCLUSION   271

who lead a NATO ally and a US strategic partner, respectively. In the case of the US, the images of supporters of defeated President Donald Trump storming the US Capitol on January 6, 2021, in a bid to halt the peaceful transition of power dealt a severe blow to US authority as a guardian of democracy,[56] while the ensuing politicization of those arrested and accused of insurrection has further divided an already intensely polarized US public. The 2024 election of Donald Trump to a second term, despite these transgressions, has vindicated Trump's own anti-systemic tactics and further emboldens the rise of right-wing populists throughout the world.

But if we look beyond the big personalities and nationalist rhetoric of all these leaders, we see that populist leaders thrive on undermining institutional checks on political power, including independent courts, civil service, and the media.[57] Their critique and even outright assault on these institutional checks often employ the techniques we have outlined in this book.[58] Stigmatizing advocates, judges, migrants, students, and/or journalists as "enemies of the people" or repurposing domestic institutions such as the courts for their own political gain is increasingly common.[59] The second Trump term appears set to actually actively target these stigmatized groups and institutions, including enacting a massive deportation program of migrants at the outset of the term and targeting media outlets that offered critical coverage of the president. Conservative politicians

---

[56] On the varying reactions to January 6 across US democratic allies, countries with populist governments, and authoritarians (Russia and China), see Gloria M. Boone et al., "International Reactions to the Capitol Attack of January 6th: A Media Frames Analysis," *American Behavioral Scientist* 67, no. 6 (2023): pp. 784–806, https://doi.org/10.1177/00027642221109121.

[57] Jan-Müller Werner, *What Is Populism?* (Penguin UK, 2017).

[58] For an overview of approaches that emphasize economic versus sociocultural grievances, see Sheri Berman, "The Causes of Populism in the West," *Annual Review of Political Science* 24 (2021): pp. 71–88, https://doi.org/10.1146/annurev-polisci-041719-102503. On the rise of populism in post-communist countries, see Maria Snegovaya, *When Left Moves Right: The Decline of the Left and the Rise of the Populist Right in Postcommunist Europe* (Oxford University Press, 2024).

[59] On how the populist backlash against domestic and international courts is intertwined, see Erik Voeten, "Populism and Backlashes Against International Courts," *Perspectives on Politics* 18, no. 2 (2020): pp. 407–22, https://doi.org/10.1017/S1537592719000975.

272 DICTATING THE AGENDA

and their public champions, including billionaire and X-owner Elon Musk, supported Trump despite his plainly authoritarian ambitions either because they think they can harness him for their own ends or because they support his program, a pattern identified by leading scholars Levitsky and Ziblatt as contributing to the death of many democracies.[60]

We have already noted how certain actors within the United States have quite willingly supported and networked with illiberal counterparts in areas such as global sport and transnational education. Some go farther. Irrespective of Trump's own political trajectory and the fate of his second term in office, what appears set to continue is a growing awareness among the US Right that finding common cause transnationally in opposing liberalism is more important than pursuing traditional US foreign policy goals. Promoting trade and financial liberalization, supporting allies within NATO and across East Asia, and promoting US active involvement in global governance institutions, let alone promoting liberal values, all appear to be anathema to powerful illiberal forces in the United States. Taken together, whereas in the 1990s liberalism appeared ascendant, today it looks squeezed from powerful forces not only in Beijing and Moscow, but also in Washington.

What Should Be Done?

Often when books like this about authoritarian politics make political, policy, or social recommendations, they focus on what democracies should do to influence authoritarians. The tyranny of low expectations means that we often assume autocrats are only targets for influence, not actors capable of changing their behavior on their own, letting them off the hook too easily. So instead we begin by making some concrete recommendations to authoritarian leaders. The recommendations most likely will be ignored, but we'll make them anyway. Authoritarian states should:

---

[60] Steven Levitsky and Daniel Ziblatt, *How Democracies Die: What History Reveals About Our Future* (Viking, 2018).

CONCLUSION   273

- *Work to ensure the liberal political rights that they have committed to through human rights treaties and their own constitutions.* Almost all authoritarian states have committed to some version of liberal political rights in some fashion, but these commitments are ignored. The treaties that they have signed committing to uphold human rights and opposing discrimination based on race, gender, ethnicity, or disability represent their own international commitments; they did not originate with Western NGOs.

- *Allow NGOs and civil society organizations to operate more freely than they do and avoid stigmatizing and repressing them.* Regulating funding and ensuring transparency of NGOs and civil society are valid activities for governments, but regulations should not be onerous, coercive, or stigmatizing. Administrative infractions should not be sanctioned by criminal penalties or state coercion.

- *Allow more foreign journalists and stop harassing them.* Of course, it is legitimate for states to regulate the entry/exit of journalists and to construct regulations about journalistic coverage. But as our ARFJ data set shows, authoritarian states routinely frustrate the work of foreign journalists for little other reason than they resent the scrutiny or reporting that they bring. The presence of foreign reporters allows a full picture of the country to be reported to the outside world—including positive stories—and should be encouraged.

- *Stop mobilizing the population for nationalistic consumer boycotts for perceived slights.* This makes the country look petty, adds to national grievances, and increases skepticism among foreign audiences. Instead of punishing companies or consumers that mobilize against forced labor and repression of ethnic minorities, governments should refrain from state-mobilized consumer nationalism that alienates foreign publics.

- *Continue to engage in transnational higher-education projects and exchange by insisting on open values across both sending and receiving countries.* Here, both democratic and autocratic governments should (1) stop monitoring and harassing students that are sent abroad—let them learn and grow; (2) recognize that academic freedom in such collaborations will ultimately help a state's higher-education sector by stimulating it with new ideas

274   DICTATING THE AGENDA

and talent; and (3) stop persecuting academics who support transnational liberal values. The pathway to mutual understanding and economic vitality is through open exchange, not repression and surveillance.

- *Invest in sports as a means of economic growth, entertainment, and health, but allow athletes and clubs the autonomy to advocate for their political beliefs if they want.* At minimum, stop trying to punish athletes and executives who are citizens of other states and make statements abroad about politics. Restraint in this area will have positive benefits by reducing skepticism about future investments and demonstrating to foreign publics that these investments really are about the economy, entertainment, and health rather than "sportswashing."

Now let's turn to the more liberal democratic end of the spectrum. Together these recommendations drive toward three overarching goals of liberal democracies: trying to be truer to their stated values, protecting their stated values from malign actors, and better promoting liberal values abroad. Rather than expect a return to the 1990s, these goals should reflect upon and embrace the challenges of this complex and emerging era of multipolarity and political contestation. They can be thought of as a blueprint for promoting "multipolar liberalism."[61] This would entail promoting liberal political values unmoored from US unipolarity.

We advocate for these points bearing in mind the challenges of a multipolar liberal vision. During the Cold War to join the "free world" all a state had to do was be anti-communist. Even odious records of political repression could be overlooked in service of the larger anti-communist cause. To join today's equivalent, one has to actually be liberal; it is not enough to just be anti-authoritarian. The standards are, for the most part, higher. This is why a state like Hungary causes so

---

[61] Cooley and Nexon look at the rise of "multipolar populism" as a set of foreign policy practices among Western countries and populist leaders that justify illiberalism in terms of embracing multipolarity. Here we consider the converse. See Cooley and Nexon, *Exit from Hegemony*; and Alexander Cooley and Daniel Nexon, "Why Populists Want a Multipolar World," *Foreign Policy*, April 20, 2020, https://foreignpolicy.com/2020/04/25/populists-multipolar-world-russia-china/.

CONCLUSION   275

much consternation in Western alliances even though it is objectively less violently oppressive than the right-wing military dictatorships of the Cold War. But on the flip side, the authoritarian world counterposed against today's liberalism has only a thin vision to offer potential adherents. The terms on offer are mostly just anti-Westernism used as a cover to protect dictatorship. Liberal democracies have a better vision to offer and should offer it without sacrificing standards or having to resort to unipolarity. We offer a few specific points:

- *Remain committed to free and fair elections and the rights that enable them to be meaningful.* The resilience of democracy stems from its ability to self-correct through periodic elections undergirded by a free press, free speech, and political parties that enable different viewpoints to be aired. Politicians, parties, and pundits within liberal democracies who try to subvert elections, denigrate them, undermine confidence in them, limit participation in them unfairly, or relativize them by claiming there are no true choices are not only wrong but singing from the authoritarian hymn sheet. Voters shouldn't fall for it.

- *Acknowledge democratic shortcomings at home while criticizing or advocating abroad.* Scholars, activists, and policymakers should routinely acknowledge their own shortcomings in the areas of democracy and governance when they advocate for these causes transnationally. The rise of illiberal policies in democracies is easily visible to the entire world, as are the public policy consequences. Democratic polities now routinely struggle to justify upholding liberal values such as institutional independence, the importance of civil liberties when confronted with a security emergency, media freedom, anticorruption standards, and maintaining the rights to mobilize and protest, even on behalf of socially and politically unpopular causes. Acknowledge shortcomings with humility in the spirit of working together to improve democracy and human rights.

- *Democracies should fund media with global reach committed to liberal values, conducting investigations and holding politicians and companies accountable.* We have noted in this study the rise of state-run media overseas outlets and, perhaps even more importantly, content-sharing agreements. Such global news feeds are vital, as they not only frame important stories, but also set the agenda by selecting the types of international stories that are even deemed newsworthy for the local, state, and regional media outlets that carry these feeds. Western-based private wire services such as Bloomberg, Reuters, Associated Press, and Agence France-Presse must charge for their content to be economically viable, while their authoritarian-based counterparts such as Xinhua and ITAR-TASS receive heavy state subsidies for these global operations. If liberal values are to actually compete for attention globally, news feeds that reflect a diversity of topics and points of view must be available across different regions.

- *Focus on global standard makers when designating the targets for advocacy.* This recommendation stems from the commonly held refrain that some domains, such as global sport, should be de-politicized as liberal influence itself overreached into areas that may not be appropriate for transnational activism. We certainly accept that not every global governance domain or global event should inherently be used as a platform for liberal activism, no matter the compelling worthiness of the cause. However, we recommend that such activism, when pursued, could target the international and global bodies that have publicly adopted such liberal values and norms in their own mission charters and public messaging in addition to focusing on the authoritarian host during the event itself. Organizations that host public campaigns on issues such as opposing discrimination or raising awareness of climate change, thereby burnishing their own reputations, should be scrutinized for their own failures to uphold these commitments in their flagship activities.

- *Recognize that liberalism promotes a range of heterogenous causes and values, not all of which can be upheld by all actors simultaneously.* A further recommendation stems from the fact that liberal activists have steadily increased the range of campaigns and causes that they advocate for in world politics. In one sense this is positive: Expanding the range of activism and issue domains can lead to progress in certain respects. But it also creates a greater potential for overreach that may lead to backlash. It also opens the door for cynical wedge strategies by illiberal actors who, through information operations, may highlight the inconsistency of any particular liberal activist in one area in order to delegitimize their advocacy in others. Demands within the transnational advocacy community for purity and consistency across advocacy domains empowers the use of wedge strategies to pick off and stigmatize liberal actors. A greater willingness to forge tactical alliances and to be forgiving of disagreements with allies in other issue areas may be helpful.

- *Leverage fractures among authoritarians by highlighting their own overreach and governance failings when dealing with one another.* A penultimate recommendation rests on how to leverage liberal issues and advocacy tactics to possibly exploit fissures among authoritarian countries in growing partnership. It will make little difference for democratic governments and advocates to make high-minded public appeals to liberal or democratic ideals when dealing with emerging partnerships among authoritarian countries. Instead, liberal democracies should look to highlight potential shortcomings in governance, specifically on issues that inform inter-authoritarian relations. For example, such a strategy would support advocacy for the legal rights of Central Asian migrants in Russia or promote investigations into the corrupt practices of Chinese business in authoritarian countries abroad, such as Russia. Ultimately, the anticorruption norm continues to resonate across publics in both democratic and authoritarian countries, even as the legitimacy of many democratic norms has eroded.
- *Avoid using authoritarian methods to fight authoritarianism.* Sometimes the only option might be to ban a media outlet or limit a research program, but authoritarian modes of response should be a last resort. These solutions are tempting in their simplicity, but a far better strategy is to figure out ways to use the openness and freedom of liberal democracy, which is its greatest resource and source of appeal.

Ultimately, politics, whether local, national, regional, or global, is about contestation. Liberal ideas about a range of issues can and should be subjected to scrutiny, skepticism, evaluation, and debate. Assuming that processes such as economic globalization, technological innovation, consumerism, and education will inevitably favor one set of political ideas and practices over another actually short-circuits this process of deliberation and competition with what has proven to be passive and unwarranted optimism. The new agendas of global governance and world politics are currently being dictated, but they are not yet published.

INDEX

Tables and figures are indicated by an italic *t* and *f*.

For the benefit of digital users, indexed terms that span two pages (e.g., 52–53) may, on occasion, appear on only one of those pages.

Abramovich, Roman, 230–232, 231*t*

academic freedom, 19, 22–23, 200, 205–207

   foreign donors and, 193–194

   Israeli-Hamas protests and, 186, 215–216

   in Singapore, 203–204

   at transnational campuses, 201–207, 214

   See also censorship; freedom of expression

Academic Ranking of World Universities, 191–192

Afghanistan, 64–65, 123–124

AFL-CIO, 158–159, 161

AI (artificial intelligence), 24, 265–268

al-Bashir, Omar, 29

Al-Rumayyan, Yasir, 250–251

Aliyev, Ilham, 184–185

All-China Federation of Trade Unions, 161–162 n.49

All-China Journalists Association, 132

Amnesty International, 3–4, 26–29, 228–229

anti-sweatshop campaigns, 22–23, 150, 153–154, 157–162

   See also cotton industry

apartheid (South Africa), 149–150, 182–183

Arab Spring, 66–67, 80

ARFJ. *See* Authoritarian Restrictions on Foreign Journalists

artificial intelligence (AI), 24, 265–268

Asian financial crisis (2007–2008), 75–76. *See also* East Asian financial crisis

Asian Infrastructure Investment Bank, 62, 74–75

authoritarian media, 122–130

   amplification of, 112–119

280 INDEX

authoritarian media, (*Continued*)
  effectiveness of, 130–138, 147–148
  global reach of, 15–17, 120f,
    112–126, 121f
  reconfiguration of, 147–148
  See also global media
authoritarian regimes, 11–12, 15–17
  contesting liberal values by, 70–78,
    101
  cooperation among, 14–17, 76–77
  emulation of, 71–73
  journalist harassment by, 138–147,
    145f, 145t
  OSF offices in, 89–90
  "sharp power" of, 98–99
  "soft power" of, 227–236
  sporting events in, 227–234
  tactics of, 81–83, 82f
  transnational networks of, 17,
    195–200, 197f
  US support of, 7–8
Authoritarian Restrictions on Foreign Journalists (ARFJ) data
  set, 142–147, 145f, 145t
authoritarian snapback, 21–22, 82f,
  79–80
  academic freedom and, 193–194
  Central European University
    and, 207–213
  in China, 31, 57, 101–109,
    239–244
  definition of, 18–19
  dictating agenda as, 96–100
  domestic success of, 100
  in global media, 135–138
  on liberal education, 186–187
  stigmatization of opponents as, 81,
    82f, 83–87
  on transnational activism, 150,
    153–156, 162–169, 179–183
  at US universities, 215–216
  on Xinjiang forced labor, 150,
    168–169, 179–182
authoritarianism, 5–17

globalization and, 14–15, 17, 33
  "offensive," 61
  resurgence of, 8–14, 51–61,
    272–278
autonomy
  embedded, 66–70
  institutional, 48
  political, 46–49
Azerbaijan, 184–185
  European Games in, 228–229,
    233–234
  Formula One racing in, 234–235
  OSF and, 89–90
  UN climate change conference
    in, 261–262

Bachelet, Michelle, 106–107
Bahrain, 234–236
Barcelona Summer Olympic Games
  (1992), 41, 220–221, 225–226
Bard College, 3–4, 213
"Beijing Consensus," 62
Beijing Summer Olympics
  (2008), 20–21, 25–29, 222,
    237
  French protests of, 104, 154–155
  global media attention on, 6–57,
    56t
  labor reforms of, 153–154
  medals awarded at, 64 n.50
Beijing Winter Olympics (2022), 4–5,
  21, 224, 237
  as "carbon neutral" event, 260–261
  corporate sponsors of, 53
  global media attention on, 6–57,
    56t
  NGOs and, 6, 53–55
Better Cotton Initiative
  (BCI), 169–175, 177, 179–180.
  See also cotton industry
Bettiza, Gregorio, 94–95
Biden, Joe, 1, 52–53, 168–169
Bienen, Henry, 200
Bjarnegård, Elin, 262–263

INDEX 281

Black Lives Matter, 64, 214–215,
  243–244
Black Power movement, 236–237
Blatter, Sepp, 226
Bletchley Declaration, 266–268
Blumenthal, Richard, 251–252
Bob, Clifford, 45–46, 49–50 n.97
Bohman, Viking, 181–182
Bologna Process, 189
boycotts, 149–151, 154–162
Boyle, Michael J., 58–59
Brazys, Samuel, 214
Brexit, 75–76, 190
BRICS New Development Bank, 62,
  74–75
Brownell, Susan, 26–28
Bucha Massacre (2022), 3–4
Bukele, Nayib, 113–114
Bush, George W., 9
Bush, Sarah, 70, 264

Cambodia, 158–159, 262
Carlson, Tucker, 212, 255–256
CCTV International, 56–57, 170–
  172, 221–222, 240–243. *See also*
  CGTN
censorship, 71–72, 193–194,
  209–210
  of advertisements, 154
  of Hollywood films, 98
  of internet, 15–17, 102, 256–258
  of journalists, 138–147, 140*f*
  at transnational
    campuses, 201–205
  See also academic freedom
Central European University
  (CEU), 41–42, 187–188,
  207–209
  accreditation loss of, 209–211, 213
  Orbán and, 23, 209–211
  Soros and, 23, 41–42, 207–208
CGTN media organization, 86,
  129–130
  global offices of, 22, 121*f*, 121–122

Potomac Radio Group
  and, 116–117
Spanish-language content
  on, 132–134
  See also CCTV International
Cha, Victor D., 25 n.1
Chan, Ronnie, 191 n.25
ChatCPT, 265, 267–268
Cheng, Joseph Yu-shek, 161–162
  n.49
Chevron Corporation, 98–99
China, 1–5, 234–235, 256–259
  AI regulation in, 265–268
  Belt and Road initiative of, 62
  consumer boycotts in, 154–156
  consumer market access in, 15–17,
    45, 175
  content-sharing agreements
    of, 122–126, 126*f*, 135–136
  control of external dissent
    by, 104–109
  control of internal dissent
    by, 101–102–P4S11
  death penalty in, 29
  global economy and, 11–12
  global media expenditures
    of, 62–63, 115–117
  India's border disputes with, 52–53
  journalists' association of, 132
  labor reforms in, 153–154, 156
  National Security Law of, 51–52
  NBA in, 23–24, 221–225, 239–244
  reframing human rights
    by, 103–109
  Russian alliance with, 5–6
  shielding of human rights
    in, 102–103
  social media of, 132–135
  after Soviet Union's collapse, 35–36
  sports apparel marketing
    in, 223–225, 238–239
  state media outlets of, 121*f*
  stigmatizing human rights
    in, 101–102

282 INDEX

China (*Continued*)
  trade unions of, 161–162 n.49
  as WTO member, 43–44, 256
China Cotton Association
  (CCA), 173–174
China Development Bank, 212–213
China Society for Human Rights
  Studies (CSHRS), 105–106
Chinese Basketball Association, 224,
  239–240
civil society, 46–47, 103–104
  leaders of, 36–37, 151
  NGOs and, 54–55
Clean Clothes Campaign, 168–169
climate change, 24, 151–152,
  260–262
Clinton, Bill, 256, 258–259
CNN (Cable News Net-
  work), 112–113, 137,
  232–233
Cold War, 5–6, 219, 227, 236–237
Color Revolutions, 66–67, 80
Columbia University (New
  York), 215–216
consumer activism, 19, 22–23
  authoritarian snapback to, 150,
    162, 179–183
  backlash against, 175–179
  global sports and, 218
  pro-authoritarian, 182–183
  repurposing of, 149–150
  transnational advocacy of, 151–156
content-sharing agreements
  with China, 122–126, 126f,
    135–136
  with Russia, 125–126, 127f,
    135–136
copyright laws, 39–41, 61–62, 258
Cornstein, David, 212
corporate social responsibility
  (CSR), 152–154, 160–161
cotton industry, 22–23, 157, 162–182
  forced labor in, 150, 168–169,
    179–182

standards of, 162–182
  See also anti-sweatshop campaigns
Cottrell, Patrick M., 237
Covid-19 pandemic, 190, 234–235
critical race theory (CRT), 214–215
CSHRS. *See* China Society for Human
  Rights Studies
Cyberspace Administration of
  China, 258

Dahlin, Peter, 104
Darfur genocide, 29
DeButts, Matt, 147 n.136
DeGioia, John J., 206
Deng Xiaoping, 221–222
Dennis, Everette, 200
DeSantis, Ron, 214–215
Deudney, Daniel, 44
dictating agenda, 80–100, 137–138,
  258
  authoritarian snapback and, 82f, 82
  by news agencies, 124–125
  on Xinjiang human rights
    and, 106–108, 181–182
dictatorships. *See* authoritarian
  regimes
"discourse power," 113 n.9
disinformation, 9, 111, 124, 135, 268
Domenicali, Stefano, 235–236
Douhan, Alena, 174

East Asian financial crisis
  (1997), 43–44, 44–45 n.77, 161
  Asian financial crisis (2007)
    and, 75–76
economic statecraft, 9–10 n.31
efficacious authority, 39–43, 61–65
Egypt, 195–200, 197f, 261–262
election observers, 74–75, 95
Elswah, Mona, 113 n.8
engagement. *See* reframing
  engagement
entertainment market, 66, 98

environmental regulations, 24,
151–152, 260–262
Erdoğan, Recep Tayyip, 113–114,
270–271
Eurasianism, 59–61
European People's Party, 211
European Union (EU), 95–96
AI regulation in, 265–267
expansion of, 39, 43–44, 209
higher education in, 189
extradition treaties, 15–17

Feritta, Tilman, 239–240
FIA (Internation Automobile
Federation), 234–236
FIFA (Fédération Internationale de
Football Association), 48–49,
217, 226
FIFA World Cup, 228
of 2002, 225–226
of 2006, 226
of 2010, 226–227
of 2018, 130–131, 226
of 2022, 23–24, 95–96, 232–
233, 238–239, 244–247, 253,
260–261
of 2034, 217, 249
Finnemore, Martha, 37–38
Forbidden Stories
(organization), 141–142
forced labor, 150, 168–169, 179–182
Foreign Agent Law (Russia,
2012), 85–86, 88–89
Foreign Agents Registration Act (US
1938), 115–117
Formula One racing, 23–24, 247–248,
272–278
freedom of expression, 19, 66–70,
113–114, 148
erosion of, 12–14
globalization of, 46–47
NBA and, 239–241

See also academic freedom; Author-
itarian Restrictions on Foreign
Journalists
Friedman, Tom, 44
Fudan University
(Shanghai), 212–214
Fukuyama, Francis, 32

Garver, John W., 71
Gaza, 215–216
gender equality, 22–23, 38–39,
209–211, 262–265
"geopoliticization," 101–104
Georgetown University, 199–200,
206
German reunification, 35
Gerschkovich, Evan, 110, 141–142
n.131, 147–148
Gewirtz, Julian, 71 n.80
Glasius, Marlies, 14–15
global activism. *See* transnational
activism
global higher education, 11–12, 19,
23, 184–189
accreditation of, 41–42
challenges of, 201–205
China and, 15–17, 197f, 192–193,
195–202
donors of, 191, 193–194
enrollments in, 15–17, 188–189,
192
expenditure on, 188–189
liberal paradigm of, 188–195,
208–209, 213–216
norms of, 200–207
rankings of, 190–192, 195
Saudi Arabia and, 15–17
transnational campuses
of, 195–207, 197f
US models of, 41–42
global liberalism, 6–8, 32–34, 49–50
authoritarian snapback
against, 18–19
norms of, 39–41, 48–49

284 INDEX

global liberalism (*Continued*)
 promotion of, 34–39
 shortcomings of, 31 n.29, 70–77
 transmitting norms of, 92–96
global media, 19, 22, 110–112
 authoritarian regimes and, 15–17,
  112–126, 135–138
 Beijing Olympic games and, 28–30,
  56t, 57
 Bukele on, 113–114
 Chinese news outlets of, 121f,
  121–122
 content-sharing agreements
  of, 122–126, 126f, 127f,
  135–136
 expenditures on, 62–63, 115–119
 Putin on, 113
 reconfiguring of, 110–112
 Russian news outlets of, 119–120,
  120f
 Western prominence in, 112–113
 See also authoritarian media
global networks. *See* transnational
  networks
global sports, 23–24, 217–219,
  229–234, 259
 "soft authoritarianism" and, 227
  n.37
 "sportswashing" in, 23–24,
  218–219, 227–236, 260
globalism, 75–76
globalization, 32
 authoritarianism and, 14–15, 17,
  33
 market power of, 43–44
 movements against, 151–152
 outsourcing and, 151–152
 of sports, 219–227
GONGOs (government-
  organized nongovernmental
  organizations), 95, 99–100
Gorbachev, Mikhail, 219–220,
  254–255, 258–259
"greenwashing," 260–262

Group of Seven (G7) summits, 46–47,
  267
Gruffydd-Jones, Jamie J., 101–104
Gui Congyou, 175–176
Gui Minhai, 175–176
Guriev, Sergei, 17, 33
Gurul, Julia, 17 n.64

H&M department stores, 157,
  175–179
 Better Cotton Initiative
  and, 22–23, 169–170
 boycott of, 178–182
Hamas, 186, 215–216
Hamilton, Lewis, 235–236
Harden, James, 240–241
Harrison, Ann, 153–154 n.13
Helsinki Accords (1975), 35 n.40
Herbert, Bob, 159–160
Hong Kong protests, 51–52,
  129–130, 153–154
 NBA support of, 239–242
HRW. *See* Human Rights Watch
Hu Jintao, 29, 66–67
Hugo Boss, 169–170, 175, 181–182
Hui Zhao, 241–242 n.90
Human Dimension Implementation
  Meeting (HDIM), 99–100
human rights, 235–236
 Beijing Summer Olympics
  and, 25–31
 "boomerang model" of, 37–38,
  164–165, 168–169
 economic sanctions for, 90–91
  n.39
 "geopoliticization" of, 101–104
 reframing of, 103–109
 in Rwanda, 69
 socialization efforts of, 6–7
 "spiral model" of, 37, 80–100
 "universal value" of, 101
Human Rights Watch
  (HRW), 26–28, 84–85
 on international students, 193, 214

on LGBTQ people, 244–245
on Uyghurs, 164–165, 167–168
Huntington, Samuel, 33–34
Hyde, Susan, 33

Ibandoghlu, Gubad, 184–185
Ikenberry, John G., 31 n.29
illiberalism, 18, 75–77, 91–92
India, 11–12
  BRICS and, 12, 62, 74–75
  ChatGPT use in, 268 n.47
  China's border disputes
    with, 52–53
  international students
    from, 190–191
  Narendra's populism in, 270–271
Indonesia, 43–44, 268 n.47
  minimum wage in, 153–154,
    158–159
  Nike factories in, 158–161
Infantino, Gianni, 217, 246–247
information warfare, 135. See also
  disinformation
intellectual property rights, 39–41,
  61–62, 258
Internation Automobile Federation
  (FIA), 234–236
International Consor-
  tium of Investigative
  Journalists, 164–165
International Criminal Court
  (ICC), 29, 47
International Federation of Journalists
  (IFJ), 123–124, 131–132,
  141–142
International Institute for
  Education, 190
International Institute of Democracy
  and Electoral Assistance, 1
international mega-events, 225–236
International Olympic Committee
  (IOC), 25–28, 30–31
  on Beijing Winter games, 53,
    55–56

charter of, 48–49, 52–53, 236
  See also global sports
internationalization of education, 186–189, 192–195. See also
  global higher education
internet, 39–41, 47–48
  artificial intelligence and, 24,
    265–268
  censorship of, 15–17, 102, 256–258
  governance of, 59–61, 74–75
Iran, 68, 128–129
  GDP of, 9–10
  journalist harassment by, 140–141,
    141–142 n.131
Iraq War, 9, 42–43, 64–65

James, Lebron, 154, 240–241
January 6th insurrection
  (2021), 64–65, 270–271
Jenne, Erin K., 209–210
Johnson, Juliet, 48
journalist harassment, 138–147, 140f,
  145t

Kaepernick, Colin, 64
Kagame, Paul, 69
Kazakhstan, 98–99, 193, 227 n.37
Keck, Margaret, 37–38, 151, 262–263
Kennedy, Paul, 34–35
Khashoggi, Jamal, 140–141
Kiseleva, Yulia, 67–68
Knight, Phil, 157–158, 160–161
Koch, Natalie, 225–226, 227 n.37
Kotkin, Stephen, 35–36 n.43, 46–47
  n.85
Krauthammer, Charles, 49–50
Kyrgyzstan, 41–42, 66–67

La Liga Party (Italy), 75–76
Lankina, Tomila, 72–73
Lavrov, Sergei, 1–2
Levitsky, Steven, 11–12, 57–58 n.23
Lewis, Pericles, 203–204
LexisNexis, 55

INDEX

LGBTQ rights, 22–23
  Qatar World Cup and, 23–24,
    238–239, 244–247,253
  Russia and, 15–17, 255, 270
  at transnational campuses, 203
liberal democracy, 32, 201–205,
    269–272
  assumptions of, 39–49
  criticisms of, 1–5, 7–10
  GDPs of, 8–10, 10*f*
  institutionalized, 212
  Putin on, 3–4, 4–5 n.14, 5–6, 270
  world populations of, 13*f*
  Xi Jinping on, 4–5 n.14, 12, 67–68,
    108–109
liberal outrage, 211–213
liberal values, 70–78, 101
Liu Jingmin, 25–26
LIV-PGA partnership, 218–219,
    250–252
Locke, Richard M., 160
LVMH (Moët Hennessy Louis
    Vuitton), 65–66, 154–155

Ma, Jack, 241–242
Major League Baseball (US), 219–220
Mandela, Nelson, 149–150, 226–227
Manning, Mary, 149–150
Mao Zedong, 122–123, 137–138,
    155, 221–222
market power, 43–46
  eastward shift in, 65–66
  leveraging of, 92–94, 98
marketization, 43–47
Masters, Richard, 243–244
McKinsey consultants, 65–66,
    250–251
media. *See* global media
Mexico City Summer Olympics
    (1968), 236–237
migrant policies, 271–272
  Chinese, 26–28, 153–154
  Emirati, 202–203
  Hungarian, 209–211

Qatari, 200–201, 246–247
minimum wage, 153–154, 158–159
misinformation, 124, 135. *See also*
    disinformation
Mohammed Bin Salman
    (MBS), 118–119
  sports sponsorship of, 23–24, 64,
    217, 247–252, 248*f*
  World Cup bid of, 217
Morey, Daryl, 239–241
multipolarity, 14, 49–50
Musgrave, Paul, 254–255
Musk, Elon, 271–272
Myanmar, 144

naming and shaming tactics, 90–91
    n.39, 182–183
National Hockey League
    (US), 219–220
National Rally Party (France), 75–76
NATO, 39, 209, 272
Nazarbayev, Nursultan, 98–99
NBA (National Basketball Associ-
    ation), 23–24, 154, 221–225,
    238–239
  broadcasting rights of, 232
  Chinese snapback on, 239–244
  "Dream Team" of, 41, 220–221
NGOs (nongovernmental or-
    ganizations), 3–4, 88–89,
    209–210
  anti-sweatshop campaigns of, 160
  Beijing Winter Olympics and, 6,
    53–55
  of Global South, 36–37, 45–46
  GONGOs and, 95, 99–100
  local advocacy by, 37–38
  in Russia, 85–86, 88–90
Nguyen, Thuyen, 159
Nike Corporation, 157–158
  advertisements of, 154
  anti-sweatshop campaign
    against, 22–23, 150, 157–162
"norm entrepreneurs," 37–38

Norman, Greg, 250
North Korea, 127, 132–134, 143, 148
Northwestern University, 199–200, 206–207
Nova Agency (Italy), 124
Nye, Joseph, 34–36

offshore campuses, 195–196, 201–202. *See also* global higher education
Olympic Games. See specific host cities
OneLove campaign, 245–247
Ong Ye Kung, 203–204
Open Society Foundations (OSF), 3–4, 41–42, 84–85, 89–90
    Central European University and, 207–208
    World Congress of Families and, 72
Orbán, Victor, 23, 255
    anti-migrant policies of, 209–211
    Fidesz Party of, 207–211
    on media bias, 113–114
    Soros and, 8–9 n.11, 89–90, 209–211
    Trump and, 70, 270–271
Organisation for Economic Co-operation and Development (OECD), 43–44
OSCE (Organization for Security and Co-operation in Europe), 99–100
OSF. *See* Open Society Foundations
outsourcing, 151–152, 158
Oxfam Clean Clothes Campaign, 160
Özil, Mesut, 242

Pakistan, 89–90, 268 n.47
Palestinians, 186, 215–216
Pashayeva, Nargiz, 184–185
"peaceful evolution," 8–9
Peng Shuai, 224
Penske Media Corporation, 118

Pew Global Attitudes Project, 42–43, 148
PGA (Professional Golfers' Association), 250–252
pharmaceutical industry, 39–41
Pils, Eva, 95–96
Podemos Party, 75–76
polarized politics, 128–129
Porter, Patrick, 85 n.17
Postolos, George, 222
Premier League, 23–24, 238–244
Press for Change (organization), 160
press freedom. *See* freedom of expression
Putin, Vladimir, 230, 255–256
    on liberalism, 3–4, 4–5 n.14, 12, 270
    on manipulating global media, 113
    Xi Jinping and, 32

Qatar
    migrant workers in, 200–201, 246–247
    Saudi disputes with, 118–119
    sport sponsorships of, 234–236, 231*t*
    "strategic engagement" with, 98–99
    tourism board of, 233–234
    transnational campuses in, 195–200, 197*f*, 200–203, 214–215
Qatar Foundation, 191, 199
Qatar World Cup (2022)
    broadcast rights of, 232–233
    as "carbon neutral" event, 260–261
    EU scandal over, 95–96
    LGBTQ rights and, 23–24, 238–239, 244–247, 253

Rassemblement National party, 75–76
reframing engagement, 90–92, 142

288 INDEX

Rassemblement National party
(*Continued*)
of human rights, 103–109
journalist harassment by, 137–138,
142, 147
over Xinjiang cotton, 180
Reporters Without Borders, 141–144
Rezaian, Jason, 141–142 n.131
right to development, 108
Risse-Kappe, Thomas, 37, 80
Rocha, Simone, 177
Rogge, Jacques, 28–30
Rohingya people, 144
RT. *See* Russia Today media
organization
Russia, 1–5, 34–35, 254–256
AI regulation in, 268
Chinese alliance with, 5–6
content-sharing agreements
of, 125–126, 127*f*, 135–136
control of dissent in, 72–73
Foreign Agent Law of, 85–86,
88–89
Formula One racing in, 234–235
"gender bashing" in, 264–265
global economic integration
of, 44–45
global media expenditures
of, 62–63, 115–117
LGBTQ rights in, 15–17, 255, 270
market transition in, 39–41
media outlets of, 22, 47–48, 120*f*,
119–120
NGOs in, 85–86, 88–90
OSF in, 89–90
sanctions against, 11–12
Sochi Winter Olympics in, 228
Undesirable Organizations Law
of, 88–89
World Cup in, 226
See also Ukraine-Russian war
Russia Today (RT) media organization, 73–74, 111,
128

effectiveness of, 130–131
Elswah on, 113 n.8
global reach of, 22, 119–120,120*f*
liberal criticisms by, 15–17
Rwanda, 69, 233–234, 263–264
Rwandan Patriotic Front
(RPF), 86–87

Sarkozy, Nicholas, 31, 154–155
Saudi Arabia, 247–252
global media expenditures
of, 118–119, 124
Public Investment Fund
of, 247–251, 231*t*
Qatar disputes with, 118–119
social media control by, 15–17
sport sponsorships of, 23–24, 64,
217–219, 234–236, 247–252,
248*f*
tourism board of, 233–234, 249
World Cup bid of, 217
Saudi Research and Media Group
(SRMG), 118–119
Schwartz, Mark Herman, 39–41
semiconductor industry, 39–41
Seoul Summer Olympics (1988), 25
n.1, 225–226
Shanghai Cooperation
Organization, 74–75
Shanghai Grand Prix, 234–235
Shanghai Jiao Tong
University, 191–192
Shanghai Pudong Development
Bank, 239–240
"sharp power," 98–99
shielding, 87–90, 137
authoritarian snapback and, 82*f*,
142
of corporate ads, 154
of human rights in China, 102–103
of journalist harassment, 147
stigmatization and, 87–88, 92,
179–180
Sikkink, Katherine, 37–38

Silver, Adam, 240–241, 243–244
Singapore, 64
 Formula One racing in, 234–235
 political dissent in, 203–205
 transnational campuses
  in, 195–200, 197f, 201,
  203–204
 universities of, 195
Singham, Neville Roy, 117
slave trade, 151
snapback. *See* authoritarian snapback
Snow, Edgar, 137–138
Snyder, Jack, 7–8 n.23, 8, 12
Sochi Winter Olympics (2014), 228
social media, 130–138, 255–256
 Beijing Winter Olympics and, 54
 censorship of, 15–17, 102–103
 Chinese, 132–135
 consumer protests on, 155–156
 "greenwashing" of, 261–262
 importance of, 132–135
 YouTube and, 132–134
soft power, 32, 34–36, 39, 228–229
 n.41
Soros, George, 23, 41–42, 207–208
 Orbán and, 8–9 n.11, 89–90,
  209–211
South Africa, 149–150, 182–183
 ChatGPT use in, 268 n.47
 global media expenditures of, 117
 World Cup in, 226–227
South Korea, 25 n.1, 158–159,
 225–226
Spielberg, Steven, 29
"sportswashing," 23–24, 218–219,
 227–236, 260. *See also* global
 sports
Sputnik news outlet, 119–120,
 130–131
Stepan, Alfred, 41–42 n.64
Stern, David, 221–222
stigmatization, 83–87, 137, 213,
 271–272

of authoritarian regimes, 81, 82f,
 83–87, 182–183
of human rights, 101–102,
 179–180
shielding and, 87–88, 92, 179–180
Sudan genocide, 29
Sudworth, John, 86
Summit for Democracy (2021), 1,
 1–2 n.4
surveillance, 256–257
 of journalists, 143
 of Uyghurs, 163–164
 See also censorship
sweatshops. *See* anti-sweatshop
 campaigns
Sydney Summer Olympics
 (1993), 25–26
Syriza Party, 75–76

Taiwan, 124 n.53, 132–134, 158
Tan Tai Yong, 203–204
Tanzania, 72
Texas A&M University, 198–201,
 214–215
Thailand, 43–44, 125
Tiananmen Square massacre
 (1989), 32, 71 n.80
Tibet protests, 26–29, 31, 51, 55, 104
TikTok, 134–135
Title IX sports programs, 184P
"traditional" values, 59–61, 70–78,
 101
 Kagame on, 69
 Orbán on, 70
 Putin on, 3–4
transnational activism, 34–39
 authoritarian snapback
  against, 153–156
 boycotts and, 157–162
 consumer activism and, 151–156
 repression of, 92–93
 See also consumer activism

transnational campuses, 195–200,
197f, 201–205. *See also* global
higher education
transnational networks, 41, 47
crackdowns on, 3–5
supply chains of, 11–12, 17
"wormhole," 48, 262–263
transnational partnerships, 205–207
transnational repression, 79–80,
92–93, 104–105, 140–141,
164–165, 263–264
Trubowitz, Peter, 58–59
Trump, Donald, 12, 58–59, 75–76
January 6th insurrection of, 64–65,
270–271
populism of, 14, 70, 270–272
Tsai, Joe, 241–242
Türkiye, 113–114
media outlets of, 113–116,
132–134
OSF and, 89–90
social media censorship by, 15–17
transnational campuses
in, 195–200, 197f
Ukraine-Russian War
and, 182–183
Turkmenistan, 193
Tutu, Desmond, 149–150

UAE. *See* United Arab Emirates
UEFA (Union of European Football
Associations), 226, 229–230,
232–233
Ukraine economy, 39–41, 66–67
Ukraine-Russian war, 3–4, 182–183,
255–256
Bucha Massacre in, 3–4
media coverage of, 59–61, 110, 128
sanctions of, 11–12, 230–232
Undesirable Organizations Law
(Russia), 88–89
United Arab Emirates (UAE)
climate change conference
in, 261–262

migration policies of, 202–203
social media control by, 15–17
sport sponsorships of, 230–232,
234–235, 231t
"strategic engagement" with, 98–99
tourism board of, 233–234
transnational universities
in, 195–200, 197f, 201–203
Ukraine-Russian War
and, 182–183
United Nations (UN), 152–153
AI resolution of, 266–267
climate change conferences
of, 261–262
Department of Economic and
Social Affairs, 258
Guiding Principles on Business and
Rights, 244–245
Human Rights Council
of, 104–108
Sustainable Development Goals
of, 266
University College Dublin, 206–207
n.79
US Olympic basketball team
(1992), 41
Usmanov, Alisher, 230–232
USSR, 34–35, 41, 254–255
during Cold War, 5–6, 219–220,
227, 236–237P
See also Russia
Uyghurs, 22–23, 51–52, 162–169
human rights of, 164–165,
167–168, 242
media attention on, 55
surveillance of, 163–164
See also Xinjiang
Uzbekistan, 89–90, 197f, 193,
195–200

Varieties of Democracy (V-Dem)
project, 8–9
GDP and, 8–10, 10f

on journalist harassment, 139–140,
140*f*, 142–147, 145*t*
on transnational campuses, 201
world population and, 12–14, 13*f*
Verbruggen, Hein, 55–56
Vietnam, 195–200, 197*f*, 262
anti-sweatshop campaigns
in, 153–154, 158–161
Vippi Media, 54
Vora, Neha, 200–201

Wa Lone, 144
Wang Yi, 1–2, 137–138
"Washington Consensus," 43–44, 62
Way, Lucan A., 11–12, 57–58 n.23
We Chat app, 102–103
Weibo app, 102–103, 242
wire services, 122–126. *See also* global
media
women's rights. *See* gender equality
World Bank, 43–44
World Congress of Families, 72
World Trade Organization
(WTO), 186
China as member of, 43–44, 256
General Agreement on Trade in
Services of, 188–189
on intellectual property, 39–41
Qatar-Saudi disputes
with, 118–119

World Wrestling Enter-
tainment, 247–248,
248*f*

Xi Jinping, 102–103, 105–106
on liberalism, 4–5 n.14, 12, 67–68,
108–109
media coverage of, 129
Putin and, 32
Xinhua media organization, 22,
56–57, 73–74
BBC and, 86
global reach of, 121–125, 126*f*
intelligence gathering by, 121–122
n.41
NBA and, 222–223
US coverage by, 128–129
on Uyghurs, 170–172
Xinjiang, 106–108, 242
forced labor in, 150, 168–169,
179–182
reframing engagement over, 180
See also Uyghurs

Yale-NUS College
(Singapore), 203–205
Yao Ming, 222–225, 239–240
YouTube. *See* social media

Zenz, Adrian, 167, 179–180
Zetterberg, Pär, 262–264
Zhao Lijian, 52–53
Ziblatt, Daniel, 271–272